KT-230-567

A regular contributor to *The Times* of London since 1969 and a foreign correspondent who has spent the better part of the last thirty-two years in Spain, Harry Debelius has been a privileged observer of the country from dictatorship to democracy.

After graduating with honours as an AB from the Johns Hopkins University in his native Baltimore, Maryland, he served as an infantry lieutenant in the US Army during the Korean War. On his return to the United States, Debelius worked briefly for the daily *Baltimore News-Post* before heading for Spain, influenced by one of his former Hopkins professors, poet Pedro Salinas. His intention was to study Spanish literature; instead he studied Spain.

Before starting to write for *The Times*, he reported wars and revolutions around the world for the American radio and television network ABC, while keeping Spain as his home base.

He is the father of eight children and the grandfather of three.

COLLINS
INDEPENDENT TRAVELLERS GUIDE

SPAIN

HARRY DEBELIUS

Series Editor Robin Dewhurst

Collins
8 Grafton Street, London
1988

Note
Whilst every effort has been made to ensure that prices, hotel and restaurant recommendations, opening hours and similar factual information in this book are accurate at the time of going to press, the Publishers cannot be held responsible for any changes found by readers using this guide.

William Collins Sons & Co Ltd
London · Glasgow · Sydney
Auckland · Toronto · Johannesburg

First published in 1988
© Harry Debelius 1988

Maps by Kevin Jones Associates

All rights reserved. No part of this publication may be reproduced, stored in a retrieval system, or transmitted, in any form, or by any means, electronic, mechanical, photocopying, recording or otherwise, without the prior permission of the publisher.

BRITISH LIBRARY CATALOGUING IN PUBLICATION DATA
Collins Independent Travellers Guide to Spain.
1. Spain—Description and Travel—1981
—Guide-books
914.6'0483   DR14

ISBN 0 00 410970 8

Typeset by Ace Filmsetting Ltd, Frome, Somerset.
Printed and bound in Great Britain by Mackays of Chatham.

Contents

Spanish Cities

Corunna
Santiago de Compostela
Pontevedra
Orense
Lugo
Oviedo
Santander
San Sebastián
Bilbao
Vitoria
Pamplona
FRANCE
Andorra
León
Logroño
Huesca
Gerona
Costa Brava
Palencia
Burgos
Saragossa
Lérida
BARCELONA
Zamora
Valladolid
Soria
Tarragona
Costa Dorada
Salamanca
Ávila
Segovia
San Lorenzo del Escorial
Guadalajara
Teruel
MADRID
Cuenca
Castellón de la Plana
Toledo
Valencia
Costa del Azahar
Balearic Islands
PORTUGAL
Cáceres
Ciudad Real
Albacete
Badajoz
Alicante
Córdoba
Murcia
Costa Blanca
Jaén
Costa Calida
Seville
Granada
Huelva
Costa de la Luz
Jerez de la Frontera
Málaga
Almería
Cádiz
Costa del Sol
Costa de Almería
Gibraltar
Ceuta
Melilla
NORTH AFRICA

Preface

As I write, workmen are putting up the log barriers blocking off the side streets along the route which the bulls will run down in the town where I live near Madrid. The new logs are smooth and white; the older ones are pale brown and splintery, some as thick as telephone poles. Men in blue coveralls slide them into supports consisting of upright parallel wooden beams with thick blocks nailed between them at intervals, like steps of a ladder. At the corners, they simply lay intersecting logs on top of each other, in the same manner that a rail fence is built.

For five days, the running of the bulls takes place here every morning. Every afternoon during that period there is a bullfight. One day there is a comic bullfight, featuring dwarfs and clowns who risk their lives to make people laugh. Another day there is a fight starring fully-fledged *matadores*. The rest of the days there are *novilladas*, in which the *toreros* are beginners who have not yet been accorded the category of *matador*.

The bulls at the *novilladas* are theoretically younger, but in fact they are generally more dangerous than the animals fought in the *corridas* by the stars of the ring. Because they are cheaper, they are often of doubtful bravery (which makes them less predictable). Sometimes, too, they have even been fought before, which is the worst thing that can happen, because such a bull quickly learns to go for the man instead of the cape.

In the mornings, anyone who wants a thrill – scores of young men, some girls and a few fit middle-aged men – runs in front of the bulls as the animals race down the three short streets lined by the school and a little park on one side and by neat whitewashed houses with green doors and window frames on the other, in the direction of the Town Hall. They then tumble and skid as they turn left to continue their race for another five streets along the Calle Real and through the Plaza Mayor to the dusty lane that leads to the portable arena.

The rest of the townspeople crowd in behind the log barriers to catch a glimpse. Little children climb between the logs, until a hand reaches out from behind and pulls them back in. Occasionally, a running bull hooks a horn between the logs, and there are screams, followed by frightened giggles as the crowd rolls back like a breaking wave. Often a runner scales the barrier with the incredible speed and agility that is born of the instinct for self-preservation, and flies over the top into the crowd. Sometimes he is pulled up high by a dozen anonymous hands reaching from behind the barrier a split second before a sharp black horn slices past.

The rest of the year, the street leading down to the Town Hall is closed on Saturdays for the weekly market. Most of the stalls sell fresh fruits and vegetables, but there are also live turtles, canaries and finches, toys, clothing, flowers and plants, kitchenware, dried fruits and nuts, herbs for cooking and for curing, and there is a big van from which delicious Granada mountain hams and cold meats are sold.

This street lies partially in the shadow of the tall square belfry of the church of San Miguel, topped on one corner by a stork's nest. Dark red tiles against a pale blue sky accentuate the uneven roofline of this great, blockish, seventeenth-century church of stone and brick, revealing the profile of its old wooden ridge-poles.

I am telling you all this because it is important to understand that Spain is not just a show for the tourists, folklore pulled out of the cedar chest, so to speak, to dust off and sell to outsiders. You will not find the town where I live, Las Rozas, mentioned in the guide because it is not particularly touristy. It is quite normal, as towns go in this area. Visitors pass it on their way from Madrid to El Escorial or as they head for Segovia and Ávila. It is very much in the twentieth century, with a municipal library and sports complex. There is a small flying field where micro-light aircraft enthusiasts do their thing at weekends. The Town Hall sponsors computer courses and other types of adult education.

Spain lives quite comfortably with all that – the bulls, the computers, the storks, the micro-light aircraft. Such incongruous combinations are what make it probably the most exotic member of the family of Western European nations, notwithstanding the tourist avalanche.

Introduction

Change or another layer?

Every year 40 million people come to Spain from abroad, which is roughly the same number as Spain's total population. Even allowing for the fact that many of these visitors stay for a short time only, their collective presence is bound to have an effect. You would think that, with so many people coming here, there would not be many places left in Spain untouched. Yet there are, because the vast majority of the visitors who stay more than one or two nights do not actually penetrate the real Spain.

Most of them spend their time on the beach, in the bar and beside the swimming pool of a coastal hotel, conversing in their own language with other people on the same package tour. Their contact with Spain is often limited to talking to the waiter, the chambermaid and the local shopkeeper who speaks English, German or whatever. They conclude that the sun always shines, Spanish beaches are clean, or dirty, the food gives you 'Spanish tummy' and the drink is cheap.

Spain deserves to be better known, and those who make the effort will have their own reward. It is a complex and varied country. Certainly it is changing, but not in the way that a primitive society does in the face of overwhelming pressure from a more dominant culture. Spain is sure of itself, and is slow to do away with ways and attitudes that have lasted for centuries. At the same time it is subject, as it has been throughout much of its history, to dramatic changes of politics and opinion, motivated by the same Manichaean tendencies that produced Torquemada and the Spanish Inquisition in the fifteenth century and the convent-burners in the twentieth.

Bare facts

Back in the 1960s, a certain Irish girl in a not very extreme green bikini was lounging by the pool atop the Plaza Hotel in Madrid. A member of the hotel staff came up to her and murmured discreetly, 'I'm sorry, Miss, but two-piece bathing costumes are not allowed.' She left him flabbergasted with the smiling reply, 'Which piece would you like me to take off?'

That whole conversation would be superfluous today, but things are still changing. The topless fashion, which predominated at pools and beaches in the early 1980s, less than ten years after Franco's death, was beginning to give way in 1986 and 1987 to the barely more modest, one-piece fashion. Paradoxically, however, Spain still has more cloistered nuns than the rest of the world put together.

The birth rate has been falling since several years before Franco's

9

death, and projections based on census statistics indicate that Spain in 1987 was on the verge of static population growth.

During nearly forty years of dictatorship, divorce was forbidden; and only those rich and powerful enough to wangle an annulment from the Roman Catholic church (and, like it or not, there was a great deal of chicanery in such dealings) were allowed to change partners legally. When, as Minister of Justice of the first Spanish Socialist Government, Francisco Fernández Ordóñez defended his proposed divorce law in Parliament, he predicted that after its passage 200,000 couples would flock to the courts asking for divorce. He was wrong. Those asking for a divorce the first year the barriers were let down could be numbered in the thousands, not the hundreds of thousands. Apparently, many people, obliged to sort out their private lives under the Franco regime without the help of clergy or courts, did not bother to seek a legal seal of approval for decisions they had taken long ago. Others, involved in marital difficulties at the time the new law was passed, did as before and saved lawyers' fees. Obviously, amicable arrangements were not possible in all cases; and there were, and still are, problems regarding widows' pensions and child custody.

Abortion is still a fiercely debated issue. The Socialist dominated Parliament legalized abortion in 1986, for cases in which the pregnancy endangers the physical or mental health of the mother, is the result of rape, or where the child is likely to be born with serious mental or physical handicaps. A great many doctors and nurses nevertheless refuse to perform abortions on grounds of conscience.

Nowadays, according to official statistics, there are fewer marriages and more and more young people are co-habiting without formalizing their relationship. Yet, contrary to these trends, Spain continues to be 90 per cent Roman Catholic.

Unemployment and crime

Unemployment probably has something to do with the unpopularity of marriage. With the jobless rate at a staggering 22 per cent nationwide in 1987, and with school-leavers being the most affected by the lack of employment, it is not surprising that few young couples are anxious to make long-term commitments.

Unemployment is also partly to blame for the amazing increase in crime since Franco died. In some places, such as the Leganés district of Madrid, there is hardly a shopkeeper who had not been held up two or three times in the past year. Chemists' shops, in particular, are boarded up like Fort Knox at night in all the cities. Those chemists which are open all night – and the law requires at least one to remain open in each area – are reminiscent of those films about speakeasies in Prohibition days in the United States. You usually have to ring a bell, and a dim figure in a white coat comes out from the depths of the semi-darkened shop and faces you behind a bulletproof glass door. You tell him through a small opening or speaker device what you want, or slide the prescription to him through a little trapdoor. He passes the medicine to you in the same way, after you have paid.

Barcelona and Madrid have the highest crime rates generally in the country, but Seville is where tourists are most often the victims of petty crime. In the section on Seville (see pp. 152–3), you will find a brief list of suggestions about how to avoid becoming a victim yourself. Those suggestions are essential to follow if you are planning to visit Seville; and they are extremely useful elsewhere, particularly in the big cities and in certain beach resorts where foreign tourists outnumber the locals. On the beaches, however, you do have the advantage in summer of thousands of extra policemen assigned to coastal resorts, specifically to deal with this problem.

Drug dependency turns many young Spaniards into criminals. An addict's need for cash to finance an increasingly greater consumption impels him to act out of desperation at times. And Spain has far too many such desperadoes. The growing drug problem has many causes, but the Government is not exempt from blame. In its headlong rush to show how 'progressive' it was, the Socialist Goverment headed by Prime Minister Felipe González revised legislation on drugs soon after it first came to power. So called 'soft' drugs were no longer prohibited, and there was no longer any penalty for people found in possession of outlawed 'hard' drugs provided they were for their own personal use.

All this is not to suggest, of course, that every outside influence on the opinions and mores of the country is to the bad. Spain has also been influenced by varying changes such as its new-found democracy and its recent membership of the European Economic Community and the North Atlantic Treaty Organization. But for the most part such changes have been superficial. There are many places in the more remote pockets of the interior where villagers are isolated, often on account of the mountainous terrain, even from their fellow countrymen, and where attitudes and customs have remained largely unchanged over the years.

The difference between such remote areas and the sophistication of large cities like Madrid, Barcelona and Seville is just one of the many contrasts to be found in Spain. Similarly, you will find ski resorts in the Pyrenees as well as the beaches on the Mediterranean; lush greenery in the Basque Country and sun-baked aridity in the Great Central Tableland; and ancient buildings and sights often jostle for your attention with the adjacent temples of modernity. Whatever you hope and expect to discover on your travels is to be found somewhere in Spain, and it is this multi-faceted appeal which is perhaps what makes it such a delightful country for the independent traveller to explore.

History

You will keep coming across reminders not only of Spain's recent history, but also of its long and eventful past, everywhere you go, from the prehistoric cave paintings such as those at Altamira near Santillana in Green Spain, to the numerous Roman bridges still in use.

While scientists believe an early ancestor of man hunted great herds of elephants on the Iberian Peninsula 200,000 years ago, the paintings in the Altamira caves are reckoned to be about 12,000 years old. From about 3000 BC, possibly with the arrival of emigrants from North Africa, there were Neolithic settlements in Spain, and soon the people began to work with bronze, and eventually with other metals.

Spain is rich in minerals, and artefacts found elsewhere show there was contact between people living in south-western Spain and in Brittany and Ireland long before the Phoenicians established themselves in present-day Cádiz, in about 1000 BC. The Carthaginians founded a colony in Ibiza in the seventh century BC. About that same time the Greeks were setting up trading posts in southern Spain. Those were also the days of Tartessos, a monarchy which probably took in most of today's Andalusia but about which little is known, including its writing which has yet to be deciphered.

Early invaders

In about 500 BC, the Tartessans rose up against their Phoenician masters, but the Phoenicians' ally, Carthage, sent troops from Ibiza and put down the revolt, destroying for ever after the political power of Tartessos. The Carthaginians spread their empire to mainland Spain and Hasdrubal, predecessor of Hannibal, founded New Carthage (Cartagena). Soon the Romans started moving in and, after some initial reverses, conquered New Carthage in 209 BC and quickly subdued the whole east coast. From then on it was Romans against early Spaniards rather than against Carthaginians.

At Numancia, near Soria, you can gaze upon the remains of a Celtiberian town whose inhabitants held out against the Roman legions for twenty years and finally committed mass suicide rather than surrender. In Corunna, you can climb to the top of the Tower of

Hercules, rebuilt by the Romans on the site of an earlier tower, and believed to be the oldest lighthouse still in use in the world.

Near Seville, you can visit the ruins of Itálica, the birthplace of the Roman Emperor Hadrian, who was later to become famous for his wall built across England to keep out the fierce tribes of what was to become Scotland. Amphitheatres and other buildings at Itálica, and at Mérida in the west; Málaga on the Costa del Sol; Tarragona on the east coast, and Segóbriga, near Cuenca, will give you an idea of how firmly the Roman Empire established itself in Spain.

In the third century AD barbarous tribes swept in across the Pyrenees and wrecked Tarraco (Tarragona). More such invasions followed in the fourth and fifth centuries AD. The Vandals established themselves in the south, and the region they dominated became known as Vandalusia, from which the modern name Andalusia is derived. Goths and Visigoths followed them in rapid succession, and the Visigoths took over control of most of the Peninsula. Leovigildo defeated the fearsome Basques, founding Victoriaco, now ironically the capital of the Basque Country, in memory of his victory. A century later, however, another Visigothic king, Wamba, had to put down the Basques once again when they rebelled.

Muslim rule

In 711, at Barbate, where today you can enjoy vast stretches of sandy beaches all to yourself, the tide of Spanish history changed. There a band of invaders from North Africa defeated the Visigoth King Rodrigo's army, and, meeting hardly any resistance, the Moors quickly conquered the whole country. The new Emir, declaring allegiance to the Caliph of Damascus, set up his capital in Toledo. Rodrigo's widow, Egilona, married the Emir, Muza Ben Nosair, and tried to convert him to Christianity, thus provoking the distrust of his closest advisers, who assassinated him as he entered a mosque to pray, just four years after the victory at Barbate. One of his successors tried to extend his territory further north, but at Poitiers in 732 Charles Martel hammered him back across the Pyrenees.

By 756 Spain was an independent Emirate ruled from Córdoba, and in less than 200 years it rose to the status of a Caliphate. The marvellous Mosque there, with its 1,000 columns, started by Abd-er-Rahman I in 785 and finished in 990, is a visible reminder of those days of splendour. But internal intrigues led to the break-up of the Caliphate, into scores of miniature independent Moorish states whose rulers spent much of their time making war on each other, thus simplifying the Christian monarchs' task. Those tiny kingdoms were called the Reigns of Taifa.

Another dynasty, the Almorávides, came across from Africa and took advantage of the situation, conquering and reuniting Arab Spain. But corruption brought about the disintegration of the union into more Reigns of Taifa; and the Almohades, who had come to power in North Africa, moved across the straits to take charge. In the meantime, Christian rulers had been steadily gaining ground. Granada was the last significant Moorish bastion.

The Reconquest

The Reconquest, which Ferdinand and Isabella finished at Granada, had begun in 718 in Covadonga in the north coastal region of Asturias, when Don Pelayo defeated a powerful Moorish contingent and remained the ruler of an independent kingdom. He credited a miraculous intervention by the Virgin Mary for his victory and the very statue he venerated is still on display at Covadonga.

From then on, for generation after generation and century after century, the movement to unseat the Moorish rulers gained momentum. By 757 most of what is now called 'Green Spain' was ruled by Christian monarchs. By 912 Christian forces were at the gates of Toledo, though Aragón was still in the hands of Muslims. By 1230 the Christians had pushed into La Mancha, and had taken Aragón and Mallorca. By 1474 only the Costa del Sol and its sierras, the Algarve and the present-day Costa de la Luz were in Moorish hands.

A legendary hero of this period was Rodrigo Díaz de Vivar, known as El Cid Campeador. You can see his tomb at the Cathedral in Burgos. The word Cid comes from *sidi*, or lord, a title which Moorish soldiers bestowed on him out of fearful respect. The word Campeador, or Battler, was pinned on him by his own troops.

A medieval sword-for-hire, El Cid always seemed to be at odds with his own king, Alfonso VI of Castile. When El Cid took on the Moorish forces at Toledo without orders from Alfonso, the monarch banished him from the kingdom. That turned out to be a mistake, because The Battler was immediately signed up by the other side. Fighting for the Moorish King of Saragossa, he defeated the Moorish King of Lérida and captured that King's Christian ally, the Count of Barcelona, but set him free soon afterwards.

When Alfonso VI was soundly thrashed by Moorish forces in the Battle of Badajoz, he decided it was time to call El Cid back from exile. Eager to please Alfonso, El Cid began taking one objective after another along the south-east coast; but when on one occasion the King wanted El Cid to go to the rescue of a besieged castle and El Cid's men arrived too late, Alfonso would not accept any excuses, and banished El Cid again.

This time El Cid simply continued the war on his own, defeating the King of Lérida once more and again capturing the Count of Barcelona. The Count decided he wanted El Cid on his side, so he put his territories under his protection. The Battler finished his conquest of Valencia in 1094. He died a natural death in 1099. Three years later Alfonso had to surrender Valencia once again to the Moors. The Muslim historian Ben Bassam wrote of the 'accursed' El Cid Campeador in 1109, 'He was always the winner, and he wiped out large armies with a handful of warriors. As much for his inexhaustible energy and clear-sightedness as for his heroic bravery, he was one of the Creator's great miracles.'

The final surrender and Columbus

By Christmas 1491, Queen Isabella, outside the walls of the Alhambra, was feeling pretty uneasy, having made a vow several months before not to change her dress until Granada fell. Finally, on 2 January 1492, after Boabdil had left the fortress-palace, the Christian troops entered. Isabella's maids hurried her to the Alhambra's sensuously decorated baths, with a sigh of relief. The harem had fled in such a rush it undoubtedly left some oriental perfume behind. Listen to the tinkling sound of the fountain in the Patio of the Lions, the very same sound Boabdil heard as he brooded over Ferdinand and Isabella's surrender ultimatum so long ago.

It was a great year for Isabella. Whether persuaded by her counsellors or merely acting on a hunch, she decided to back a sea captain's dangerous and costly experiment, even if it meant pawning her own jewels to finance it. You can still pray where Columbus did near Huelva, just before leaving Europe on a wild hunch that he could establish new and lucrative trade routes by sailing west – provided he was right and the world really was round. If he was wrong. . . .

In Villajoyosa, near Benidorm, you can take part in the riotous annual *fiestas* in which battles between Christians and Moors are re-enacted.

In the name of God

The role of the church was strengthened by the long Christian–Muslim confrontation and during this period a number of religious orders were established. The discovery in Galicia early in the ninth century of what, according to tradition, was the burial place of St James the Apostle, resulted in the creation of a much-travelled pilgrims' route to the apostle's shrine in Santiago.

Some of the solid old hostels and hospitals built for the pilgrims have since been turned into luxurious modern hotels, such as the Hostal de San Marcos in León and the Hostal de los Reyes Católicos in Santiago.

A byproduct of the long Crusade to put the Iberian Peninsula in the hands of Christian rulers was intolerance and mistrust of anyone holding other beliefs. Muslims, Jews and Christians lived in harmony under most Moorish rulers, but such was not the case on the other side of the battle lines. Even before the Moorish invasion, the Visigothic King Sisebuto ordered Jews to convert to Roman Catholicism or get out of the country in the early seventh century. He expelled 60,000 of them and allowed 90,000 to stay after they became converts. When the Moors invaded, North African Jews were suspected of being involved in the invasion plan; it would hardly be surprising if they were.

The final, definitive order expelling Jews from Spain was not actually issued until 1492, but before that the political climate of the final years of the Reconquest severely restricted unorthodox thinking or beliefs. Between 1481 and 1482, about 2,000 people were burned for Jewish practices or beliefs, mostly in Andalusia. Those who did not leave were obliged to take up the Catholic faith, and little mercy was shown to anyone who secretly tried to cling to his old faith.

Quite apart from the catastrophic effects the order had on countless families whose ancestors had lived in Spain for many generations, it did not do much good for Spain either. Many of the Jewish families were engaged in commerce, and many Jews were of a cultural level far above the norm for the times, when most Christian kings could not even write their own names. By persecuting them Spain lost the Jews' potential contribution to society.

Muslims were treated much the same way. In Granada, the Moorish people were guaranteed the right to keep their homes and customs, according to the terms of Boabdil's surrender. However, just seven years later, the powerful Cardinal Cisneros began seizing and burning their Arab books and manuscripts, and exerting considerable pressure on them to convert or be expelled. His tough measures provoked a riot in the Albaicín quarter of Granada, and while the Cardinal was lucky to escape, his two servants were killed.

The Catholic monarchs, Isabella and Ferdinand, put several of the ringleaders in prison; and the great majority of the Moorish population of the city of Granada, about 50,000, agreed to be baptized. The Albaicín still looks Middle-Eastern today, but the inhabitants you will meet there are not descendants of these Moorish Christians, who were known as Moriscos.

In the Andalusian mountain villages, unlike in the city, the problems were not over. There the Moorish people, including many who had agreed to conversion to avoid trouble, revolted. It took several battles to subdue them, and the royal army suffered heavy casualties. In 1502 Ferdinand and Isabella signed an order obliging all Moors to adopt the Christian faith or leave Spain. Most chose to pay lip-service to their conquerors' religion.

Another uprising in 1568 led to the deportation of the Moorish Christians and the recolonization of southern mountain villages with Christians from the north. Between 1609 and 1614, Philip III, convinced that the Morisco population in various parts of the country was full of spies and plotters, carried out another relentless and thorough campaign of expulsion.

The Inquisition carried out its grim task in Spain from 1480, killing and torturing people in the name of God. The 'executions', however, were carried out by civil authorities on the recommendation of the Inquisition's secret tribunals. Its most ignominious period was in the sixteenth century, when it zealously pursued Protestants, heretics, pro-Jews and witches. One of the favourite places where victims were burned to death was the Plaza Mayor of Madrid. The Inquisition was largely organized by Dominican friars and thus they came to be known as the Domini Cane – Latin for 'Hounds of the Lord'. The Protestant Reformation never reached Spain, with the exception of a few martyred foreign preachers and a few proscribed renegade monks; indeed, Philip II of Spain had been an important force in the Counter Reformation.

An empire gained and lost

It was a period of expansion. At the end of the fifteenth century and beginning of the sixteenth, Spain colonized the Canary Islands, some of which had been in the process of colonization since 1402, and captured the North African coastal strongholds of Orán, Bugia and Tripoli. A policy of astute marriages engineered by the Catholic monarchs for their children greatly increased the Spanish holdings. An aggressive policy building on the discoveries made by Columbus and subsequent explorers soon gave Spain control over most of the Americas.

By the sixteenth century, Philip II ruled an empire far vaster than any that had ever been put together before. Spain controlled what is now Belgium and the Netherlands, much of what is now Italy, part of modern-day France, all the Iberian Peninsula (Portugal being briefly united with Spain), Sardinia and Corsica – and of course most of South America and much of North America. Philip was also active against the Muslims when he put the Turks to flight at Vienna in 1532. In 1571 he wrecked the Turkish fleet at Lepanto. In that battle

Cervantes, who called it 'the greatest day's work of all times', lost his left hand, which did not keep him from going on to become the literary star of Spain's Golden Age.

A Protestant uprising in Holland destroyed more than 400 churches and convents in 1566. The Duke of Alba suppressed it and beheaded its leaders. Unrest continued. In 1588 Philip II sent the supposedly invincible Armada to punish England's Queen Elizabeth I for helping the rebels of Flanders. The expedition was a disaster, being overwhelmed both by Sir Francis Drake and a heavy storm. The defeat of the Armada was the first sign of the decline of mighty Spain.

A war of succession in the beginning of the eighteenth century, which other European powers took advantage of to take over Spanish possessions, resulted in the loss of Naples, Tuscany, Belgium, Sardinia, Sicily, Menorca and Gibraltar. The last named, having been captured in 1704, was formally ceded to England with certain specific conditions under the Treaty of Utrecht in 1713, and Spain today bases its arguments for return of The Rock on that treaty. The dispute about sovereignty over the British colony continues, but there are no restrictions other than normal passport controls on travelling between Gibraltar and the adjoining Spanish territory.

A series of wars in the eighteenth century resulted in further losses in the New World and caused Florida, the Louisiana territory and parts of California to change hands several times. In 1783, the Treaty of Versailles confirmed Spain's rule over Menorca but did not give back Gibraltar, which had been the subject of an unsuccessful siege from 1779 to 1782. In 1805 Admiral Nelson smashed the combined French and Spanish fleets at Cape Trafalgar, off the still undeveloped, beautiful sandy beach known as Los Caños de Meca.

One hundred years of troubles

That famous naval battle set a sour keynote for the next hundred years. The nineteenth century was one of unceasing wars and revolutions. The weak Bourbon King Charles IV granted Napoleon's troops the right of passage to attack Portugal, and of course they occupied parts of Spain. The Spaniards, however, were braver than their King. On 2 May 1808, the people of Madrid rose up against the French, and that spark set off a chain reaction all over the country.

At the Prado in Madrid, and not to be missed, is Goya's painting of the executions in Madrid on 3 May 1808, in which a patriot with panic in his eyes falls in front of a French firing squad by the light of a lantern. The Prado Museum itself suffered from Napoleon's occupation when French cavalrymen stabled their horses in the elegant building by Villanueva, which had been built for an academy of sciences.

Napoleon named his brother, Joseph, king, and the French usurper made a ceremonial entrance into Madrid on 20 July 1808, only to pull out a few days later when Napoleon's army was trounced at Bailén. In December of that same year, Napoleon personally came to Spain to reinstate his brother on the insecure throne, but it was a lost cause.

The Cortes (Spanish Parliament) met in Cádiz and named a Regency Council pending the return of a legitimate heir to the throne, and rejected the authority of Joseph Bonaparte. The Cortes also drew up a short-lived liberal constitution in 1812. Meanwhile, the Spanish people, with the military assistance of the British forces under the Duke of Wellington, kept up the pressure on the French invaders. Among places where important battles took place are Corunna and Ciudad Rodrigo, near Salamanca.

The Carlist Wars

No sooner had a Bourbon, Fernando VII, been restored to the throne than he nullified the Constitution of 1812 and tried to rule as an absolute monarch. After the discovery of several conspiracies against him, the king agreed to abide by the 1812 Constitution, but his promise turned out to be empty as he called on France to send troops in his aid. It took the so-called '100,000 Sons of St Louis' only a few months to restore order and firmly install Fernando on his throne. The king had no male descendants but did have one daughter, Isabel, which led him to repeal the Salic Law that barred women from inheriting the crown.

Meanwhile, taking advantage of the chaotic situation in Spain during the War of Independence, as the war against Napoleon is called by Spaniards, though in Britain it is better known as the Peninsular War, and the years immediately afterward, all of Spain's colonies in the Americas declared their independence except Cuba and Puerto Rico. The Philippines also remained loyal to Spain.

When Fernando died, a long list of short-lived governments, of varying political hues from despotic to liberal, took power one after the other during the regency of Queen María Cristina before Isabel II came of age. From 1830 to the end of the century, there were numerous outbreaks and uprisings, including two hard-fought wars of succession between those who supported Fernando's brother Carlos and those who accepted the idea that a woman, Isabel, could inherit the throne. They were called the Carlist Wars, and those who supported succession through the male line only were called Carlists.

The Jesuits were suppressed in 1835 and church property was seized in 1835 and 1836. A general named Espartero forced the abdication of the queen regent and took over the regency himself in 1840. (His equestrian statue in the main square in Logroño achieved notoriety, but for a different reason, as you will discover in the section on Green Spain. See p. 276.)

The Primo de Rivera dictatorship

The coming of age of Isabel II in 1843 did not bring political stability and, in 1868, there was a revolution and the royal family fled to France. Two years later, a provisional government declared Amadeo of Savoy, son of King Victor Manuel II of Italy, King of Spain. Before he even reached Madrid, his principal supporter, General Prim, was assassinated and the carriage in which he was bombed can still be seen at the Army Museum in Madrid. Amadeo abdicated after three short years, and the first Spanish Republic was declared the very same day. This did not, however, last even one year. A general, Pavia, rode into the Parliament on horseback and told the lawmakers to go home. The regime which his action fostered called in the Pretender of the Isabelina line, Alfonso, and proclaimed him King Alfonso XII in 1874. Alfonso died in 1885, and his widow María Cristina took over as regent, already bearing the royal heir, the future King Alfonso XIII.

On the other side of the Atlantic, the US battleship *Maine* was blown up in the Havana harbour in 1898 after several uprisings in Cuba. Who set off the bomb was never proved, but the US Government had been waiting for an incident to justify its entry into the Cuban struggle for independence. When war broke out with the United States, the outmoded Spanish ships were quickly defeated by the more modern American Navy. Thus did Spain lose the last of its possessions in the New World, Cuba, and in the same year in the Far East the Philippines were also lost.

The regency ended in 1902, when King Alfonso XIII officially came of age. At the time troops in Spanish North Africa were warding off ever stronger attacks from the rebels, and on the Spanish mainland, there were riots and general strikes. Spain was able to maintain neutrality throughout the First World War, but in 1921 a Moroccan attack caused 14,000 Spanish casualties in North Africa. The King and the people were understandably anxious for peace and order to be restored.

So, when General Miguel Primo de Rivera issued a proclamation in 1923 that he was taking control of the country long enough to set things right, Alfonso XIII, rather than resist, welcomed him and appointed him as Prime Minister. General Primo de Rivera's statue today adorns the Plaza del Arenal in his hometown, Jerez. For a time, the dictator succeeded in bringing peace, albeit rather fragile, to Spain. In 1930 he retired and his successor, another general appointed by the King, was less proficient at controlling the unstable Spanish nation.

Franco's pacification methods

In nation-wide municipal elections on 12 April 1931, there was a land-slide in favour of Republican candidates. Alfonso XIII interpreted the result to mean that his subjects no longer wanted a monarchy. Hoping to avoid more bloodshed, he drove to Cartagena on the east coast and embarked for France, never to return.

The Second Republic was proclaimed on 14 April, and promptly received diplomatic recognition from France, Britain and the United States. From the start, however, it was troubled by riots, uprisings and other signs of discontent. The Azaña Law, named after the Prime Minister who introduced it, antagonized military officers because it was designed to reduce their power and privileges; and, in 1932, in Seville, there was an army uprising. This was successfully put down but, in 1933, the Cortes alienated another powerful force in Spanish society by nationalizing church property and banning religious orders from teaching. The Government also clipped the wings of trade unions and limited efforts to expand home rule in places like Catalonia and the Basque Country.

When 30,000 miners took part in a revolt in Asturias, the Government called in a military man who had distinguished himself in battles in Morocco and had risen to be Spain's youngest general. He was Francisco Franco Bahamonde, soon to become known simply as Franco. As the commander of units made up of Moroccan soldiers in the Spanish Army, Franco quickly crushed the Asturias revolt with brutal efficiency.

The Civil War

A Popular Front government elected in 1936, uniting Socialists, Communists and members of the Republican Left, dedicated considerable effort to controlling the Fascists as the disturbances continued. On 7 April 1936 right wing parties walked out of the Parliament. On 13 July, a member of Parliament and leader of the Monarchist coalition Bloque Nacional, Jose Calvo Sotelo, was assassinated.

Four days later, Spanish Army garrisons in Morocco rebelled; and the next day, 18 July 1936, General Franco announced the beginning of the uprising over the radio from Tenerife in Spain's Canary Islands. He then flew to North Africa in a private plane chartered by his supporters, and, with several other generals, began the hostilities that were to last three years, leave one million dead and leave the already weakened Spanish economy devastated.

It was a war which was to attract world-wide attention, largely because of the ideological conflict between Communism and Fascism which caught the imagination of European intellectuals. As a result it was chronicled by writers of unusual stature, like Hemingway and Orwell. But it was also a war which was to scatter Spain's best creative talents around the world in exile, like poet Pedro Salinas, or turn them into sanguine sacrifice, like Federico García Lorca, who was shot in 1936 by Nationalist forces. As a Civil War it pitted brother against brother and was a grim prelude to the Second World War. In Guernica, the world's first major bombing raid on a civilian target was carried out. At the Casón del Buen Retiro, an annexe of the Prado in Madrid, you can see Picasso's artistic interpretation of that attack. Near Granada, you can visit the grave of García Lorca.

Franco clung to power from the time he won the war, 1 April 1939, to 20 November 1975, when he died at the age of eighty-two. You can see his tomb, as well as that of Falange founder José Antonio Primo de Rivera, at the immense Valley of the Fallen mausoleum near Madrid. Also near the capital, you can visit the El Pardo Palace where the Generalissimo lived, which has been turned into a museum and a residence for visiting dignitaries. Franco survived a United Nations embargo, international snubs, various assassination attempts and pressures from his own countrymen, retaining a tight control over Spain.

The dictator's determination to hold onto power became the subject of many jokes, such as the one in which a salesman called at the Pardo Palace and offered Franco a turtle for a pet: Franco asked how long the turtle could be expected to live. 'Oh, they live a hundred years or more,' explained the salesman. 'In that case I'm not interested,' said Franco; 'just when I get accustomed to him, he'll go and die.'

In 1953, induced by the Cold War, the United States was the first country to help Franco break out of international isolation. The United States made a deal with the Franco regime allowing them to establish military bases there. This not only gave Spain much needed economic aid, it also indirectly reinforced Franco's internal political position. General Franco's opponents have never forgiven the United States for this action, which they believe helped him to remain in power for as long as he did. This partly explains the reason for today's opposition to the US military presence in Spain and the Spanish Government's ambivalent attitude towards NATO.

Changing times

In the 1960s, fuelled in part by tourism, a new phenomenon in Spain, and in part by the plans of 'technocrat' ministers, the Spanish economy started to pick up. The long-awaited recovery from the ravages of the Civil War began to take place. At the same time, foreign influences, brought by increasing numbers of holiday-makers from abroad, Spanish emigrant workers returning for holidays, and growing trade exchanges, made inroads on the psychological defences of the Franco regime, whose supporters considered it the moral bastion and spiritual reserve of the west.

By the mid-1960s there were simply too many girls in bikinis for the Civil Guard to bundle them all up in blankets and hustle them off to the police station. There was so much British and American music being played on the radio that the Government ordered that Spanish music must be broadcast more frequently than foreign tunes.

Prior censorship was abolished, but not the control of ideas. Books were still subject to censorship and editors were liable to prosecution. The evening newspaper *Madrid* was subjected to a number of fines and temporary closure orders and was finally shut down permanently. Journalists were fined, jailed and barred from working. Many foreign correspondents were expelled or had their permits withdrawn. Foreign publications with anti-government stories simply did not appear on the news-stands.

After unacknowledged fighting in Sidi Ifni in Morocco in the early 1960s, Spain began to pull out of its last colonies and in 1968 granted independence to the small African nation of Equatorial Guinea. Franco then made plans to withdraw from the Spanish Sahara, promising the desert-dwellers a referendum as to possible independence. Those plans collapsed when Franco was on his deathbed and his closest advisers, desperate to avoid any unnecessary conflicts at a time when the domestic situation was very uncertain, yielded to Moroccan and American pressure to give Morocco and Mauritania, two of the nations bordering on the territory, administrative control over it. Spain has never formally disputed Morocco's subsequent claim to sovereignty. The only colonial territories Spain retains today are the free-port and garrison cities of Ceuta and Melilla, enclaves set into Morocco's northern coast.

The making of a king

By means of a pact with his enemy, the pretender to the throne, Don Juan of Bourbon, a son of Alfonso XIII, Franco arranged for the education in Spain of the then Prince Juan Carlos, his son, at all three military academies. Don Juan was interested in the arrangement because he wanted his son to be in close contact with the reality of modern Spain; Franco, for his part, wanted to keep the Prince under his wing. When the Prince's education was completed, Franco appeared before his rubber-stamp Parliament and named Juan Carlos his future successor. To this day, and for all his democratic beliefs, the King has never spoken badly of Franco, who, Juan Carlos once admitted privately, 'acted like a father to me'.

The *éminence grise* of the regime and the dictator's most trusted confidant was Admiral Luis Carrero Blanco. When the extremist organization ETA (Basque Homeland and Liberty) blasted the admiral in his heavy black Dodge over the top of a six-storey building in Madrid in 1973, the regime was deeply shaken.

Final years of Franco regime

In the latter years of the Franco regime, several political trials brought Spain unwanted international attention. Communist Julián Grimau was tried by court martial in the early 1960s for offences committed at the time of the Civil War, more than twenty years before, and was executed by firing squad within hours of his conviction. Leaders of trade unions, which were outlawed, were in Madrid's Palace of Justice awaiting the opening of their trial, the very day Admiral Carrero Blanco was killed, and were later given long prison sentences. They had been arrested while meeting in a monastery in Madrid, for the church in Franco's final years was a strong supporter of democratic reform. The first important trial of ETA members took place in Burgos in 1970, when nine of them were accused in connection with the killing of a police chief and were condemned to death by a military court. This sentence was later commuted to life imprisonment as a result of a Christmas reprieve from Franco. In his final year, four members of left-wing revolutionary organizations were court-martialled and executed by firing squads.

Violent opponents of the regime retaliated by shooting three policemen dead in different parts of Madrid on the morning of what turned out to be the General's last public appearance, on 1 October 1975. More than 100,000 people (official estimates said one million) chanted 'Franco, Franco, Franco!' as he waved weakly from the balcony of the Royal Palace facing the Plaza de Oriente.

Franco had fallen gravely ill, though official sources denied it, in autumn 1974, but he had recovered. Then in 1975 he suffered a heart attack during a cabinet meeting, though the official version was that he had a cold. He went from bad to worse, undergoing operations for a variety of ailments. Wired up, covered in tubes and surrounded by the most sophisticated medical equipment available, the tough old man clung to life with the same tenacity with which he had kept all Spain in his cold grip for decades. On 20 November 1975, before dawn, his death was finally announced, though for many days he had been kept alive only by a life support machine.

Hundreds of thousands of Spaniards waited in long queues to file past the coffin in the huge Royal Palace and to pay their last respects to a man who was bitterly hated by many and – to judge from the tears – loved by some too. In spite of make-up, the face of the corpse was purple; not even the embalmers could erase the marks of his final suffering, prolonged, ironically, by those who most wanted to keep him alive, but for reasons of their own. When the half-ton slab was slid into place over his coffin at the Valley of the Fallen, the joke going the rounds in Madrid was a warning to opponents of the regime: Wait until the third day to make sure he does not rise again.

The post-Franco era

Juan Carlos was formally installed as King by the Cortes, as Franco had planned. In his inaugural speech, the monarch said he wanted to be 'the King of all Spaniards'. This turned out to be more than rhetoric; and, to everybody's surprise, the dictator's protégé revealed himself as a man committed to democracy. But the first six months and more after Franco's death were marked by disturbances and demonstrations, as pressure built up for a more rapid transition to democracy. King Juan Carlos replaced General Franco's last Prime Minister, Carlos Arias, with a dynamic young political unknown, Adolfo Suárez. Suárez dismantled the bureaucratic machinery of the Franco regime, persuaded Franco's rubber-stamp Parliament to vote itself out of office and call new elections, and won the first post-Franco general elections himself in 1977. Members of the newly-elected parliament drew up a constitution, which was approved in a referendum and came into effect in 1978.

Regional self-government, authorized by the constitution, gave certain regions, such as the Basque Country, Catalonia and Galicia, considerable autonomy and it partially decentralized control over the affairs of the fourteen other regions. Basques and Catalans, among others, still want a greater degree of home rule, and some parties that are represented in Parliament are demanding independence for their respective regions.

The man in the patent leather hat

The winner of the next elections as well, Suárez shortly saw his hastily-formed party, the Centre Democratic Union, disintegrating as a result of internal power struggles. In a surprise move, he resigned as Prime Minister. He was succeeded by another member of his own party, Leopoldo Calvo Sotelo, without further elections at that time.

On 23 February 1981, as Calvo Sotelo was delivering his inaugural address in the Parliament, some soldiers led by Colonel Antonio Tejero, in his green Civil Guard uniform complete with patent leather hat, seized the Cortes and held the entire Parliament and Government at gunpoint throughout a tense night. It was only the King's direct appeal to military district commanders that thwarted the attempted coup. Marks left on the ceiling by bursts of machine-gun fire, used to intimidate the parliamentary deputies, have been left unrepaired, as a reminder that democracy in Spain still has its opponents.

NATO and defence

Later in 1981, the Cortes voted in favour of joining the North Atlantic Treaty Organization, in spite of strong objections from the left. Socialist leader Felipe González warned Parliament that if a simple majority in the Cortes was all that was needed to put Spain into NATO, then a simple majority could take it out again the day his party came to power. He did not have to wait long for that day to come. In the 1982 elections, the Socialists won by an overwhelming majority and Felipe González headed Spain's first Socialist government. One of his campaign promises had been a referendum on NATO, but once in power, González had second thoughts about withdrawing. He delayed the referendum as long as he could. Then, to make the NATO pill more palatable to his leftist supporters, the question the referendum put to Spaniards, in paraphrase, was: Do you want Spain to form a part of the western defence alliance, reduce the American military presence in this country, and remain out of the military structure of NATO? Answer yes or no.

Spaniards voted to remain in NATO – but with those restrictive conditions. On 1 January 1986, Spain became a member of the European Economic Community. In June 1986, the Spanish Socialist Workers' Party again won general elections, with a large majority, sufficient to be able to continue to govern alone. A split between the party and the trade unions, including the Socialist-led General Workers' Union, became worse as the Government continued, in its second term, to pursue economic policies that the unions considered antisocial.

Spain Today

How Spain is governed

Modern Spain is a constitutional monarchy with a bicameral parliament. The lower and more powerful house is the Congress of Deputies. The upper house, the Senate, was originally conceived of as a chamber in which the interests of the various regions would be represented, but it has not turned out that way, and is more or less a duplicate of the lower house as far as its political composition is concerned. The Parliament is often referred to as the Cortes, the old Spanish word for it.

The normal parliamentary term of office is four years, but it can be less. In general elections, Spaniards do not vote for individuals. Rather, they must choose a group of candidates from among the various lists, each compiled by a particular party or coalition. It is not possible to vote for a candidate on one list and another on a different one. Local and regional representation is somewhat frustrated by this system, since there are no residency requirements for candidates standing for election as deputies from the various regions. As a result, most lists are made up at the parties' national headquarters in Madrid, and for the most part they include politicians who belong to the central power structure of any given party. It is thus possible for a person to hold a seat in Parliament without ever having lived in the region which he theoretically represents.

The Government is chosen by the Prime Minister, who is nominated by the King, and whose appointment must be approved by the Parliament. The King, as Chief of State, has no real constitutional powers, but, in fact, his influence has been crucial on a number of occasions since the constitution came into effect.

Spain is made up of seventeen 'autonomous regions', each of which contains one or more provinces. Each region has its own local government. Certain regions, like Catalonia, the Basque Country and Galicia, have a greater degree of self-government than the others. For instance, the Basque region and Catalonia have their own police forces.

The Socialists can now be expected to remain in power until 1990, unless early elections are called. Felipe González, a lawyer from Seville with a convincing manner, is the Prime Minister for a second

Regions

term and though his cabinet has undergone some changes, it remains wholly Socialist. The major opposition party is the conservative Popular Alliance, headed by another young Andalusian lawyer, Antonio Hernández Mancha. Adolfo Suárez, the first Prime Minister of the post-Franco era, leads the Social Democratic Centre, a centre-left party which has shown significant gains in the last two elections. Among other principal parties or coalitions with representation in the Cortes are the Popular Democratic Party (Christian Democrat), the Liberal Party, the United Left (a Communist-led coalition) and a number of regional parties, particularly from the Basque Country and Catalonia. The economy, which has been depressed for the last decade, has recently shown signs of picking up. There have been well-founded hopes that the unemployment level, one of Europe's highest at 22 per cent, has been about to drop. Government efforts to curb inflation also seemed to be working, with a rate of a little over 5 per cent in 1987, down from the 1986 rate of approximately 8 per cent.

Social changes

Few Spaniards had much time for frivolity, and indeed it was actively discouraged, during at least the first half of Franco's long rule. Reliable unemployment figures were not available then, but the job shortage was severe enough to cause hundreds of thousands of Spaniards to leave their families and emigrate, mostly to other parts of Europe, to take even the hardest, most menial jobs.

At the end of the 1960s and in the early 1970s that situation started to change as Spain began to become industrialized. Cheap, and ugly, blocks of flats were built on the outskirts of the large cities, as families moved out of the poor villages to be near the factories – and jobs.

In the schools, from the first form to university level, students were required to study the 'Three Marias': religion (the Roman Catholic one, of course, which was the official creed of the state); political science (the regime's own version of its glorious contribution to history); and physical education.

Crime was not, at least apparently not, the problem it is today. In the first place, the police could do pretty much what they pleased, and their word was usually sufficient to have a person convicted. There were certainly no investigations into police maltreatment of prisoners. In the circumstances, cases were often solved in record time. In the second place, not all crimes were revealed, presumably because they reflected badly on the Government. Publisher Eugenio Suárez, the founder of *El Caso*, a weekly tabloid dedicated to reporting crimes in the most lurid fashion, was for many years restricted to one murder case per week and censored at that; usually there was no limit on reporting other types of crime, except where reports would cause unwanted scandal, such as those about crimes committed by priests or Government officials. There was little pornography and no casinos. Pages ripped out of *Playboy* magazine were peddled under the counter at Madrid's flea market. Paradoxically, prostitution was relatively free from persecution.

Pio Cabanillas, one of General Franco's last Ministers of Information and Tourism, was sacked, reportedly because one of Cabanillas' enemies presented the General with a dossier of revealing photos of pretty girls, which Cabanillas had allegedly allowed to be printed. Franco never found out that not all the photos had actually been published in Spain.

There was an incipient drug problem. Marijuana smoking was fairly common and it had begun to be sold illegally at schools in Madrid in the mid-1960s. Religious holidays were public ones. Carnival *fiestas* were forbidden. In Holy Week, everything that smacked of enjoyment was closed, except the bars and cinemas which showed films with approved religious themes. The only entertainment allowed was football and bullfights, *tapas* and conversation in the bars, card games and an occasional night at the theatre, censored, of course. Television did not reach Spain until the late 1960s – and there was initially only one channel. Then came Sunday traffic jams, and the littering of all beauty spots within easy reach of major towns, as Spaniards, schooled in the Three Marias but not in civic duties, began to have family cars.

As Franco grew older, it became harder for him to resist the impetus of change, and when he died it was though a dam had burst.

There is high unemployment today but less hunger than before because, though not every jobless family benefits, there are various kinds of aid for the unemployed. In contrast there are more beggars on the streets, as the authorities now make little effort to prevent begging, as the police used to. The flow of people from villages to the cities has stopped, and is actually going into reverse in some places as a result of the prolonged recession, which has reduced the number of industrial jobs in the cities.

Entertainment is now big business. There are discos everywhere, catering to a vast young crowd with nothing to do, because unemployment is worst among school-leavers. Plays are uncensored and there are more of them, with local governments sponsoring more musical and theatrical events. Football and the bullfights are bigger than ever. Pornography is now widespread and casinos are to be found all over Spain.

Women's rights and attitudes towards women have changed considerably. While it is fair to say that Spanish women had access to certain professions such as the law and engineering under Franco, and also that Spanish women have always retained their maiden names on marriage, there is no doubt that women are much freer and their horizons are much less restricted today, than they were previously. No longer does a married woman need her husband's authorization to open a bank account and no longer are women arrested for wearing daring fashions or for bathing topless. Barriers to career opportunities for women are falling so fast that even the paramilitary Civil Guard police has announced it will soon be admitting women.

Weekly church attendance has remained fairly static since the last few years of the Franco regime, estimated at about 20 per cent of the baptized population, but most people still christen their children and arrange funeral masses for their dead. There have been fewer marriages in recent years; and birth control methods forbidden by the church are widely accepted. Religions other than Roman Catholicism are no longer suppressed or barred from proselytizing. The assortment of sects that had sprung up in the United States during the past generation has spread to Spain, and has met little legal resistance.

Crime rates soared after Franco's death. Officials brandish statistics to show things are no worse here than, say, in London or Rome, but that is small consolation to the victim. Companies offering anti-theft equipment and private security firms are doing a roaring trade. The law is partly to blame: at present a suspect whose offence would normally bring a sentence of fourteen months or less is generally freed pending trial, with the result that petty criminals keep on stealing even after repeated arrests.

Official holidays no longer necessarily coincide with religious holy days, though most towns still celebrate their annual *fiestas* around the feastday of their patron saints. Since some holidays are declared by the central government and some by the respective regional government, a holiday in one place is not always a holiday elsewhere. Carnival time and other celebrations suppressed by the previous regime because of their presumed subversive or immoral nature are unhindered today.

There are problems in education, which led to strikes and violent demonstrations in Madrid and some other cities in 1987, but they are not about the Three Marias. Religion classes are optional. Propaganda for the regime is no longer a classroom affair. Physical education is still on the school timetables, however.

Siesta

Modern life has taken its toll on the siesta. Very few people now have the opportunity to take an afternoon nap. Among reasons for this are the time it takes to travel even in medium-sized cities between home and work and the uninterrupted work shifts at most factories and many offices. Another reason is that with so many women now working there is often no one at home to prepare a big midday meal and hustle the snoozers off to their jobs again after their rest.

By the same token, Spanish eating habits are changing. Working women have less time to prepare the slow-cooking, traditional stews that also take hours to prepare. More and more, they rely on frozen and convenience foods, though not yet to the extent that housewives of more northerly countries do.

Remnants of more leisurely working hours exist here and there, however. All shops, apart from major department stores and the big supermarkets, pull down the shutters and close between about 1.30 and 5 p.m. all over the country, as do some offices. Also, hours for doing any official business with government departments are usually restricted to between 11 a.m. and 1 p.m.

In summer, however, things become more confusing. The offices of most companies then work an uninterrupted shift which normally begins at about 8 a.m. and continues until about 3 p.m., but a minority still stick to traditional times. Museums and such almost invariably close for the siesta hours, and some are open in the morning only.

Staying awake

With or without a siesta, Spaniards are night owls. They are a gregarious people and they tend to keep late hours. The simple truth is, Spaniards probably sleep less than people north of the Pyrenees; the meal times should give you a clue to that. Climate probably has as much to do with this as custom.

You may be surprised to find children with their families in bars, or late at night at a *fiesta*. This is especially so when there is no school the next day, for Spaniards love to be with their children as often as possible. Notwithstanding the falling birth rate, there is still a strong family tradition. Although children are barred from bullfights and X-rated films, you will see them at the race track, at fairs at all hours and playing outside long after dark.

Living standards

Even in the villages, the average Spanish family today has at least standard modern conveniences, such as a car, a refrigerator, a washing machine, a television set and a telephone – and many also have videos, freezers, personal computers and private swimming pools. The per capita income is £2,700 ($4,470) per year, compared, for example, with the United Kingdom's £5,200 ($8,530). On average, wage levels are about 60 per cent of what they are in Britain, but there are marked differences between the two countries in some categories. For instance, though top Spanish business executives earn less than their British counterparts, good Spanish secretaries earn more on average than they would in Britain.

Spanish salaries seem low to the outsider, but they are, in fact, higher than they appear because of the universal practice of paying employees an extra month's pay at least twice a year. Some companies hand out four or even more extra months' paycheques per year. Salaries vary from one part of the country to another, but in Madrid, for example, unskilled labourers and cleaners earn about 55,000 pesetas a month upwards; skilled industrial workers generally earn from 90,000 to 140,000 pesetas a month.

Spain does have a free public health service, but it does not cover the full cost of medicines, and its coverage for psychiatric illnesses is extremely restricted. To receive free treatment, you must show a *cartilla*, a type of identity card, which is given to wage-earners and their families. There are long hospital waiting lists and they are getting longer. Private medicine, clinics and health insurance coexist with the public health system.

Most Spanish families live in flats, but there is a growing tendency, particularly in the upper-middle income bracket, towards individual houses either terraced or detached. It is common for the new estates to have community swimming pools and tennis courts.

Most Spanish families take a one-month holiday, and nearly all of them take it entirely in the month of August, with the effect that the whole country, including the Government and the civil service, just about shuts down for those four weeks.

Spain used to have the reputation of being a cheap country. While it is not expensive compared with, say, Britain or France, it is more expensive than Portugal or Greece. Some package holidays can be extremely economical, primarily because of the huge volume of trade handled by the tour operators and hotel chains which cater for this type of tourism. Hotels generally offer good value for money, but internal air fares are on the high side.

National and regional characteristics

Generalizations are always risky, but they are especially so in Spain, where there are pronounced regional differences. But I will offer a few in an attempt to portray some of the common factors. The average

Spaniard is a very helpful, open person, welcoming strangers, but generally he (or she) invites home only close friends. He makes an effort to understand foreigners, which cannot be said for many countries. He spoils children but is not keen on pets. This, however, seems to be changing fast, to judge by the sharp increase in pet food sales and in dog-do on the pavements. He can be opinionated and hot-headed, but he seldom resorts to force. He likes wine, and, increasingly, beer, but there are few drunks on the streets, which is perhaps because of the custom of having a *tapa* with a drink.

He is more amused than scandalized by the antics, misdemeanours or aberrations of the famous and powerful. He is quick to belittle and disparage anything Spanish and to praise foreign innovations or inventions, though deep down he is emotionally tied to his own ways and customs. He thinks of himself first as a Basque, an Andalusian, a Catalan or whatever rather than as a Spaniard.

A Spanish friend of mine explained the question of regional autonomy to me this way: the Basques want to be alone to concentrate collectively on their navels until everybody in the Basque Country knows the word for 'navel' in their language, Euskera. The Catalans want more home rule so they can run Spain's affairs as well as their own and handle all the business deals. The Galicians want more self-government so Madrid will leave them alone, while the Andalusians feel the central government has left them alone too long, and for that reason they want more self-government.

That is a gross simplification, of course, but it gives you an idea of the collective temperament of the people of some of Spain's most characteristic regions.

Women travelling alone

Modern Spain accepts the woman business executive, the woman in a liberal profession, policewomen, female taxi drivers, and even firewomen. There are still a lot of Don Juans around, but women need have no fear of travelling alone these days in Spain. Many Spanish girls travel without male accompaniment, though usually they travel in small groups of two or three.

Dangerous situations for a woman travelling alone, or two or three women travelling together, are similar to the kind women are familiar with in more northerly countries. In other words, hitch-hiking, accepting invitations from male strangers, and the like, are to be handled with due caution.

In trains, couchette compartments have six to eight bunks. Tickets are sold to individuals and to groups of either sex, so you are likely to find both men and women in the same compartment for which you have a reservation. The custom is to sleep clothed in the couchettes.

It costs a bit more to book a 'tourist' bed in a Wagon-Lit sleeper coach, but there are advantages. The compartments are segregated by sex, except in the case of a family taking a whole compartment, the beds are more comfortable, and it is customary to sleep in night-clothes. You can also, of course, have a compartment to yourself if you travel first class.

Unmarried couples and homosexuality

For the most part, Spaniards are not concerned about the marital status of couples travelling together. In years past, some hotels were stuffy about this matter, but this is no longer the case. Furthermore, since Spanish women retain their maiden names after marriage, hotel clerks are accustomed to seeing different surnames on a couple's identity cards. However, you shouldn't try to bring a friend of the opposite sex to your room unless he or she is registered with you. Most hotels do not allow this.

Homosexual and lesbian couples may attract attention in certain places and situations, but they are not prosecuted or, as a rule, harassed. These days attitudes towards gays in Spain are generally more liberal, and there are certain bars where they tend to gather in most cities.

Police

In most of Spain there are three kinds of uniformed policemen: the Municipal Police, who wear blue uniforms, the National Police, who wear khaki or brown army-style uniforms with berets and the Civil Guards, who dress in green and wear either a distinctive black patent-leather hat or a green overseas cap.

If you need help in the city, call on the Municipal Policemen (*Policía Municipal*), who usually direct city traffic and patrol in white or blue cars. However, to report a theft or almost any other type of crime, you should go to the nearest station of the National Police. These policemen patrol on foot in pairs and in vehicles, which may be either white or tan.

The Civil Guard (*Guardia Civil*) forces are responsible for traffic control, rural law enforcement and customs and excise. Report road accidents to them.

If your wallet or purse is stolen, do not forget to make a formal complaint at the nearest *comisaría* (police station), where you will be given a copy of the statement you made. This is required in order to make any insurance claim and to apply for another passport if yours has been stolen. Spanish cities are no more crime-free than London or Melbourne, so take elementary precautions: see pp. 152 to 153.

In the Basque Country, Catalonia and Navarra there are also regional police forces, which are gradually assuming the responsibilities of the Civil Guard and the National Police. In any case, you should still ask for the *policía*, or the *comisaría de policía*.

Customs and courtesies

In Madrid they say Spain has been on the threshold of a new era for a long time; but it remains there, because the average Spaniard is so insistent on stepping aside to allow others to pass through a door first. That is not altogether true. Because men hold doors open for ladies, it is the Spanish women who have entered a new era and they are waiting for the men to stop quibbling and catch up.

Polite as they are in many respects, Spaniards are incapable of forming or keeping to a queue. Whenever you go to, say, the Post Office, or the cinema, there will always be a queue-jumper. And, so far as catching a bus in a town is concerned, it is every man or woman for himself. You should keep an eye out for the queue-creeper, who edges forward bit by bit, taking advantage of the ragged nature of Spanish queues.

You are not expected to pay for your drinks each time you are served at a Spanish café, bar or pub. (Yes, they have lots of pubs, with wood-panelled décor, modelled on the typical English public house.) The custom is to pay only when you have finished and are ready to leave. This is one reason why some people nurse a coffee for an hour or so, using a café table as a desk to do their office work or simply pass the time of day.

Other customs which may surprise you are the kisses exchanged between male and female acquaintances whenever they meet: a kiss on both cheeks in Madrid and in the north, and on one cheek only in the south. Men friends simply embrace and pat each other on the back.

In the lift, in shops, on the streets, people often say '*Buenos días*' (Good morning) to strangers. This is especially so in smaller towns. In restaurants, strangers are never seated together at the same table, as they are in some other countries. Even if there are many seats vacant because a number of tables are occupied by a single person each, you should wait until a table is free for you or your group.

A few words of Spanish

Everybody in Spain can speak Castilian, but in parts of Spain the people have their own languages. This situation has become more pronounced since the granting of regional autonomy. However, it is not necessary for you to speak Catalan, Basque or Galician. English is the most commonly understood foreign language in Spain, but here are a few common Spanish words and phrases. See also pp. 55 to 57 for more words relating to food and drink.

One	*un, uno*	Twelve	*doce*
Two	*dos*	Twenty	*veinte*
Three	*tres*	Thirty	*treinta*
Four	*cuatro*	Forty	*cuarenta*
Five	*cinco*	Fifty	*cincuenta*
Six	*seis*	Sixty	*sesenta*
Seven	*siete*	Seventy	*setenta*
Eight	*ocho*	Eighty	*ochenta*
Nine	*nueve*	Ninety	*noventa*
Ten	*diez*	A hundred	*cien*
Eleven	*once*	A thousand	*mil*

Adaptor plug	*enchufe adaptor*
Aeroplane	*avión*
Airport	*aeropuerto*
Bank	*banco*
Beach	*playa*
Bridge	*puente*
Bullring	*plaza de toros*
Bus	*autobús*
Bus station	*estación de autobuses*
Bus stop	*parada*
Chambermaid	*camarera*
Church	*iglesia*
Doctor (medical)	*médico*
Drink (noun)	*bebida*
Beer	*cerveza*
Coffee	*café*
Milk	*leche*
Mineral water	*agua mineral*
Soft drink	*refresco*
Water	*agua*
Electrician	*electricista*
Ferry	*transbordador*
Food	*comida*

Butcher's shop	*carnicería*
Fish shop	*pescadería*
Food shop	*ultramarinos*
Greengrocer's	*frutería*
Supermarket	*supermercado*
Gas (bottled)	*butano*
Golf course	*campo de golf*
Help!	*¡socorro!*
Hospital	*hospital*
Hotel	*hotel*
Inn (state-run)	*parador*
Boarding house	*pensión*
House	*casa*
How much is it?	*¿cuánto vale?*
I need ...	*necesito ...*
Information office	*oficina de información*
Mechanic	*mecánico*
Medicine	*medicina*
Money	*dinero*
Mosque	*mezquita*
Motor car	*coche*
Museum	*museo*
Petrol	*gasolina*
Petrol station	*gasolinera*
Please	*por favor*
Police	*policía*
Police station	*comisaría*
Post Office	*oficina de correos*
River	*río*
Road	*carretera*
Square	*plaza*
Street	*calle*
Strolling area	*paseo*
Speak slowly (request)	*hable despacio*
Swimming pool	*piscina*
Synagogue	*sinagoga*
Thank you	*gracias*
Tobacconist's	*estanco*
Toilet	*retrete*
Tourist Office	*oficina de turismo*
Town Hall	*ayuntamiento*
Train	*tren*
Train station	*estación de ferrocarril*
Transformer	*transformador*
Waiter	*camarero*
What?	*¿cómo?*

What is this?	¿esto qué es?
When?	¿cuándo?
Where is...?	¿dónde está...?
Who?	¿quién?

Pronunciation

Spanish is not hard to read or understand because it is pronounced as it is spelt. Here are a few fundamental rules to get you started:

● The vowels are a, e, i, o, u, pronounced ah, eh, ee, oh, ooh.

● The consonants are the same ones used in the English language, except for:

W, which technically does not exist, plus –

CH, which is considered just one letter and is pronounced like the 'ch' in 'chocolate';

LL, which is considered one letter and sounds something like the 'y' in 'young',

Ñ, which is pronounced with an 'ny' sound, as in 'vineyard', and

RR, which is considered one letter and is simply trilled more than the single 'r'.

● R is spoken at the front of the mouth, making the tongue vibrate.

● C is pronounced hard, as in 'cad', except when it precedes 'e' or 'i'. In that case it sounds like 'th' in 'thistle' in Madrid and northern areas, or like the 's' in 'sister' in the south.

● G is pronounced hard, as in 'regain', except when it precedes 'e' or 'i'. In that case it sounds something like an aspirated 'h', as in 'heat'. When G is followed by a 'u' and another vowel, the 'u' is not normally pronounced but the G remains hard.

● H is normally not pronounced.

● J sounds like an aspirated 'h'.

● Q, almost invariably followed by 'u', is pronounced like a hard 'c'.

● Z is pronounced like 'th' in the north and like a soft 's' in the south.

● All the other consonants sound pretty much like their counterparts in English.

The Weather and When to Go

Spain is so big and has so many different climates that any time is a good time to visit. However, when to go may depend on what you expect to do. Putting it very succinctly, if beaches and water sports are what you want, the Costa del Sol and the east coast south of Tarragona are fine from May to the end of September, with good spells in March and April. The same sort of timetable applies to beaches in the south-west.

If it is ski-related activities that you seek in Spain, then you should go between December and March, although November, April and May are often all right as well. That is equally true of the Pyrenees ski resorts and the ones as far south as Granada.

If hunting and fishing attract you, you should time your holiday to coincide with the open season for the catch you expect to get. To do that, contact one of the Spanish National Tourist Offices, or the Spanish Hunting Federation (Federación Española de Caza, Calle Ortega y Gasset 5, 28006 Madrid), to find out the dates.

If you are planning to walk or camp, late spring and summer are best in the centre and north, and late spring or early autumn in the south. If you are touring a number of inland places in the northern half of the Peninsula for whatever reason, avoid late December, January and February if you are travelling by car, because mountain passes are then frequently closed or difficult to cross. Remember, Spain is the second highest country, in terms of average altitude, in Europe, next to Switzerland.

To give you an idea of the temperature range in various parts of Spain, here were the maximum and minimum Centigrade temperatures for a number of places, measured in July (usually the hottest month) and February (usually the coldest) in 1986:

Place	February Max/Min	July Max/Min
Barcelona	21.4/−3.2	33.4/16.4
Cáceres	16.4/−1.6	39.2/13
Corunna	17/1.6	28/12.6

Madrid	14/−3.2	37.5/14
Málaga	25.6/1.8	37.2/16.4
San Sebastián	18/−5.8	34/13.6
Saragossa	18.6/−2.4	37/14.5
Seville	20.6/−0.4	40.6/15.6
Toledo	16.9/−5	40.8/13.3
Valencia	23/0.6	41.8/17

Average number of rainy days and hours of bright sunshine per year (1940–80):

Place	Rainy days	Hours of sunshine a year
Barcelona	100	2,476
Cáceres	97	2,730
Corunna	194	2,047
Madrid	98	2,864
Málaga	62	3,023
San Sebastián	197	1,830
Saragossa	94	2,728
Seville	71	2,892
Toledo	96	2,894
Valencia	94	2,631

Travelling Around

No matter how you travel around Spain, you will gain from it. The visitor who goes to only one or two places, and stays put, learns a lot less about the country than the one who moves around. Depending on how much time you have, you will find it rewarding to see a variety of places. This is the best way to get an idea of Spain's tremendous variations in landscape, climate, architecture, customs and languages. You will also get more of a chance to meet the people.

You will find most Spaniards friendly and very willing to help. Do not hesitate to ask directions or small favours. Generally, a Spaniard will go out of his way to be courteous to a stranger. Another good trait is that they make an effort to understand you if you do not speak their language.

There are all sorts of ways to get around, from bicycle or burro to private jet.

By car

Documents
The ideal way to get around is by car since it offers flexibility in timing and flexibility as far as the route is concerned. If you use your own car, you should have the 'green card', which is an international insurance guarantee (see p. 68). Whether you use your own or a hired car, you should have an international driving licence, which is issued by Automobile Clubs in most countries on production of a valid national licence. If your stay is short, however, your normal driving licence is acceptable.

Driving habits
In Britain, they drive on the left. In the United States they drive on the right. In Spain they drive on both sides and in the middle, preferably simultaneously. Drive defensively in Spain. Every Spaniard behind the wheel of his or her little Seat has a Formula-1 complex. Watch out for the following unnerving driving habits, which are not exclusive to Spaniards but typical of them:

● Whizzing through lights as they change to red. Defensive action: Do not stop on amber or you stand a very good chance of being rammed from behind.

● Double and triple parking, and leaving their cars unattended that way for long periods, thus blocking others who are parked by the kerb. Defensive action: If you are going to stop briefly, double-park yourself

Distance Chart

Albacete	Alicante	Almería	Ávila	Badajoz	Barcelona	Bilbao	Burgos	Cáceres	Cádiz	Castellon	Ciudad Real	Cordoba	Corunna	Cuenca	Gerona	Granada	Guadalajara	Huelva	Huesca	Jaen	León	Lérida	Logroño	Lugo	Madrid	Málaga	Murcia	Orense	Oviedo	Palencia	Pamplona	Pontevedra	Salamanca	San Sebastián	Santander	Segovia	Seville	Soria	Tarragona	Teruel	Toledo	Valencia	Valladolid	Vitoria	Zamora	Saragossa (Zaragoza)
171
369	294
366	537	663
525	696	604	318
540	515	809	717	1022
646	817	958	401	694	620
488	659	800	243	536	583	158
504	675	651	229	89	918	605	447
617	688	484	618	342	1284	1058	900	389
256	231	525	532	805	284	607	524	701	873
207	378	407	256	318	811	585	427	324	464	463
354	525	332	457	272	908	795	637	319	263	610	201
860	1031	1172	538	772	1118	644	535	683	1072	1026	799	995
142	313	511	282	555	562	562	404	451	708	305	244	445	776
640	615	909	817	1122	100	720	683	1018	1384	384	911	1008	1218	662
363	353	166	534	438	868	829	671	485	335	584	278	166	1043	479	968
309	480	621	173	459	563	396	238	355	721	396	248	458	667	186	663	492
506	703	516	552	251	1140	939	781	323	219	856	433	232	1006	677	1240	350	690
495	570	830	490	798	274	322	359	694	1060	355	587	797	905	406	374	831	339	1029
264	415	228	435	376	804	730	572	423	367	520	179	104	944	380	904	99	393	336	732
584	755	896	255	496	784	359	201	407	796	725	511	733	334	500	884	761	391	730	560	668
515	490	802	558	866	156	464	427	762	1128	259	655	865	973	472	256	861	407	1097	118	779	628
578	653	899	358	676	468	152	115	595	999	455	526	736	650	464	568	770	278	968	244	671	316	312
762	933	1074	440	674	1020	546	437	585	974	928	696	897	98	678	1120	945	569	908	807	846	236	875	552
251	422	563	115	401	621	395	237	297	663	417	190	400	609	167	721	434	58	632	397	335	333	465	336	511
473	482	219	644	436	997	939	781	506	265	713	388	187	1153	615	1097	129	602	313	941	209	877	1009	880	1055	544
150	75	219	516	675	590	796	638	654	613	306	357	444	1010	292	690	278	459	628	611	340	734	583	694	912	401	407
772	943	1084	443	645	1027	605	447	556	945	938	699	921	175	689	1127	955	579	879	803	856	271	871	562	95	521	1065	922
702	873	1014	373	614	902	304	322	525	914	868	641	851	340	618	1002	885	509	821	626	786	118	703	391	242	451	995	852	337
491	662	803	168	461	669	244	86	372	761	596	424	640	450	407	769	674	298	695	442	575	130	513	201	352	240	784	641	361	248
598	673	970	437	755	437	159	203	650	1070	458	597	807	738	535	537	841	349	1039	163	742	404	281	88	640	407	951	714	650	463	289
874	1045	1186	545	747	1129	707	549	658	1047	1040	701	977	121	791	1229	1057	681	981	905	957	373	973	664	148	623	1153	1024	102	390	463	752
463	634	763	97	299	778	395	237	210	599	629	353	529	473	379	878	631	270	533	554	532	197	622	352	375	212	756	613	346	315	162	440	448
691	766	1032	475	768	529	119	232	679	1132	551	659	869	763	636	629	903	441	1101	255	804	433	373	169	665	469	1013	807	679	423	318	92	781	469
644	815	956	369	662	693	108	156	573	1056	680	583	793	547	560	793	827	394	962	430	728	293	537	225	449	393	937	794	544	207	201	267	666	363	227
338	509	650	67	385	650	355	197	296	750	504	277	497	560	254	750	521	145	619	426	422	245	494	299	462	87	631	488	467	363	158	370	569	164	429	359
492	609	422	493	217	1046	933	775	264	125	762	339	138	947	583	1146	256	596	94	935	242	671	1003	874	849	538	219	534	820	789	636	945	922	474	1007	837	560
473	548	794	261	579	453	257	141	490	894	383	421	631	676	359	553	665	173	863	229	566	342	297	105	578	231	775	589	574	463	213	176	676	325	268	297	194	769
443	417	711	649	935	98	555	518	831	1059	186	649	796	1064	464	198	770	476	1029	209	707	719	91	403	966	534	899	492	962	835	604	372	1064	713	464	628	585	949	388
242	317	577	417	703	409	488	372	599	873	152	397	596	907	153	509	605	244	842	253	506	573	319	336	809	302	715	358	805	694	444	356	907	514	449	528	389	748	231	311
240	411	526	137	368	692	466	308	264	583	437	119	320	675	187	792	397	129	552	468	298	392	536	407	577	71	507	390	580	510	305	478	682	234	540	464	158	458	302	605	340
191	166	460	467	716	349	633	517	636	808	65	398	545	961	220	449	519	410	791	398	455	685	324	481	863	352	648	241	873	803	592	501	975	564	594	673	439	697	376	251	145	372
444	615	756	121	414	663	280	122	325	714	563	377	578	455	360	763	627	251	648	439	528	134	507	237	357	193	737	594	356	252	47	325	458	115	354	248	111	589	210	598	441	258	545
602	739	914	357	650	530	66	114	561	1014	574	541	751	549	518	630	785	352	919	256	686	315	374	86	451	351	895	752	561	340	200	93	663	351	118	174	311	825	191	489	422	422	576	236
499	670	811	159	361	759	376	218	272	661	665	415	616	411	415	859	682	306	595	535	583	135	603	333	313	248	792	649	284	253	143	421	386	62	450	344	182	536	306	694	537	296	600	96	332
423	498	758	418	726	296	324	287	622	988	283	515	725	833	334	396	759	267	957	72	660	488	140	172	735	325	869	539	731	604	373	175	833	482	268	397	354	863	157	231	181	396	326	367	258	463

even if there is an empty space at the kerb. Otherwise you might be trapped until you can find the owner of the double-parked car which will invariably block your exit.

● Ignoring lines painted on the street. Spanish drivers frequently make four lanes out of three, and the crosshatched lines at junctions that indicate areas which should be left clear seem to be little more than decoration. Defensive action: Take a taxi in rush hours; you won't get there any faster, but your nerves will be in better shape.

● Disdain for zebra crossings. Defensive action: Never trust a zebra or else don't be a pedestrian.

● Overtaking blind on narrow roads, or overtaking near the top of a hill. Many Spanish lorries are underpowered, and impatient drivers often overtake other vehicles in dangerous circumstances. Defensive action: Pray.

Speed limits
Unless otherwise posted, these are 120 km/hour on motorways, 100 on good normal roads (110 for overtaking) and 40 in built-up areas.

Tyre chains
The roads in Spain can be treacherously slippery, so do not travel in winter without tyre chains.

Petrol
There is no point in looking for a bargain in petrol (*gasolina*) prices. It costs the same everywhere because there is a petroleum monopoly in Spain. Do not expect service at petrol stations. It is practically non-existent. Only if an attendant helps you to put air in your tyres or performs some other minor maintenance chore should you give a tip of a few 5-peseta coins or a 25-peseta piece, depending on what he does. Do not let your petrol supply fall below one-fourth of a tank; in some remote areas petrol stations are few and far between.

When travelling at night, order petrol in exact cash amounts, for example 2,000 pesetas worth; some petrol stations will not give change late at night as a defence against robbery.

There are two basic grades of petrol, Super and Regular (both spelled this way in Spanish too). Most modern cars, manufactured for fuel with an octane rating in the upper 90s, use Super. Unleaded fuel is available at extra cost at only a very few stations. Diesel fuel is available almost everywhere; not only lorries but many Spanish passenger cars use diesel fuel (*petroleo* or *gas-oil* in Spanish) for reasons of economy. Super petrol costs about 78 pesetas a litre, Normal costs about 72 pesetas and diesel fuel costs approximately 58 pesetas.

Repairs
Breakdowns are not the problem they used to be. Since Spain entered the Common Market, all the major west European car manufacturers have dealerships in principal cities, so there is more of a chance of finding the parts you need. This is not true of Japanese-made cars, however.

Roads
All motorways – and there are not very many – are toll roads. Each toll road has its own fee structure, so it may cost more per kilometre in one part of Spain than in another. Ordinary main roads exist parallel to toll roads in all cases. The toll roads are excellent for getting from

one point to another: faster, with less traffic and less strain on the driver. The others, of course, are better for seeing the country and the towns. As a general rule, roads are well surfaced, although they are often narrow and winding. The warning signs use standard international symbols. Watch out at night for bicycles, motorbikes, burros and carts without lights. Watch out by day for slow-moving tractors and sheep and cattle.

Hire cars

These are expensive (compared to Britain) or very expensive (compared to the United States), though they have come down a bit since the Government reduced the IVA (VAT) from 33 to 16 per cent. Shop around unless you book before you come, but be careful; some small local companies charge less but their cars may not be in as good condition as those of the large companies. Check your car before accepting it. Some travel agents offer fly-drive deals that usually represent a considerable saving. If you plan to travel around, the unlimited mileage rate is generally more favourable than the daily rate plus a per-kilometre charge. Most companies offer special deals by the week or the month.

Travel time

Because of the nature of the roads and the terrain, you should base your journey time on an average estimate of about 70 km an hour.

Seat belts

These are obligatory on the road but not in town.

By train

Spain has an extensive rail network, and basic ticket costs are quite reasonable. Trains are generally clean and comfortable, though they do sway and bounce around a lot partly because of Spain's many old-fashioned track beds. There are two classes on long-distance trains, only one on locals.

For overnight travel there are couchettes (*literas*) and sleepers (*coche-cama*). There is also the option of *coche-cama* in tourist class, which means you share a sleeper compartment with two or more strangers of the same sex. By contrast, there are usually eight couchettes per compartment and the sexes are not segregated.

Cut-rate fares and supplements

There are so many different discount schemes on RENFE, the Spanish National Railway Network, that only the RENFE information desk and ticket counter staff, and travel agents, can sort them all out and advise you on what is best. Sometimes your journey might even qualify for two different discounts. Among the many schemes are: the Eurail pass (available only outside Europe but for use in Europe); the *kilométrico* (a card entitling you to travel up to a certain total distance, which works out less than the normal per-kilometre rate); youth card; family card; golden card (for those over sixty-five); and a *cheque-tren* (a document which you buy for 15 per cent less than its face value and which can be exchanged for railway tickets). There are train-hotel combinations, reduced rates for transport of your car depending on how many people are travelling, reductions for groups of more than ten, and *'dias azules'*, or 'blue days' (an automatic reduction for travel on other than peak days).

There are supplements for special trains, such as the fast, low-slung Talgos which connect major cities with the capital daily, or the electrified Ter, which speeds between Madrid and Valencia. There are also supplements for air-conditioned coaches. Discounts do not always apply to the supplements, and supplements can sometimes amount to more than 50 per cent of the basic fare.

Types of trains

The fastest are the Talgo and the Ter. Next are the *expresos*, then the *rápidos* (which are not very rapid), and finally the *correos*, which are very slow. Local trains are designated as *tranvías* (the same word as for a tram) or, sometimes, *ferrobuses*.

For long-distance journeys buy your ticket in advance; otherwise you might not get the accommodation you want. Also, there is usually a long queue at the ticket counter and if you leave it to the last minute, you could miss your train, even in the main stations, where there is a window marked *Salida Inmediata* (Immediate Departure).

Refreshment

Most overnight passenger trains between Madrid and coastal cities have dining cars; there is at least a bar and café car on all long-distance passenger trains. On medium-distance trains, from Madrid to León, for instance, there is a man with a sandwich and refreshment trolley aboard if there is no buffet car.

Time

Apart from Madrid, most of Spain's principal cities are on the coasts. Bearing in mind that the distance from Madrid to any city on the coast is at least about 400 km, and that the omnipresent mountains limit speed, it takes from four and a half to nine hours for the fastest trains to make the run to or from Madrid and the coast.

Other trains

RENFE offers some package excursions, with a round-trip ticket, guided tour and sometimes lunch thrown in. Most of these operate from Madrid. There are also two trains dedicated exclusively to tourist routes. One is the Al Andalus Express, which offers a week-long tour of Andalusia, combining visits to places of interest and luxury hotels with first-class train service. The other is the Cantabrian Express, which does a circuit of the north central coast. Narrow-gauge railways serve some parts of Spain, mostly for local traffic.

By air

Spain's two airlines with regularly scheduled domestic flights are Iberia and Aviaco. Aviaco is owned by Iberia and Iberia is owned by the state.

Which airline? The main difference between the two is that Iberia is the flag airline for international flights, whereas Aviaco's international activities are basically restricted to charters and cut-price group-fare flights. Inside Spain you normally have no choice. Aviaco flies to certain destinations and Iberia to others. On routes where they both operate, the fares are the same. In-flight service on domestic routes is minimal. Most principal cities have airports, with at least daily flights to and from Madrid and/or Barcelona, which are the most important airports. There is a shuttle service between Madrid and Barcelona, with flights leaving in both directions every half hour to every hour on weekdays and less frequently on Sundays and holidays.

Fares Domestic flights are not cheap. The cost of flying from Madrid to Barcelona or Seville, one way, for example, is about 10,000 pesetas. Iberia offers reduced-fare stopover deals in Spain for round-trip travel beginning abroad; but, once you are in Spain, there are no special deals on domestic fares, other than package deals through travel agencies. There is only one class on domestic flights, except to and from the Canary Islands and except on combined domestic-international flights.

Aircraft Almost all domestic scheduled flights are by jet. The exceptions are those that land at a few airports which are not equipped to handle jets, such as Corunna. The flight time between Madrid and Barcelona, Seville or Málaga is about fifty minutes.

Reservations Generally, you should make reservations in advance as flights are often fully booked one or two days ahead. You do not need a reservation, however, for the shuttle (*puente aéreo*) between Barcelona and Madrid; just buy your ticket and go to the check-in counter. Iberia does not assign seats by number on domestic flights; Aviaco does. Non-smokers should bear this in mind when boarding Iberia planes in Spain, in order to find a seat in the non-smoking section.

Credit cards Iberia accepts most major credit cards; Aviaco does too, with the exception of American Express.

Planes and helicopters for hire If you win the lottery or inherit an oil well or want to get somewhere in a hurry to clinch a huge business deal, you will be pleased to know that a number of companies rent out small jets, turbo-props and helicopters, with crew, which will take you to any destination you like. In Madrid, such private flights land and take off from the North Terminal of the Barajas Airport. Among companies offering such services is Tahis, with offices in the North Terminal; Tel. (91) 416 8612 or 416 8799.

By bus

Bus is the cheapest form of travel and the best way to get around if you do not have a car. Fares vary, but a rule of thumb is that it will cost you about 5 pesetas per kilometre, but not less than 50 pesetas no matter how short the trip. For example, the fare from Madrid to Málaga, a distance of 532 km, is 2,500 pesetas. The fare on city buses varies from place to place, even from one type of city bus to another, but usually it is not more than 60 pesetas.

Bus stations and stops
Some Spanish cities have a central bus station, though there are usually other points in the city from which buses leave for certain destinations. Buses go everywhere, even to the smallest villages. There are regular stops along medium- to long-distance routes, but they are not always marked, so it is best to ask. City bus stops and some suburban route stops have bus-stop signs. In the cities, the bus route is often painted on the signpost at the bus stop.

Getting the right bus
Tourist offices can usually give you information about which buses to get and where. Standards of comfort are reasonably good. Most medium- to long-distance buses are air-conditioned in summer and heated in winter. City and commuter buses are frequently not air-conditioned.

By taxi

Finding them
Taxis are relatively inexpensive in Spain, and there are plenty of them. The word 'taxi' is spelled the same and pronounced almost exactly the same as in English. In most Spanish cities the taxis with meters are painted black or white with a broad, coloured horizontal or diagonal stripe on the side.

An increasing number are butane-gas-powered, and the gas bottles take up most of the room in the boot, leaving little space for your luggage. Most have roof racks, where the drivers perilously stack your bags. Not all of them have a sign on top of the roof reading 'Taxi', but in most places they have a green light on the roof, which is lit at night if the taxi is available. By day, a big sign on the windscreen, usually in green letters, reads '*Libre*' if it is unoccupied. In small towns, unlike the cities, the taxis do not cruise, but wait at taxi ranks for customers.

Gran Turismo
For in-town use, metered taxis are best, because there are no unpleasant surprises when it comes to paying the bill. *Gran turismos*, which are taxis without meters, are generally very comfortable cars, such as Mercedes or big Citroëns, and are outwardly indistinguishable from ordinary cars. It is preferable to hire one of these for out-of-town or long-distance travel if you do not drive yourself. If you decide to do so, you will have to negotiate beforehand what it is going to cost you, including the driver's meal allowance. Most *gran turismo* drivers speak some English.

By other means

Hitch-hiking

Very few Spanish girls hitch-hike. Young men occasionally do. Few Spaniards pick up hitch-hikers. Hitching is easier in coastal areas and other places where there are a lot of foreign visitors. As almost anywhere else, girls are wise to avoid hitch-hiking alone.

On horseback

Several companies organize riding tours of parts of Spain. If you are an experienced horseman or horsewoman and would like to try this novel way of seeing much of Spain that those on wheels will never see, contact: Rutas a Caballo SA, Calle Augustina de Aragón 14, Madrid-28006.

On a bicycle

The possibilities are unlimited, but to make it easy for you, if you are a fit and fun-loving bike rider, Spanish tourist authorities have mapped out a route which takes you through some of the loveliest spots in Andalusia, most of which are not on main roads. They have broken down the route into an eighteen day trip, from Granada to Palos de la Frontera, from where Columbus set sail. The distance to be pedalled per day ranges from 29 to 68 km. If you are interested, ask at tourist offices abroad or in Spain for the booklet, *Ruta Colombina en Bicicleta* from the series, *Deporte y Turismo para Todos*. It also lists lodgings along the route and the outstanding sights.

Where to Stay

Good value   Generally speaking, accommodation is good value for money in Spain. Because Spain is so tourist-oriented, you can usually find lodgings to suit your budget anywhere. Hotels and pensions are all subject to official controls and are classified by category and subjected to regular inspections to ensure that minimum standards are maintained. All such establishments are required to report to the authorities their prices for the year to come.

Apartments   Another important type of lodging on offer is the tourist apartments, some of which are officially registered. Because of the difficulty of locating and classifying such apartments, they are not listed in the gazetteer section, as a selection of hotels is.

Grass roots Spain   The least known tourist lodging facility in Spain is the private farmhouse. Tourist authorities periodically compile lists of inspected and approved farmhouse rooms or whole houses in rural areas, which are published annually in a book called *Vacaciones en Casas de Labranza*. The guidebook does not list prices, but it does indicate what services are available in each place (such as running water, electricity, and so on) and the name of the owner. This type of lodging usually puts the visitor in close contact with a Spanish family or families. Prices are negotiated with the family in question, but they are invariably economical and often include meals. Ask for a copy at Spanish Tourist Offices abroad or in Spain if you are interested. The book costs only 200 pesetas.

Picking the best   All hotel prices listed in this book are for a double room with bath unless otherwise indicated. Where there are maximum and minimum prices depending on the type of room or the season, this is indicated. Please note that high-season prices often apply during the week before Easter and local *fiestas*. Some hotels charge the same prices all year round. You will find that you get more for your money in some parts of the country than in others.

To make it convenient for readers, most of whom probably have a fixed holiday budget, hotels are classified in this book as top range, mid-range and bottom range, usually without reference to their official classification. Top range hotels are those which cost more than 8,000 pesetas per night for a double room. Mid-range hotels are those which cost more than 2,000 but not more than 8,000 pesetas for a double room. Bottom range hotels charge 2,000 pesetas or less. This classification is as exact as possible, but it does not take into account the tax which may be added to your bill. It also does not take into account the annoying practice of some hotels, particularly on the Costa Brava, of not accepting reservations for the high season, unless customers book half-pension, that is, with one meal included.

Finally, many of the hotels in the bottom range have been included with fear and trepidation, since 2,000 pesetas does not buy much. Some economical lodgings, particularly in small towns, are a joy and a bargain. Others, especially in big cities, have little to recommend them but the price. A great many one-star establishments should be rated with one falling star. To make it easier, hotels are listed in this book in order of my preference within their respective category.

Hotel prices

The hotel prices listed in this book were the official prices at the time of going to press as reported to tourist authorities and published in the official hotel guidebook. Since the annual inflation rate is running at about 5 per cent, those prices are not likely to go up very much. Moreover, they are published as a guide, not a guarantee. In fact, you may pay less in some places, since hotels sometimes set official prices higher than they actually charge, so that they will not have to inform the government of an upward revision at a later date. Also, most hotels offer reduced rates for stays of one week or more, and some offer various other reductions. Bear in mind in any case, however, that the prices quoted in this book do not always include IVA (VAT), which varies from 6 to 12 per cent depending on the category of the establishment. Some hotels quote prices including IVA when you make an inquiry about prices; others add it to the price quoted when the time comes to pay your bill.

Official classifications

The state tourist department classifies hotels and the like, and requires them to display the appropriate symbol outside the main door. Starting with the best, they are as follows:

H = Hotel. This symbol is accompanied by one to five stars. A few exceptional hotels (for example, the Ritz of Madrid) are authorized to display the 'H' above the five stars and the letters 'GL' below. Those letters stand for *Gran Lujo* (Great Luxury).

HR = Residence Hotel. This symbol is also accompanied by one to five stars, though a five-star residence hotel is a rarity. Residence hotels are generally cheaper than hotels. The principal difference is in the variety of services offered and the size and number of public lounges.

HA = Apartment Hotel, also accompanied by one to five stars. Apartment hotels generally offer good weekly or monthly rates and little service, since rooms contain kitchenettes.

RA = Residence Apartments, which are also rated with one to five stars. These are similar to ordinary apartments except they are destined primarily for the use of tourists. Minimal service.

M = Motel. One to five stars, roadside lodgings designed for brief stays.

51

Hs = Hostel. A bare-bones kind of place, which may nevertheless be comfortable and clean, usually family-run. No public rooms as such, though there is probably a television in the dining room. Rated with one to three stars.

P = *Pensión,* or boarding house. These can have up to three stars.

HsR = Residence Hostel. Similar to the hostel but theoretically for longer-staying guests. One to three stars.

F = *Fonda.* Similar to a *pensión*, but generally smaller. No stars.

CH = Guest House. More often than not a private home where one or more rooms are let. No stars.

Seeing stars   Since the criteria for classification include such things as the space dedicated to public rooms, lifts, twenty-four-hour reception, or whether there is a restaurant, or telephones in the rooms, some charming places get fewer stars than they deserve. A lot of one-star pensions are much better value than some three-star hotels. Star for star, hostels are cheaper than hotels, and they can be just as pleasant. A galaxy of stars is not necessarily a guarantee of a good place to stay; it is only a rough indication. Of course, it is also a rough indication of price.

Paradors   The term parador literally means inn, but it is reserved exclusively for the state-run or, more rarely, province-run inns. The standard of quality and comfort is high and their restaurants usually serve good regional food. Many of them are in old palaces, castles or other historic buildings. Most of them are in towns or areas where rooms are otherwise scarce. They are invariably good value. Some paradors on well travelled roads were formerly known as *albergues*, or wayside inns, but the distinction is no longer made. *Hosterías* are the restaurant equivalent of paradors but do not offer accommodation.

Spas   Hotels at spas are generally better priced than hotels elsewhere, and they are usually in very scenic places. The old-fashioned image of the spa as a retreat for dowagers and the decrepit is no longer applicable to Spain's spas, which are frequented by slimmers and the health-conscious.

Avoiding the mob scene   All large Spanish hotels in holiday areas today book in package tours if they can, even five-star hotels. So it is hard to get away from the mob in the lobby at 5 a.m. or the ranks of suitcases you trip over when going out to dinner. The best insurance against that is to choose a small hotel whenever possible.

Another tip: Many resort hotels have noisy discotheques. Insist when you book or check in that you want a room which will not vibrate all night long with the disco. Again, smaller hotels do not usually have discotheques.

Camping   Camping grounds are classified and inspected by the authorities, in a manner similar to the hotels. There are about 500 authorized camping grounds. Site standards are generally high, though many camping grounds, particularly those on the east coast, tend to be overcrowded in mid-summer. They are rated as luxury, first, second or third class, depending on the facilities and services, location and space. Even third-class camping grounds must meet the following minimum requirements: watchmen on duty twenty-four hours a day; area completely fenced in; unlimited supply of drinking water; first aid kit and fire precautions; toilets, washing, washing-up and shower installations; and rubbish collection. Many have sports facilities, some have discos, supermarkets, restaurants, shops, hairdressers and so on.

Prices depend on the category and popularity of the site, the number of people in the party, the number of vehicles, the number of tents and the particular services used such as direct water, and electricity to your caravan or near to your tent. As a yardstick, a couple with a small tent and one car could probably stay overnight at most second- or third-class sites for a total of about 800 pesetas or less. Tourist authorities publish a full list of all authorized camping grounds every year. Camping on your own, rather than at an organized camping ground, is not prohibited, provided the owner of the property does not object, and provided you do not cause a nuisance or hazard. In summer, it is generally forbidden to light fires.

Eating and Drinking

Businessmen and journalists who often travel to Spain know what a good country it is for eating; yet there is a popular misconception in Britain that Spanish food is awful and monotonous, and in North America that it is like Mexican food. It is time to dispel those misconceptions, which probably resulted from poor package-tour meals on the one hand and confusion on the other. Spain has not one style of cooking, but several. Its many distinct regions provide delicious variety.

Regional dishes

Spaniards say of their climate and their cooking that in the north they stew, in the centre they bake and in the south they fry. That is not altogether inaccurate, but it is, of course, a generalization. In the north-west Galicians stew things like their *caldo*, which is broth flavoured with ham and turnip greens. The most typical dish of the Asturians in the north is *fabada*, a hearty stew of white beans with an assortment of Spanish sausages and ham.

The Basques do not fit the pattern, for their cooking is based on sauces rather than stews; it is fairly delicate and complex, and many dishes which are considered French are in fact Basque in origin. In the centre it is true that they roast – and how they roast! There is no meat so tender and delicious as a roast suckling pig in Segovia or a roast baby lamb in Cuenca, or roast kid in the Valley of the River Tietar on the south side of the Gredos Mountains.

They do fry in the south. Fried fish of all kinds is typical of all of Andalusia, but there is more to their cooking than just fried fish. *Gazpacho* (a cold tomato soup), for instance, is Andalusian. This comparison also fails to take into account the rice zone, all down the east coast, or Catalonia's distinctive and delicious sauces and sausages.

If there is one dish which can be called all-Spanish because it is cooked in all the regions, it is the *tortilla*, the Spanish potato omelette, which has nothing at all to do with the Mexican dish of the same name. The *tortilla* is a culinary triumph because it makes something very special out of quite ordinary ingredients: eggs, potatoes, onions and oil. What makes it especially good is the way it is done.

Another misconception about Spanish cooking is that it is greasy and uses too much olive oil. Properly prepared Spanish food, even fried Andalusian fish dishes, are not greasy, and olive oil is often not used because chefs use cheaper vegetable oils.

Tapa

The *tapa* is a Spanish custom that visitors from abroad usually latch onto quickly. *Tapas* are small morsels of usually hot food, served in infinite varieties, usually accompanied by a *chato* (small glass) or two of wine and some amenable conversation. You can spend hours in the *tascas* (taverns) sampling the *tapas*. And, of course, if you do, you have no inclination to sit down to a meal because you have already had one, bit by bit.

Restaurants

For sit-down meals, even the humblest Spanish restaurants spread white tablecloths on the table. You can eat a good three-course meal, plus wine and bread, for as little as 500 pesetas in many restaurants if you order the menu of the day. In this book, restaurants listed in the gazetteer section have been classified as follows:

Pricey   The kind of place where, even if you do not choose the most expensive thing on the menu or order a bottle of very special wine, the bill will inevitably come to more than 2,000 pesetas per person for à la carte fare, and sometimes a lot more.

Moderate   The sort of place where you can eat well and, unless you order the most expensive items on the menu, can have a three-course meal with wine for not more than 2,000 pesetas per person on average.

Economical   A restaurant where you can eat satisfactorily, including a starter and a main dish, a sweet and a drink (wine, beer, mineral water or refreshment) for 1,000 pesetas or less, choosing from the à la carte menu. This is the type of restaurant where you can eat for 500 or 600 pesetas if you stick to the menu of the day.

Menu and dining vocabulary

Starters

Broth with potato and greens	*caldo gallego*
hors-d'œuvres	*entremeses*
Bread and garlic soup	*sopa castellana*

Eggs and omelettes

Fried eggs	*huevos fritos*
Fried eggs with tomato sauce and peas	*huevos a la flamenca*
Scrambled eggs	*huevos revueltos*
Spanish omelette	*tortilla española*

Vegetables

Onion	*cebolla*
Runner beans	*judías verdes*
Lettuce	*lechuga*
Potatoes	*patatas*

(Sweet) peppers	*pimientos*
Cabbage	*repollo*
Tomato	*tomate*

Seafood

Clams	*almejas*
Tunnyfish	*atún*
Cod	*bacalao*
Squid	*calamares*
Prawns	*gambas*
Sole	*lenguado*
Mussels	*mejillones*
Hake	*merluza*
Grouper	*mero*
Monkfish	*rape*
Turbot	*rodaballo*
Red mullet	*salmonete*
Trout	*trucha*

Meat

Roast	*asado/a*
Kid (goat)	*cabrito*
Tripe	*callos*
Pork	*cerdo*
Lamb chop	*chuleta de cordero*
Veal chop	*chuleta de ternera*
Suckling pig	*cochinillo*
Veal scallop	*escalope*
Cured ham	*jamón*
Boiled ham	*lacón*
Chicken	*pollo*
Fillet steak	*solomillo*

Desserts

Crème caramel	*flan*
Fruit	*fruta*
Ice cream	*helado*
Apple	*manzana*
Peach	*melocotón*
Orange	*naranja*
Pineapple	*piña*
Cheese	*queso*
Watermelon	*sandía*

On the table

Oil	*aceite*
Spoon	*cuchara*
Knife	*cuchillo*

Butter	*mantequilla*
Mustard	*mostaza*
Salt and pepper	*sal y pimienta*
Napkin	*servilleta*
Fork	*tenedor*
Vinegar	*vinagre*

Meal times

Spaniards eat late. The midday meal is usually served any time between 1 and 4 p.m. and the evening meal is served any time from 9 p.m. to 11.30 p.m. or midnight.

Wines and spirits

Spanish wines are very reasonably priced for their quality. Sherry is the best known and comes only from the sherry district, which surrounds the city of Jerez de la Frontera (see p. 154). The variety of grape used is the Palomino. Sherry is matured by the *solera* system, a traditional method of fractional blending, which means there are no sherries from exceptional years. Owing to the presence of a natural yeast which contributes to the process of maturation of the wine, and to the alcoholic content, the same must produces three different basic types of dry wine: *fino* (pale dry), *amontillado* (medium) and *oloroso* (brown sherry). Sweet wine from Pedro Ximénez or Moscatel grapes, grown in the district as well, is blended with the dry sherries to make sweet ones. Manzanilla is a type of pale dry sherry, which comes only from Sanlúcar de Barrameda in the sherry district. Sherry is generally drunk with *tapas*, or as an apéritif or dessert wine.

Spain's *Cava* (sparkling wine made by the Champagne method) outsells Champagne by volume in several European countries and in the United States. Most of it comes from the north-eastern region of Catalonia.

Riojan wines , especially the reds, are rapidly gaining prestige outside Spain. Spaniards have always known how good they are. They come from a district around Logroño in north central Spain. There are so many other good wines in Spain that they cannot all be listed here. Let yourself be guided by the recommendations of the waiters, particularly with regard to the local wines of where you happen to be. Among other important wine districts are the Penedés in Catalonia, Rueda in old Castile, Málaga, Valdepeñas in La Mancha, Cariñena in Aragón, Jumilla in the south-east and Montilla-Moriles in Córdoba.

Spain also produces a number of spirits, the most popular of which are brandy and anise. Brandies from Jerez are the most widely distributed and are of good to excellent quality. Unlike brandy in some other countries, the law requires Spanish brandy to be made only from wine alcohol, not alcohol of any other kind. Most Spanish bodegas welcome visits, provided you telephone ahead. Several suggested wine visits are included in the gazetteer. Local tourist offices will also provide information on request.

Entertainment

Bullfights These represent the most uniquely Spanish entertainment you will come across. The ritual killing of the bull is rooted in the history of Spain. Until a few centuries ago, however, bullfighting was a game played only by noblemen on horseback. If you do not like Spain's 'National *Fiesta*', you are in good company: Queen Isabella (the one who sponsored Columbus) detested it. Pope Gregory V excommunicated performers and spectators alike, but the art of tauromachy not only survived, it developed, becoming more refined, more ritualized and orderly. King Charles V enjoyed fighting bulls himself. His son Philip II prevailed upon the Vatican to lift the excommunication against bullfighters and fans. By the early eighteenth century, the nobles had lost interest but the commoners had not. That was the beginning of the spectacle of bullfighting on foot. Later, in stages, rules were laid down, establishing the various phases of the fight.

Bullfighting is considered an art rather than a sport. It is reported on different pages from sports events in the newspapers. Perhaps the word in English – bullfight – is misleading as to the nature of the spectacle. Rather than a fight it is more like a ballet, but with the element of danger thrown in, in which the *torero* must get the bull to cooperate in a series of properly executed passes within a certain time limit. First-time spectators never appreciate the beauty of the spectacle; they are usually horrified and disgusted by it. There is some opposition to bullfights from animal lovers in Spain, but such opposition has proved very ineffective so far. King Juan Carlos is a bullfight fan.

Not many bullfights are good ones from the fans' point of view. With luck, maybe one out of ten fights featuring major figures of the ring is memorable. The ideal *corrida* is the result of the perfect combination of the right bullfighter and the right bull on the right day. The number of fights and spectators has been growing for the past few years. The most important rings are the Maestranza of Seville and the Monumental of Madrid. Rings at Benidorm, Marbella and other places where a large percentage of the audience are tourists occasionally draw top figures, but tourism does not support the bullfighting business. In addition to permanent rings, town squares all over Spain are converted into improvized rings during local *fiestas*; and portable bullrings bring 'road show' fights to many towns.

Prices are high for ringside seats at a major fight, especially if the touts get hold of the tickets; but acceptable seats in the lower part of the *tendidos* (stands) on the shady side of the main Madrid ring can be bought for as little as 600 pesetas for some *novilladas* (fights featuring apprentice *toreros*). The same seat for a fight with bulls from a good ranch and renowned *matadores* would cost 3,000 or 4,000 pesetas, provided you could buy it at the official price. No single *matador* dominates the profession today, but the level of talent and ability among prominent *toreros* is high. There are usually six bulls at a fight, and they are dispatched – two each – by three bullfighters. For each bull there are three short acts:

● The bull comes out and is caped and led to the mounted *picador*, who jabs his lance into the bull's hump as it charges the padded side of the horse on which he is mounted. He often plunges the lance into the bull's back several times. The *picador* is usually unpopular with the crowd.

● An assistant of the bullfighter whose turn it is, or sometimes the bullfighter himself, faces the animal on foot and places barbed sticks, decorated with colourful paper curls, in the bull's back. Usually three pairs of sticks, known as *banderillas*, are placed.

● The bullfighter takes the red *muleta*, the small cape, and tries to perform a series of passes with the bull. Then he kills it with his sword.

Nightlife   There are shows and activities for all tastes in the big cities, except in August, when even restaurants and cinemas shut down in cities in the centre of the country. Madrid and Barcelona offer theatre the year round, however. There are bullfights twice weekly from spring through autumn in Madrid (and daily in May), and weekly in various other cities in the summer. Nightclub shows, featuring flamenco dancers, comedians, magicians, and other acts, go on until the small hours nightly all along the south and east coasts from June until September, and in some places, like Marbella and Alicante, all year round.

Shopping

Alcohol   Taxes are considerably lower on alcohol in Spain than in the UK. Spanish shop prices are sometimes cheaper than the duty-free shops at London airports, even for Scotch whisky. Sherry, Riojan wines of good vintages, brandy from Jerez and *Cava* (Spanish bubbly made by the Champagne method) are worth taking back home.

Cigars   The finest Havana cigars are available at bargain prices at tobacco shops everywhere in Spain, as well as good Canary Islands cigars.

Virgin olive oil   The very best, the first pressing, is excellent for salads and *gazpachos*; it is much cheaper than abroad and not subject to duty in most countries. Make sure the label says '*Aceite Virgen de Oliva*'.

Saffron   This is real vegetable gold, a costly colouring and seasoning item which lends aroma and a yellow hue to certain dishes. It is indispensable for a good *paella*. There are other, cheaper, yellow colourings but there is nothing like the real thing. Spain is a major producer of saffron, which is nothing more than the stigmas of a certain variety of crocus. It takes 8,000 flowers to make 100 grams of saffron. Prices abroad are usually at least double those in Spanish grocery shops. It makes a great gift for friends who like to cook.

Clothes   Spain makes good quality **leather goods**. Leather and suede jackets, suits, skirts and the like are of good quality, but no longer always cheap compared with similar items north of the Pyrenees, though you still find the occasional bargain.

Spanish fashion styles are in, and you can buy the real thing at major department stores and boutiques. In Madrid, the best shopping street for fashions is Calle Serrano. In Barcelona it is Paseo de Gracia.

Flamenco dresses   These colourful, frilly dresses are real conversation pieces for any party. It is best to buy them in Andalusia, but they are available in department stores in other parts of the country as well.

Mantillas, lace and embroidery goods are available at good prices at department stores and women's clothing shops in varying degrees of quality. If you want good quality at a good price, do not buy at bargain and souvenir shops, where the quality is generally poor.

Ceramic ware   There is a vast variety, all low priced. Glazed porcelain statuary, particularly that made by Lladró, is a popular item with visitors from abroad. La Cartuja is an excellent brand for tableware. Sagardelos designs are particularly good. Buy them at department stores all over the country.

Small gifts   *Chisqueros*, which are cigarette lighters incorporating a length of rope, never fail and always amuse. *Botas*, the wineskins you see people drinking from at *fiestas* and bullfights. They are available at souvenir shops everywhere. See p. 243 for advice on how to 'cure' a bota.

Firearms   Finely tooled and well priced, Spanish guns have a good reputation among hunters and collectors abroad.

General Basics

Cinemas

Every city has cinemas where films are shown regularly with the original soundtrack. These films are advertized with the abbreviation 'v.o.', which stands for 'versión original'. Otherwise, and nearly always on television, films are dubbed into Castilian Spanish.

To find out what's showing, check one of the local English-language publications mentioned on p. 70. Spanish daily newspapers also carry a list of cinemas and the films showing at each. You will be able to spot the English titles and letters 'v.o.'.

Documents needed to enter Spain

EEC citizens do not need a passport if they have valid national identification cards. Citizens of the UK and Eire, since they do not have such a card, do need passports, like all other foreign visitors. Visas are not generally necessary but citizens of Australia, New Zealand, South Africa and some other Commonwealth countries do need one. Apply for one in advance at a Spanish consulate in your own country.

Visitors from the United States may stay six months; others may stay three months, but extensions are normally granted on request. Tourists are not authorized to work at all in Spain; for that you need work and residence permits.

Electrical current

Throughout most of Spain, the current is 220 V, 50 cycles, though in a few places the current is 110 V. Hotel sockets usually indicate which voltage applies. If in doubt, ask. American 60-cycle, 110 V, appliances, like hair-driers, electric razors and radios, will work with transformers, but not things like clocks or tape recorders, which are more affected by differences in cycle.

Normal British plugs, like thin-bladed American ones, do not fit standard Spanish sockets. In case you forget to bring an adaptor plug, they are readily available at any electrical shop. Rather bulky small transformers are also available.

Embassies and consulates

An embassy is a diplomatic representation of one country in another. A consulate, often part of an embassy, normally deals with trade, business relations and personal matters. If you need help in a foreign country, call on your consul.

Great Britain and some other countries have more than one consulate in Spain. New Zealand, however, has neither an embassy nor a consulate in Spain. Its affairs are handled by Great Britain. The word for consul in Spanish is spelled exactly the same, and pronounced almost the same, as in English. The word for consulate is *consulado*. Following are the addresses of consulates you might need:

● **Australia:** Consulado de Australia, Paseo de la Castellana 143, 28003 Madrid. Tel. (91) 279 8504.

● **Canada:** Consulado de Canadá, Calle Nuñez de Balboa 35, 28001 Madrid. Tel. (91) 431 4300.

Vía Augusta 125, Atico 3, 08006 Barcelona. Tel. (93) 209 0634.

Plaza Malagueta 3, 1°, 29016 Málaga. Tel. (952) 223 346.

Avenida de la Constitución 30, 2°–4, 41001 Seville (Sevilla). Tel. (954) 229 413.

● **Great Britain:** Consulado de Gran Bretaña, Calle Fernando El Santo 16, 28010 Madrid. Tel. (91) 419 0200.

Avenida de las Fuerzas Armadas 11, 1°, 11014 Algeciras, Cádiz. Tel. (956) 661 600 or 661 604.

Paseo de Calvo Sotelo 1, 03001 Alicante. Tel. (965) 216 190 or 216 022.

Avenida Diagonal 477, 13°, 08036 Barcelona. Tel. (93) 322 3169.

Alameda de Urquijo 2, 8°, 48008 Bilbao, Vizcaya. Tel. (94) 415 7600 or 415 7711.

Edificio Duquesa, Calle Duquesa de Parcent 8, 29001 Málaga. Tel. (952) 217 571 or 212 325.

Paseo de Pereda 27, 39004 Santander. Tel. (942) 220 000.

Plaza Nueva 8 Duplicado, 41001 Seville (Sevilla). Tel. (954) 228 875.

Calle Real 33, 1°–1, 43004 Tarragona. Tel. (977) 220 812.

Plaza de Compostela 23, 6° izq, 36201 Vigo, Pontevedra. Tel. (986) 437 133.

● **South Africa:** Consulado de Africa del Sur, Calle Claudio Coello 91, 28006 Madrid. Tel. (91) 227 3156.

Gran Vía de les Corts Catalanes 6, 6° C, 08007 Barcelona. Tel. (93) 318 0797.

Edificio Abra, Calle Las Mercedes 31, 4° A, Las Arenas (Bilbao), Vizcaya. Tel. (94) 464 1830.
- **United States:** Consulado de los Estados Unidos de América, Calle Serrano 75, 28006 Madrid. Tel. (91) 276 3600 or 276 3400.
Vía Layetana 33, 08003 Barcelona. Tel. (93) 319 9550.
Avenida del Ejército 11, 48014 Bilbao, Vizcaya. Tel. (94) 435 8300.

Emergency messages

The state-run Radio Nacional offers a year-round emergency message service. At the end of news bulletins, Radio Nacional often broadcasts messages asking someone to telephone home because of serious illness or accident in that person's family and so forth. Foreigners as well as Spaniards may use the service. If you need it, or if someone in your home country needs to reach you in an emergency, the message to be transmitted should be given to the Spanish police, with the request that they pass it on to the radio. It can be given to the Red Cross in your home country, with the request that it be transmitted to Spanish police for broadcast in Spain.

Finding your way around

Spanish addresses are written with the number placed after the name of the street. Thus, for example, the address of the tourist office in the centre of Madrid is Plaza Mayor 3. Quite often a building does not have an assigned street number. If that were the case with regard to the tourist office above, the address would be written: Plaza Mayor s/n. 'S/n' means *sin número* (without a number).

Some addresses give a road designation followed by a certain number of kilometres, for example: N-VI, km 105; or N-234, km 67, or Carretera Buendía-Huete, km 12. Interpreting that is easy once you know how. To begin with, the principal national motorways all radiate from Madrid to some point on the perimeter of Spain. These highways are designated by a capital 'N' (for *nacional*) followed by a Roman numeral, for example, N-IV. Distances on those roads are always calculated from the Puerta del Sol in Madrid, where there is a bronze 'kilometre 0' marker embedded in the pavement. Thus an address at the centre of Aranjuez would be N-IV, km 47, as it is 47 km from Madrid on N-IV.

Other major roads are designated by a capital 'N' and an Arabic number, such as N-420. The starting point of each of these is not so easy to determine, but the distance from the road's starting point is always indicated on kilometre stones or signs all along the road. Thus N-420, km 18, would be the address of a place 18 km along the N-420 road, counting from its starting point.

In the third example above (Carretera Buendía-Huete, km 12), the address means '12 km along the road from Buendía to Huete'. If it had simply been 'Carretera de Huete, km 12', it would have meant '12 km along the road to Huete' from wherever you are.

Addresses of museums, hotels, tourist offices and other places mentioned in this book appear in Spanish. Words such as *calle* (street) *carretera* (road) and *plaza* (square) have not been translated. This is so that if you show the address of any given place to a Spaniard he or she will understand it.

What's in a name? You may run into some difficulty with street names. Streets which bore the names of heroes of the Nationalist side in the Civil War and leading lights of the Franco regime were renamed in most of Spain in the first years following General Franco's death in 1975. In most towns, the main streets up to that time carried the names of General Franco, José Antonio Primo de Rivera, founder of the Falangists, and generals, like Mola, who played a prominent part in the military uprising against the Spanish Republic of the early 1930s.

The trouble is that not everybody refers to the streets by their new names, and some towns never did change the names, so that General Franco, for example, still has streets named after him. In most places, however, the principal roads and squares now bear the names of new heroes and newly honoured concepts. As a rule of thumb, streets named after Franco and José Antonio have been renamed after King Juan Carlos or the Constitution. Other main streets, in places where regional nationalism is strongly felt, bear the name of that region or of its own heroes. Bear this in mind when using city maps. Not all of them have been sufficiently updated.

Health

No vaccinations are needed.

The two major problems which particularly affect visitors from less sunny climes are overexposure to the sun and upset stomachs.

Sun Many people, anxious to take advantage of the good weather, soak up all the sun they can at once – with unpleasant consequences. It is much better to stay in the sun for only a short time at first and, as most of Spain has consistent good weather, there is no danger of missing out later. A bad case of sunburn is painful and can spoil your holiday. Suntan lotions and oils are a good investment, as is a hat or parasol. Sunstroke is more serious, and it could put you in hospital.

Ice cold drinks when you are in the hot sun, particularly if you have been exercising, are bad for you. Take that cool drink slowly and in the shade when you've settled comfortably into your hammock or chair.

Spanish tummy

The other problem, diarrhoea, often called Spanish tummy though it is really a universal travellers' scourge, can usually be avoided. It has probably more to do with water than food. The drinking water may be perfectly safe – it usually is anywhere in Spain nowadays – but nevertheless differs everywhere you go, and it can upset you even though it is perfectly all right. It is wiser to stick to bottled water throughout your holiday, and if possible to the same brand. All brands are subject to health ministry control, so take your pick.

Bear in mind also that ice cubes are generally made from tap water. Moreover, they may have been frozen in unwashed ice trays, have picked up debris from ice-cube bins, and they are usually handled by someone before they go into your glass. So, if you are worried about Spanish tummy, don't take ice in your drink.

Eating sensibly will help keep you from becoming ill too. Don't look for the cheapest food; look for the best you can afford. Take it easy on foods that are hard to digest or that are very greasy. Don't overeat. Gradually work up to dishes with seasonings and spices to which you are unaccustomed. Don't overtax your body, and the chances are it won't break down.

In hot weather, certain foods go off quicker, even if they are put back in the fridge as soon as they are removed from the table. One frequent offender in cases of food poisoning is mayonnaise. If in doubt, or merely to play safe, steer clear of mayonnaise except in the best places.

Shellfish can cause stomach upsets and itchy rashes, if it is not perfectly fresh – or if it has been treated with boric acid. Such treatment is forbidden, but it still occurs occasionally in Spain, as a way of preserving fresh seafood longer. If you have any doubts about shellfish on your plate, or if there is even the slightest hint of a smell of ammonia, do not eat it. On the other hand, it goes without saying that better restaurants generally have good fresh food.

Maltese Fever

Maltese Fever still crops up in Spain. It comes from unpasteurized milk and milk products. Packaged brand-name milk and cheese are safe, but be careful if you are offered any homemade cheese.

Drink

Another health problem is self-induced. The abundance of good wine and the cheapness of drink generally in Spain often lead visitors to over-indulge. A word to the wise is sufficient.

Sea nettles

Sea nettles occasionally annoy bathers at some Atlantic beaches. At every protected public bathing beach there is a first-aid station. A bit of ammonia usually takes away the sting.

Chemists

Many common remedies, such as aspirin and liniments, are sold without prescription, but medicines of the kind a doctor might prescribe may not be bought without a prescription. Rules in this regard were lax in the past but are now strictly enforced. For minor complaints, the person on duty at any chemist's shop can usually recommend something. The law requires one chemist's shop to stay open all night and on Sundays and holidays in every town and in each section of every city. A list posted on the door of every chemist's shop at night will tell you the nearest chemist on 'guard duty'.

Doctors   If you need a doctor in a hurry, ask at any hotel, which all have house doctors on call, or ask the police. Many hotel doctors speak some English. Spanish public health clinics and hospitals, as well as private medical establishments, normally admit anybody for emergency treatment, but if you do not have a card entitling you to Spanish public health service, you will have to pay in either case. The level of medical training is quite satisfactory; many Spanish doctors practise in the United States, and in Britain.

Hunting, fishing, shooting

Spain offers more opportunities to hunters and fishermen than most other European countries, and the variety of game is considerable. You need a licence to engage in such activities. Normally, licences are issued within a day or two, provided your papers are in order.

Some big game animals you can hunt are deer, ibex, wild boar, mountain goat, mountain sheep, lynx and roebuck. Small game includes, but is not limited to, partridge, various kinds of water fowl, hare, rabbit and quail.

Hunting licences are granted by the conservation section at agriculture departments of most regional governments (and this section has different names in the various regions), though in some cases the issuing agency is still ICONA, the central administration's conservation agency. The kind of licence depends on whether you are gunning for big or small game. In any case you also must have hunters' insurance, covering third-party liabilities. Details about information and documents you have to furnish are available from Spanish National Tourist Offices abroad, and it is strongly recommended that you ask the nearest of those offices to help process your application before you come to Spain; otherwise you may find yourself wasting valuable holiday time sorting out permits.

You also need a licence for river and lake fishing. The normal issuing agency again is the agriculture department of the region or regions where you intend to fish. Apply before you come, as above. Licences for underwater fishing and other sea fishing are issued by the Comandancia de Marina, the naval authorities in the area where you intend to fish. Sort it out ahead of time, as above.

Seasons vary from year to year, species to species, and from one part of Spain to another; and, of course, failure to respect hunting and fishing regulations is punishable. Certain endangered or protected species may not be hunted at all. Some others, like the brown bear, are on a temporary protection list, which is reviewed and changed, as conditions indicate, periodically. When you request your permit, ask for the relevant information about hunting seasons.

There are companies which specialize in hunting and shooting trips; most travel agencies can put you in touch with them. So can Spanish National Tourist Offices abroad.

Insurance

The standard 'green card', used throughout the European Community, provides sufficient insurance cover for your car. If you are not sure whether you have the 'green card', check with your insurance company before leaving for Spain. If you do not have the 'green card', you can get one at the border. There are insurance agents' offices for this purpose near the customs post at major points of entry by road. The cost varies, depending on how long you want it for, but it is not very expensive.

If you hire a car in Spain, it is best to ask for full coverage. It costs a bit more, but it may save you a lot of money and grief.

Travel insurance is certainly a good thing to have. Make sure it covers illness as well as accident. Remember, if you are hurt or are taken ill, you will have to pay for treatment.

Either your car insurance will include coverage for such things as bail bonds in relation to serious traffic accidents, or such a provision can and should be added to the policy. A bail bond is a guarantee of payment of bail.

Laundry and dry-cleaning

Most dry-cleaning shops in Spain do a good job, but are slow. One-day service is a rarity, except in good hotels, and even there you will usually find that there is no service on Sunday and possibly little or none on Saturday. There are hardly any do-it-yourself type launderettes in Spain, except at camping grounds. Hotel laundry prices are usually quite high. You may find it best to wash some things yourself.

Money matters

Major international credit cards, such as Visa, Access, American

Express and Diner's Club, are widely accepted in Spain. Travellers' cheques in any west European currency or US dollars are acceptable at any bank, in shops used to dealing with foreigners, in department stores, in all but the economical restaurants, and at most hotels. The Eurocheque is also widely used.

Whenever possible, change your money at a bank. Banks give the best exchange rate, and they all use the daily rate quoted by the Bank of Spain, the only difference being that the charges for the service are calculated differently at different banks.

Most banks are open from 9 a.m. to 2 p.m. on weekdays and until 1 p.m. on Saturdays. During local *fiestas* and in summer they sometimes close earlier. There are plans for some banks in key locations to remain open until 5 p.m. from Monday until Thursday.

The abbreviation for pesetas is pta. Spanish banknotes come in denominations of: 10,000 pesetas (blue and larger than a £20 note); 5,000 pesetas (purple and a trifle smaller than a £20 note); 2,000 pesetas (reddish-orange and about the size of a £5 note); 1,000 pesetas (green and larger than the old £1 note); 500 pesetas (blue and smaller than a £1 note); 200 pesetas (red and even smaller); and 100 pesetas (brown, smaller still, and going out of circulation).

Coins are issued in denominations of: 200 pesetas (similar to a 20-pence coin); 100 pesetas (roughly similar to the £1 coin); 50 pesetas (silvery looking and bigger than a 10-pence coin); 25 pesetas (about the size and colour of a 10-pence coin); 10 pesetas (small, like an American 10-cent coin but a little thicker); 5 pesetas (similar to the 5 pence coin); 1 peseta (either copper-toned or aluminium and similar in size to the 1 pence coin).

Taxi drivers are reluctant to change more than a 1,000-peseta note, and at times they even complain about that. Because of the danger of robberies, petrol stations which remain open at night will normally not accept anything but the exact amount after about 10 p.m. So, at night, remember to ask for how many thousands of pesetas worth of petrol you want, rather than the number of litres. Drivers of city buses, who usually have to collect the fare as well as drive, will not change anything higher than a 500-peseta note as a general rule.

You can change money at Spanish airports on arrival or departure or any time during normal banking hours, and also at Madrid's Chamartín Railway Station.

Newspaper, radio and television

British newspapers and international editions of certain American newspapers are available on news-stands in the centre of major cities and coastal resorts. Some are on sale the morning of the date of publication; others do not arrive until late afternoon or the next day.

There are a number of English-language publications in Spain. All carry information about what to do and where to go, but most of them give thorough coverage for their own area only. The *Iberian Daily Sun* publishes international and Spanish news. The weekly *Guidepost* covers Madrid primarily. Also weekly is the *Costa Blanca News*, published in Benidorm, which prints mostly local coastal news, but with front-page attention to foreign affairs. The monthly *Lookout* covers all Spain, but especially the Costa del Sol, where it is published.

The major daily newspapers, in the order of their circulation, are: the left-leaning independent *El Pais* of Madrid; the conservative monarchist *ABC* of Madrid; the conservative Catalan nationalist *La Vanguardia* of Barcelona; the sports daily *As* of Madrid; the politically moderate pro-Catalan *El Periódico* of Barcelona; the liberal and slightly sensationalist *Diario-16* of Madrid; the centralist-oriented *El Correo Español-El Pueblo Vasco* of Bilbao; the sports paper *Marca* of Madrid; and the Roman Catholic *Ya* of Madrid.

Radio and television
Radio 80, a Spanish station, broadcasts news in English in Madrid between 7 and 8 a.m. daily except Sundays, on 89 FM.

The American Armed Forces Network broadcasts all day for US military personnel, in English of course, at Torrejón (near Madrid). You can tune in if you are in the vicinity, on 100.2 FM.

On the Costa Blanca, Radio Benidorm broadcasts a chatty show of news and music, every Friday at 3 p.m. for an hour, and has another half-hour programme every Monday and Wednesday at 10 p.m., on 102.9 FM. Radio Denia broadcasts *Take to the Air* every Tuesday, Thursday, and Saturday at 3 p.m., a show of news, talk and local information at 92.5 FM.

You can pick up Gibraltar television on the western end of the Costa del Sol, which features news, local stories and some re-runs of popular British programmes. Many hotels all over Spain offer closed-circuit television with films in 'original version', and/or international satellite broadcasts. Spanish television consists of two state-run Spanish-language channels with nationwide coverage and, in some parts of the country, one or more additional channels run by regional governments, broadcasting mostly in regional languages. Commercial television has long been promised but has not yet materialized.

Place names

The names of places in Spain are often written in more than one way, depending on the regional language used. This may cause you some confusion, particularly with signposts. The spellings of place names in this book are either the English spelling, such as Saragossa for

Zaragoza, or the most commonly used spelling, such as Gerona rather than the Catalan spelling, Girona. Most maps will reflect the spellings used in this book. Here, however, are the alternative spellings of some of the places you might pass through:

Alcira	Alzira
Almusafes	Almussafes
Bagur	Begur
Bilbao	Bilbo
Carcagente	Carcaixent
Castelldefels	Casteldefels
Castellón de la Plana	Castelló de la Plana
Castillo de Aro	Castell d'Aro
Cestona	Zestoa
Ciudadela (Menorca)	Ciutatella
Corunna	La Coruña, A Coruña
Finisterre	Fisterra
Fuenterrabía	Hondarríbia
Gerona	Girona
Guernica y Luno	Gernika-Lumo
Játiva	Xátiva
Jávea	Xábia
La Junquera	La Jonquera
La Puebla	Sa Pobla
Lérida	Lleida
Lluchmayor	Llucmajor
Los Nogales	As Nogais
Noya (Galicia)	Noia
Onteniente	Ontinyent
Pamplona	Irunea
Pollensa	Pollença
Puerto Marín	Portomarín
Ribas de Freser	Ribes de Freser
Rosas	Roses
San Carlos de la Rápita	Sant Carles de la Rápita
San Sadurní de Noya	Sant Sadurní d'Anoia
San Sebastián	Donostia
Sangenjo	Sanxenso
Seo de Urgel	La Seu d'Urgell
Vallfogona de Riucorp	Vallfogona de Riucorb
Villafranca del Panedés	Vilafranca del Penedés
Villanueva de Arosa	Vilanova de Arousa
Vinaroz	Vinaros
Vitoria	Gastéiz
Zarauz	Zarautz

Photography

Photographing policemen is forbidden because terrorists sometimes use snapshots to single out their victims. Photographs of army, navy or air force installations are also forbidden. Last, but not least, you are not allowed to take photos of runways and planes at any airport without permission. The same goes, of course, for home video cameras.

Only professional photographers are allowed in the *callejon* (the alleyway around the inside of the bullring), and only by special arrangement.

In most churches and museums, flash devices are not authorized. In certain museums, no photography at all is allowed except by professionals, with special permission.

Places of worship

Brief or beach-type attire is frowned on when visiting places of worship. In some, people dressed inadequately are not allowed to enter. Shorts are usually unacceptable, whether worn by men or women. Universally acceptable dress is a blouse and skirt or a dress for women (in some places the shoulders should be covered) and trousers and shirt for men. Women do not have to cover their heads in Spanish churches.

Talking loudly is taboo, as is anything that might disrupt services or interfere with the normal use of the place by the faithful.

Post offices

Except for one central post office in each city, which is open for stamp sales from 9 a.m. until 8 p.m. on weekdays (but with shorter hours for most other services), post offices are normally open from 9 a.m. to 2 p.m. You have to go there to send or receive money orders, send registered mail (*correo certificado*) and send packages. Telex and fax services are only available at the central post office in each city, but in Madrid the latter services are open all night. Spanish post offices have no connections with the telephone service. See 'Telephoning' below.

If all you want to do is buy stamps, there is no need to go to the post office. You can do that at any tobacconist's shop, and normally the assistant there will have a small scale to weigh your letter. There is usually less of a queue at a tobacconist than at a post office. The former can be identified by the red and yellow sign *Tabacalera SA*.

Public holidays and fiestas

There are fourteen official holidays in Spain per year, not counting extra ones which coincide with the feastdays of local patron saints and are more *de facto* than declared. Of the fourteen, there are seven which are celebrated nationally:

- **1 January,** New Year's Day.
- **Good Friday,** a moveable feast.
- **1 May,** Labour Day.
- **15 August,** Assumption of the Virgin Mary.
- **12 October,** National Day, Day of Hispanic Culture and feastday of Spain's patroness, the Virgin of Pilar.
- **8 December,** Feast of the Immaculate Conception of the Virgin.
- **25 December,** Christmas day.

Five others are widely observed, but regional authorities are entitled to substitute dates of regional or local interest for any three of these five:

- **6 January,** Epiphany.
- **19 March,** St Joseph's feastday.
- **Holy Thursday,** a moveable feast.
- **Corpus Christi,** a moveable feast.
- **25 July,** Feastday of Santiago, patron saint of Spain.

Finally, governments at regional or municipal level add two more *fiestas* to the list, to commemorate dates of local importance.

There is a *fiesta* every day somewhere in Spain. Local celebrations are generally colourful and exciting; some of the better known are:

January

5 Eve of Epiphany parade in every Spanish city; members of the pageant mounted on floats throw sweets to children.

19 Tamborrada, Traditional Drummers' Festival, San Sebastián.

February

2 Endiablada, Ceremony of the Devils, Almonacid del Marquesado, Cuenca province.

(Moveable) Carnival pre-Lenten festivals, Cádiz and Santa Cruz de Tenerife.

(Moveable) Pero Palo, controversial pre-Lenten festival, Villanueva de la Vera in Cáceres province.

(Moveable) Passion Play, every Sunday of Lent, at Ulldecona, Esparraguera in Barcelona province and Cervera in Lérida province.

March

9–19 *Fallas, fiestas* in honour of St Joseph, outstanding fireworks and bullfights, in Valencia.

(Moveable) Holy Week processions in Seville, Valladolid, Málaga and Jerez de la Frontera. Holy Week Religious Music Festival, Cuenca.

(Moveable) Holy Thursday, Los Empalaos procession, in which men are tied to crosses, Valverde de la Vera, Cáceres province.

(Moveable) Good Friday, flagellations of penitents in Holy Week processions, San Vicente de la Sonsierra, Logroño province.

April

23 St George's Day and Book Fair, Barcelona.

(Moveable) Spring Fair, Seville.

May

15 San Isidro *fiestas* in Madrid, featuring one month of daily bullfights plus numerous other cultural events and entertainments.

(Moveable) Horse Fair, Jerez de la Frontera.

(Moveable) Moors and Christians, at Alcoy in Alicante province.

June

21-30 San Juan bonfires and fireworks all along the Costa Blanca.

23-24 Firewalkers' festival at San Pedro Manrique in Soria province.

29 Wine battle at Haro.

(Moveable) Rocío Pilgrimage, Whitsunday, at Almonte.

(Moveable) Corpus Christi procession and celebrations, Toledo. Also on Corpus Christi is the El Colacho festival in Castrillo de Murcia, Burgos province, in which a man representing the devil leaps repeatedly over a mattress covered with babies.

July

13 Tribute of the Three Cows, in which residents of several French Pyrenees villages give three cows annually to residents of the Roncal Valley.

6-14 San Fermín bull-running festivities, Pamplona.

15-16 *Fiestas* in honour of the Virgin of Carmen at: San Fernando in Cádiz province; San Pedro de Pinatar in Murcia province; and Nerja, Rincón de la Victoria, Torremolinos, Fuengirola and Estepona. Waterborne processions.

24 Stilt-dancers in Mary Magdalene festivals at Anguiano in Logroño province.

24-31 Moors and Christians at Villajoyosa, province of Alicante.

(Moveable) First Saturday, Sunday and Monday of July, round up of wild horses in San Lorenzo de Sabucedo-La Estrada, Pontevedra province.

August

4-10 White Virgin festivals at Vitoria.

11-15 Mystery of Elche, medieval morality play performed in the Cathedral at Elche.

(Moveable) *Vaqueiros* mountaintop wedding celebrations near Luarca, Oviedo province.

September

20-27 *Fiestas* of Our Lady of Mercy in Barcelona, Tarragona and Jerez de la Frontera.

(Moveable) River Guadalquivir Festival, first week of September, featuring horse races on the beach at Sanlúcar de Barrameda.

(Moveable) Sherry Grape Harvest festival at Jerez de la Frontera, with ceremonial blessing of the grapes, parade, horse show and other events.

(Moveable) Toro de la Vega celebrations in which a bull is fought in a pasture at Tordesillas.

(Moveable) Goya-style bullfight in mid-September at Ronda.

October

9–16 Festivals of the Virgin of Pilar, with bullfights, processions, and traditional dancing at Saragossa.

(Moveable) Shellfish Festival, second Sunday, at El Grove, Pontevedra province.

November

30 Pilgrimage in honour of St Andrew at San Andrés de Teixido in Corunna province.

(Moveable) Jubilee Bull *fiestas*, in which flaming torches are attached to a bull's horns at night, at Medinaceli.

December

24 Christmas Eve all over Spain is a time for a big special dinner and family reunion, comparable to dinner on Christmas day in the UK.

28 Feast of the Holy Innocents, the Spanish equivalent of April Fool's Day all across the country.

31 New Year's Eve, celebrations similar to those in Anglo-Saxon countries.

Shoeshines

There is something delightfully luxurious about sitting down and having your shoes shined while you wait. You can do it in Spain, and the bootblacks do a better job on your footwear than you do. The cost is usually about 200 pesetas. Many bars and *tapa* bars have a regular bootblack.

Telephoning

To phone outside Spain, wait for the dialling tone, then dial 07; then wait for a high-pitched tone and dial the code for the country and city; then, without further interruption, dial the number itself.

You are not allowed to make reverse (*cobro revertido*) charge calls from a pay phone. These should be made from the telephone company offices. Ask for the *locutorio*, which is the room with one or more operators on duty, from where you can make long-distance calls.

As a rule, coin-operated phones take coins of 100, 25 and 5 pesetas. Brief local calls will ordinarily cost about 25 pesetas at least.

Here are some of the country codes:

- **United Kingdom and Northern Ireland:** 44
- **Eire:** 353
- **United States and Canada:** 1
- **Australia:** 61
- **New Zealand:** 64
- **South Africa:** 27
- **Hong Kong:** 852

If you do not know the code of the city you want to call, there is a list of them in the introductory pages of the Spanish telephone directory. Codes for capitals of the countries mentioned above are as follows:

London: 1
Dublin: 1
Washington DC: 202
Ottawa: 613
Auckland: 9
Pretoria: 12
New Territories (Hong Kong): 0

Inside Spain   Each Spanish region has its own telephone code, which begins with a 9 and has two or three digits and which should be prefixed to the number if you are calling within Spain to a place in another province. When telephoning from outside Spain, you should drop the 9.

Provincial codes appear in the front of the directories and they are pasted on the sides of most coin-operated public phones. All telephone numbers listed in this guide are preceded by their provincial codes in parentheses.

Terrorism

Don't worry unduly about it. It is real, but the favourite targets of ETA are Spanish police, military men and business and political leaders. Several beach-bomb campaigns in recent years have produced no fatalities among holiday-makers but lots of headlines – which is undoubtedly what the terrorists want. There are no special precautions to be taken by foreign holiday-makers, except of course, the obvious, like never accepting a package from a stranger to take aboard a plane.

It is no doubt small consolation to say that Spain is not the only place troubled by political extremists in our times, but the point is worth making nevertheless. Also, more commonplace dangers, such as accidents and heart attacks, are statistically much more of a threat than terrorism.

Time differences

Clocks in Spain are one hour later than in the UK and Eire (except for a brief period when clocks are changed over from summer to winter time and vice versa, at which time for a few days or a few weeks Spain and the British Isles have the same hour).

It is six hours later in Spain than on the east coast of the United States and Canada in winter, and five hours later in summer.

Tipping

By law, service is included on Spanish hotel and restaurant bills, but it does not appear on the bill as a separate item. Tax (VAT, or IVA in Spanish) often does. Nevertheless it is customary to leave up to 10 per cent in restaurants, and to tip hotel staff.

Tips at hotels depend on the services you ask for and get, but if you stay for more than a few days in a hotel, you should remember the chambermaid when you go. If she has been particularly helpful, you might leave her 500 pesetas. You are under no obligation to leave anything.

In a great many Spanish hotels, the concierge, or hall porter is a veritable mine of information. Tip him 100 pesetas or so for a special favour. However, remember that if he gets you tickets for any kind of show or bullfight, or if he arranges the hire of a car for you, he is no doubt already collecting a commission, so a tip is unnecessary.

Taxi drivers will not snarl if you fail to tip them, but a few five-peseta coins will be greatly appreciated.

Porters at airports and railway stations (and there are never enough of them to go around) charge a fixed fee per piece of luggage carried. It varies from one place to another, but you are entitled to ask for the receipt (*recibo*), which will assure you that you are paying the official rate. As a general guideline, more than 100 pesetas per bag is a lot.

Doormen who open car doors can be given one five-peseta coin each. Barbers and hairdressers are usually tipped; the maximum in this case is about 15 per cent. It is customary to leave a very small tip even when you are served at the bar.

Toilets

There are not many public conveniences in Spain, but every bar, café, restaurant and petrol station has toilets. The standard of cleanliness in the few public facilities is generally very good. That includes airports and railway stations. However, the privately owned toilets, all too often, are dirty. As a general rule, the more expensive the establishment, the cleaner the loo, though there are honourable exceptions among some modestly priced restaurants and cafés. Where there is an attendant, it is usual to leave a tip of not less than five or ten pesetas.

Take note that sometimes there is not even any paper, so it is worth while carrying your own when travelling around. There is frequently no waste bin for soiled sanitary towels, babies' nappies and the like either, so carry a few plastic bags with you. There is no special table for changing babies' nappies in the toilets, with the exception of some at cafés on motorways.

Urgent shipments

If you have to get something from one end of Spain to the other in a hurry, the domestic courier service with the most extensive network and the best guarantee of speed in Spain is Seur, with offices in every principal town. The same company also has an international courier service and local motorcycle messenger service.

Wildlife

There are some dangerous animals in Spain, and, though they are not very common, you will want to know about them.

Scorpions   There are scorpions in the south, particularly in the mountains. The locals call them *alacranes* (singular: *alacrán*). These creatures, which in Spain rarely measure more than about seven centimetres long, look something like a tiny lobster with a long tail, which is curved up at the end. Their colour is a dusty brown and the tail is almost transparent. At the end of the tail is the stinger. The sting of the scorpion is extremely painful and, very occasionally, fatal. Scorpions live under rocks and tend to come out only at night in search of their prey, which are usually insects. Don't look under rocks.

Tarantulas   The tarantula is a hairy spider. The adult in Spain measures about two centimetres across. Its bite is not fatal – contrary to popular belief – but it is very painful. It is native to the south and south-west, but is not very common.

Eels   There is a type of eel, known locally as the *morena* (moray in English), which lives in rocks underwater along the Atlantic coasts of the south and which will bite if disturbed in its lair. It has very sharp teeth that can cause serious injury. Normally, it feeds on small fish. To avoid it, stay away from underwater rock formations.

Sharks   There are sharks on the Atlantic side of the Straits of Gibraltar. The danger is minimal, since they do not normally come close to the coast. Nevertheless young sharks are frequently netted by tuna fishermen at Zahara de los Atunes near Cape Trafalgar. Don't swim out too far in this area. (You can eat young shark, *escualo*, at *tapa* bars in Zahara; it is a tasty, meaty kind of fish.)

Bulls   Fighting bulls are bred to attack. They are raised primarily in western Andalusia, in Extremadura, around Salamanca and in the mountains north of Madrid. If you are hiking or camping, never climb over a fence into a pasture or a sparsely wooded area, without being absolutely certain there are no bulls.

Wild horses   Horses breed wild in Galicia and in forested land in the mountains of the province of Ávila. They do not normally come close to humans, but if you are camping, do not make them nervous; a runaway herd could trample you.

Bears, wolves, wildcats and other forest animals   Spain has more wildlife in its big forests, particularly in the mountains, than other west European countries. While such animals rarely represent a threat, campers and hikers who go deep into the wilderness should be aware that not all the sharp-toothed creatures are fenced in in safari parks.

Insects   The climate in most of Spain is propitious to the proliferation of a number of insects. Depending on where you are, you may run into mosquitoes, horseflies, wasps, sand fleas, ants or other annoying bugs. It is a good idea to carry with you some product to soothe the itch and pain of insect bites. You can buy them at Spanish chemists' shops. Mosquito-repellant lotions are also available.

Snakes   There are no poisonous snakes in Spain.

Glossary

Some historical, cultural or geographic terms used in this book may not be familiar to readers.

Alcazaba   a fortified garrison area inside a walled town.

Alcázar   a fortress, particularly a royal castle.

Banderillas   barbed sticks, usually adorned with coloured paper frills, which a bullfighter on foot stabs into the back of a bull.

Baroque   a highly ornamented style of decoration commonly used in the seventeenth and first half of the eighteenth century.

Bodega   a place where wine is matured.

Calle   street.

Celts   an Indo-European people who in pre-Roman times inhabited Spain and other parts of west and central Europe.

Celtiberians   the Celtic people who inhabited the Iberian Peninsula in ancient times.

Churrigueresque   a variant of the Baroque style named after Spanish architect José Churriguera.

Cistercian   a religious order for monks and nuns founded in 1098 which follows a strict form of the Benedictine rule.

Cloister   a colonnaded, covered walk around an interior courtyard of a church, a monastery or a convent.

Conquistador   conqueror, especially of South America.

Corrida   bullfight.

Dolmen   a Neolithic stone formation, consisting of a large horizontal stone supported by several vertical ones.

Gothic   an architectural style prevalent in Europe from the twelfth to the sixteenth centuries, characterized by pointed arches, ribbed vaults and flying buttresses.

Herrerian an austere style named after its originator, architect Juan Herrera.

Iberians members of a group of ancient Caucasoid peoples who inhabited the Iberian Peninsula in preclassical and classical times.

Levant (or Levante) the east coast of Spain, particularly from the province of Valencia southward.

Matador a fully-fledged bullfighter.

Meseta plateau.

Mezquita mosque.

Monstrance a receptacle, usually of gold and silver, with a transparent container in which the consecrated Host is placed.

Morisco nominally Christian Moor in territory gained by the Reconquest.

Mozarabic characteristic of Christians living in Moorish Spain; or a particular religious rite.

Mudéjar characteristic of Moors living under Christian conquerors in Spain; an architectural style which flourished in the thirteenth to the sixteenth centuries and incorporated Arabic decorative elements.

Necropolis a burial site or cemetery.

Neolithic a cultural period which lasted in Europe from about 4000 to 2400 BC.

Novillero apprentice bullfighter.

Paleolithic Stone Age.

Paseo promenade.

Picador a man on horseback who, in a bullfight, lances the bull.

Plateresque a Spanish decorative style modelled on silversmiths' adornments in the sixteenth century that combined Moorish and Christian arches.

Reconquest (or *Reconquista*) the gradual recovery of the Iberian Peninsula by Christian rulers from the Moors, mostly by force, over a period of nearly eight centuries.

Refectory dining hall of a religious building.

Renaissance the historic period marking the waning of the Middle Ages and the embracing of new ideas, particularly in arts and sciences.

Reredos altarpiece.

Ría   estuary in Galicia.

Romanesque   a simple architectural and artistic style characteristic of the ninth to the twelfth century.

Taifa   in the phrase 'reinos de Taifa', a term used to describe a collection of tiny, disunited kingdoms under Moorish rule in medieval Spain.

Talayot   prehistoric stone monument in the form of a tower.

Visigoths   western Goths who sacked Rome in AD 410 and established a kingdom in southern France and Spain that lasted until 711.

Gazetteer

Introduction: the many Spains

In times past, chroniclers referred to this country as 'Las Españas' ('The Spains'), and they were not far wrong. In an area not quite as big as France or, if you like, slightly larger than California, Spain crams in a lot of variety. There are pronounced differences between regions in terms of history, customs and even language.

Although this guide deals only with the mainland territory on the Iberian Peninsula, which it shares with Portugal, Spain also consists of: the Canary Islands in the Atlantic, off the African Coast; the Balearic Islands in the Mediterranean; and two cities on the north coast of Morocco.

This gazetteer does not always follow the regional divisions on the Spanish map. It often lumps more than one region together or deals with parts of regions individually and is divided into:

Madrid and Environs, including such historic cities as Toledo, Segovia and Ávila.

The **Great Central Tableland**, which extends for hundreds of kilometres north and south of the capital.

South and South-west, including Extremadura and most of western Andalusia, the land of sherry, flamenco dancing, bulls, horses and vast empty beaches.

Costa del Sol and its Sierras, which covers the southern coast of Spain from Gibraltar in the west to Almería in the east and takes you back from the coast for a look at some inland places of interest.

The **Levante**, from the Costa Dorada southward along the coast to Almería, with a few trips inland into the mountains.

Barcelona and the Costa Brava, with a close look at the city of the 1992 Olympics.

The **Pyrenees**, where nature conspires against change.

Green Spain, from the Basque Country at the western end of the Pyrenees to Galicia in Spain's north-west.

Madrid
and Environs

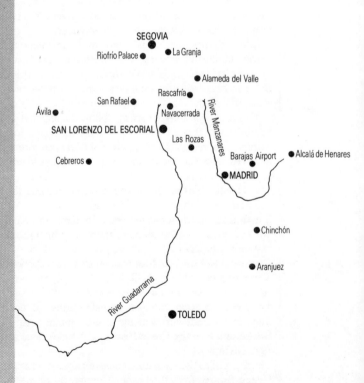

Sepúlveda ●   ● Riaza

SEGOVIA ●
Riofrío Palace ●   ● La Granja

                           ● Alameda del Valle
           Rascafría ●
San Rafael ●
Ávila ●   Navacerrada
SAN LORENZO DEL ESCORIAL ●
                  Las Rozas ●
Cebreros ●   Barajas Airport ●   ● Alcalá de Henares
                              ● **MADRID**

River Manzanares

                                ● Chinchón

                                ● Aranjuez

River Guadarrama

● **TOLEDO**

Madrid
and Environs

Introduction

As Spanish cities go, Madrid has few old monuments. In fact, it is a newcomer among the metropolises of the Iberian Peninsula. It owes its present importance to the decision of a bureaucratic king, Philip II (the one who built the Monastery of the Escorial), to establish his capital in the geographic centre of the Peninsula.

That was in 1561, when the humble little village of Magerit, as the Arabs had called it, was significant only because the Emir of Córdoba, Mohamed I, had established a fortress there on the heights overlooking the puny trickle known as the River Manzanares. In recognition of this central position, a stone marker in Madrid's Puerta del Sol plaza is known as 'kilometre zero'. The kilometres were invented later, but the point from which all distances within continental Spain were measured has not changed.

Modern Madrid is big and bustling, but it has grown gracefully, at least in the centre. As the capital of a fair-sized country – and one which once controlled a global empire – Madrid naturally has a lot of ministries and administrative offices, along with their corresponding civil servants. However, once General Franco embarked on a plan to make Madrid an industrial rival of Barcelona and Bilbao, the city started to grow in a big way. From a population of about one and a half million in the mid-1950s, it has grown to nearly four million.

The greatest period of growth was in the mid-1960s. In recent years the population has stabilized, and has actually diminished slightly as some of those who migrated from their villages to seek factory jobs were obliged by rising unemployment to return.

Lying just south of the impressive Guadarrama mountains, which are snow-capped until June, the city occupies a generally sloping plain draining into the system of the Tagus (Tajo). Madrid's climate is continental, which means cold winters and hot summers. Many people who come here for the first time do not realize how cold it gets in Madrid in the winter, though Centigrade temperatures in the summer, frequently in the upper thirties (about 100°F), do not surprise them. Madrid is 650 m above sea level and parts of it are higher. It is about as far as you can get from the sea in any direction on the Iberian Peninsula. Thus it is dry. To make it even drier, the mountains to the north and west of the city serve as a barrier to the humid winds that bring rainstorms sweeping across the peninsula. Below-freezing temperatures are common in the winter, but the strong sun shining out of a Velázquez-blue sky quickly takes the chill off you.

Madrid is the big show in central Spain, simply because it is populous, literally in the middle, and is the focal point of political and cultural influences. Which is not to say that there is nothing else to see but Madrid in the centre. On the contrary, there are many other towns and areas within easy reach of the capital that should not be overlooked and, in their own way, may prove more interesting.

This section will deal not only with Madrid but also with its immediate environs. As Hemingway pointed out, few cities have so many lovely places surrounding them. Each of them is worth at least a day.

Madrid

Getting there Madrid is on the routes of most large international airlines, with flights several times daily to and from major European cities. There are also scheduled airline services connecting Madrid with principal cities in North and South America, Africa, the Middle East and Asia. Flying time from most European capitals is, very roughly, two hours. Trains run directly between Madrid and Paris, with the fastest ones making the trip in a single day and night. Trains via Barcelona connect without change with Geneva. Within Spain, Madrid is the hub, with the main lines spreading out from it like spokes on a wheel.

For those coming by road from somewhere north of the Pyrenees, the main border crossings are at Irún (Hendaye on the French side) and La Junquera (Le Perthus, via Perpignan); the Irún crossing offers a more direct route to Madrid. For those entering via Portugal it is simple. The most direct route by road from Lisbon to Madrid is via the road to Elvas, crossing to Badajoz.

As for reaching Spain by sea, there is a regular car-ferry offering departures between Santander on Spain's northern coast and Plymouth, England. The road from Santander to Madrid is even more direct than the one from Irún, but, except for a short stretch in the Basque Country in the case of the Irún route, neither is a motorway.

Buses run between Madrid and many European cities daily during the tourist season and, in some cases, all year round. Bus is generally the cheapest form of transport.

Getting about Once in Madrid, you can use the Metro. It is cheap and it covers much of the city. A flat fare gets you to any destination on the network, except those on the outskirts, which are serviced by commuter trains. Maps are displayed inside the Metro stations.

Public buses are another option for getting around the city, but since Madrid is quite large, this method is less advisable for those who do not know the city and the routes. But, of course, hotels can advise on which buses to get for specific destinations.

You can get to and from Madrid's Barajas International Airport (11 km from the centre) by the yellow airport bus. The bus leaves from a station in the parking area under the Plaza de Colón at half-hourly or less intervals throughout the day. Coming from the airport, the bus leaves you at the same central point. It will not pick up passengers with luggage along the route, so you should board it at the beginning of its run.

Taxis are either black or white with a red stripe. They are entitled to charge supplements, in addition to what is shown on the meter, for each piece of luggage, for airport trips and for certain other extras, all of which are supposed to be displayed on a list inside the cab. Since the fare system may seem complicated to a person who is not used to it, the best thing you can do if in doubt about whether you are being charged the correct fare is to ask your hotel.

Main areas To find your way around in Madrid, bear in mind that the main north–south thoroughfare is the broad, tree-lined Castellana Avenue, which is known in its various segments, from north to south as far as the Atocha Railway Station, as Castellana, Paseo de Recoletos and Paseo del Prado. The principal east–west thoroughfares are María de Molina, which connects with the airport road, Avenida de América, and which changes its name to Abascal west of the Castellana; and the Calle de Alcalá, which passes through the Plaza de Independencia, the Plaza de la Cibeles and the Puerta del Sol. Between Cibeles and Sol, however, it intersects with a wide street branching off to the right, the Gran Vía, which is another section of a cross-city route and which changes its name to Princesa past the Plaza de España and leads on to the University of Madrid and the Corunna road (N-VI).

The airport lies east of the city, on the road which goes to Barcelona, the Avenida de América. Travel time to or from the airport obviously depends on the time of day, though normally one-half to three-quarters of an hour is enough time to get there from most central hotels by taxi.

There are three main railway stations, Chamartín (from which north and eastbound trains depart), Atocha (for southbound trains) and Príncipe Pio (for trains going north-west). The Metro goes to all three. Chamartín Station, the newest and biggest, is a few blocks north of the Plaza de Castilla, and just off the Castellana, the north–south axis on which the Atocha Station is situated several kilometres further south. For those who have to change trains from north to south or vice-versa, there is a railway line (in addition to the Metro)

MADRID STREET MAP

PLACES OF INTEREST

1 Tourist Office
2 Tourist Office
3 Municipal Tourist Office
4 Prado Museum
5 Casón del Buen Retiro
6 Royal Palace
7 Army Museum
8 Contemporary Spanish Art Museum
9 Sorolla Museum
10 Carriage Museum
11 Wax Museum
12 Royal Tapestry Factory
13 Liria Palace
14 Hermitage of San Antonio de la Florida
15 Plaza Mayor
16 Debod Temple
17 Archaeological Museum
18 Bullring

RAILWAY STATIONS

19 Atocha
20 Chamartin
21 Principe Pio

University of Madrid

Casa de Campo Park

Castellana Avenue

Calle Serrano

Calle Velázquez

Avenida de América

Calle de José Abascal

Calle de María de Molina

Calle de la Princesa

Paseo de la Florida

Plaza de España

Gran Via

Plaza de Colón

Plaza de la Cibeles

Paseo de Recoletos

Plaza de la Independencia

Calle de Alcalá

Retiro Park

Carrera de San Jeronimo

Paseo del Prado

River Manzanares

Santa María de la Cabeza

running under the Castellana that connects the two stations.

The Príncipe Pio Station is near the River Manzanares, at the inter-section of the Paseo de la Florida and the Paseo de Onésimo Redondo, which runs downhill from the Plaza de España and alongside the northern side of the gardens of the Royal Palace.

Many of the major hotels are on or near the Castellana and Paseo del Prado. There are also several hotels near the airport, but they will not interest you if you are planning to see Madrid.

There are Tourist Offices at the international arrivals hall of Madrid's Barajas Airport; at the Chamartín Railway Station; at Calle Duque de Medinaceli 2 (across the street from the Palace Hotel); and in the Torre de Madrid, the tallest building on the Plaza de España at the foot of the Gran Vía. The municipal Tourist Office is at Plaza Mayor 3.

Madrid's museums are quite scattered. The only important ones reasonably close to each other in the centre are the Prado, with its annexe known as El Casón del Buen Retiro (where Picasso's *Guernica* hangs), the new Reina Sofía Museum, the Army Museum, the Navy Museum and the Palacio de Cristal (an exhibit centre in the Retiro Park). Taking the Prado as a reference point, since it is easy to locate on the Paseo del Prado, the Casón del Buen Retiro is up the hill in the street running past the north side of the Prado. The Army Museum is two streets north of the Prado. The Navy Museum is two streets north but on the Paseo del Prado. The Reina Sofía Museum is at the Plaza del Emperador Carlos V (also known as Atocha), down the Paseo del Prado and in front of the Atocha Railway Station. The Palacio de Cristal is in the Retiro Park, one entrance to which is directly across the street from the east side of the Casón del Buen Retiro.

History Madrilenians, a great many of whom were not born in Madrid, have a saying: *De Madrid al cielo, y un agujerito para verlo.* (After Madrid, heaven, and a peephole to look down on it.) Others, however, would say that you only get to heaven after spending some time in purgatory.

As you can see, Madrid has its admirers and its detractors, as does any large city. However, it is lively, attractive and relatively clean. Although the people of Madrid enjoy the city's beauty, they do not have a reputation for being very grateful to the people who embel-lished it with noble buildings, tree-lined boulevards and graceful stat-ues and fountains. Charles III, referred to in the history books as Madrid's best mayor, built the beautiful Alcalá Gate, the building which today houses most of the paintings of the Prado Museum, and the building which now serves as headquarters of the Madrid regional government in the Puerta del Sol, among other things. He also estab-lished the state-run lottery, lit the streets of Madrid, built the first part of the lovely, broad Castellana Avenue, ordered the construction of several fountains, including the Cibeles, a useful landmark, and the Neptune near the Prado.

In a word, Charles III gave Madrid style. So it is ironic that the cause of a revolt in 1766 against his Prime Minister, the Marqués de Esquilache, was the bitter objection of Madrid's *caballeros* (gentle-men) to a decree prohibiting the use of long capes and extremely broad-brimmed *sombreros*. The point of the decree was to cut down on crime by muggers and murderers who did their dirty work and got away by hiding their swords and their identity under their ample capes. They were so serious about it that the King decided to take a six-month sojourn outside Madrid and eventually he had to dismiss his Prime Minister, before the 'Esquilache Mutiny' could be forgot-ten.

Napoleon's allegedly alcoholic brother, Joseph Bonaparte, nick-named Pepe Botella by the Spanish, also did a lot for Madrid, though the city's inhabitants were in no mood to acknowledge it. He author-ized bars and cafés to stay open until the small hours, built several of Madrid's finest plazas, and arranged daily theatre performances with free admission for workers. Madrilenians repaid Pepe Botella with the uprising of 2 May 1808, of which Goya was the graphic reporter. With Pepe Botella still in power, Madrid endured what has gone down in history as 'the year of hunger', 1811, when 20,000 of its citizens died of starvation and disease rather than accept food and medical care from the French troops.

In the latter half of the nineteenth century, Isabel II brought abun-dant mountain water to Madrid through the construction of a pipeline that to this day is known as the Canal of Isabel II. Then she decided to sell off the Royal Patrimony and give 75 per cent of the proceeds to the Spanish people. Were they happy? No. They wanted it all. After a few years of turmoil, there was a revolution in 1868, followed by Spain's First Republic. Isabel slipped across the border to France from the northern city where she had been spending her summer holidays, San Sebastián.

In 1906, Alfonso XIII, grandfather of the present Spanish King, Juan Carlos, took an English bride, the lovely 'Princess Ina', Victoria Eugenia de Battenberg. Unfortunately, their wedding day was some-what marred when an anarchist threw a bomb hidden in a bouquet of flowers as their carriage clattered by on the Calle Mayor. The royal bride's wedding gown was splattered with the blood of the victims, but she and the King escaped harm. Alfonso XIII survived at least one other assassination attempt, seven years later. The heads of two of his successive governments were assassinated. He and Ina enjoyed con-siderable popular support, but he knew which side the royal bread was buttered on; so, in 1931, when municipal elections brought a landslide vote in favour of Republican candidates, and they ran up the purple, red and yellow Republican flag on the Post Office flagpole, he dis-creetly slipped out of the country, never to return. He did not abdi-cate: he just left.

In 1975, General Franco, who had held power as dictator since 1939 when he won the Civil War that toppled the second Spanish Republic, died. King Juan Carlos, and a democratic system, succeeded the Generalissimo. On 23 February 1981, a pistol-packing Civil Guard colonel, Tejero, leading a small group of troops, held the entire Parliament, including the Prime Minister and all his Cabinet, at gunpoint for one long, tense night, while tanks rumbled through the streets of Valencia, thousands of known opponents of the Franco regime went into hiding or even crossed the borders, and many a military leader pondered about whether to join the rebels. Only the King's personal intervention, demanding pledges of loyalty from key military officers, averted a *coup d'état*.

In 1981, Spain joined the North Atlantic Treaty Organization, and in 1986, became a member of the European Economic Community.

What to see

There is so much to see and do in Madrid that this section is intended only to stimulate you to look for more. You will not have to look far.

There are scores of museums in the Spanish capital, including one of the world's greatest, the Prado; there are many historic or otherwise important buildings; there are trade fairs on an almost continuous basis throughout the year; there are two major football clubs, and outstanding teams and players in a number of sports. There is a motor racetrack, a greyhound track, and a racecourse. Bullfights take place throughout the season (from spring until early autumn) twice-weekly at Madrid's main bullring, Las Ventas, and daily for almost the entire month of May during the *fiestas* in honour of St Isidro, Madrid's patron saint. In addition, there are fights at other rings on the outskirts of the capital in conjunction with local *fiestas*.

There are many lovely parks in Madrid too, including the Retiro, a huge central park with ancient trees, a boating lake, a bandstand, an exhibition hall, an astronomical observatory, two restaurant nightclubs, and elegant treelined avenues for walking. It was once the garden of the (former) royal palace. There is also El Pardo, which used to be General Franco's private hunting grounds, a vast natural park full of deer and other wildlife on the northern edge of the city, reaching up to the mountains. The Casa de Campo Park, a large natural park, reaches almost to the centre of the city and spreads out along its west side. It contains a zoo, an amusement park, a boating lake and a large fairground. The Rosales Parque del Oeste starts near the central Plaza de España and spreads northward to join the green campus of the University of Madrid.

Visitors will do well to consult lists and schedules of events that appear in a number of publications, some in English. Such English-language publications include: *Lookout* (an excellent national magazine, but since it is monthly it may offer less detail on events); *Guidepost*, a Madrid weekly; and the *Iberian Daily Sun*.

Try to see at least the following:

Prado Museum

This is on Paseo del Prado. Open daily from 10 a.m. to 6 p.m. and from 10 a.m. to 2 p.m. on Sundays. Closed on Mondays. The museum closes at 5 p.m. on weekdays in winter. Do not even dream of 'doing' this museum in a couple of hours; you would regret it if you tried. If you have little time to dedicate to this incredible collection of the world's greatest masters of painting, limit yourself to Velázquez and Goya, both of whose work is on the same floor and relatively near to each other (not Goya's Black Paintings; they are on another floor). That way you will be able to take in a few of the most famous master-pieces, such as Velázquez's *Las Meninas* and *Surrender at Breda* (also known as 'The Lances') and Goya's *Majas* (both the clothed and the naked ones) and his dramatic painting of the execution of Spaniards involved in the uprising against Napoleon's troops on 2 May 1808.

If you have more time, get an eyeful of more of this huge treasure trove of painting up to the latter part of the last century. To be crimi-nally brief, the museum's tens of thousands of pieces of art include enviable collections of not only the two artists mentioned, but also of Titian, Zurbarán, the Flemish school and El Greco. Many people make a point of going to the **Casón del Buen Retiro**, which is part of the Prado but in a different building, to see Picasso's *Guernica* because of its historical significance, or the ballyhoo that surrounds it. If you don't like abstract art, it's probably not worth making a big effort to see this particular painting; it leaves a lot of people cold.

Royal Palace

This Palace (Palacio Real) is at Plaza de Oriente. Open daily from 10 a.m. to 12.45 p.m. and 4 to 5.45 p.m. and from 10 a.m. to 1.30 p.m. on Sundays and holidays. In winter, the afternoon hours on weekdays are from 3.30 to 5.15 p.m. This is one of the most magnificent royal palaces in Europe, with 2,000 rooms (not all of them open to the pub-lic). Used only for state receptions and as a museum since Juan Carlos and his family do not live there, the palace itself is worthy of study in addition to its contents. Begun in 1738 and completed (with a parade square added as an afterthought) in 1831, it is an impressive structure. Philip V ordered the start of construction after a previous fortress-pal-ace on the same site had burned down in 1734. The original architect was called Juvara, but the building was continued after his death by Juan Bautista Sachetti and Ventura Rodríguez, who probably greatly influenced the final design.

Army Museum

(Del Ejército) Calle Méndez Núñez 1. Open daily from 10 a.m. to 5 p.m. and from 10 a.m. to 2 p.m. on Sundays. Closed on Mondays. One of the more ghoulish items here is the big black bulletproof Dodge car in which General Franco's most trusted deputy, Admiral Luis Carrero Blanco, was blown sky-high by Basque extremists in Madrid in 1973. The explosion tossed the car over the top of a six-storey building and into an interior patio. It is impressively flattened. Also on display is the carriage in which General Juan Prim, prime mover of the 1868 revolution which obliged Queen Isabel II to flee and, at the time of his death, premier, was assassinated by anarchists in Madrid three days after Christmas, 1870.

Contemporary Spanish Art Museum
Avenida Juan de Herrera 2 (Ciudad Universitaria). Open daily from 10 a.m. to 6 p.m. and from 10 a.m. to 3 p.m. on Sundays. Closed on Mondays. Modern painters' and sculptors' work, mostly Spanish. Exhibits change frequently and artists are top-rank.

Sorolla Museum
General Martínez Campos 37. Open daily from 10 a.m. to 2 p.m. Closed on Mondays. A little gem for fans of this Valencian painter who brought the light of the Mediterranean to his canvas.

Some of the many other museums:

Carriage Museum
(De Carruajes), Calle Vírgen del Puerto s/n. Open daily from 10 a.m. to 12.45 p.m. and 4 to 5.45 p.m. in summer, and from 10 a.m. to 12.45 p.m. and 3.30 to 5.15 p.m. in winter. Open from 10 a.m. to 1.30 p.m. on Sundays and holidays. Closed whenever the carriages are needed for official events. These beautiful, ornate carriages are not fossils but are all in good working order, even though some of them are of a very respectable age.

Wax Museum
(Museo de Cera), Paseo de Recoletos 41. Open daily from 10.30 a.m. to 1.30 p.m. and from 4 to 8.30 p.m. They're all there in painstakingly realistic images – a celebrated bullfighter being gored horribly in the eye; a famous murderer doing his thing, with blood all over the place, and, of course, kings, queens and princesses. Kids love every gory bit of it.

Archaeological Museum
(Museo Arqueológico), Calle Serrano 13. Open daily from 9 a.m. to 1.30 p.m. Closed on Mondays. It contains a reproduction of the cave paintings of Altamira, a good collection of ancient coins and, perhaps the most interesting item, the stone head of the Dama de Elche dating from pre-Phoenician times.

Other places of interest or permanent exhibits:

Royal Tapestry Factory
Calle Fuenterrabía 2. Open daily from 9.30 a.m. to 12.30 p.m. Closed on Saturdays, Sundays and holidays and for the entire month of August. Watch the tapestry weavers at work; order one for yourself if you feel flush.

Liria Palace
Calle Princesa 20. Visitors are allowed on Saturdays, but only after applying for permission by letter, addressed to the Duke and Duchess of Alba, who live in this palace built over two centuries ago. This lovely building, tucked away in its garden, almost out of sight in the very heart of Madrid, was badly damaged in the Civil War but has been carefully restored. The Albas' private art collection includes some of Europe's finest works of the past few centuries.

Hermitage of San Antonio de la Florida
Glorieta de San Antonio de la Florida. Open daily from 11 a.m. to 1 p.m. and from 3 to 6 p.m. Closed on Wednesdays, and also on Sunday afternoons. Goya frescos cover the dome. A great time to visit this chapel is on 13 June, the feast of St Anthony, when, following tradition, Madrid's seamstresses file in by the hundreds, light a candle and

pray to the saint to find them a boyfriend, then walk out of a side door, where many of them find the answer to their prayers, for it seems that unattached young men also know about the tradition.

Plaza Mayor   A monumental seventeenth-century porticoed square with nine arched entrances, which was in times past the scene of *autos-da-fé* and bullfights; still used for special events in connection with various *fiestas*. A good time to go is at night, when outdoor restaurants and pavement cafés fill up.

Debod Temple   Parque del Oeste, Paseo del Pintor Rosales. A charming little Egyptian temple of golden-coloured stone, saved from being swallowed up by the waters behind the Aswan High Dam, which was donated to Spain by the Egyptian Government, brought here and reconstructed stone by stone.

What to do   Madrid used to be the capital and Barcelona the cultural centre of Spain. Such is the case no longer. Madrid has undergone a rejuvenation since the advent of democracy, and the *movida*, as it is called, has got the city moving. There is more music, theatre, participant-sports, and other leisure activity than ever before.

If you are a passive holiday-maker, try people-watching from the vantage point of a seat at one of the pavement cafés that line the Castellana for several kilometres.

Casa de   Take the cable car from the Paseo de Rosales at the intersection of
Campo Park   Calle Marqués de Urquijo to the huge Casa de Campo Park. It runs daily from 11.45 a.m. to 7 p.m. and from 10.45 a.m. to 8 p.m. on Sundays and holidays. There you will find a big, modern Amusement Park, which is open daily from 4 to 11 p.m., from midday to midnight on Saturdays and from 11 a.m. to 11 p.m. on Sundays and holidays; closed on weekdays in winter. The Park also offers free shows featuring top entertainers.

Zoo   Or – also at the Casa de Campo – visit the Zoo (open daily from 10 a.m. to 9 p.m.), also very modern, where a great deal of attention has been paid to the animals' habitats. Ask at the gate for times of the trained-bird show and the hilarious antics at feeding time of the seals and walruses. There is also a new dolphin show.

The chances are that there will be some kind of commercial fair going on at the exhibition grounds of the Casa de Campo. Check with the Tourist Office to see if you might be interested in seeing it.

Go to this park early in the morning and you will see young would-be bullfighters practising their passes with their red capes and lunging at unseen taurine enemies with their wooden swords. They often work in pairs, with one taking the part of the bull and the other avoiding the simulated deadly horns. If the bulls fascinate you even more, you can enrol at one of the capital's schools of tauromachy.

Cultural   Theatre, concerts, recitals, art exhibitions, lectures and other such
events   events take place throughout the year – except in August, when just about everybody packs up and goes to the beaches or the mountains.

Thanks to kind-hearted municipal planners, however, there is now theatre in August and, to make it more delightful, it is usually staged outdoors in one or more of Madrid's many plazas.

Sports If you feel energetic, try a round of golf at the city-owned **Puerta de Hierro** course or at one of the private ones; or go rowing on the lake at Retiro Park or on the bigger one at the Casa de Campo Park.

In winter, skiers, sledgers, snowball throwers and the like can indulge themselves at any of several winter sports resorts within an hour or two's drive from Madrid, namely La Pinilla (112 km), Valcotos (82 km), Valdesqui (73 km) and Navacerrada (75 km).

Despite its distance from the sea, Madrid has water sports too. A number of large mountain lakes within easy driving distance of the capital offer opportunities for sailing, windsurfing, swimming, fishing, rowing, boating and water skiing. The best known of the chain of artificial lakes are the Lago de San Juan, the Embalse de Alberche and the Entrepeñas-Buendía system. If you are in the neighbourhood of the San Juan or the Alberche lakes, stop off at the co-operative winery in San Martín de Valdeiglesias and pick up some of the local brew, red, white or rosé; you can buy it by the gallon jug and it is good stuff.

Bullfights There are daily bullfights at the Las Ventas bullring for about one month, beginning on or about 15 May, the feast of St Isidro, Madrid's patron saint, whose claim to fame is that he meditated under a tree while the angels did his ploughing for him. There are fights usually twice weekly or more often throughout the season, which in Madrid begins in March or April and continues until September. Local *fiestas* in most towns and villages around the capital feature bullfights, often offering a chance for the local lads, and lasses, to jump into the ring, which is frequently an improvised one in the main square. Visitors too are usually welcome to have a go.

Shopping Good buys are women's fashions, leather goods and gold jewellery. The most elegant shops are mostly along the Calles of Serrano and Velázquez. Don't miss Madrid's fabulous **Flea Market**, the **Rastro**, in the streets going downhill from the Plaza del Cascorro. You can buy just about anything there, from old airplane parts to Indian perfume. But it is not all junk. Some extremely valuable antiques and works of art change hands at the Rastro. It is best on Sunday morning, but go before 11 a.m. or you will find you can hardly move in the mob.

Nightlife To mention just a few:

Flamenco **Venta del Gato**, Avenida de Burgos, km 7.7 (just before the entrance to Royal Oaks US military dependents' housing area). Tel. (91) 766 6060 or 202 3427. If you are not into flamenco, this may be a bit too authentic for you. You can have supper here before the show. Moderately expensive, but top talent.

Zambra, Calle Velázquez 8 (in the Wellington Hotel building). Tel. (91) 435 5164 or 435 4928. A new flamenco supper club with the same name as one that was Madrid's best about twenty years ago.

Music hall   **Scala Meliá Castilla**, Capitán Haya 43 (in the Meliá Castilla Hotel). The best Madrid has to offer in this type of spectacle. You can have dinner as well, starting at 8.30 p.m., with the first show at 10 or 10.15 p.m. Moderately expensive but worth it.

Florida Park, Retiro Park, entrance on Avenida Menéndez y Pelayo, opposite intersection of Calle Ibiza. Tel. (91) 273 7804 or 273 7805. A supper club in the park, offering two shows nightly and dancing. Frequent appearances by top stars.

Nightclubs   **Xénon**, basement of the Callao Cinema at the Plaza de Callao. Tel. (91) 231 9794 or 521 2506. Top Spanish performers and dancing.

Pasapoga, Gran Vía 37. Tel. (91) 521 5027. Frequented by a middle-aged crowd. Variety show and dancing.

Red light district   Madrid's principal red-light districts, which have really come to life since the end of the Franco dictatorship, are the 'Costa Fleming', the area including and surrounding the Calle Dr Fleming in the upper reaches of the Castellana, near the Eurobuilding and Cuzco Hotels; and the area centred on the Calle Ballesta near the Gran Vía. Transvestites ply their trade along the Castellana, particularly in the vicinity of the Miguel Angel and the Castellana Intercontinental Hotels.

Live jazz   **Whisky Jazz Club**, Calle Diego de Léon 7. Tel. (91) 261 1165. Open from 7 p.m. to 3.30 a.m., with music from 11.30 p.m. Very reasonable, and one of Madrid's veteran jazz clubs.

El Despertar, Torecilla del Leal 18. Metro Antón Martín. Tel. (91) 230 8095. Open from 7 p.m., music from 8.30 p.m. Thursday to Saturday.

Beer halls, special bars   **Cervecería Alemana**, Plaza de Santa Ana. The hangout for Madrid's young foreign writers, actors and emigrés. Hemingway drank here, but the prices are still low.

Viva Madrid, Calle Manuel F. González 7 (just off the Plaza Santa Ana). Impressive tiled walls and a university crowd, including many foreigners. You may have seen this bar if you saw BBC television's production of Laurie Lee's *As I Walked Out One Midsummer Morning*. Cheap.

Live Latin American music   **La Carreta**, Calle Barbieri 10. Metro Chueca. Tel. (91) 232 7042. Open from 8 p.m. to 5 a.m. Argentinian music, live, and Argentinian steaks too. Moderate prices.

Don Alberto, Manuel Silvela 6. Tel. (91) 446 0110. Caribbean rhythms.

Arara, Comandante Zorita 8. Tel. (91) 254 9437. Current Brazilian music, open from 9 p.m. to 3.30 a.m., music from 11.30 p.m. Closed on Sundays.

Discotheque   **Pachá**, Barceló 11. Metros Tribunal and Bilbao. Tel. (91) 446 0137. Open every night and Saturday and Sunday afternoons as well. Young crowd and the latest and loudest music.

Casino   **Casino de Madrid**, Carretera de La Coruña, km 28.3

Tasca-hopping

Where to stay
Top range

Mid-range

(Torrelodones). Roulette, blackjack – the lot – plus a restaurant and nightclub with show.

This is a favourite nocturnal activity of Madrilenians and foreigners alike. It is Spanish for wandering, in company, from bar to bar (*tasca* to *tasca*), sampling a *tapa* or two in each place, along with a small glass of wine or beer. *Tapas* are snacks in the Spanish style, more often than not hot from the cooker. Some bars specialize in certain types. The best area in Madrid for *tasca*-hopping is that roughly between the Plaza de Santa Ana and the Carrera de San Jerónimo, near the Puerta del Sol. Having tried it you won't ever want another sit-down meal.

Castellana Intercontinental, Avenida de la Castellana 49. Tel. (91) 410 0200, telex 27686. A fine hotel with spacious rooms, direct-dial telephones and good service, on the lovely Castellana Avenue. It has one of the most attractive lobbies of any Madrid hotel. From 21,000 ptas.

Ritz, Plaza de la Lealtad 5. Tel. (91) 221 2857, telex 43986. Madrid's poshest, with a good restaurant too, and, in summer, a pleasant garden to dine in. Be forewarned: it is the kind of place where men must wear ties. Once, the Ritz used to refuse to admit actors and other riff-raff. The only way James Stewart could get a room was to register as a military officer, which, by the way, he was entitled to do, being a general in the US Air Force Reserve. Now even journalists are allowed in; just another sign of these decadent times! From 28,000 ptas.

Wellington, Calle Velázquez 8. Tel. (91) 275 4400, telex 22700. A businessmen's and bullfighters' hotel, with a good restaurant and a pleasant bar, and videos and critiques of the afternoon's bullfight. Very cosy and central, with all facilities. From 15,200 ptas.

Alcalá, Calle Alcalá 66. Tel. (91) 435 1060, telex 48094. Near the cool, green Retiro Park and close to the elegant shopping area of the Calles Serrano and Velázquez. Good Basque restaurant and a favourite stopping place for Basque politicians. Garage, sauna, good bar. From 8,970 ptas.

Victoria, Plaza del Angel 7. Tel. (91) 231 4500. A great old hotel, with many of its rooms overlooking the fascinating Plaza de Santa Ana. It is close to the stately old Plaza Mayor, the Puerta del Sol plaza, which is generally acknowledged as the centre of Madrid, and to the best area for *tapas*. From 5,990 ptas.

Zurbano, Calle Zurbano 79. Tel. (91) 441 5500, telex 27578. Excellent value for money. It is situated on a narrow street and has an unimpressive reception area, but it is clean and quite comfortable. From 5,800 ptas (December to February) to 6,800 ptas (rest of the year).

Bretón, Calle Bretón de los Herreros 29. Tel. (91) 442 8300. A smallish residence hotel offering good value for money. It is not far from the Castellana. From 7,500 ptas.

Colón, Dr Esquerdo 117. Tel. (91) 273 5900, telex 22984. A good four-star hotel with all sorts of conveniences, but a bit out of the way. However, the price makes up for that: 6,600 ptas.

Aristos, Avenida de Pio XII 34. Tel. (91) 457 0450. This only has twenty-five rooms and is in a pleasant residential area, but it is nowhere near the centre. There is a Metro stop (Pio XII) nearby, and city buses run past the door. It is also handy for the Chamartin Railway Station. From 7,000 ptas.

Conde Duque, Plaza Conde Valle Súchil 5. Tel. (91) 447 7000, telex 22058. A pleasant residence hotel on an attractive and quiet square in the centre of town. From 5,665 ptas.

Bottom range   **Marbella**, Plaza de Isabel II 5. Tel. (91) 247 6148. Central. There are only eight rooms and it is virtually impossible to find anything more economical in Madrid. From 700 (without private bath) to 1,700 ptas.

Mary Ely, Conde de Romanones 11. Tel. (91) 239 4458. Near the Plaza Santa Ana and Madrid's best district for *tapas*. The street is noisy until late at night, but for the price you could hardly expect more. There are only eight rooms. From 1,700 (without bath) to 2,000 ptas (with bath).

Where to eat
Pricey   **Zalacaín**, Calle Alvarez de Baena 4. Tel. (91) 261 4840. Closed Saturday at midday and all day Sunday; also closed during August and the Holy Week. International cooking with Basque specialities. Superb but prices are on the high side. This is the only restaurant in Spain rated with five stars in the *Michelin Guide*, which is not to say it is the only one that deserves such consideration. Outstanding service, food and cellar.

El Bodegón, Calle Pinar 15. Tel. (91) 262 8844. Closed on Sundays, holidays and during August. Mouth-watering Spanish cuisine, with specialities like roast sirloin in red wine sauce and, for dessert, almond pastry. Excellent selection of wines, particularly Spanish ones.

Jockey, Calle Amador de los Rios 6. Tel. (91) 419 2435. Closed on Sundays, holidays and during August. The classic place for high-class group lunches, particularly of businessmen, this restaurant has a number of private dining rooms and very discreet service plus exquisite food. Spanish and French cooking, impeccable wine list.

La Dorada, Calle Orense 64. Tel. (91) 270 2004. Closed on Sundays and during August. A large but very good seafood restaurant. Specialities include sea bass baked in salt paste.

Moderate   **La Gran Tasca**, Calle Ballesta 1. Tel. (91) 231 0044 or 221 6805. Midday meals only. Castilian cooking. A great restaurant in a terrible neighbourhood. The house rosé wine is very good and so is the service. The lamb chops are lovely.

Solchaga, Plaza Alonso Martínez 2. Tel. (91) 447 1496. Closed all day Sunday and Saturday at midday and during Holy Week. Basque cooking and a lot of class for your money. Some private dining rooms.

Specialities include stuffed peppers and hake in squids' ink.

Jai Alai, Calle Balbina Valverde 2. Tel. (91) 261 2742. Closed on Mondays and during the latter half of August. This restaurant had a reputation for being a centre of conspiracy before the end of the Franco regime. Good Basque cooking, friendly service, terrace for dining on a summer evening. Good wine selection.

La Barraca, Calle Reina 29. Tel. (91) 232 7154. Levante cooking, which means all kinds of rice dishes: paella, rice *abanda*, rice in broth and many other variations on the theme. Foreigners who tend to die of hunger before most restaurants in this country serve lunch or dinner will like this place. It is open from 12.30 to 4 p.m. and from 8.30 p.m. to midnight.

Casa Paco, Plaza Puerta Cerrada 11. Tel. (91) 266 3166. Closed on Sundays and for all of August. Do not fail to phone ahead for reservations in this, Madrid's most popular steak house. You'll still have to wait when you get there, but the wait would be a great deal longer if you failed to book ahead. The old-fashioned zinc-topped bar at the entrance, where customers knock back *chatos* of the house red while waiting, is a prelude to the simplicity and genuine old-time atmosphere throughout. A word of warning: do not touch your plate; the meat is served sizzling hot on plates straight out of the oven.

Botín, Calle Cuchilleros 17. Tel. (91) 266 4217. After 250 years, Botín continues to produce excellent roast suckling-pig and baby lamb. The restaurant is full of atmosphere, just behind the Plaza Mayor. Inspired by Hemingway, tourists flock to this place; but don't get the idea that it is more of a curiosity than a good eatery. Standards remain high. A *tuna*, which in Spanish is not something on the menu but a band of student troubadors, will serenade you while you dine.

Economical   **China King**, Calle Ponzano 34. Tel. (91) 442 3851. As at most Chinese restaurants, you don't need to be a millionaire to fill your stomach here, but at the same time both the décor and the food are a cut above average. They do fried wan-ton well, and Mongolian-style veal. Some of the staff speak English. The service is quite good.

El Huevo de Colón, Calle Santa Engracia 15. Tel. (91) 447 5016. The name refers to an apocryphal story about how Columbus managed to stand an egg on its butt to illustrate his theory that the earth was round, and hence to any kind of difficult feat, which here appears to be how they can serve good food for an average of 1,000 ptas per person.

Casa Ciriaco, Calle Mayor 84. Tel. (91) 248 0620. Closed on Wednesdays and during August. Home-style Spanish cooking at prices everyone can afford. Friendly service. Specialities include *cocido*, that Madrilenian stew of chick-peas and everything else that fuelled the reconquest of Spain from the Arabs and the conquest of the Americas, and would probably also serve as rocket fuel for the conquest of space.

Around Madrid

Madrid is a marvellous base for excursions. All around it, in a radius of little more than 100 km, are lovely spots to visit, eat, ogle at, play in and rest. If you don't have a car, there are guided bus-tours of most of the following places with buses leaving either daily or several times a week from principal Madrid hotels. They usually offer a complete guided tour of the town or place you want to see for a reasonable price, often with lunch included. For timetables and route details, contact the Tourist Office, any travel agent in Madrid or ask at your hotel. Most of the towns mentioned have frequent daily train links with Madrid as well. Each of the places described here can be visited in one day, with time to return to Madrid for the night; however, in some you may want to stay at least overnight.

Toledo

Toledo (population 57,769) is 70 km south of Madrid on the N401. A fortified city dating from Roman times, it was the capital of Visigothic Spain and still looks today exactly as El Greco painted it in the six-teenth century. Toledo has a history of spine-chilling battles even in modern times. During the siege of the Alcázar (which you can visit) by Republican forces in the Spanish Civil War, the son of Colonel Moscardó, the Alcázar's commanding officer, was captured. The Republicans called the pro-Franco colonel on the telephone. (Tele-phone lines were frequently left in place during that war and used for transmitting ultimatums.) They let the colonel's son speak. 'Dad,' he reportedly said, 'they say they'll shoot me if you don't surrender the fortress.' Colonel Moscardo allegedly replied, 'Son, die like a man.'

What to see

In Toledo, don't miss the **Cathedral**, begun in the sixth century, converted into a mosque when the Arabs took over, then restored to its status as a church when the Christian forces finally recaptured Toledo. Most of the present structure dates from that period, the early thirteenth century. The cathedral and cathedral museum are open daily from 10.30 a.m. to 1.30 p.m. and from 3.30 to 6 p.m.

Other 'must' visits include:

● **Santo Tomé Church**, where El Greco's large canvas of *The Burial of the Count of Orgaz* hangs. Open daily from 10 a.m. to 1.45 p.m. and from 3.30 to 7.45 p.m. (winter to 6.45 p.m.).

● **Gothic Church and Monastery of San Juan de los Reyes**, dating from the fifteenth century with its lovely cloister. Open daily from 10 a.m. to 2 p.m. and from 3.30 to 7 p.m.

● **El Tránsito Synagogue**, dating from the fourteenth century which was converted into a Christian place of worship after the expulsion of the Jews from Spain in 1492 but was happily left largely unchanged by its new tenants. Open daily from 10 a.m. to 1.45 p.m. and from 2 to 6.45 p.m.; in winter from 10 a.m. to 1.45 p.m. and from 3.30 to 5.45 p.m.; closed Mondays and Sunday aftenrnoons.

● **House of El Greco**, with a good collection of some of the paintings he did in Toledo. Open daily from 10 a.m. to 2 p.m. and from 4 to 7 p.m. Closed Mondays and Sunday afternoons.

● **Santa Cruz Museum**, a repository of master paintings in a sixteenth-century hospital building with a Plateresque façade, and, in fact, the whole city, with its walls, its gates, its bridges and its outlying Romanic churches. The best place to get a breathtaking view of this city, which rightly has been declared a national monument in its entirety, is from the parador across the river. The Santa Cruz Museum is open daily from 10 a.m. to 7 p.m.; closed Mondays, Sunday afternoons and from 25 December to 2 January.

Tourist Office: Puerta de Bisagra s/n. Tel. (925) 22 0843.

Shopping

Toledo is a good place to buy handicrafts, particularly Damascene-type Toledo-ware and steel swords. Remember Toledo steel was famous in the Middle Ages because of a secret tempering process. The celebrated Toledo marzipan is also a good buy if you've a sweet tooth.

Where to stay
Top range

Parador Conde de Orgaz, Paseo de los Cigarrales. Tel. (925) 221 850, telex 47998. There is a fabulous El Greco view of Toledo. Swimming pool. Restaurant with local specialities. Huge terrace. From 8,500 ptas (January to March) to 10,000 ptas (rest of year).

Mid-range

Alfonso VI, General Moscardó 2. Tel. (925) 222 600. Within walking distance of all the places you want to see. Ample rooms at a very reasonable price: 4,850 ptas.

Where to eat
Moderate

Hostal del Cardenal, Paseo Recaredo 24. Tel. (925) 220 862. Full of the flavour of Toledo, this restaurant-inn is in a seventeenth-century cardinal's palace right by the city walls, and in good weather – which means five months of the year at least – you can dine in the old gardens. Spanish and international cooking.

Casa Aurelio, Calle del Sinagoga 6. Tel. (925) 222 097. Typical old Castilian architecture and good Castilian cooking. Game in season. Try the garlic soup.

San Lorenzo del Escorial

San Lorenzo del Escorial (population 9,518) is 49 km from Madrid via the N-VI motorway, turning left on C-505 at Las Rozas. This is the site of the huge but austere seventeenth-century monastery palace built by Philip II, Spain's monk-king and ruler of a vast empire. The monastery is still in use, so parts of it are closed to the public, but there is plenty to see nonetheless. The library is one of the most complete ones left from the time of Philip II; scholars may use it by putting in an advance request. The monastery is open from 10 a.m. to 1 p.m. and from 3.30 to 6.30 p.m.; winter from 10 a.m. to 1 p.m. and from 3 to 6 p.m. The pine-forested slopes surrounding the monastery and the town are delightful in summer but icy in winter. Signposts indicate the way up the mountainside to the carved stone chair above the monastery from which Philip watched the progress of construction during the thirty-one years it took to build it. To get to the chair, take the road leading out of Escorial in the direction of/Ávila; you will see a sign indicating the direction of the chair on an unpaved road to your left within about 1 km.

Tourist Office: Floridablanca 10, Tel. (91) 890 1554.

Valley of the Fallen War Memorial

This is just 12 km to the east of El Escorial. Its 150-m-high stone cross and the basilica carved out of solid rock make this complex, designed by General Franco to be his final resting place, a mausoleum comparable in its grandiose proportions only to the pyramids of Egypt.

Where to stay
Mid-range

Victoria Palace, Juan de Toledo. Tel. (91) 890 1511, telex 22227. A delightful, old-fashioned hotel with all comforts, within walking distance of the El Escorial monastery-palace. It has a tiny garden bar in front of the main entrance, under ancient trees. Swimming pool and restaurant too. From 5,500 ptas (September to June) to 6,750 ptas (July and August).

Ávila

Ávila (population 41,735) is 113 km north-west of Madrid via the N-VI motorway, then left on the N-110. Snug behind its marvellously intact eleventh-century walls with their round watchtowers, standing high on the treeless plains of Old Castile, Ávila resists change, and its city fathers seem to remember no other prominent son or daughter than the strong-willed mystic, St Teresa. Its twelfth-century Cathedral, forming part of the city walls, looks more like a fortress than a church. Built on the remains of an ancient Iberian settlement, Ávila is in the centre of an area which was populated in the Iron Age, as is witnessed by the numerous artefacts found in the area, which include life-sized carved stone animals like the renowned Bulls of Guisando.

Ávila is the highest city in Spain and one of the coldest.

Tourist Office: Plaza de la Catedral 4. Tel. (918) 211 387.

Where to stay
Mid-range

Parador Raimundo de Borgoña, Calle Marqués de Canales y Chozas 16. Tel. (918) 211 340. Central and in scenic surroundings, just a garden away from the marvellous twelfth-century walls. The parador is in a tastefully restored and enlarged fifteenth-century palace. The dining room offers St Teresa's stew and St Teresa's candied egg yolks, just in case anyone visiting here could have forgotten for a moment that Ávila is the home of that great and gutsy mystic of the sixteenth-century. From 6,000 ptas (November to June) to 7,500 ptas.

Where to eat
Moderate

Mesón del Rastro, Plaza del Rastro 1. Tel. (918) 211 218. This restaurant, in an austere old palace, offers good Castilian cooking at a price that will not strain your budget. The good house wine is from Cebreros, the nearby home town of Spain's first democratically elected Prime Minister of the post-Franco era, Adolfo Suárez. Sweetbreads are a speciality.

Segovia

Segovia (population 53,237) 88 km from Madrid via the N-VI motorway and a local road to the right at San Rafael. A city characterized by two very different things: its perfectly preserved Roman aqueduct, which vaults over the town centre, and its mouth-watering roast suckling-pig and baby lamb. Apart from the hearty wines of the region, you can wash down your meal with water which even today is carried across the top of that tall and graceful aqueduct. The only difference nowadays is that, since 1929, the water has been carried in pipes which lie on the top of the structure, in the trough where the water used to flow freely.

Pliny wrote of Segovia that it resisted Roman attacks until 80 BC, when the Consul Tito Didio destroyed it, only to rebuild it later. It was one of the key cities of the Iberian Peninsula in Roman times. In the Middle Ages also it was important as the capital of Castile.

Alcázar

Its fabulous spike-spired Alcázar, a fortress-palace, was rebuilt several times on the ruins of previous ones. The present building, with its formidable walls, its deep moat crossed by a drawbridge and its conical towers, was built in the twelfth and thirteenth centuries and enlarged in the fifteenth. It looks like a fairy-tale castle and some say it inspired Walt Disney. You can roam through much of its interior and climb the high tower overlooking the drawbridge, if you are in shape, but you can no longer visit the dungeons. Open on weekdays from 10 a.m. to 2 p.m. and from 4 to 6 p.m.; on Saturdays and holidays from 10 a.m. to 6 p.m.

Tourist Office: Plaza Mayor 10. Tel. (911) 430 328.

Excursions
Riofrío Palace

Just 11 km away is the Riofrío Palace built by Philip V's widow Isabel de Farnesio, which houses a Hunting Museum. Children will be delighted to see the large number of deer in the woods surrounding the palace. Open daily from 10 a.m. to 1 p.m. and from 3 to 7 p.m.; in winter to 6 p.m.

La Granja

Some 11 km away on the other side of Segovia is La Granja (population 4,588), also known as San Ildefonso, where there is a delightful airy summer palace now used only as a museum. The dozens of large fountains are turned on only on special occasions. Open daily from 10 a.m. to 1 p.m. and from 3 to 5.30 p.m. It is 77 km from Madrid.

Where to stay
Top range

Parador de Segovia, Carretera de Valladolid s/n. Tel. (911) 430 462. A striking, modern brick building on high ground overlooking the city. Indoor and outdoor pools, spacious rooms, simple but tasteful furnishings, beautiful slate-floored lounge. Away from all traffic noise. From 7,500 to 9,000 ptas.

Mid-range

Los Linajes, Dr Velasco 9. Tel. (911) 431 201. A little gem, this hotel in an old house on a narrow street of Segovia, with all the charm of arched doorways, zig-zag passageways, lots of thick stone and brick walls that will stand until doomsday, attentive service and, surprisingly, even a place to park the car. From 4,975 to 6,575 ptas.

Roma, Calle Guardas 2, La Granja (11 km south-east of Segovia). Tel. (911) 470 752. In the centre of San Ildefonso, and in an attractive location near the summer palace. Although the hotel is cheaper in the winter, there is likely to be snow, and it is quite a long way from the ski-runs. In the other seasons, however, this is a pleasant base for trips in the area. From 3,600 ptas (October to May) to 4,000 ptas.

Where to eat
Moderate

Mesón de Cándido, Plaza Azoguejo 5. Tel. (911) 428 102. Do not miss the roast suckling-pig at this justly proud restaurant in the shadow of the ancient Roman Aqueduct. It is so tender, they cut it with a plate. Castilian cooking at its best, abundant servings.

Alcalá de Henares

A city (population 142,862) which lost much of its charm as industry grew up around it and the population increased. It is 30 km east of Madrid on N-II. Its main attraction is the Hostería del Estudiante, a state-run restaurant in an ancient student hostel. Part of the town walls are still standing. The university attended by Cervantes, which was originally founded in the twelfth century, has only recently been reestablished there.

Tourist Office: Callejón de Sta María 1. Tel. (91) 889 2694.

Where to eat: moderate

Hostería del Estudiante, Plaza de Cervantes. Tel. (91) 888 0330. In a dining hall of the sixteenth-century university of this town where Cervantes was born, the Hostería naturally specializes in typical Castilian cooking. Try the *entremeses*, a selection of tiny plates of just about everything in the kitchen. Henry VIII's first wife, Catherine of Aragón, came from this town, which, incidentally, also produced the world's first polyglot Bible in 1520.

Chinchón

Quite a lovely little whitewashed town (population 3,900) in the farmland south-east of Madrid. It is 45 km from Madrid. Its large wooden-balconied square, dominated by a high, reddish stone church, is the scene of a popular annual benefit bullfight in September. It was also featured in the film *Around the World in Eighty Days*. On 25 July, the feast of St James, patron saint of Spain, there is also a special *corrida*, preceded by the running of the bulls through the streets, as in

Pamplona, a 300-year-old tradition here. A seventeenth-century convent with a charming little cloister as well as some late additions, which the nuns never had (such as a terrace bar and a swimming pool), is a good place to stay (see below). The town is famous for its aniseed liqueur, some of which is distilled in a castle that you can visit. The Chinchón Extra Seco is mindblowingly powerful.

Where to stay:
top range

Parador de Chinchón, Avenida del Generalísimo 1. Tel. (91) 894 0836. This gracious seventeenth-century building and its grounds have been lovingly restored, but where the vegetable garden used to be there are now flower beds, and where the trough for doing laundry by hand in cold spring water used to be, there is a swimming pool. The building went through some hard times. In 1835, when a law allowed the seizure of church properties, it was turned into a prison and later a court-house. The restorers of our times could not resist an insiders' joke. If you look at the murals on one wall of the glassed-in cloister, you will see a number of monks holding T-squares, triangles and the like. Read the Latin inscriptions; they tell you about the people who restored the convent. From 7,500 ptas (January to March) to 8,500 ptas.

Aranjuez

Site of a lovely summer palace of the kings of Spain, built in the sixteenth century and enlarged in the eighteenth, now used only as a museum, and of adjacent historic buildings and gardens. Aranjuez (population 35,936), 47 km south of Madrid on A-4, is famous as the site of an uprising in 1808 and for its fertile vegetable plots along the banks of the River Tagus (Tajo) and especially for its strawberries and asparagus, which are marketed in Madrid. Local authorities have done a great deal to accentuate the charms of this old royal residence in the country but there is not much they can do about the facts that the river is polluted and that the main highway between Madrid and Andalusia runs smack through the most monumental part of town. Stopping at a certain riverside restaurant mentioned by Hemingway is not recommended.

'Strawberry
Train'

For fun take the old-fashioned 'Strawberry Train', with its well-preserved wooden carriages and its un-upholstered benches, which runs to and from Madrid. It leaves from the Delicias Station in Madrid (on Paseo de las Delicias, six streets – or two Metro stops – south of the Atocha Station) every Saturday, Sunday and holiday, except in winter, at 10.15 a.m. and gets you back to Madrid by 8.20 p.m. Its old-fashioned style is a reminder that the line between Madrid and Aranjuez was Spain's first stretch of railway. Girls in period costumes offer strawberries to travellers as the train, pulled by an old steam locomotive which has been reconverted to diesel without changing its external appearance, rattles through the countryside. The Aranjuez municipal band oom-pah-pahs the train into the quaint little station with its wrought-iron supports for the platform roof.

Tourist Office: Plaza de Santiago Ruisiñol. Tel. (91) 889 2694.

Where to eat:
moderate

El Castillo, Jardines del Príncipe. Tel. (91) 891 3000. Closed from 20 December to 20 January. Castilian cooking, with emphasis on small game and fresh locally grown fruits and vegetables. Scenic surroundings.

Guadarrama Mountains

The high mountains to the west and north of Madrid offer opportunities for skiers in winter and excursionists the rest of the year. Among mountain towns close to ski resorts are:

● **Navacerrada**, 50 km north-west of Madrid (on N-601, via A-6), in the vicinity of the ski area of the same name;

● **Rascafría**, 84 km north of Madrid (by local roads, via Colmenar Viejo, where you turn right on the road to Miraflores de la Sierra, and Miraflores, where you turn left on the road to Puerto de la Morcuera and Rascafría), near the Cotos ski runs;

● **Sepúlveda**, 120 km north of Madrid (N-I to Cereza de Abajo, then left on C-112, then right on a local road at Perorrubia), not too far from the La Pinilla ski slopes;

● **Riaza**, 118 km north of Madrid (on N-110 via N-I), near the La Pinilla slopes.

Where to stay:
Top range

Santa María del Paular, El Paular, Rascafría. Tel. (91) 869 3200, telex 023 222. An elegant mountain hotel in a former monastery, and next door to an existing monastery, this hostelry is not far from the Valcotos ski-runs. Restaurant, heated pool, air so unpolluted that your lungs will be shocked, horseback riding and the sound of birds singing, all for 10,500 to 12,000 ptas.

Mid-range

Arcipreste de Hita, Praderas de San Sebastián, Navacerrada. Tel. (91) 856 0125. Situated not far from ski-runs, with a swimming pool for warmer seasons and tennis. Eight bungalows and thirty hotel rooms. From 3,400 ptas.

La Trucha, Avenida del Dr Tapia, Riaza. Tel. (911) 550 061. Swimming pool, bar, restaurant. It isn't fancy but it is near the La Pinilla ski-runs. From 3,350 to 4,125 ptas.

Where to eat:
Moderate

Hostal del Marqués, Alameda del Valle, Carretera Lozoyuela-Navacerrada, km 2 . Closed on Mondays and from 20 December to 24 January. Tel. (91) 869 3045. A reservation is essential at weekends. This surprisingly elegant small country restaurant offers first-rate Castilian cooking, with specialities like garlic soup and, on Saturdays, *cocido Madrileño*, that solid chick-pea stew characteristic of Madrid.

Figón Zute el Mayor, Calle Tetuán 6, Sepúlveda. Tel. (911) 540 165. Book in advance by telephone. Just about the only thing on the menu is roast lamb, with salad and bread, served with palatable local red wine. Order a quarter, a half or a whole lamb depending on the size of your party and the size of their collective appetite. A simple culinary triumph worth making the pilgrimage for from Madrid even if you do not ski.

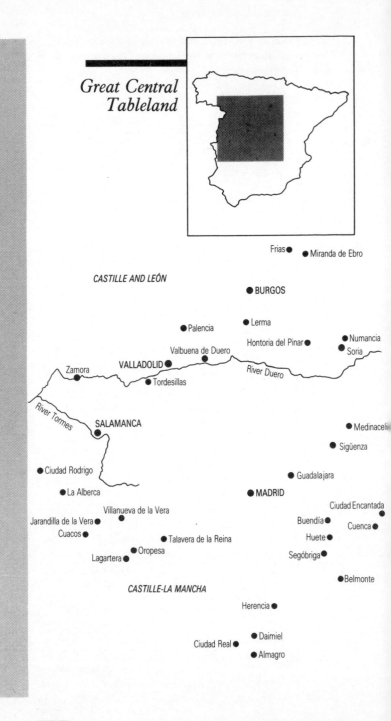

Great Central Tableland

Frias ● ● Miranda de Ebro

CASTILLE AND LEÓN

● **BURGOS**

● Lerma

Palencia ●

Hontoria del Pinar ● ● Numancia

Valbuena de Duero ● ● Soria

Zamora ● **VALLADOLID** ● River Duero

Tordesillas ●

River Tormes

SALAMANCA ●

● Medinaceli

● Sigüenza

● Ciudad Rodrigo

● Guadalajara

● La Alberca

● **MADRID**

Ciudad Encantada ●

Villanueva de la Vera ●

Buendía ● Cuenca ●

Jarandilla de la Vera ●

Cuacos ● Huete ●

● Talavera de la Reina

Segóbriga ●

● Oropesa

Lagartera ●

● Belmonte

CASTILLE-LA MANCHA

Herencia ●

● Daimiel

Ciudad Real ●

● Almagro

Great Central Tableland

Introduction

The central part of Spain consists of two great plateaus, separated by a range of mountains, which stretches roughly from north-east to south-west, passing just north of Madrid. The region known as Castille and León covers the northern *meseta* (tableland), and the region known as Castille–La Mancha covers the southern.

These modern administrative regions correspond roughly to the traditional division of the high central plains into Old Castile (north of Madrid) and New Castile (south of Madrid). The descent from these high tablelands can be quite dramatic in places, such as at Despeñaperros, where La Mancha stops and Andalusia begins.

Although Madrid and some towns around it such as Toledo, Ávila and Segovia come within this region, they are covered in a separate chapter. Nonetheless, the territory to be covered is quite large and there are no motorways. For the convenience of such explorers, and the word is appropriate, for many of these places are off the beaten track, the various cities and towns are described in a sequence which follows a circle around but keeps some distance from Madrid. It takes eight days and eight nights at the very least to cover the whole circuit thoroughly by car. If you can spare the time, however, it would be wiser to allow a fortnight. Although travelling around the area by bus will require constant changing, the local services are very convenient for excursions from the town where you might be staying.

For those visitors who do not want to follow the circular route, the distance from Madrid is given for larger places as well as the distance from the preceding town.

A friend recently asked me wistfully, 'Where can I find the real Spain?' For many years he has lived in a Spanish village near the southern coast, not as yet discovered by package tours but unmistakably influenced nonetheless by the tourist influx. 'Nobody in my village plays a guitar,' he said; 'and I don't know a single bullfighter.'

The real Spain is certainly here, in this broad central tableland, but whether he would swap his pleasant Andalusian village for sleepy Soria, Spain's coldest and smallest provincial capital, or for some dusty, treeless *pueblo* in Don Quixote's very flat old stamping ground of La Mancha, where bullfighters perform in a portable ring, is doubtful.

The area to be dealt with here is not a region but rather it includes parts of several regions. Some of the towns are agricultural, some are industrial; some are historic, others are modern; but what they have in common are the consequences of being close neither to Madrid nor the coasts. That distance greatly reduced their exposure to the upheaval in customs and attitudes that shook Spain in the years immediately following General Franco's death. Because of this 'the real Spain' can still be found here for better or for worse, if that means unchanged.

Salamanca

If the following route were a clock, with Madrid at its centre, Salamanca would be at 10 o'clock and this is where I will begin. Salamanca (population 167,131) lies on the right, or north bank of the River Tormes, a tributary of the River Duero or Duoro. It is situated in an important wheat-farming and cattle-raising area, which produces a large number of Spain's specially-bred fighting bulls.

You should plan to stay at least two nights in Salamanca, which is often referred to as 'Roma la Chica' (Little Rome) because of its monumental character.

Salamanca is 210 km west of Madrid (via the A-6 to Sanchidrián, then south-west 28 km on a local road to N-501, then right [west] to Salamanca). The driving time from Madrid is about two and a half hours. Also, anyone considering coming back from Galicia should bear in mind that the distance from Vigo to Salamanca is 453 km.

Salamanca does have an airport, at Matacán, 14 km to the east, but flights are very infrequent and flying there is not recommended. There are several trains daily between Madrid and Salamanca. There is also a bus service, with several departures every day.

Main areas The Plaza Mayor marks the centre of the city, geographically, socially and culturally. The road running across the Puente Nuevo Bridge, as you come in from Madrid, leads you right to it and there are more than enough signposts along the way to keep you from getting lost in the city.

There is also a convenient route around the periphery of the old town; in most parts it is a broad street. This street changes its name several times. It begins with the first principal street to your right as you come off the Puente Nuevo Bridge, Paseo del Rector Esperabé, and continues (anti-clockwise) as Paseo de Canalejas, Avenida de Mirat, Avenida de Alemania, Paseo de San Vicente, Calle del Desengaño, and Calle San Juan del Alcázar, where it intersects with the Puente Romano (which is still in use), ending at Rivera del Puente, where it joins back up with the Paseo del Rector Esperabé.

Just about everything you will want to see in the city is within that roughly drawn circle. The railway station, however, is at Calle Onésino Redondo 10, in the north-east part of the city, almost 1 km outside the circle.

There is no one main bus station. Most of the city's many restaurants are in the centre, especially in the area around the Plaza Mayor, where you will also find some of the best hotels. The regional Tourist Office is at Plaza Mayor 10. Tel. (923) 218 342, and the municipal Tourist Office is at Gran Vía 39. Tel. (923) 243 730; both are within the circle.

History

Hannibal took this city in 217 BC. The Romans fortified it. However, practically nothing remains from before the thirteenth century (with the exception of the Puente Romano), because the city was razed to the ground in the long struggle between Christian and Arab forces. King Alfonso IX of León is credited with the final reconquest of Salamanca from the Moors in the twelfth century. Its university, founded in about 1218, is said to be one of the oldest in Europe. The Battle of Arapiles, a few kilometres to the south, in July 1812, was the beginning of the end of Napoleon's conquest of Spain.

What to see

Salamanca is rich in buildings of architectural interest which, being fairly closely grouped together, can easily be seen on foot.

A convenient starting point is the magnificent **Plaza Mayor**, which was built in the first half of the eighteenth century to the design of Alberto Churriguera. This not quite rectangular square is made of a warm and golden local stone and is one of the most outstanding examples of Baroque architecture in Spain. Between the columns of the arcades are carved stone medallions. The surrounding buildings are three storeys high with a stone balustrade running round the top. The Grand Town Hall is on one side of the square. The many cafés, shops and restaurants mean that this area is always lively.

Just to the south of the Plaza Mayor is the Convent of the **Agustinos**. This church contains one of the finest religious paintings of the seventeenth century, the *Immaculate Conception* by Ribera.

Going south towards the river you come to the **La Clerecía** Church, which was founded by Philip III in 1617 as a Jesuit school. It has a gilt wooden altarpiece and a much prized tenth-century sculpture of the Flagellation of Christ by Luis Salvador Carmona. Opposite this building is the picturesque fifteenth-century **Casa de las Conchas**. This takes its name from the hundreds of stone scallop shells (*conchas*) that decorate its façade, symbols of the Order of Santiago, of which the house's original owner was Chancellor.

Salamanca has two Cathedrals which are both a short walk south of the Casa de las Conchas. The first one which you come to is the **New Cathedral** (Catedral Nueva) which was begun in 1512 and took 220 years to finish. In spite of the date the overall style is Gothic and the grandiose exterior is certainly very impressive. It is apparent from looking at the side chapels that the builders were running out of money as they neared its completion. The first two on the left and the first three on the right were built first, because construction of the Cathedral began at the back.

The **Old Cathedral** (Catedral Vieja) is somewhat smaller and was built in the tenth century in the Romanesque style with early Gothic influences. Among some fine works of art to be found within the Cathedral is a superb series of fifty-three panels behind the altar by Nicolás Florentino. There is also a particularly fine copper and enamel statue of the Virgin Mary, which dates from the thirteenth century. In some of the side chapels there are some interesting early stone sarcophagi. The adjoining diocesan museum contains, among other exhibits, documents relating to El Cid.

Both Cathedrals are open daily from 10 a.m. to 1 p.m. and 3.30 to 5 p.m. in summer and from 9.30 a.m. to 1.15 p.m. and 3.30 to 5.45 p.m. in winter.

Nearby is the **University** whose sixteenth-century façade is a classic exposition of the Plateresque style. It also has an important library of over 50,000 books and manuscripts. Open daily from 9.30 a.m. to 1.30 p.m. and from 4.30 to 8.30 p.m.; closed Saturday afternoons.

A curious reminder of England in the south-east corner of the old city is a small Romanesque chapel built in 1175, **Santo Tomás Cantaburense**, which claims to be the first church to be dedicated to St Thomas Becket.

One of the bridges over the River Tormes is Roman and has twenty-three arches.

Excursions

If you have time, the following make pleasant excursions from Salamanca:

Ciudad Rodrigo

Ciudad Rodrigo (population 14,766), 88 km south-west of Salamanca on N-620, is an attractive walled town originally settled in Roman days, but founded in the twelfth century by Count Rodríguez González. It has a fine, Gothic Cathedral, which contains some beautiful choirstalls.

An ivy-covered castle with a crenellated keep, now part of the parador chain, was built at the orders of Enrique of Trastamara. Tour buses stop for lunch at the moderately priced parador restaurant.

Wellington earned the titles of Duke of Ciudad Rodrigo and Grandee of Spain when he forced Marshall Ney's French troops to abandon the city in January, 1812. Tourist Office: Arco de las Amayuelas 6. Tel. (923) 460 561.

The Carnival *fiesta*, which takes place just before the beginning of

Lent, includes bullrunning, but with a difference. The bulls are turned loose in the streets at night, while street dances are taking place, and then it's every man and woman for him or herself!

La Alberca La Alberca (population 1,357), 77 km (C-512 south to Miranda del Castañar, then right on a westbound local road which passes through Las Casas del Conde). This lovely, photogenic village has been declared a national monument because of its distinctive architecture with wooden balconies and wood and stone arcades. It is 8 km from the Las Batuecas Valley, where citrus trees and other subtropical plants grow, and where there are Palaeolithic cave paintings and a hunting reserve. La Alberca has a *fiesta* commemorating the Feastday of the Assumption of the Virgin in mid-August with processions and religious ceremonies and everyone wearing traditional dress. The town also celebrates 'The Day of the Drink' on Easter Monday, when wine is served free to all-comers.

Shopping Good buys include ceramics from Alba de Tormes and Vitigudino; handwoven cloth from Macoteras and El Bodón; riding boots from Bejar, Macoteras and Salamanca; silverware from Ciudad Rodrigo, Tamames and Salamanca, and cane furniture and basketware from Villoruela. These items may be bought in the villages of origin or in Salamanca. The main shopping area is on and in the vicinity of the Gran Vía, which runs north and south three streets to the east of the Plaza Mayor.

Nightlife in Salamanca A university town, Salamanca is full of students, so there is plenty of life late at night in the taverns around the Plaza Mayor; but it is mostly a matter of drinks and *tapas*. Pavement cafés are open morning, noon and night on the Plaza Mayor in good weather; and here that means most of the year.

The presence of the university also means there are always lectures, concerts, recitals and other cultural activities going on, mostly in the old university buildings.

Some of these take place in the municipal Cultural Centre, a beautifully-restored, modernistic-style mansion from the beginning of this century, overlooking the river near the Puente Romano. The Tourist Office should have details.

Where to stay There are several good hotels near the Plaza Mayor, and many small ones in the old quarter. Across the river, some distance away, are the Parador de Salamanca and another good hotel, the Regio.

Top range **Monterrey**, Calle Azafranal 21. Tel. (923) 214 400, telex 26809. Very central, bar. From 5,400 to 8,100 ptas.

Gran Hotel, Plaza del Poeta Iglesias 5. Tel. (923) 213 500, telex 26809. Right next door to the Plaza Mayor, this is the hotel preferred by cattle ranchers, bullfighters and literary figures. Old-fashioned charm, intimate bar, garage. From 6,480 to 8,640 ptas.

Mid-range **Regio**, Carretera Salamanca-Madrid, km 4. Tel. (923) 200 250, telex 22895. Plenty of parking, swimming pool, children's playground, bar, restaurant, but out of town on the other side of the river. From 5,000 ptas (November to February) to 6,000 ptas (rest of the year).

Parador de Salamanca, Teso de la Feria 2. Tel. (923) 228 700. An eyesore on the lovely landscape of Salamanca, even though it is quite a distance from the centre on the other side of the river, this functional, dun-coloured modern building is quite comfortable inside, and does offer good views of the city. Pool, bar, restaurant, parking. From 7,000 ptas (January to March) to 8,000 ptas (rest of the year).

Alfonso X, Calle Toro 64. Tel. (923) 214 401, telex 26809. Very central, comfortable. From 3,800 to 5,950 ptas.

Condal, Santa Eulalia 3. Tel. (923) 218 400. Central, in a historic building, bar. From 3,875 to 4,275 ptas.

Ceylán, San Teodoro 7. Tel. (923) 212 603. Central. From 2,700 ptas (mid-October to June) to 3,025 ptas (rest of the year).

Emperatriz, Calle Compañía 44. Tel. (923) 219 200. In the heart of the old town. Garage. From 2,550 ptas (November to 10 April) to 2,925 ptas (rest of the year).

Bottom range **Los Charros**, Calle Pollo Martín 12. Tel. (923) 252 204. Central, only five rooms. From 850 ptas (without private bath, November to May) to 1,700 ptas (rest of the year, with bath).

Where to eat
Moderate **Venecia**, Plaza del Mercado 5. Tel. (923) 216 744. Closed on Sunday evenings. A well-established, fine restaurant featuring international and Spanish cooking.

El Candil Viejo, Calle Ruiz Aguilera 10. Tel. (923) 217 239. Castilian cuisine, good *tapas*.

Chez Victor, Calle Espoz y Mina 26. Tel. (923) 213 123. French cuisine.

El Candil Nuevo, Plaza de la Reina 1. Tel. (923) 219 027. Similar fare to the other Candil, which is owned by the same family. This one, however, is only a restaurant, not a *tapa* bar.

Zamora – Tordesillas – Valladolid

Zamora Zamora (population 59,734), 61 km north of Salamanca on N-630, deserves a visit. Its *fiestas*, including those dedicated to St Peter at the end of June, are lively; its wine, notably that of **Toro** (33 km east of Zamora) is very good; and the city and its surroundings contain a number of interesting monuments. How about this one for a starter? The Zamora prison was where General Franco put priests who stepped out of line. They were segregated from other prisoners so as not to scandalize anyone.

The Cathedral and several other churches date from the twelfth

century. The seventh-century San Pedro de la Nave Church, 20 km
west of Zamora at **Campillo**, is considered one of the most important
Visigothic churches in Spain.

Tordesillas   Tordesillas (population 6,681) is 66 km east of Zamora on N-122; or
181 km north-west of Madrid on N-VI. This is where Iberian diplo-
mats divided up the world. On 7 June 1494, representatives of Spain
and Portugal signed a pact, with the blessings of Pope Alexander VI,
under which Spain was 'entitled' to all newly-discovered lands west of
an imaginary line drawn from pole to pole 370 leagues west of the
Cape Verde Islands, and Portugal was 'entitled' to everything to the
east of that line; thus Brazil became Portuguese.

Santa Clara   This is also where Joan the Mad, daughter of Ferdinand and
Convent   Isabella, spent the last forty-six years of her life in a nunnery, incapable of recovering from the shock of the death of her husband Philip
the Fair, Philip I. Part of the Santa Clara Convent, where she stayed,
is open to the public on weekdays from 9 a.m. to 1 p.m. and from 3 to
6 p.m. Cloistered nuns who live in the other part of the convent sell
sweets, which they make, to visitors by means of a small turntable in
the wall. You put your money on the round wooden shelf and someone
inside, whom you cannot see, turns it around and puts the sweets in its
place. The part of the convent which you can visit has a multi-coloured tiled stone façade and delicately carved and moulded Mudéjar
ceilings. In the chapel there is a fifteenth-century polychromed image
of the Virgin. The convent, built by Alfonso XI in the fourteenth century as a palace, was later inhabited by Pedro I, The Cruel, who
ordered it to be turned into a convent.

The *fiesta* of the *Toro de la Vega* (The Bull in the Pasture), which
begins on the Sunday after 8 September, provides a variation on the
bullfight theme. It begins in the brightly decorated Plaza Mayor. A
banderilla, or dart, is stuck in a bull's hump; then the bull is turned
loose to race through the streets, with the young men of the town running in front, and across the bridge to fields on the other side of the
River Duero, where men on horseback fight it.

Tourist Office: at the Town Hall. Tel. (983) 770 061.

Where to eat: **Hostal Juan Manuel**, Carretera Burgos-Portugal (N-620), km
pricey   151. Tel. (983) 770 911. Castilian cooking; good local wines.

Valladolid

Valladolid (population 330,242), 30 km north-east of Tordesillas on
N-620, or 184 km north-west of Madrid on N-403, is both an industrial town and the centre of a farming area, and it is the capital of the
province of the same name. Wheat is a major crop on the plains and
grapes for wine are grown along the banks of the River Duero.

Valladolid lies on a tributary of this river, called the Pisuerga. Some of Spain's most beautiful castles are close by. Valladolid itself is reasonably clean and neat, and it occupies a prominent place in Spanish history – but it takes itself a lot more seriously than other Spanish towns. As a result it is 'Dullsville', except during *fiestas* and Holy Week.

Getting there

It has an airport, at Villanubla, 14 km distant, but the only daily flights are to Barcelona, Vigo and, in summer, Palma de Mallorca. It is on the major rail line from Madrid to Santander.

Main areas

The monumental part of the city lies on the right, or east, bank of the Duero. A good starting point for finding your way around is the triangular-shaped park near the Estación del Norte Railway Station. The apex of the triangle, at the Plaza de Zorrilla, points north towards the old section of town, which begins right there, with its many short, narrow streets. The bus station is at Puente Colgante 2. The Tourist Office is at Plaza de Zorrilla 3. Tel. (983) 351 801.

History

The history of Valladolid before the time of the Moorish domination is obscure, but soon after its reconquest, it became the capital of Castile, and it remained so until Philip II decided to move the seat of government to Madrid. It was the capital once again briefly during the reign of Philip III, but his successor, Philip IV, moved back to Madrid.

Columbus died here and Cervantes was briefly imprisoned here. Their respective houses can be visited. Columbus' house is a museum devoted to the theme of discovery. Cervantes' is a library and literary museum.

What to see

National Sculpture Museum

(Museo Nacional de Escultura), Calle Cadenas de San Gregorio 1 (open daily from 9 a.m. to 2 p.m. and 5 to 8 p.m. and from 9.30 a.m. to 2 p.m. on Sundays and holidays), in the old quarter, contains what is reputed to be one of the finest collections of religious, polychromed statuary in the world. The museum is housed in the elaborate **Colegio de San Gregorio**, built between 1488 and 1496, whose façade is profusely covered with detailed carvings.

Churches

Noteworthy churches, all in the old quarter, include the twelfth-century **El Salvador** with Flemish school paintings; **San Pablo** with its late Gothic façade; **Santiago** with its prized altarpiece by Alonso Berruguete, *The Adoration of the Magi*; and the thirteenth-century **Santa María la Antigua** with its lovely Romanesque tower.

Valladolid's still unfinished **Cathedral**, in the middle of the old part of town, is not one of Spain's most noteworthy, but it has a lovely sixteenth-century Renaissance altarpiece by Juan de Juni; and its choir stalls, similar to those at the El Escorial monastery, were carved from designs made by the famous Spanish architect Juan de Herrera. Original plans for the Cathedral were drawn up by Juan de Herrera at the end of the sixteenth century; but the bulk of construction did not take place until the early eighteenth. Open daily from 7.30 to 11.30 a.m. and from 5 to 9 p.m. in summer, and 3 to 5 p.m. in winter.

Excursion

If you have time for an excursion, visit the charming little fifteenth-century Fuensaldaña Castle, just 6 km north-west of Valladolid on a local road. It has been the home of the Regional Parliament since 1983, when Castille and León was granted the status of autonomous region.

Alternatively, you could visit Palencia (population 76,100), 43 km north of Valladolid or 228 km north of Madrid, which lives on the agriculture of the surrounding flatlands and on its furniture factories. Off the beaten tourist track, it is a quiet town of pre-Roman origin which, in 1208, boasted the first university on the Iberian Peninsula. It is surrounded by villages containing the most impressive collection of Romanesque architecture in Spain. In the city, one of the loveliest Romanesque churches is that of San Miguel, on the Plaza San Miguel, where El Cid, the legendary hero of the Reconquest, got married. A landmark on a ridge on the outskirts, the Cerro de Otero, is a modern statue of Christ, 20 m. high and made of reinforced concrete. Tourist office: Calle Mayor 105. Tel. (988) 740 068.

Fiestas

Holy Week is a good time to visit Valladolid. Its people pride themselves on having the best images of Christ and the saints, and on imbuing their processions with an air of solemnity which is quite different from the relaxed attitude that prevails in the south of Spain.

In September there are bullfights and sports events as part of the *fiestas* to celebrate the feastday of St Matthew. September is also the month of the Regional Trade Fair of Old Castile and León.

Where to stay

Mid-range

Most of the better hotels are near the triangular park, which the Tourist Office faces. Many smaller hotels are in the old quarter.

Felipe IV, Calle Gamazo 16. Tel. (983) 307 000, telex 26264. Garage. From 6,765 ptas.

Olid Meliá, Plaza San Miguel 10. Tel. (983) 357 200, telex 26312. Central, garage, restaurant. From 7,500 ptas.

Meliá Parque, Calle García Morato 17. Tel. (983) 470 100, telex 26355. Around the corner from the bus station. Garage, bar, moderate restaurant. From 6,350 ptas.

Roma, Calle Héroes del Alcázar de Toledo 8. Tel. (983) 354 666. Central, garage, restaurant. From 3,850 ptas (November to February) to 4,400 ptas (rest of the year).

Bottom range

Los Arces, Calle San Antonio de Padua 2. Tel. (983) 353 853. A central pension. From 1,600 ptas.

Where to eat

Pricey

Mesón Panero, Calle Marina Escóbar 1. Tel. (983) 301 673. Closed on Sunday evenings; closed all day Sunday in July and August. Castilian cooking, and homemade desserts.

La Fragua, Paseo de Zorrilla 10. Tel. (983) 337 102. Closed on Sunday evenings. Castilian cooking, good local wines.

Moderate

La Goya, Calle Puente Colgante 79. Tel. (983) 355 724. Closed on Monday evenings, all of August and Christmas season. Castilian cooking. Popular with locals. Good and inexpensive local wine.

Valbuena de Duero – Lerma – Burgos

Valbuena de Duero

Valbuena de Duero, 40 km east of Valladolid (N-122 to Quintanilla de Onésimo, then left – north – across the river to Olivares de Duero, then right – east – to Valbuena). This is the town from which Spain's most highly priced table wines come, but they are worth every penny.

Bodegas Vega Sicilia SA, Carretera Valladolid-Soria, km 40.2. Tel. (983) 680 147. Every bottle they put on the market is good, but unless it is an exceptionally good year, they do not use the Vega Sicilia label. Most years the wine bears the label of Valbuena. Visits are by prior appointment, from 9 a.m. to 1 p.m. and from 2 to 6 p.m., Monday to Friday. Call Pablo Alvarez to arrange it. You can buy these wines at wholesale prices here.

San Bernardo

There is also a beautiful Cistercian monastery above Valbuena, very much off the beaten track, the Monasterio de San Bernardo, founded in about 1144, with a church from approximately that date and a beautiful cloister from the thirteenth and sixteenth centuries.

Lerma

Lerma (population 2,591), 97 km north-east of Valbuena on N-I via Aranda de Duero. Also known as Villa del Duque, Lerma has a charming, beautifully preserved seventeenth-century nucleus behind its eleventh-century walls. Its stone-paved streets are lined with brightly-coloured flowers growing in front of the houses, in all kinds of containers, from old tin cans to plastic pails and rusty pots. Here are the ruins of the once sumptuous **Palace** to which the Duke of Lerma, who greatly enriched himself and his relatives at the expense of the kingdom while acting as Válido, or Prime Minister, for King Philip III, retired in 1618 as a cardinal when his own wily son unseated him to become himself the king's most trusted deputy. The palace can be seen from 9.30 a.m. to 1 p.m. and from 4 to 7 p.m. Monday to Friday except holidays. Here too is a magnificent **Church** (**Colegiata de San Pedro**) built by the Duke's uncle, Cristóbal de Rojas y Sandóval, Archbishop of Seville.

Burgos

Burgos (population 156,449) is 37 km north of Lerma on N-I; or 242 km north of Madrid.

Getting there

Burgos has no airport, but it is the main road and rail hub for the Old Castile highlands. Rail lines from Madrid to several northern destinations pass through it, as do lines connecting it with Palencia and points west, and with Soria and points east. The streamlined Talgo train takes about three hours to reach Burgos from Madrid. The city sits astride N-I, Spain's main north–south highway. It is the terminal of motorways connecting it with the Basque Country and Saragossa. It is 233 km from the French border at Irún.

Main areas

Finding your way around in Burgos is easy because the Cathedral's incredible forest of intricate stone spires, which is visible from almost anywhere, lies in the centre of the most interesting part of the city, on the north side of the River Arlazón. Most important shops, hotels and restaurants are also on the north bank.

The bus and railway stations are on the south side. The railway station is at the southern end of the Avenida del Conde Guadalhorce and the bus terminal is at Calle de Miranda 4, across the street from the Provincial Museum. The Tourist Office is at Plaza Alonso Martínez 7. Tel. (947) 203 125.

History

This industrial town in the midst of an agricultural area was founded in 887. It took on more importance from 1037, when it became the residence of kings of Castile and León (though the definitive fusion of those two kingdoms was not to come until four centuries later). El Cid, Spain's legendary warrior from the times when Spain was winning back territory from the Moors, is buried in the Cathedral here, which is one of the country's most beautiful and a fine example of Gothic architecture. The fact that El Cid was basically a mercenary and was just as happy fighting for the Moors is, not surprisingly, kept rather in the background.

In 1813, Burgos, which was the general headquarters of Napoleon's Peninsular army, was captured by Wellington, having been under siege for a year.

During the Spanish Civil War, 1936–39, Burgos was General Franco's capital. Burgos was also the scene of the military trial of the first members of the Basque extremist organization ETA to be sentenced to death. The court convicted them in 1969 of murdering a police chief and passed nine death sentences on the six defendants, but General Franco himself commuted these to life imprisonment. Some of those original defendants, pardoned after Franco's death, are now active politicians.

What to see

The artistic riches of the **Cathedral** are immense, but one of the most delightful details, at the back of the church and on the left-hand side as you face the main altar, is the *Papamoscas* (Flycatcher), a sixteenth-century clock with the bust of a figure which opens its mouth when the clock strikes the hours.

Other places of interest

Besides the Cathedral, Burgos' most important monuments include:

● The fourteenth-century **Santa María Gate**, adorned with sixteenth-century statues, which faces the bridge nearest to the Cathedral.

● The **Casa del Cordón**, now a bank, so called because of the

119

Franciscan rope belt which has been carved around its doorway. It was where Columbus was received by Ferdinand and Isabella in 1496, following his second expedition to the New World.

● The fascinating **Monasterio de Las Huelgas**, 1.5 km from the town centre on the Valladolid road, was built in the twelfth century and was a convent for noble ladies.

● Also worth seeing is the fifteenth-century **Charterhouse (Cartuja) of Miraflores**, 3 km east, which contains the alabaster tombs of King Juan II and his wife Isabel of Portugal.

What to do

Fiestas

Many towns in the Burgos area have their own lively *fiestas* and, should your visit coincide with one, it would make an excellent excursion.

In Burgos itself, there are several days of celebrations coinciding with the feast of Saints Peter and Paul, 29 June, with bullfights, street fairs, traditional music and dancing, cooking competitions and a live-stock fair. On 25 July, garlic-growers from miles around come to town to get wind of new developments at the Garlic Festival.

At **Hontoria del Pinar**, 67 km south-east of Burgos on N-234 (the road to Soria), eight men in regional costume dance the ancient *Paloteo* to the music of a flute and castanets in the church, on the Sunday before the beginning of Lent. Ancient feats of warfare are re-enacted on 24 June in the medieval village of **Frias**, 79 km north-east of Burgos (N-I to Cubo de Bureba, then take a local road north, passing through Ranera). The *pueblo* is full of astonishing sights, ideal for the photographer, such as a ridge-running castle, houses clinging to a cliffside in seeming defiance of nature, and a Roman bridge topped by a medieval tower.

The colourful San Juan del Monte Pilgrimage, on the first Sunday and the following Monday after Pentecost, fills the streets of **Miranda de Ebro** (78 km, north-east on A-1) with crowds dressed in bright traditional costume, dancing, singing and playing all kinds of musical instruments, some on foot and some in beautifully decorated, horse-drawn carriages.

Shopping

Good buys are leather goods from Covarrubias, available in Burgos shops, and, if you or anyone you know owns a horse, bridles, saddles and the like from Poza de la Sal.

Music

Annual events for music-lovers are the religious music week during Holy Week and international ancient music week in late July or August.

Where to stay

Top range

Probably the greatest concentration of hotels is close to the Cathedral.

Landa Palace, Carretera Madrid-Irún, km 236. Tel (947) 206 343. Easily recognizable because of its newly-built 'medieval' tower. Linen sheets, heated swimming pool, garage, garden – but it is on the outskirts. From 10,900 ptas (November to May) to 12,000 ptas (rest of the year).

Mid-range | **Almirante Bonifaz**, Calle Vitoria 22. Tel. (947) 206 943. Central, recently redecorated. From 5,600 to 7,000 ptas.

Corona de Castilla, Calle Madrid 15. Tel. (947) 262 142, telex 39619. Garage, moderate restaurant, bar. From 4,500 ptas (January to 12 April) to 5,500 ptas (high season).

Fernán González, Calle Calera 17. Tel. (947) 209 441. Central, garage, bar, moderate restaurant. From 4,900 ptas (October to 12 April) to 5,500 ptas (rest of the year).

Mesón del Cid, Plaza de Santa María 8. Tel. (947) 208 715. On the Plaza Santa María facing the Cathedral. Garage, disco, pricey restaurant. From 5,600 ptas (10 October to 12 April) to 6,700 ptas (rest of the year).

España, Paseo del Espolón 32. Tel. (947) 206 340. Central, moderate restaurant. From 3,675 ptas (October to May) to 3,975 ptas (rest of the year).

Rice, Calle Reyes Católicos 30. Tel. (947) 222 300. Central, bar, From 4,100 ptas (October to May) to 4,700 ptas (rest of the year).

Bottom range | **Ambos Mundos**, Plaza Vega 27. Tel. (947) 206 130. Central, only three rooms, without private bath. From 1,800 ptas.

Where to eat
Pricey | **Hostal Landa**, Carretera Madrid-Irún 236. Tel. (947) 206 343. Superb regional and international fare with a great wine cellar and attentive service. The best place to eat in Burgos by far. Specialities include stuffed partridge, roast lamb and Burgos black pudding.

Los Chapiteles, Calle General Santocildes 7. Tel. (947) 201 837. Closed on Sunday evenings. Castilian cooking, good local wines.

Mesón del Cid, Plaza de Santa María 8. Tel. (947) 205 971. Closed on Sunday evenings. Regional cooking, with such delicious dishes as Olla Podrida (literally, 'Rotten Stew', but far from it), a hearty dish of beans and local sausages. In a fifteenth-century building, which also houses a hotel of the same name, in front of the Cathedral.

Soria – Medinaceli – Sigüenza

Soria | Soria (population 32,039), 141 km east of Burgos on N-234. The capital of Spain's most sparsely populated province, Soria is the centre of an agricultural region, which almost seems untouched by the passage of time. An ancient town, it was resettled in the early twelfth century by King Alfonso I, The Battler, of Aragón and later ceded to Castile.

Numancia | Less than 9 km to the north lie the remains of Numancia, a Celtiberian town remembered for its valiant stand against Roman attacks over a period of twenty years from 153 to 133 BC. Eventually, in 133, Roman troops under the command of the victor of Carthage, Scipio, laid siege to the town. Rather than surrender, the Numantines set fire to their houses and possessions and preferred to commit suicide than to die at the hands of their enemy. Only a few people were still alive when Scipio marched in and razed the town to the ground.

What to see

Soria itself is full of perfectly preserved sixteenth and seventeenth century buildings and several from the twelfth and thirteenth centuries. The San Juan de Duero monastery, founded by the Knights Templar, has a unique late Romanesque cloister reflecting an oriental influence, whose intertwining arches are redolent more of wickerwork than of stone.

Tourist Office: Plaza Ramón y Cajal s/n. Tel. (975) 212 052.

Fiestas

At San Pedro Manrique, 48 km north of Soria (N-111 to Garray, C-115 to Huerteles, then 11 km on a local road to San Pedro), the young men walk barefoot across a 2-m bed of glowing coals, carrying their sweethearts on their backs, on the night of 23 June, eve of the feastday of St John, in an ancient tradition known as *Las Móndidas*.

In Soria, the San Juan festivities begin on the first Thursday on or after 24 June and they last five days, with bullfights, processions and other events.

Where to eat

Pricey

Maroto, Paseo del Espolón 20. Tel. (975) 224 086. Elegantly decorated dining area. Delicious regional cooking.

Moderate

Mesón Castellano, Plaza Mayor 2. Tel. (975) 213 045. Regional cooking, good house wine from Cariñena at a very low price.

Parador Antonio Machado, Parque del Castillo s/n. Tel. (975) 213 445. Pleasant views from this hilltop hotel of the state's parador chain, whose restaurant offers regional food.

Medinaceli

Medinaceli (population 1,036), 76 km south of Soria, just to the right of N-111. This is a stately old town of dark-coloured stone houses on the edge of a plateau, with sweeping views incomparably framed by the only three-arched Roman gateway to remain in Spain. Quite a few artists have settled in this quiet place, fascinated by its small, stone-paved, partially colonnaded main square in front of the church, the remains of its old Arab walls and its wholly unspoilt medieval character.

Old Medinaceli was spared because no main road passes through it, and the more modern part of the town grew up 3 km away, at the bottom of the mountain, alongside the Madrid–Saragossa motorway.

Fiesta

On 13 November, the people of Medinaceli celebrate the night of the 'jubilee bull' as part of their annual *fiestas*. Iron sheaths covered with tar are fitted over each horn. The tar is then set alight and the bull is turned loose in the main square for the locals to fight. The fire does not burn the bull but it does turn the animal into a living torch. At one stage, for fifteen years, this spectacle was prohibited as a result of pressure from the Spanish Society for the Protection of Animals.

During the last week of August, Medinaceli is the scene of a series of concerts of medieval and Renaissance music.

Sigüenza

Sigüenza (population 5,656), 31 km south-west of Medinaceli (N-II south to Fuencaliente; then right, or south-west, on a local road, passing through Torralba del Moral); or 121 km east of Madrid (N-II to intersection with C-204; then left on C-204 northbound). We are now in so-called New Castille.

Inhabited from pre-Roman days, Sigüenza changed hands several times between Christians and Arabs. Even El Cid lost it once. An agricultural town, off the main tourist routes, it preserves a certain aloofness. Among its proudest possessions is its Cathedral, a great fortress of a church, with a dark interior, which was begun in 1150 and shows a strong French influence, but was not finished until the end of the fifteenth century. There is a reclining statue on the tomb of Comendador Martín Vázquez, known as El Doncel (The Page), by an artist identified only as Maestro Juan. El Doncel was a favourite of Queen Isabella who was killed outside the walls of Granada in 1486. The statue is reckoned by some to be the most outstanding work of Renaissance funerary art in Spain.

The Castle was built and rebuilt by Romans, Visigoths and Moors before Bishop Bernardo de Ayén turned it into an episcopal palace in 1124.

Where to stay
Mid-range

Parador Castillo de Sigüenza, Plaza del Castillo s/n. Tel. (911) 390 100, telex 22517. Central, parking, good and moderately priced restaurant – try the superb local mushrooms if they are in season – views, bar. The rooms are spacious and comfortable; some look out over the town, a cascade of red-brown tile roofs and ochre buildings against a background of green and straw-yellow fields and dark red earth. Furnishings are regal. It is impossible not to be aware that you are but the most recent of guests who have come to stay in this former castle over several hundred years, and who have included Ferdinand and Isabella, Joan the Mad and the Cardinals Mendoza and Cisneros. From 6,500 ptas (November to June except in Holy Week, when top rates apply) to 7,500 ptas (rest of the year).

El Doncel, Calle General Mola 1. Tel. (911) 390 190. Central, bar, economical restaurant. From 2,600 ptas.

El Motor, Carretera de Madrid s/n. Tel. (911) 390 827. A residence hostel with only eight rooms. From 2,300 ptas.

Bottom range

Elias, Calle Alfonso VI 6. Tel. (911) 390 090. Central, economical restaurant, no frills, no private baths. From 1,300 ptas (16 September to 14 June) to 1,450 ptas.

El Mesón, Calle Román Pascual 14. Tel. (911) 390 649. Central, economical restaurant, only twelve rooms, no private baths. From 1,300 ptas.

Venancio, Calle San Roque 1. Tel. (911) 390 347. Central, scenic, economical restaurant, no private baths. From 1,800 ptas.

Where to eat
Moderate

El Motor, Calle Calvo Sotelo 12. Tel. (911) 390 343. Closed Sundays, 16–30 April and 1–15 November.

Sánchez, Calle Calvo Sotelo 11. Tel. (911) 390 545. Closed all of September and every Tuesday. Specialities of La Mancha, including roast kid and roast lamb.

Economical

El Moderno, Calle General Mola 1. Tel. (911) 390 001. Closed 9 June to 9 July and every Friday. The best place in town for *tapas*. Castilian cooking.

Guadalajara

Guadalajara (population 56,922), 73 km south-west of Sigüenza via C-204 and N-II, is not worth the detour. It is an ancient place but it has traded its patina for the facelessness of an out-of-the-way industrial town.

Buendía – Cuenca

Buendía

Buendía (population 465) is 104 km south of Sigüenza (C-204 south to Sacedón, bordering on the big Entrepeñas Lake, then south on a signposted local road through fields and pine forests bordering another lake for the last 20 km).

This charming, but dusty, little town, with its enormous yellow sandstone church for ever circled by swallows, and its stone and timber houses, now stands on a peninsula jutting into the vast man-made Buendía Lake in the high and almost rainless province of Cuenca. It depends on agriculture and its fair-weather inhabitants, that is those who return only at weekends and in the summer, and the small number of families from Madrid and Guadalajara who have 'discovered' it. Curiously, many of the city visitors seem to be taxi drivers. A handful of Spanish and foreign writers and artists also live in refurbished old houses.

The tranquillity and lack of traffic noise can be positively nerve-wracking. The *siesta* is certainly alive and well here. People leave their doors not only unlocked but wide open. The town crier and postman has a little brass horn that he blows before reading out mayoral proclamations.

The heat in summer, reflected off the yellow earth, can be searing, but inside the traditional stone and adobe houses, rather than the two or three modern apartment blocks, it is cool. Under every house is a cave that served as a wine cellar before phylloxera and before the artificial lake covered the old vineyards. Huge brown clay *tinajas*, jugs taller than a man, still stand in the cobwebby cellars.

The lake is refreshingly cool and perfect for a dip at any hour. Swimming and fishing are the only activities that take place here. The level of the water tends to drop in summer, since this is a reservoir, but the lake covers over 100 square kilometres, so it makes little difference. It simply means you have to walk, or drive, a little farther along old rutted lanes which, in winter, are underwater, to get to the water's edge. Farmers are the main beneficiaries of this extra land which they use for cultivating wheat.

Cuenca

Cuenca (population 41,791) is 103 km south-east of Buendía (southward on a local road to Garcinarro, then left on a westbound local road to the junction with C-202, then right on C-202 southbound to Carrascosa del Campo, then left on N-400 eastbound); or 165 km east of Madrid via N-III to Tarrancón and N-400.

Once you have seen Cuenca you will understand the fascination that it exercised over contemporary Spanish painters such as Antoni Tápies, Francisco Zóbel and others; a fascination which led Zóbel to found the Spanish Abstract Art Museum in the death-defying Hanging Houses (*Casas Colgades*) on Calle Canónigos s/n (open from Tuesday to Friday, 11 a.m. to 2 p.m. and from 4 to 6 p.m.; Saturday until 8 p.m., and Sunday 11 a.m. to 2.30 p.m. only).

Cuenca is a surrealistic city. Even after you have seen it you find it hard to believe. Teetering on a high ship-shaped promontory at the junction of two river canyons, its buildings reach to seven storeys high on the river side and to three on the town side, perched on, or even leaning out from the high rock over the abyss. A springy footbridge leads across a deep gorge to the seminary. (Don't look down!) The main square (*Plaza Mayor*) is at the top of the main street (Calle Alfonso), through a triple arch and in front of the Cathedral.

Main areas

Owing to the shortage of room at the top of the hill, most of Cuenca's hotels are not cliff-hangers; they are solidly planted in the valley below, where the more modern part of the city lies. The railway station, predictably, is also at the bottom, at the south end of Avenida General Moscardó, in the southern part of the city. The bullring is in that area too, on the Avenida Reyes Católicos. The Tourist Office is at Dalmacio García Izcara 8. Tel. (966) 220 062.

The Cathedral was begun at the end of the twelfth century, has some Anglo-Norman features and has a partially restored façade following damage at the beginning of this century. Cuenca's Holy Week processions are unusual in that it is the only place in Spain where the crowd mocks and derides the image of Christ on his way to the cross on Good Friday, blowing wrong notes on trumpets and banging discordant drums, as they act out the role of the mob. The landscape lends a dramatic atmosphere to the processions of hooded penitents as they climb the steep main street by the light of flickering candles. Holy Week is also the occasion of a major religious music festival.

Excursions
Ciudad Encantada

The capital of one of Spain's largest and most sparsely populated provinces, Cuenca is a good base for excursions for nature-lovers. The 'Enchanted City', 36 km north of Cuenca (via the road which runs north up the Júcar Valley past Villalba de la Sierra), consists of 20 square km of capricious rock formations, as if wind, water and time were guided by an unseen artist's hand to carve out forms resembling ships, a man's face, city streets and many other objects.

Villar del Humo

If you have a day or two to spare, Cuenca also offers eye-openers for archaeology and history buffs. There are some very clear Palaeolithic paintings in red, representing bison, boars, bulls, horses and archers, near Villar del Humo, a village 80 km to the east (via N-420 and a southbound local road to the right at Carboneras de Guadazón and another local road to the left at Cardenete).

Segóbriga

The remains of an entire Roman city, Segóbriga, lie near Saelices, 77 km west of Cuenca (N-400 west to Carrascosa, then left for the final 20 km on a local road).

The excavation has been going on slowly for many years. So far a very complete amphitheatre has been uncovered as well as the remains of a number of houses. Some statues, mosaics, coins and jewellery are on display at a small museum on the site, but other valuable pieces may be lost because the digs have not been adequately protected from souvenir-hunters. Aerial photographs of the flat-topped hill where the excavation has started show intersecting parallel depressions, which may be streets.

Huete

Huete, a town dating at least from Roman times, bears the marks of successive waves of conquerors; its sixteenth-century colonnades still shade doorways around the main square; this town 71 km west of Cuenca (via N-400 and C-202, turning right at Carrascosa) was part of the dowry brought by the almond-eyed Princess Zaida, daughter of the Moorish King Al-Motamid of Seville, when she officially became the concubine, and later Queen, of King Alfonso VI of Castile.

Shopping

Good buys in Cuenca or its surrounding towns are ceramics from Cuenca and Priego and Arab-style pottery from Mota del Cuervo; guitars and other string instruments from Casasimarro; handmade rugs from Cuenca, some copying the unusual designs of antique carpets in the Cathedral, and wickerwork from Villalba de la Sierra and Priego.

Where to stay
Mid-range

Posada de San José, Calle Julián Romero 4. Tel. (966) 211 300. This former convent high above the river has views that only a hawk would normally share, and a tiny garden too, but only twenty-five rooms. From 2,100 ptas (without private bath, October to June) to 3,900 ptas (rest of the year).

Alfonso VIII, Parque de San Julián 3. Tel. (966) 214 325. In the modern part of town, garage, bar, pleasant service. From 4,040 ptas (15 October to June) to 4,600 ptas (rest of the year).

Figón de Pedro, Calle Cervantes 17. Tel. (966) 224 511. Comfortable, modern, with a superior, moderately priced restaurant. From 2,640 to 2,870 ptas.

Torremangana, Calle San Ignacio de Loyola 9. Tel. (966) 223 351, telex 23400. In the modern part of town, with garage, moderate restaurant, television in rooms, and bar. From 5,800 to 6,700 ptas.

Cortés, Calle Ramón y Cajal 59. Tel. (966) 220 400. Garage, bar. From 2,285 ptas (October to June) to 2,640 ptas (rest of the year).

Cueva del Fraile, Carretera Cuenca-Benache 7. Tel. (966) 211 571. Closed 9 January to beginning of March. In the valley out of town, but a charming place with scenic views, garden, pool and a moderate restaurant. Walnut trees line the road up the valley. From 4,000 to 4,400 ptas.

Where to eat

Pricey

Mesón Casas Colgadas, Canónigas s/n. Tel. (966) 220 876. Closed on Wednesdays and the second half of December. Recently reopened by the owner of the Figón de Pedro restaurant (see below).

Moderate

Figón de Pedro, Calle Cervantes 15. Tel. (966) 226 821. Closed Mondays, Sunday evenings and the second half of December. The best place to eat in Cuenca, serving regional food. Good wine selection.

Mesón Los Claveles, Calle 18 de Julio 32. Tel. (966) 213 824. Closed Thursdays and all of September. Regional dishes.

Daimiel – Almagro

Daimiel

Daimiel (population 16,260) is 212 km south-west of Cuenca on N-420. This is real Don Quixote country, deep in La Mancha, that treeless, wide-open land with nary a hill in sight. Vineyards stretch from one flat horizon to another.

Some 100 km along the road to Daimiel, you pass one of Spain's most beautiful castles, at **Belmonte**, where the tournament scenes were shot for the film *El Cid*. French Empress Eugenia de Montijo spent part of her days of exile there. It is open daily for visits from 9 a.m. to 2 p.m. and from 4 to 6 p.m.

Herencia

Herencia, 169 km along the route from Cuenca to Daimiel, is a little Mancha *pueblo* famous for its cheeses. Manchego sheep's milk cheese comes in several varieties: mild, aged, and cured in oil. There are shops in town and along the road.

Daimiel boasts a lovely Plaza Mayor and two fifteenth-century churches, but it is noteworthy primarily because of its proximity to the Tablas de Daimiel, a National Park covering 2,750 hectares, which is a nesting place and point of passage for much of Europe's waterfowl. The Tablas are virtually treeless marshlands formed by waters of the Rivers Ciguela and Guadiana. The Park, 11 km from Daimiel on an unpaved road, is closed on Mondays and Tuesdays, but is otherwise open daily from 9 a.m. to 8 p.m. in summer and from 10 a.m. to 5 p.m. in winter.

Visit to a bodega

Cooperativa del Campo la Daimieleña, Plaza del Carmen s/n. Tel. (926) 852 100. This winery does not have the capacity to store as much liquid as the Tablas de Daimiel, but it comes close. It ages and sells forty-five million litres of wine per year, and has its own vineyards that cover five times as much surface area as the Tablas de Daimiel

Park. Among brands which it sells in the EEC and the States are Castillo Daimiel and Clavileño. You can buy the stuff at special prices at the bodega. Telephone Rafael Díaz Salazar to arrange a visit, Monday to Friday, from 9 a.m. to 1 p.m. or from 4 to 7 p.m.

Almagro

Almagro (population 8,364) is 23 km south of Daimiel on C-147; or 190 km south of Madrid via N-IV to Puerto Lapice, N-420 to Daimiel and C-417 to Almagro. Before the Spanish administration opened a parador there in 1979, about all most Spaniards knew about Almagro, if only one thing, was that it produces tons and tons of fiery hot pickled aubergines. Since then Almagro has had its second Renaissance, calling attention to its first.

What to see

This small agricultural town has an elegant elliptical main square (Plaza Mayor) dating from the twelfth century, with two storeys of glassed-in galleries above the colonnades, a mute reminder of its powerful families of the Middle Ages, who were bankers from Flanders. Another Flemish reminder is the handmade-lace industry, which has persisted for centuries. Coats of arms still adorn the doorways of noble buildings.

Other monuments include: the Calatrava Convent with its extraordinary Renaissance cloister; the ponderous Mother of God Church, believed to have been erected by Diego de Almagro, the Conquistador of Chile, a native son; and the San Francisco Monastery – now the parador – all from the sixteenth century. Last but not least, there is a courtyard-type theatre from Spain's Golden Age of Literature, the only one left intact. Today it is once again the scene of performances.

Obviously, lace is a good buy here. Almagro is also a good place to buy Manchego cheese. There are shops on the Plaza Mayor. The Tourist Office is at Calle Carnicerías 11. Tel. (926) 860 717.

Fiestas

The St Bartholomew *Fiestas*, 23–28 August, bring bullfights and theatre to Almagro. *Fiestas* in Ciudad Real (24 km west on C-425) in honour of the Virgin of the Meadow, are the occasion for bullfights, a poetry contest and other events around 15 August. In Valdepeñas, a wine town 36 km to the east on C-415, there are *fiestas* 1–18 August, with bullfights, traditional dancing and other events.

Where to stay

There is only one hotel in Almagro, the fifty-five room Parador. In case you cannot get a room there, two hotels in Ciudad Real are included in the following list. Ciudad Real is 24 easy km to the west.

Mid-range

Parador de Almagro, Ronda de San Francisco. Tel. (926) 860 100. The barefoot Franciscan monks who lived in this monastery would recognize the building but they would find it hard to get the habit. There are the same sixteen interior courtyards, giving every cell a garden view, but there are easy chairs in the oratory and lace doilies everywhere, white linen in the refectory, and there is certainly no mortification of the flesh when it comes to the amount of good food

served, the swimming pool, air-conditioning and central heating.
From 6,500 ptas (November to June) to 7,500 ptas (rest of the year).

Castillos, Avenida del Rey Santo 5, Ciudad Real. Tel. (926) 213
640. Central, garage. From 4,500 ptas.

El Molino, Carretera Córdoba-Tarragona, km 242, Ciudad Real.
Tel. (926) 223 050. Simple, on the outskirts, disco, moderate restaurant. From 5,830 ptas.

Talavera – Jarandilla

Talavera de la Reina

Talavera (population 64,136) is 210 km north-west of Almagro (C-425
west to Ciudad Real, N-430 west to Piedrabuena, right on C-403
northbound to La Puebla de Montalbán, and left on C-502 westbound).

This is a long drive from Almagro, but the countryside is not as
monotonous as parts of La Mancha. The route to Talavera takes you
over two very manageable mountain passes and through country wat-
ered by quite a few streams and rivers. There are fewer vineyards
here. There are vast fields of bright yellow sunflowers, herds of sheep,
olive groves that impose their geometric patterns on rolling red hills,
and extensive wooded areas, many of which are large private hunting
estates. On the tower of every village church there is a stork's nest.

Las Ventas con Peña Aguilera, 80 km past Piedrabuena, is well
known for its handmade accessories for hunters and harnesses and
other gear for horses. Nearby are dolmens and prehistoric caves.

Talavera, originally a Roman city, has been famous for eight
centuries for its ceramics. Today it is also an important furniture-
manufacturing centre, and it retains its traditional role as a market
town for the cotton and tobacco farmers and livestock breeders in the
fertile valley it dominates.

What to see

Its Ruíz de Luna Museum contains potteryware made between the
sixteenth and nineteenth centuries. Other monuments include the
thirteenth-century Romanesque El Salvador Church, the Gothic
Collegiate Church, the Mudéjar-style Santiago Church, and the
chapel of Nuestra Señora del Prado, which has beautiful glazed tiling
from the sixteenth to the eighteenth centuries.

Ceramics are the thing to buy. There are countless pottery shops on
your way through the city and on the outskirts.

Where to eat: pricey

El Anticuario, Avenida de Madrid s/n. Tel. (925) 807 600. Delu-
sions of grandeur here, but some of the dishes, especially game, are
quite good. International cooking. Pleasant service, parking area.

El Arcipreste, Calle Bandera de Castilla 14. Tel. (925) 804 092.
Closed on Sunday evenings. A Castilian inn with regional food.

Un Alto en el Camino, Carretera Madrid-Lisboa, km 119. Tel.

(925) 804 107. Closed on Tuesdays and all of November. Mancha regional cooking, and wines from the region.

Jarandilla de la Vera

This town (population 3,144) is 99 km west of Talavera (C-502 north to Ramacastañas, then through Arenas de San Pedro to C-501 westbound); or 206 km west of Madrid (A-5 south-west to Alcorcón, then right on C-501 westbound).

Jarandilla is an important stop not so much for itself, since it is a very small town, but for its surroundings. Alfonso VIII founded this town, and you will see a number of sixteenth-century coats of arms emblazoned on its houses. The fifteenth-century castle, with its glassed-in Renaissance galleries, is now a lovely parador.

This is no longer Castile. It is the pleasantest corner of Extremadura, the region from which the most famous of the Conquistadores came. The valley of the River Tietar, where Jarandilla stands, and the nearby Jerte Valley, are both sheltered by mountain ranges so they enjoy a surprisingly mild climate in the very shadow of snow-capped mountains. The Jerte district is famous for the beauty of its cherry blossoms. In the Tietar Valley, and particularly in the Vera district, orange trees blossom. Bougainvillaea splashes the walls of the parador with crimson.

Within easy reach by car or local bus are such places as:

Cuacos

Yuste Monastery (at Cuacos, 13 km west of Jarandilla), to which Spain's King Carlos I (Karl V of Germany) retired in 1557, abdicating in favour of his son Philip II. Also in Cuacos is the humble house in which Don Juan of Austria, victor of the naval Battle of Lepanto against the Turks in 1571, lived as a child.

Oropesa

Oropesa, 61 km to the east (south-east to Navalmoral de la Mata on a local road and left on N-5 eastbound), is a town (population 3,069) with a distinctive medieval air and a magnificent fourteenth-century castle, half of which has been converted into a parador and the other half of which is a Civil Guard Police barracks. St Teresa lived in this castle for a while.

Lagartera

Lagartera, 61 km east of Jarandilla (same road as for Oropesa, but take the signposted turn-off to the right 28 km past Navalmoral), is a town (population 1,980) renowned for its handmade lace and embroidery. You can buy from women tatting lace in their doorways or from shops; great value for money.

Villanueva de la Vera

Villanueva de la Vera, 30 km east of Jarandilla on C-501, was where in spring 1987 *Daily Express* reporter Edward Owen engaged in fierce competition with *The Sun*. Blackie the burro, according to the British tabloid press, was destined to be crushed beneath the weight of the fattest man in town and beaten to death by the villagers in the annual Pero Palo *fiestas* if humanitarian tabloids had not intervened. Both Owen and a *Sun* reporter offered cash ransoms for the animal.

Both claimed in print to have bought the beast, but in the end only Owen produced the authenticated one for delivery to a burro-lovers' association, and *The Sun*'s ass was out. Villagers claim they cannot remember when a burro was killed in the *fiestas* which take place at carnival time, in the week preceding Ash Wednesday.

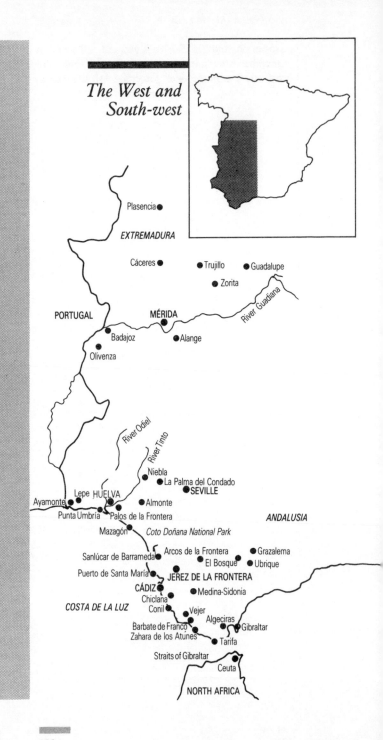

The West and
South-west

EXTREMADURA

Plasencia

Cáceres ● ● Trujillo ● Guadalupe
● Zorita

PORTUGAL   MÉRIDA   River Guadiana

● Badajoz   ● Alange

Olivenza

River Odiel

River Tinto

Niebla
● La Palma del Condado
Lepe HUELVA   SEVILLE
Ayamonte ● Almonte
Punta Umbría   ANDALUSIA
● Palos de la Frontera
Mazagón ● Coto Doñana National Park

Sanlúcar de Barrameda   Arcos de la Frontera   ● Grazalema
● El Bosque ● Ubrique
Puerto de Santa María   JEREZ DE LA FRONTERA
CÁDIZ
Chiclana   ● Medina-Sidonia
COSTA DE LA LUZ   Conil   Vejer
Algeciras
Barbate de Franco   ● Gibraltar
Zahara de los Atunes   Tarifa

Straits of Gibraltar
Ceuta

NORTH AFRICA

The West and South-west

Introduction

No part of the country gives you more of a feeling of being in Spain than do western Andalusia and Extremadura. I would be hard put to explain why for, in one sense, the west and south-west are not at all representative of the rest of the country. The area has a strong personality – or rather, personalities – of its own. It is partly because it is here that you will come across those aspects that form part of every foreigner's idea of Spain, that is: flamenco dancers, gipsy bullfighters, girls in polka-dotted skirts and high combs with mantillas. All that this proves, however, is that things typical of this part of Spain are identified with Spain as a whole, and leaves unanswered why it is that this should be so.

Whatever the reason, here you will find the essence of colourful Spain. Yet, surprisingly, to a considerable extent it remains unvisited by foreign tourists and is only just beginning to prepare for the anticipated tide of tourism to be generated by the 1992 World's Fair, Expo 92, in Seville. There's still time to get there ahead of the mob.

The area covered in this section is bounded on the south by the Atlantic, from the Straits of Gibraltar to the River Guadiana; on the west by the border with Portugal; on the north by the region of Castille and León, and on the east by the region of Castille-La Mancha and by an imaginary line running roughly from the northernmost point of Andalusia, near the La Mancha mining town of Almadén, southward to Gibraltar. It is a vast area, with a road distance from the northernmost city, Plasencia, to the southernmost, Algeciras, of well over 500 km, and an average width of over 150 km.

To help you make the most of your visit to the west and south-west, the principal places of interest have been organized into four separate areas: Extremadura, beginning in Trujillo, and for which you will need three days' minimum to see; Costa de la Luz, starting at Huelva – again three days are necessary; Seville; and Jerez – Solera, Sand and Sierra.

It is quite likely that you will decide to stay in one of the many lovely and intriguing places along the routes described, rather than merely in the cities. For this reason, hotels are listed, where satisfactory, even for small towns.

To make it easier to join the route along the way, distances for the main towns are given from Madrid as well as from the previous town mentioned.

The routes are laid out on the assumption that you are using a car. There are local bus services throughout the area, but obviously they will slow down your coverage of any given route. It is not possible to cover the area by rail, since the railway lines link the major cities only.

If you arrive by plane, you can land in Madrid or Seville, which has frequent flights from European capitals as well as domestic cities. Jerez also has an airport, with at least four flights to and from Madrid each day in addition to some flights to other Spanish cities.

Extremadura

Trujillo
Trujillo (population 9,445) is 253 km west of Madrid on N-5. Trujillo has an impressive number of monuments for its size. Since its population has been shrinking rather than growing in recent years, due to the lack of job opportunities, there is not a great deal more to it than the old section, which has typically narrow and winding streets. The Plaza Mayor lies in the centre and the main Madrid–Mérida highway skirts the east edge of town. There is no airport or railway station. Of its five hotels, two are on the main road and one is on the Plaza Mayor; not all of them can be recommended. The Tourist Office is at Plaza Mayor 18. Tel. (927) 320 653.

History
The Celts lived here, and the city came under the control of the complete succession of invaders who occupied Spain. The most brilliant chapter in its history was the era of Spain's conquest of the New World. No city was home to more prominent Conquistadores than Trujillo, including Francisco Pizarro (c. 1478–1541), whose main achievement was the conquest of Peru.

What to see
The Plaza Mayor is where most of the places of interest are to be found, among them the sixteenth-century Palacio del Marqués de la Conquista, which was built by Pizarro's son-in-law to commemorate the Conquistador and is soon to be occupied by the Extremaduran Academy of Arts and Letters. The square also contains the sixteenth- and seventeenth-century Palace of the Dukes of San Carlos; two privately-owned and occupied palaces dating from the same periods, and the San Martín Church, which was rebuilt in the sixteenth century and contains a priceless eighteenth-century organ in working condition. An equestrian statue of Pizarro in bronze, by American sculptors Charles Rumsey and Mary Harriman, stands in the middle of the

plaza. A twelfth-century Arab fortress dominates the city. Four of the city's seven old gates are intact.

What to do

Fiestas in honour of Our Lady of Victory in the second week of September include a ladies-only bullfight open to volunteers. There are also processions, traditional dancing and costumes.

Nightlife

The locals gather in bars in the town centre for *tapas*, or in one of several music bars and discos on the outskirts. Trujillo is not exactly the most exciting place for nightlife in Spain.

Where to stay: mid-range

The parador is well signposted and most hotels on the road are visible as you pass. There is one on the Plaza Mayor too.

Parador de Trujillo, Plaza Santa Clara. Tel. (927) 321 350. A modern building that blends in perfectly with, and forms a part of, the restored sixteenth-century Santa Clara convent. Paintings on the walls recount moments of importance in local history. This parador has a pleasant garden, pool, lovely Renaissance cloister and a good, moderately-priced restaurant. From 7,500 ptas.

Las Cigüeñas, Carretera Madrid-Lisboa, km 253. Tel. (927) 321 250. Moderate restaurant, bar, air-conditioning. From 4,800 ptas.

Where to eat: moderate

Mesón Pizarro, Plaza Mayor. Tel. (927) 320 255. Regional cooking, with an emphasis on delicious ham from Iberian-breed pigs. Local wines. Parking.

Casa La Pata, Calle Domingo de Ramos 2. Tel. (927) 320 337. Midday meals only. Closed in June. Extremaduran cooking. Specialities include *criadillas* – try them first before you ask what they are – and fried lamb.

Guadalupe

Guadalupe (population 2,765) is 78 km east of Trujillo (C-524 south-east to Zorita, then continue on same road, which now becomes C-401 heading roughly north-west).

This quaint village with its twisted old wooden balconies has an impressive Hieronymite monastery, which was much visited by explorers and the Conquistadores, including Hernán Cortés, who founded its namesake in Mexico. It contains a famous wooden statue of the Virgin Mary. Legend has it that it was dug up by a shepherd in the thirteenth century who had been told where to dig by a vision of the Virgin herself. The monastery was founded on the site of the discovery. The statue is small, squat and black, and is kept in its own chamber at the back of the high altar on a turntable, so that it can be swivelled around and displayed on important occasions. Among things to see at the monastery are the cloisters and eight famous paintings by Zurbarán.

There is also a colourful procession on 8 September, feastday of Our Lady of Guadalupe, and a festival on 12 October, the day dedicated to all Spanish-speaking nations.

Where to stay: mid-range

Hospedería del Real Monasterio, Plaza Juan Carlos I s/n. Tel. (927) 367 000. The rooms are very simple, but, after all, this is a still functioning monastery, though ladies are admitted too. However, no one wakes you up for Matins or Lauds. The monks pray, you pay – but not much. From 3,850 ptas.

Parador Zurbarán, Calle Marqués de la Romana 10. Tel. (927) 367 075. A little fancier. In a fifteenth-century hospital. Pool, tennis court, garage. From 6,000 ptas (November to June) to 7,500 ptas (rest of the year).

Where to eat:
moderate

Hospedería del Real Monasterio. Tel. (927) 367 000. Closed second half of January to first half of February. Extremaduran cooking. Good service, local wines.

Mesón El Cordero, Calle Convento 11. Tel. (927) 367 131. Closed all of February and every Monday. Regional cooking.

Alange

Alange (population 2,186) is 143 km south-west of Guadalupe (C-401 south-west to Majadas, where the same road becomes N-V, then left on a signposted southbound local road from Mérida).

This is one of the three spas in Extremadura. Its waters bubble with calcium, magnesium and sodium bicarbonate, which people immerse themselves in, spray themselves with, drink and inhale, in the hope of curing minor nervous disorders among a long list of other ailments.

The waters work wonders, if we are to believe the testimony of a Roman family who had their thanks to the goddess Juno for curing their daughter, Varinia Serena, chiselled into a stone plaque which is set into the wall there. Two indoor pools, covered by cupolas, in which Ms Serena undoubtedly treated her acne or whatever, are still in use.

Where to stay:
mid-range

Macías, Avenida de Juan Carlos I 11. Tel. Alange 11. Closed from January to June. Historic building, views, garage, bar, moderate restaurant, but kind of countrified. From 4,500 ptas.

Bottom range

Juan de Dios, Calle José Antonio 36. Tel. Alange 15. Closed from October to June. Old building, garage, in the centre of town, economical restaurant. From 1,530 ptas (without bath).

Mérida

Mérida (population 41,783) is 18 km north of Alange on a local road. An agricultural city, Mérida has lost many of its architectural glories owing to wars, the pillaging of old stones for new buildings and, today, the bulldozer.

Founded in 25 BC on the site of a Celtiberian village as a place of retirement for distinguished veterans of Octavio Augustus' Roman Legions V and X, as *Emerita Augusta*, Mérida got a head start in life. Mérida was the capital of Lusitania, most of which today is Portugal. Such a major Roman city required a vast amount of public building, much of which is still visible today as a reminder of its magnificent past.

Main areas

The main roads bypass Mérida, which looks quite prosaic as you pass. If you enter the city from the south via the Roman bridge over the Guadiana, you immediately find the Moorish Alcázar fortress on your right. Follow that street in the same direction until you come to a landscaped triangle on your left. Turn right, and you will shortly come to a park at the end of which you can see the famous theatre. Most of the other monuments are nearby. There are several restaurants around the various squares in the old quarter. There are Tourist Offices at the Roman theatre and at Calle del Puente 9. Tel. (924) 303 161.

What to see

Notable among these are the ruins of the so-called Miraculous Aqueduct; the Prosperina Reservoir; a noble bridge over the River Albarrega and a monumental one over the Guadiana. This latter comprises over sixty granite arches, each originally carved from a single block. There is also a circus where Christians were thrown to the lions (Mérida's patron saint, Eulalia, was a local martyr), a magnificent amphitheatre, a much-deteriorated memorial arch for the Emperor Trajan, and statues, colonnades and lesser works all over the city. The most beautiful monument is, however, the 6,000-seat Roman theatre, whose stage in particular has survived astonishingly intact; so much so in fact that Spain's most important festival of theatre is held here every summer. Mérida is also the scene of an annual gipsy fair in October.

Where to stay

Top range

Hotels tend to be on or near plazas in the old part of town or else beside main roads on the outskirts.

Parador Vía de la Plata, Plaza de la Constitución 3. Tel. (924) 313 800. This is in the fascinating Baroque sixteenth-century San Francisco convent, which was partly built with columns and stones from an earlier building. In the early 1960s, General Franco went to meet his fellow dictator, Rafael Salazar of Portugal, at the Mérida parador. While the *Generalissimo* was entertaining him, a lift in the parador plummeted to the ground. The news report of this event was censored and it was probably one of several unrevealed assassination attempts. From 7,500 ptas (January to March) to 8,500 ptas (rest of the year).

Mid-range

Las Lomas, Carretera de Madrid, km 338. Tel. (924) 311 011, telex 28840. Air-conditioning, parking area, children's playground, moderate restaurant. From 5,250 (January to March) to 6,000 ptas (rest of the year).

Emperatriz, Plaza de España 19. Tel. (924) 313 111. This hotel is in a former sixteenth-century palace with garden in its centre. Moderate restaurant. From 4,000 ptas (January to March) to 4,500 ptas (rest of the year).

Nova Roma, Calle Suárez Somonte 42. Tel. (924) 311 201. Modern, near the Roman theatre, bar. From 4,200 ptas (January to 23 March) to 4,725 ptas (rest of the year).

Bottom range **Guadiana**, Plaza de Santa Clara s/n. Tel. (927) 313 200. A small, simple residence hostel, very central. From 1,800 ptas (January to March) to 2,000 ptas (rest of the year).

Where to eat: **Parador Vía de la Plata**, address as above. Tel. (924) 313 800.
moderate The locals flock here too. Extremaduran food, including Extremadura stew and rabbit, with local wines.

Cáceres Cáceres (population 71,852) is 68 km north of Mérida on N-630. Capital of the province of the same name, this city is in the middle of a cattle-ranching area. Its name comes from the Arabian Cazris, but it was originally founded by the Romans. Most of the sights are inside the walls of the old town, which is on a hill, largely surrounded by the modern city. A complicated one-way system makes it difficult for drivers to reach the old town, but keep on heading up hill and you won't go far wrong. Follow the signs for *centro urbano*; the Town Hall is on the Plaza Mayor, from which you can enter the old quarter. The Tourist Office is also on the Plaza Mayor. Tel. (927) 246 347.

Moorish walls still completely encircle the surprisingly small old town, which should be visited on foot. Roughly five streets long by four streets wide, it has perfectly retained its medieval character and is full of old fortress-palaces and churches and delightful little squares.

Where to stay There are several hotels in the vicinity of the Parque de Calvo Sotelo and also around the Plaza de Italia, and a few smaller ones close by the outside of the walls.

Mid-range **Alcántara**, Avenida Virgen de Guadalupe 14. Tel. (927) 228 900. A residence hotel in the new part, with shops and bar. From 4,750 ptas (January to March) to 5,160 ptas (rest of the year).

Extremadura, Avenida Virgen de Guadalupe 5. Tel. (927) 221 604. Air-conditioned, garage, garden, pool, moderate restaurant. In the new part of town. From 4,800 ptas (January to March) to 5,230 ptas (rest of the year).

Alvarez, Calle Parras 20. Tel. (927) 246 400. Simple, central, with bar and economical restaurant. From 3,200 ptas.

Bottom range **Adarve**, Calle Sánchez Garrido 4. Tel. (927) 244 874. Central. From 1,500 ptas.

Where to eat: **El Figón de Eustaquio**, Plaza San Juan 12. Tel. (927) 248 194.
moderate Right outside the walls. International and regional cooking, very popular with the locals. Specialities include Extremaduran stew and pork dishes.

Delfos, Plaza de Albatros 3. Tel. (927) 225 026. Regional dishes, such as fried lamb and ham from Montánchez.

Badajoz Badajoz (population 114,361) is 89 km south-west of Cáceres on N-523; or 401 km west of Madrid on N-V.

History This city has changed hands so many times in so many battles that there is not much left to recall its past. For several centuries before 1230, when it was definitively conquered by Christian forces, it was lost and won by both sides time after time. The Portuguese laid siege to it in 1660, and it was besieged again in the War of Succession in 1705. In 1810 Napoleon's forces managed to enter the city after forty-two days of fighting; then in 1812 the French forces occupying it surrendered to Wellington after repeated attacks. In 1936 Republican forces put up a brief but bitter resistance to an attack by Nationalist troops, but they lost.

What to see

The building in which the Archaeological Museum is housed is a collection of exhibits in itself. The columns are Roman, the capitals are Visigothic and the decoration is Arabic. It is inside the fortified area known as the Alcazaba, along with a tower which has become the symbol of the city, the Torre de Espantaperros (Dog-frightening Tower). No one seems to know why it is called that. The thirteenth-century Cathedral is dark and blockish.

Where to stay: mid-range

Gran Hotel Zurbarán, Paseo de Castelar s/n. Tel. (924) 223 741. Garage, pool, tennis, television in rooms, shops, moderate restaurant, disco. From 6,160 ptas (January to August) to 6,530 ptas (rest of the year).

Lisboa, Avenida Elvas 13. Tel. (924) 238 200. Garage, television, disco, economical restaurant. From 4,000 ptas.

Rio, Avenida Elvas s/n. Tel. (924) 237 600. Garage, pool, garden, disco. From 3,475 ptas (January to March) to 3,950 ptas (rest of the year).

Bottom range

De las Heras, Calle Pedro de Valdivia 6. Tel. (924) 224 014. Basic, economical restaurant, no private baths. From 990 ptas.

Where to eat: moderate

La Toja, Avenida Elvas 21. Tel. (924) 237 477. Closed on Sunday evenings. Galician food.

Los Gabrieles, Calle Vicente Barrantes 21. Tel. (924) 224 275. Closed on Sundays. Among popular dishes is oxtail soup (called 'bull's-tail' in this part of the country).

El Tronco, Calle Muñoz Torero 16. Tel. (924) 222 076. Closed on Sundays. Regional food.

Olivenza

Olivenza (population 9,837) is 25 km south of Badajoz on C-436. What makes this moderately prosperous farming town interesting is that Portugal wants it back. Olivenza became a part of Spain after the seventeen-day War of the Oranges in 1801, instigated by Spain's Premier Godoy in league with the French. The idea was to force Portugal to promise not to let the British use its ports. When the Portuguese government gave that promise, the war ended, but Olivenza, with its olive and orange groves in gently rolling countryside, remains under the Spanish flag to this day. It was called the War of the Oranges because the haughty Godoy presented his queen with a branch full of them from a tree in Olivenza.

The twisting Manueline columns in the Santa María Magdalena Church in Olivenza are typically late Portuguese Gothic. Its tower also looks more Portuguese than Spanish. The town's castle is from the late thirteenth century, with a fifteenth-century keep.

Costa de la Luz
Huelva

Huelva (population 127,806) is 223 km south of Olivenza (C-423 east to Almendral, then right on N-435); or 604 km south-west of Madrid. An earthquake in 1755 left few ancient buildings standing. The city itself is not particularly attractive, but its surroundings are.

Main areas

Huelva occupies a southward-pointing peninsula bounded on two sides by the Rivers Tinto and Odiel, which have a common delta on the Gulf of Cádiz, which is known as the Costa de la Luz (Coast of Light). All main roads and the railway enter it from the north. Residential areas and the better hotels tend to be in the higher parts, particularly on the River Tinto side. Docks are on the south and west sides.

The railway station is at Avenida Italia s/n. The provincial Tourist Office is at Calle Plus Ultra 10. Tel. (955) 245 092. The regional Tourist Office is at Calle Vázquez López 5. Tel. (955) 257 403.

Excursions

Monasterio de la Rábida

This is 10 km to the east of Huelva via a road that leaves from the Punta del Sebo at the south end of the city. This Franciscan monastery near Palos de la Frontera, across the River Tinto, is where Columbus and his crew attended Mass in its fourteenth-century chapel before setting out on his first voyage of discovery.

Niebla

Niebla is 28 km to the north-east of Huelva on N-431. This small town, slumbering behind its red-brown Arab walls by the side of the road, was originally an Iberian settlement. Under Arab rule it became a small emirate, eventually paying tribute to the crown of Castile. But the Emir Aben Mofad rebelled, and Alfonso X, The Wise, of Castile, besieged the town for nine and a half months before it fell in February 1262. The battle was no doubt prolonged by the Emir's formidable secret weapon, the cannon, which was being used for the first time in the Iberian Peninsula.

This largely unchanged and seldom visited town guards such treasures as the Mozarabic interior of the Santa María de la Granada Church, and – a few kilometres down the road on the right-hand side as you return to Huelva – a grotto known as the Dolmen de la Lobita with prehistoric wall paintings. Ask at the Niebla Town Hall or the Huelva Tourist Office how to get permission to see these paintings, since they are on private property.

Shopping

Ham from Jabugo, a town in the north of the province of Huelva, is the king of hams, made only from the black-footed Iberian breed of pigs, fattened on acorns and cured high in the mountains. It is expensive compared to other hams, but it has reason to be. However, it is cheaper in this area than in other parts of the country. Try some in a good *tapa* bar before you buy, in order to convince yourself. By the same token, Spanish sausages, such as *chorizo* and *lomo*, made from this breed are superior to the less expensive varieties.

Boots from the Huelva town of Valverde del Camino are fashionable and useful. There are styles for country and for city wear, for riding and walking, for men and women.

Wrought-iron work from Cortegana and pottery from Cortegana, La Palma del Condado and Trigueros are also much appreciated.

Where to stay

Huelva does not have many hotels, since visitors tend to head for the long, long beaches on the Gulf. Better hotels in the city are mostly on the higher ground and on the east side of the Peninsula. The Hostería de la Rábida at the monastery where Columbus prayed is included in this list because, though it is across the river, it is just 6 km from the centre.

Mid-range

Luz Huelva, Alameda Sundheim 26. Tel. (955) 250 011, telex 75527. Garage, pool, tennis, bar. From 8,000 ptas.

Tartessos, Avenida Martín Alonso Pinzón 13. Tel. (955) 245 611. Central, bar, air-conditioned. From 4,650 ptas.

Costa de la Luz, Calle José María Amo 8. Tel. (955) 256 422. A central residence hotel. From 3,600 ptas.

Hostería de la Rábida, Paraje de la Rábida, Palos de la Frontera (6 km to the east). Tel. (955) 350 312. The view is somewhat spoiled by a refinery, but the place is historic, the garden is pleasant and there is a moderately-priced restaurant on the premises. Only five rooms. From 3,600 ptas.

Bottom range

Calvo, Calle Rascón 33. Tel. (955) 249 016. Plain lodging at a minimal price. No private baths. From 1,250 ptas (10 September to June) to 1,300 ptas (rest of the year).

Where to eat

Pricey

Las Meigas, Plaza de América s/n. Tel. (955) 230 098. Closed on Sundays in July and August. Spanish cooking with Galician specialities, especially seafood. Sample dishes: squid in their ink, boiled ham shoulder with turnip greens. Catalan and Riojan wines. Parking area, terrace.

Moderate

Doñana, Gran Vía 13. Tel. (955) 242 723. Closed on Sundays. International cooking, good fish and stews.

Los Gordos, Calle Carmen 14. Tel. 246 266. Seafood, perfectly fresh and simply prepared. Local and Riojan wines.

Punta Umbría

This town (population 9,480) is 26 km south of Huelva (west on a local road across the Odiel estuary, then left at the T-junction on a southbound local road for 9 km to another T-junction, where you turn left again and continue to the end of the road).

This has been a traditional Spanish family resort since the great-grandfathers of the present batch of holiday-makers first dipped their toes in the water. It is a favourite with families from Seville and Jerez. Non-Spaniards are a rarity.

The Club de Mar y Ténis de Punta Umbría operates a small yacht basin for pleasure craft. It is at the mouth of the Ria (estuary) de Punta

Umbría. With 20 km of sandy beaches, a mild climate and usually gentle winds, this place also attracts an increasing number of wind-surfers every year.

There's plenty of entertainment in the summer, especially at week-ends, when there are at least a dozen discos throbbing away, and gre-garious young Spaniards talk late into the night. When they do decide to go to bed, they walk back to their houses or hotels singing and clapping their hands to the beat of Sevillanas. Some of the bars and discos offer live music.

Where to stay   The most built-up part of town is at the end of the road, on the point. Most of the hotels are there. Don't expect luxury, but you will find comfort in the mid-range places.

Mid-range   **Pato Amarillo**, Urbanizacion Everluz s/n. Tel. (955) 311 250. Closed from November to March. This Yellow Duck is the most com-plete hotel in town, with garden, pool, children's pool, disco and a moderate restaurant. From 4,200 to 5,280 ptas.

Pato Rojo, Avenida Oceano. Tel. (955) 311 600. On the beach, parking. Half or full board in high season, meaning you have to pay for meals whether you eat in the hotel or not. Rooms cost from 4,000 ptas (16 September to end of June) to 5,000 ptas (rest of the year). Standard meal prices are moderate.

El Ayamontino, Avenida Andalucía. Tel. (955) 311 450. In the centre of town, near the beach, with garage, bar and a moderate res-taurant. From 2,550 ptas (October to February) to 3,475 ptas (rest of the year).

Ayamontino-Ria, Plaza Pérez Pastor 25. Tel. (955) 311 458. A small central hotel. From 2,550 ptas (October to February) to 3,475 ptas (rest of the year).

Where to eat: **Don Diego**, Avenida Oceano s/n. Tel. (955) 312 868. Closed
moderate   October to June. Spanish cooking, especially seafood.

Lepe   Lepe (population 13,669) is 30 km west of Punta Umbría (local road west to Cartaya via El Rompido, then left on N-431 westbound). This is another town patronized by Spanish families, but in this case most of them stay in their own or rented houses on the beach a few kilometres from the centre, which is inland and surrounded by melon fields. Small houses, painted in different colours but otherwise very much alike, stand alone, marshalled in rows on the sand dunes, with streets running in front of them but not a blade of grass to be seen. At nearby El Terrón the | local fishermen's catch is auctioned off twice daily, late in the morning and in the afternoon.

Ayamonte   Ayamonte (population 16,216) is 22 km west of Lepe on N-431. This is the last Spanish town before the Portuguese border. It has 7 km of fine beaches. Many people going to or coming from the Portu-guese Algarve, particularly Britons, use this route. If you are thinking of doing so, don't, at least not in summer. Cars have to queue for up to twelve hours for the ferry across the river from Ayamonte to the Portuguese village of Vila Real de Santo Antonio in July and August.

Ayamonte has a small fishing port at the mouth of the River Guadiana with a customs post for maritime as well as road traffic. At low tide the port is almost dry. In recent years, alleged violations of a Spanish-Portuguese fishing agreement have even resulted in some shooting incidents here. A popular ballad tells the sad tale of Portuguese María, who fell in love with a Spanish langoustine poacher; she went aboard his boat with him one night, but he was shot dead by the Portuguese Coast Guard.

Where to stay:
mid-range

Parador Costa de la Luz, El Castillito. Tel. (955) 320 700. Pleasant views, pool, garden, moderate restaurant serving good seafood. Only twenty rooms, so reserve well in advance. From 6,000 ptas (November to June) to 7,500 ptas (rest of the year).

Don Diego, Calle Ramón y Cajal s/n. Tel. (955) 320 250. Central, bar. From 4,000 ptas (October to June) to 4,500 ptas (rest of the year).

Where to eat:
moderate

Barbieri, Paseo de la Ribera. Tel. (955) 320 298. Closed for two weeks in October and every Tuesday except in July and August. Fresh seafood accompanied by wines of nearby La Palma del Condado.

Isla Cristina

Isla Cristina (population 16,335) is 22 km east of Ayamonte (N-431 east to El Empalme, then right on a local road passing through Pozo del Camino). This is Huelva's second largest fishing port. It was founded a century and a half ago by fishermen from the east coast of Spain. It is an island, but only just. You enter by crossing a short iron bridge over a narrow delta-type channel. It has good beaches and is a very attractive town with flowery doorways. There are only a few hotels, but many families rent out rooms in their homes to tourists in the summer.

Where to stay:
mid-range

Los Geranios, Carretera de la Playa. Tel. (955) 331 800. Pool, garden, bar, pine-shaded surroundings. From 3,200 ptas (October to May) to 3,600 ptas (rest of the year).

Pato Azul, Gran Vía. Tel. (955) 331 350. Central, garden, pool, bar, moderate restaurant. With fifty-eight rooms, the largest hotel in town. From 3,000 ptas (17 September to 15 July) to 3,800 ptas (rest of the year).

Where to eat

Every bar, even the discos, in Isla Cristina offers a selection of *tapas*, mostly seafood, and all delicious.

Moderate

Casa Rufino, Carretera de la Playa s/n. Tel. (955) 330 565. Freshly-caught fish, big portions. Local and Riojan wines.

Mazagón

Mazagón (population 104) is 101 km east of Isla Cristina (eastward on a local road along the beach to La Antilla, then left to Lepe, then right on N-431 to Huelva, then east on N-442).

This is a summer resort patronized mostly by well-to-do Spaniards. Their homes are set in pine forests and their gardens are bright with flowers. Beyond Mazagón there are dunes, dunes and more dunes. Away from the built-up area, the beaches of powder-fine white sand are absolutely deserted.

Coto Doñana National Park

About 16 km further down the beach is the last town, Matalascañas. Beyond that, to the far shore of the mouth of the River Guadalquivir, there is no human habitation – only the huge Coto Doñana National Park. Further construction at Matalascañas has been halted in order to maintain the wild beauty of this reserve, a blend of shifting dunes, marshlands, pine forests and grasslands, where the majority of Europe's migratory birds feed, breed or rest. The long list of wildlife living there includes the lynx, various species of eagle, deer, boar, camel, viper, fox, badger, weasel and mongoose.

From Mazagón, there are roads leading to small villages and settlements in the interior, mostly outside the boundaries of the Park. Part of the land is farmed, but much of it is as wild as the Park itself. A warning: some of these roads are mere tracks in the wilderness and not suitable for ordinary motor cars at all. You can go on guided tours of the Coto Doñana from Almonte (see below).

Where to stay: top range

Parador Cristobal Cólon, Carretera de la Playa. Tel. (955) 376 000. Pool, tennis, garden, sweeping views of the beach, moderate restaurant. From 7,000 ptas (November to June) to 8,500 ptas (rest of the year).

Almonte

This town (population 12,959) is 41 km north-east of Mazagón (C-442 east to Matalascañas, then left on a local road passing through the village of El Rocio, leading to Almonte).

Except for its connection with the Pilgrimage of the Rocio, Spain's largest and most colourful popular religious celebration, Almonte would remain an undistinguished little Andalusian farm town. The Rocío Pilgrimage draws hundreds of thousands of Andalusians at Whitsuntide to Almonte and the shrine of the Virgin of the Dew (Rocío), 11 km further south. Dressed in traditional Andalusian garb – the girls in white blouses and bright-coloured, polka-dotted skirts and the men in the grey or black riding trousers and short jacket of the *traje corto* – they converge on Almonte, crossing the countryside on foot, on horseback and in gaily decorated carts drawn by horses or oxen, singing and dancing all the way to the sound of fifes, guitars and castanets for three days in a row. The highlight of the *fiesta* is the *paseo* of the Virgin of the Dew, when the brotherhoods of Almonte – which have the privilege of carrying 'The White Dove', as the Virgin is called, on their shoulders – jostle and tug and push to get close as the image goes rocking and dipping by above a sea of humanity. The few houses around the shrine of El Rocío, as you will see when you pass it, are practically deserted for the rest of the year.

From Almonte, it is possible to make guided tours of parts of the Coto Doñana in a four-wheel drive vehicle with the blessings of ICONA, Spain's official wildlife conservation department. The cost of such tours varies. Contact the Huelva Tourist Office or telephone the park's service office, (955) 430 432, for information. Remember to take a telephoto lens if you have one.

Where to stay   Hotels in La Palma del Condado, 16 km north of Almonte, are included in the following list, since there is only one small, simple hostel in Almonte itself. Needless to say, every hotel for miles around is booked at the time of the Rocío Pilgrimage, though the vast majority of the pilgrims simply sleep in the fields, if they sleep at all.

Many carry sleeping bags on their horses and in the carts; and, hidden underneath the decoration, the carts are laden with hams, big jugs of wine and other provisions. If you want to see the Rocío, book at least a year ahead.

Mid-range   **La Viña**, Carretera Huelva-Sevilla, km 601 (La Palma del Condado). Tel. (955) 400 273. Scenic surroundings, pool, children's pool, bar. From 1,500 ptas (October to March without private bath) to 2,500 ptas (high season, with bath).

Los Morenos, Calle Huelva 3 (La Palma del Condado). Tel. (955) 400 438. Central, garage, bar. From 1,200 ptas (without bath) to 2,200 ptas (with bath).

Bottom range   **Endrina**, Calle Concepción 9 (Almonte). Tel. (955) 406 120. Central, with economical restaurant. From 950 ptas (September to June, without private bath) to 1,740 ptas (rest of the year, with bath).

Seville (Sevilla)

Seville (population 653,833) is 68 km east of Almonte (north on a local road passing through Bollullos Par del Condado to La Palma del Condado; then right on N-431 eastbound); or 538 km south-west of Madrid on N-IV.

The capital of Spain's biggest region, Andalusia, old Seville is very beautiful, but the most modern parts are totally uninspired and uninspiring. Turning a blind eye to the uniformly ugly rows of blocks of flats on unlandscaped earth in the modern part of Seville, this is the loveliest city in Spain. The number of museums, monuments and historic or artistic structures is overwhelming. You need the very minimum of one day to see the city. Seville's climate is mild in winter, with a moderate amount of rainfall, and very hot and dry in summer.

Getting there   Seville's airport, 14 km to the east at San Pablo, is one of the country's busiest, receiving frequent international as well as national flights. Seville is a major railway junction for Andalusia. Motorways reach to Cádiz in the south and Huelva in the west, but roads to the other Andalusian capitals are less satisfactory, considering the distances involved and the mountainous terrain. Seville is also a port, but the Guadalquivir, the region's main river, is not deep enough for very large ships to sail as far as Seville. There is a yacht club, the Club Náutico Sevilla, Margen Derecha del Guadalquivir. Tel. (954) 454 777.

SEVILLE STREET MAP

PLACES OF INTEREST

1 Tourist Office
2 University (former Tobacco Factory)
3 Cathedral and Giralda
4 Santa Cruz quarter
5 María Luisa Park
6 Alcázar
7 Casa Lonja and Archive of the Indies
8 Plaza de España
9 Real Maestranza Bullring
10 Hospital de la Caridad
11 Alameda de Hércules
12 Museum of Fine Arts
13 Archaeological Museum
14 Town Hall
15 Casa de Pilatos
16 Torre del Oro (Naval Museum)

CHURCHES AND CONVENTS

17 Basilica de la Macarena
18 Convento de Santa Clara
19 Monasterio de San Clemente
20 Iglesia de la Magdalena
21 Basilica de Jesus del Gran Poder

RAILWAY STATIONS

22 Bus Station
23 La Cádiz
24 Córdoba

Main areas

Seville stands mostly on the left, or east, bank of the Guadalquivir in its fertile valley. Its identifying landmark is the Giralda, the graceful Moorish belltower of its grandiose Cathedral. Since the Giralda can be seen from just about anywhere in the centre of the city, it is a useful reference point.

The Cathedral faces the Avenida de la Constitución; and one street to the south, on the same side of the road, is the Casa Lonja, inside which is the Archive of the Indies (Archivo de las Indias). The Alcázar, the ancient Moorish stronghold, lies just past the next street, and behind the Archives.

The charming and extensive old Santa Cruz quarter, much of which is closed to cars because of its narrow streets, lies behind the Cathedral and just north of the Alcázar. The famous Triana gipsy quarter, where renowned bullfighter Juan Belmonte came from, lies on the opposite side of the river, across the Isabel II, or Triana, Bridge.

Of Seville's many restaurants, there are quite a few near the Cathedral and there are several on the right-hand side of the river opposite the distinctive thirteenth-century Torre del Oro, now a Naval Museum. The narrow Calle Sierpes (north on the Avenida de la Constitución and past the Town Hall), for pedestrians only, is the heart of the shopping and business district, and it is lined with cafés and *tapa* bars too.

There are two railway stations, the Cádiz, Calle San Bernardo 13; and the Córdoba, Plaza de Armas 56, on the east bank, a few streets north of the Isabel II Bridge. The bus station is at Diego de Riano 2.

The regional Tourist Office is at Avenida de la Constitución 9 (near the Alcázar); Tel. (954) 221 404; the municipal Tourist Office is at Plaza de los Marineros Voluntarios, in María Luisa Park; Tel. (954) 234 465.

History

In about 1000 BC, it was called Hispalis by the Phoenicians. Then came the Greeks, the Carthaginians and the Romans, who built a large temple on what is now the Calle de los Marmoles (so called because of the huge marble blocks found there), and made Seville the capital of the province of Bética.

Later the Vandals destroyed Seville, but then the Visigoths made Seville the capital of the local kingdom. In AD 712 the Arabs took Seville, which they called Xibilia, causing more destruction; but they built anew, creating some priceless monuments. In 1248 Christian forces conquered the city, which they called Sevilla, and repopulated much of it, demolishing the great mosque, except for its minaret, to build a cathedral on the same site. With the discovery of the New World, Seville reached its greatest splendour, as the sole port of entry for the gold and silver. It also received all manner of exotic merchandise such as huge sacks of pearls from Darien, emeralds from Colombia and colourful silks from the Philippines. Its decline began in 1649 when its population was decimated due to plague. In 1717 it lost the exclusive right to New World freight, but made a comeback later, in the eighteenth century, with the construction of the tobacco factory (Fábrica de Tabacos), a huge, elegant stone building where 3,000 people were employed to make cigars for export all over Europe. The splendid old building, which until 1950 was the second largest in Spain, surpassed only by the Escorial, is now the home of the University of Seville.

What to see

Santa Cruz quarter

This quarter, part of which was the old Jewish neighbourhood, is cool and shady with narrow, twisting streets, which are closed to cars, and delightful small squares, full of flowers. Murillo was buried in the old church of Santa Cruz in 1682.

María Luisa Park

The María Luisa Park, with its majestic buildings built for the 1929 World Fair, is uniquely beautiful. Its eighteenth and nineteenth century surroundings overflow with geraniums and charm.

Cathedral

The Gothic Cathedral, which contains a vast wealth of artistic treasures, is one of the largest in Christendom, rivalling St Peter's in Rome and St Paul's in London. Columbus is buried here. Its tower, the Giralda, with a belfry and a huge bronze weathervane in the form of a human figure added in the sixteenth century, is the old minaret. The Orange-Tree Patio was the site of a bazaar in Moorish times.

Alcázar

This is a fortified area containing an eleventh-century Mudéjar palace which has undergone several reformations. The Hall of the Ambassadors, the gardens and the tilework generally are noteworthy. Open daily from 9 a.m. to 1 p.m. and from 3 to 5 p.m. Entrance on the Plaza del Triunfo s/n.

Archive of the Indies

In the Casa Lonja, Archivo de las Indias is an incredibly valuable repository of ancient documents relating to the discovery and conquest of the Americas. Not all of the documents have been fully studied yet: it is not open to the general public, only to scholars.

Bullring

The Real Maestranza Bullring, where Carmen's former lover Don José stabbed her to death according both to Bizet's opera and to local legend, is the most ornate in Spain.

Hospital de la Caridad

This Hospital (Plaza de Jurado), which houses one of Seville's most important collections of art, was founded to care for the poor and the sick and to bury the dead. Today it is an old people's home. It contains numerous artistic treasures, including paintings by Valdés Leal and Murillo. It was founded in the seventeenth century by a wealthy wastrel, Miguel de Mañara (1626–79), after a bad binge in which he imagined men were coming to pick him up off the street and put him in a coffin.

Calle Bustos Tavera

Seville is full of romantic legends, one of which may have been the inspiration for Schubert's opera *Alphonso and Estrella*. In the thirteenth century, so the story goes, King Sancho IV was quite taken with a young lady of Seville, Estrella Tavera, but as she was in love with a handsome nobleman, Sancho Ortiz de Roelas, she spurned the royal advances. One night King Sancho slipped out of the palace alone and bribed servants at Doña Estrella's house, where she lived virtuously with her brother Bustos Tavera, to let him in. Unfortunately for the King, Bustos discovered the intruder and threw him out. Enraged at being treated like a commoner and afraid that the story would be made public, the King ordered Bustos Tavera's execution, and haughtily commanded Estrella's fiancé, Sancho, to carry it out. Torn between loyalty to his King and his own conscience, Sancho obeyed, but left Seville immediately afterwards, never to return. Brokenhearted and left without a brother or a husband, Estrella turned her home into a convent and became a nun. Whether or not the story is true is a matter of conjecture. Certainly, there is a convent on the Calle Bustos Tavera, dedicated to Our Lady of Perpetual Help, but the records say it was not founded until 1552. However, the then King was Philip II, and Venetian ambassadors have written of Philip's amorous adventures, before he chose a monk's life.

Alameda de
Hércules

The Don Juan legend is also thought to be based on real life. A small chapel dedicated to Our Lady of Carmen, at the end of the Alameda de Hércules, erected by the forebears of the Dukes of Medinaceli, stands on the spot where the locals say the first-born son of the Marqués de Tarifa (the Medinacelis' line) died in a sword-fight at the foot of a wayside cross, done in by the family of a woman he had abducted from a convent.

Calle Cabeza
del Rey
Don Pedro

Another of the legends which refers to something you can see concerns King Pedro I, The Cruel, curiously known in Seville as The Just, who went out alone one night and became involved in a dispute with another *caballero*. They pulled out their swords and in a brief struggle the King ran his sword through his opponent's body. At that moment an old woman leaned out of a window, lighting up the street with an oil lamp she held in her hand, to see what was going on. The victim, it turned out, was a son of the extremely powerful Guzmán family, so the King, believing no one had seen him, offered a fabulous reward of one hundred gold coins to anyone who could identify the killer. To placate the Guzmán family, the King promised to place the killer's head in a niche in the wall at the spot where Guzmán's death occurred. A coal merchant named Juan, a son of the old woman who had leaned out the window, went to the palace and was admitted to the King's presence because he said he had information about the slaying. Pointing to a mirror, he told the King, 'If you look through that window you will see who killed Guzmán.' The King, realizing he had been caught out, looked at the mirror and said, 'It's true. The gentleman who can be seen in the window is the one who killed Guzmán.' He ordered a servant to pay the man the reward as promised – in exchange for his silence.

When the niche was made, the King sent a wooden box, which he said contained the head of the slayer, to be inserted in it; but he ordered the niche to be sealed up, saying the head was of a very prominent person and that civil disorders might occur if his identity became known. After the King's death, the Guzmáns opened the niche. Inside was the stone bust of Pedro I, which to this day stands in a hollow in a wall on a street called Calle Cabeza del Rey Don Pedro (King Don Pedro's Head) near the junction with the Calle Candilejo (Oil Lamp).

Museum of Fine Arts

Other sights to see include two excellent museums, the best of which is the Museum of Fine Arts (Museo de Bellas Artes), in the former Merced Convent, Plaza del Museo 9 (open daily from 10 a.m. to 2 p.m. and from 4 to 7 p.m.; closed on Sunday afternoons and Mondays). It contains a large selection of Murillos, Riberas and other master painters.

Archaeological Museum

The other unmissable museum is the Provincial Archaeological Museum, Plaza de América s/n (open 10 a.m. to 2 p.m. and from 5 to 8 p.m. including Sunday; closed on Mondays and holidays), displaying some of the varied finds in this province associated with Tartessos one or two thousand years before the Phoenicians arrived, and with the many other cultures since then.

Churches and convents

There are churches and convents galore, full of paintings, statuary, great architecture and curiosities. Most of the churches are open to the public for daily religious services. Also, most convents and monasteries are open for daily masses from about 8 to 10 a.m. The following are among the better known.

● **Basilica de la Macarena** (Calle Bécquer 1), which houses the most famous statue in Seville's Holy Week processions, the tearful Virgin of Sorrows, the Macarena, by an unknown sculptor.

● **Convento de Santa Clara** (Calle de Santa Clara), where Doña María Coronel, a noble fourteenth-century lady, sought refuge from the amorous advances of King Pedro I, The Cruel, who had even killed her husband in an effort to achieve his ends. When he tried to have her removed from the convent, she was so distraught that she disfigured her pretty face by pouring burning oil on it.

● **Monasterio de San Clemente** (Calle de Santa Clara 91), which houses the sepulchre of Queen María of Portugal and works by Valdés Leal.

● **Iglesia de la Magdalena** (Calle Bailén 5), notable for its multi-coloured cupolas on the outside and for three Mudéjar-style cupolas inside from the fourteenth or fifteenth century.

● **Basilica de Jesús del Gran Poder** (Plaza San Lorenzo 13), where one of the most revered images of Seville's Holy Week processions is kept, a statue of Jesus carved in 1620 by sculptor Juan de Mesa.

Palaces

There are also many palaces of great beauty. One of the most famous is **Casa de Pilatos** (Plaza de Pilatos; open daily from 10 a.m. to 8 p.m. in summer and to 6 p.m. in winter), an airy, sixteenth-century mansion which combines classical Roman and Greek elements with Mudéjar, Gothic and Renaissance styles. Many other lovely old homes are still lived in by both the powerful and the humble, and you can catch glimpses of their flower-filled courtyards through wrought-iron gates as you walk along narrow streets in the older parts of the town.

Excursions

Itálica

Scipio Africanus founded the city of Itálica (8 km north on N-630, turning off at Santiponce) in 250 BC for veterans of his campaigns against Carthage. Roman Emperors Trajan and Hadrian were born here. The Vandals later destroyed it. The amphitheatre, mosaic tile floors of Roman villas and other ruins can still be seen.

What to do

River cruises

Short river cruises: daily, on boats leaving from the dock in front of the Torre del Oro. Check times and prices by calling (954) 211 396 or 721 934.

Dance of the
Seises

During the eight-day festival (octave) of Corpus Christi in June, ten choir boys, dressed as sixteenth-century pages, dance and sing every day in front of the high altar of the Cathedral, where a consecrated host is on display. By special dispensation, they do not have to remove their plumed hats, just as the Grandees of Spain are allowed to keep theirs on in the presence of the King.

Flamenco

In the latter years of the Franco regime it became fashionable in Spain to snub Andalusian music, both the hoarsely oriental strains of flamenco and the popular, contemporary *tonadilla* tunes, but the appointment of Sevillan lawyer Felipe González as Prime Minister, and his re-election, was to make Andalusian music the 'in' thing. Only wallflowers cannot dance the rhythmic Sevillana today. Spaniards are tickled when foreigners try it.

Los Gallos, Plaza Santa Cruz 11. Tel. (954) 216 981. Moderate prices.

El Tablao de Curro Velez, Calle Rodo 7. Tel. (954) 216 492. 'Pure' flamenco, more exciting for the initiated than for tourists.

Classical music
and ballet

Frequent concerts by the Bética Filarmónica Orchestra. Music and dance festivals take place in May and in summer. Check dates and times at the Tourist Office. Music and dance performances are given in July and August at the Roman amphitheatre in nearby Itálica.

Bullfights

During the Feria de Abril these take place daily, featuring the top *toreros*, and weekly or more often for the rest of the summer at the Maestranza.

Fiestas

The world-famous **Feria de Abril** takes place from Tuesday to Sunday two weeks after Easter. It consists of continuous dancing and singing, eating and drinking considerable quantities of sherry and other local wines, at the brightly lit and gaily decorated fairgrounds. Well-to-do families, social clubs and businesses set up private *casetas* or tents where they entertain guests non-stop. Interiors of the *casetas* are often decorated with chandeliers, antique furniture and priceless paintings. Visitors come from all over Europe as well as people from all over western Andalusia, who are decked out in traditional costume. Girls with carnations in their hair, wearing flouncy flamenco dresses in bright reds, greens, yellows and blues, ride around the fairgrounds on beautiful horses sitting behind Andalusian gentlemen in the saddle, who wear the broad-brimmed Córdoban hat and the tight-fitting *traje corto* (short jacket). The wail and stomp of flamenco music goes on till dawn every day.

No other city in Spain can offer as much pageantry as Seville does during its **Holy Week** processions. Each of the fifty-five brotherhoods parades its favourite statue or statue-group through darkened streets in one or more of over a hundred processions during the week, on flower-decked, often canopied, platforms crowded with glowing candles. A wealth of antique vestments, jewellery, and gold, silver and bronze-work adorn the statues. Members of the brotherhoods work in teams, or *cuadrillas*, carrying these platforms on their backs, but you won't see them because they are hidden under the skirts that hang down from the edges. Some of the statues weigh over a ton. From time to time a lone, spontaneous singer will bring a procession to a halt as he or she chants from a balcony a haunting *saeta* dedicated to the Virgin Mary or Christ. Marching bands play tunes of varying tempos depending on the procession and the images, and the Virgins are made to dance in time to the music.

Shopping

Mantillas and flamenco dresses: Feliciano Foronda, Calle Alvarez Quintero 52. Or Pardales, Calle Cuna 23. Modern tapestries: Julián Ruesga, Calle San Diego 8. Chinaware, ceramics: shops along the Calle Sierpes. La Cartuja tableware is of excellent quality. Bridles, saddles and other horse-related items: Guarnicionería San Pablo, Calle Bailén. Or El Caballo, Calle Antonio Díaz 7.

Markets

Handicraft, antiques and junk: Sunday mornings at Alameda de Hércules. Flea market: Thursday mornings at Calle Feria. Pet market including birds, dogs and cats: Sunday mornings at Plaza de la Alfalfa.

What NOT to do

A word of advice: both by day, and especially by night, be on your guard in Seville against petty crime. Handbag-snatching, pickpocketing and thefts of and from cars, are not at all exceptional in Seville, whose underworld regrettably has earned it the reputation for being the worst town in this respect in Spain. The better hotels post warnings to guests. Basically, these are the rules you should follow for your own safety and security anywhere, but especially in Seville:

● Leave your passport, jewellery and all but a small amount of cash in the hotel safe.

● Make sure you have a record of the numbers of your credit cards and the numbers to call if they are stolen.

● Do not carry a handbag on the street, but if you do, do not carry anything of value in it. If someone grabs the strap, let it go as there have been many cases of women being dragged along the street and injured by a purse-snatcher riding on the back of a motorcycle. This is, in fact, the most common form of robbery; it is known as the *tirón* (pull).

● Do not leave anything of value in sight in your car, even when you are in it. A common method of robbery is for a man on a motorcycle to smash a window – even in the brief moments a car is stopped at a traffic light – grab the loot and roar off. They will try for anything that looks remotely promising.

● Do not leave anything in your car, including the car radio, even if it is screwed down, when the car is parked in the street. Seville's thieves will select cars with out-of-town or foreign number plates because they assume there may be luggage inside. Too often they are right.

● Do not park your car in the street. The best solution is a hotel garage. Never leave the car unlocked, not even for a moment.

● Do not wear a necklace. Seville's small-time crooks have become very skilled at removing a necklace with one quick, sharp jerk. Apart from losing it, you could be hurt or pulled to the ground as the thief tugs at it.

Nightlife

Nightclubs (among others): **Califas**, Calle Menéndez y Pelayo 50; **Escala's**, Calle Asunción 79.

Live music bars: **Patio de San Laureano**, Calle Alfonso XII, corner of Calle Torneo. Mostly jazz. **Líneas**, Calle Castilla 145. Jazz at weekends, flamenco on Thursdays. **La Carbonería**, Calle Levies 18. Modern, pop and oldies.

A few of the many discotheques: **Maestranza**, Carretera de Jerez s/n. Dine and dance. Live music occasionally. **Piruetas**, Calle Asunción 3. Popular with the young crowd. **El Coto**, Calle Luis Montoto 118 (basement of Hotel Los Lebreros). Mixed crowd but lively.

Where to stay

The area with the most hotels lies within a radius of about four streets from the Cathedral, but there are hotels all over the city.

Top range

Alfonso XIII, Calle San Fernando 2. Tel. (954) 222 850, telex 72725. The best hotel in Seville. Built for the 1929 World's Fair in neo-Mudéjar style, it exudes a feeling of luxury. Central, air-conditioned, with pool, shops, lively bar, television in rooms, good but pricey restaurant, efficient service. And the stand for horse-drawn taxis is right outside the door. From 15,000 to 22,000 ptas.

Macarena, Calle San Juan Ribera 2. Tel. (954) 375 700, telex 72815. In the Macarena district near what is left of the old walls. Pool, air-conditioning, garage, pricey restaurant. From 8,800 to 16,000 ptas.

Inglaterra, Plaza Nueva 7. Tel. (954) 224 970, telex 72244. Old but classic on a pretty square in the centre, garage, pricey restaurant. From 8,300 to 12,300 ptas.

Los Lebreros, Calle Luis Morales 2. Tel. (954) 579 400, telex 72772. A convention hotel, above all, in the modern part of town. Garage, air-conditioning, pool, bar, pricey restaurant. From 11,500 to 19,000 ptas.

Mid-range

Bécquer, Calle Reyes Católicos 4. Tel. (954) 228 900. Just across the bridge from Triana, near the Córdoba Railway Station. Pleasant service, garage, air-conditioning, bar. From 4,900 ptas (November to 11 April) to 7,400 ptas (high season).

Fernando III, Calle San José 21. Tel. (954) 217 307, telex 72491. Garage, pool, bar. From 5,500 ptas (6 May to March) to 8,000 ptas (rest of the year).

Monte Carmelo, Calle Turia 9. Tel. (954) 279 000. In the modern part of town near the fairgrounds. The bullfighters' favourite in Seville. Garage, bar, air-conditioning. From 5,000 ptas (5 May to 11 April) to 7,700 ptas (rest of the year).

Where to eat
Pricey

Rincón de Curro, Calle Virgen de Luján 45. Tel. (954) 540 251. Closed on Sunday evenings. One of the finest places to eat Spanish food in Seville. Good meats, very complete wine cellar, very good service.

La Dorada, Calle Virgen de Aguas Santas 6. Tel. (954) 455 100. Closed on Sunday evenings and all of August. Fresh fish as you like it, fried, baked in salt, grilled, in fish soup or otherwise.

Moderate

Casa Serna, Calle Bécquer 4. Tel. (954) 370 338. Closed on Sundays. In the heart of the Macarena district, patronized by bullfighters, this place has good *tapas*, atmosphere and accessible prices. Tends to be crowded. Bull's tail soup, fish dishes are best.

Sand, Sierra and Solera
Jerez de la Frontera

The biggest city in the region of Cádiz (population 176,238), it is 108 km south of Seville on the A-4; or 646 km south of Madrid on N-IV to Seville and A-4 to Jerez. The centre of the sherry industry, Jerez is a very beautiful, very old town (the Romans imported vinum ceretanum) full of flowers and streets lined with orange trees and, in the autumn, heady with the aroma of the wine fermenting in the bodegas all over town.

The old Arabic name for Jerez was Scheris and it is its anglicized version, Sherry, which has become famous as the fine wine. Unlike most other wines, sherry needs to be in contact with the air to mature; so bungs are placed only loosely over the hole in the top of each butt. Between 5 and 10 per cent of the wine evaporates away every year. The winemakers refer to this as 'the angels' share'. With nearly 500 million litres of wine waiting quietly to be old enough and good enough to leave the bodegas of Jerez, Puerto de Santa María and Sanlúcar de Barrameda, the angels' cut is almost forty million litres each year.

Main areas

Jerez is an old city with many narrow, winding streets, still surrounded in part by its medieval walls. In contrast, more modern areas of the city are crossed by broad boulevards. The principal route through the centre begins on the north side with the wide Avenida Alvaro Domecq, a continuation of the N-IV that starts beside the Hotel Jerez and continues past the González Hontoria Park and El Bosque restaurant, the Plaza del Caballo, the Sherry Council headquarters, all on the left, into a plaza in front of the Santo Domingo Church. It then goes on to the Calle Larga and the Plaza del Arenal, and on to the Calle Pérez Galdós, which passes by the Alcázar on your right, and on to Cuatro Caminos, the intersection of roads leading to Puerto de Santa María, Sanlúcar and other nearby towns.

The Calle Larga is in the commercial part of town. Shops line both it and the streets on either side. The main square, with a series of arcades on its west side which are now being restored, is the charming Arenal Plaza. In its middle there is a statue of General Primo de Rivera, a native son and the dictator of the early part of this century (see p. 20) and fountains in the gardens. The railway station is on the east side of town, 1 km from the centre. The airport is 9 km to the north, just off the east side of the N-IV. In addition to El Bosque, already mentioned, there are several restaurants and *tapa* bars in the vicinity of the Plaza del Caballo, and a few outside town on the road to Sanlúcar. There is, however, no clearly defined restaurant area.

The bodegas are all over town and many of them are in historic buildings. The fairgrounds are in the González Hontoria Park. There is a partial ring road that skirts Jerez to the west, which reduces the amount of through traffic in the town. This links up with the road leading to the A-4 motorway near the Hotel Jerez. There is also a formula-one automobile race track a few kilometres east of the city, and the way to it is adequately signposted.

History

Jerez may have been an Iberian community and its grape vines were probably brought by Phoenicians. It is not until Roman times, however, that the existence of this city is certain. From that time on, Jerez has been dedicated primarily to the production of wine, and proof of sherry's popularity in ancient times has been found on amphoras from wrecked Roman ships, which bear inscriptions indicating that they contained wine from Jerez. Pliny also mentioned it. Even under Arab domination Jerez continued to produce and export wine. José María Quiros, a chemist from Jerez who has spent a lot of time researching the subject, says the typical stemmed, thin, slightly bulbous sherry glass, the *catavinos*, was invented by the Arabs because, since drinking is prohibited by their religion, they could inhale the aroma, and drink such a small quantity that their sin would be only a small one.

England has imported sherry since the twelfth century, and still remains a most important export market. Shakespeare, Baudelaire, Washington Irving and Edgar Allan Poe have all sung the praises of Jerez and its wine.

What to see

Above all, the bodegas! This is not just a wine visit. The wineries are

Jerez's *raison d'être*. The bodegas in Jerez are not cellars; rather, the wine is matured above ground in large brick, stone and masonry buildings with high ceilings. Inside, it is cool; and straw mats, placed over a few, usually round windows, high in the walls, filter the sunlight and let in the air. The butts are lined up in long rows on their sides, stacked in tiers, three or four rows high. The sand floor of the passageways between the rows of butts is regularly sprinkled with water from a clay jug to maintain the right level of humidity.

Most of the bodegas admit visitors, but you should telephone ahead to arrange your visit. Most of them also sell wine to visitors at low prices. Here is a list of just a few of the many sherry bodegas, large and small, from each of the three towns of the sherry district. If the one which produces your favourite brand is not on this very brief list, ask at the Tourist Office or at your hotel for its address and telephone number.

Jerez de la Frontera

Emilio M. Hidalgo SA, Calle Clavel 29. Tel. (956) 341 078.

González Byass SA, Calle Manuel María González 12. Tel. (956) 340 000. Visits by prior arrangement, from 11 a.m. to 1 p.m. Monday to Friday except in August.

John Harvey & Sons (España) Ltd, Calle Arcos 53. Tel. (956) 346 000. Visits by prior arrangement, from 8 a.m. to 1 p.m. Monday to Friday except in August.

Pedro Domecq SA, Calle San Ildefonso 3. Tel. (956) 331 800. Visits by prior arrangement from 10 a.m. to 2 p.m. Monday to Friday except 25 July to 18 August.

Sandeman Coprimar SA, Calle Pizarro 10. Tel. (956) 301 100. Visits by prior arrangement from 9 a.m. to 1 p.m. except 20 July to 20 August.

Puerto de Santa María

Duff Gordon & Co, Calle Fernán Caballero 6. Tel. (956) 855 111.

Osborne y Cía SA, Calle Fernán Caballero 3. Tel. (956) 855 311. Visits by prior arrangement, from 9 a.m. to 2 p.m. Monday to Friday except in August.

Sanlúcar de Barrameda

Antonio Barbadillo SA, Calle Luis de Eguilaz 11. Tel. (956) 360 894. Telephone in advance.

Bodegas de los Infantes Orleans-Borbon SA, Calle Baños 1. Tel. (956) 360 352. Visits by prior arrangement, from 11 a.m. to 2 p.m. Monday to Friday.

You should also see:

Alcázar

This eleventh-century Moorish fortress originally contained a mosque which was converted into the Chapel of Santa María la Real by its Christian conquerors. It is in the process of being restored at present.

Churches

● **San Dionisio** (Plaza de la Asunción) is in Jerez-type Mudéjar style, with eighteenth-century Baroque modifications. It has a solid Mudéjar tower, more a watchtower than a belltower.

● **Santiago** was built in stages between 1430 and the late eighteenth century, with beautiful Gothic doorways.

● **San Miguel** (Plaza Primo de Rivera), perhaps the loveliest of them all, was begun in 1482 and added to, right up to the last century. It has fascinating sculptures forming part of the ceiling of one of the cupolas, Plateresque doorways and a mammoth, carved altarpiece.

● The glorious, Gothic **Cathedral** (Plaza de Arroyo), formerly known as La Colegiata, with a stairway leading up to the front door that is a monument in itself, was built between the sixteenth and eighteenth centuries.

● The **Carthusian Monastery**, 5 km east of Jerez, was built in 1477 with later Baroque additions, and with a charming Gothic patio. Sorry, men only for this visit! Women are not allowed inside the monastery.

Excursions

Puerto de Santa María

This town (population 54,437), 11 km south on N-IV, is an ancient port still in use for shipping wine abroad, though much of it now goes overland. It has several long beaches of fine sand. Its streets are characteristically narrow but curiously as straight as a die. Among its historic buildings are the twelfth-century Cathedral, the small San Marcos Castle whose battlements are adorned with words of prayer (open Saturdays only, from 10 a.m. to 1 p.m.), and the century-old bullring, one of Spain's largest.

One-way streets and streets that go nowhere will frustrate you everywhere in Puerto de Santa María. If you are driving, you would do well to park your car outside the town and take a taxi to wherever you want to go.

The Valdelagrana beach area, where many houses and blocks of flats have been built over the past twenty years, forms part of Puerto de Santa María, but the best way to get there, coming from Jerez, is to go past the indicated turn-off for Puerto de Santa María and to turn right about 1 km further south, at the junction where the Hotel Caballo Blanco stands.

The opening in the summer of 1986 of Puerto Sherry marked an important step in realizing the tourist potential of this area with its year-round mild climate. Puerto Sherry, on the coast near Puerto de Santa María, is a complete yachting base with space for 1,000 vessels of varying sizes, which will eventually become a completely self-contained resort. It will have a 300-room hotel, an eighteen-hole golf course, tennis courts, indoor and outdoor swimming pools, theatre, shops, houses and flats. There is no other facility on Europe's Atlantic coast to compare with this ambitious project, financed by Spanish and Arab capital.

Sanlúcar de Barrameda

Some 23 km north-west of Jerez on C-440, or 21 km north of Puerto de Santa María on a local road, this is one of the most beautiful old Andalusian towns you will ever find. The population is 40,496. On the way, whether you come from Jerez or from Puerto de Santa María, you will pass kilometres and kilometres of vineyards, stretching over the rolling white hills as far as you can see. This is because the vineyards lie mostly on the west, or seaward, side of Jerez, where they benefit from the mists at night.

Sanlúcar is a town of fish and wine, and the majority of its working population dedicates itself to one or other of those activities. Its human sized main square, lined by green-shuttered, whitewashed buildings not more than three storeys tall, is for pedestrians only, to stroll around or sit at a table in the shade of towering palms, sipping the light, dry manzanilla wine that Sanlúcar is famous for, while children play around a tinkling fountain. Manzanilla is similar to a fino sherry, but differs in that it has benefited from being matured in the bodegas of Sanlúcar, where the natural yeasts are different, and some claim to be able to taste the influence of the salty sea breezes.

The modern part of town is equally delightful, consisting mostly of houses in flowery gardens close to the beaches. Sanlúcar's tiny yacht club perches on the only rock in sight on the coast at the mouth of the Guadalquivir. In summer, beach shelters, in colourful striped canvas, ranged in rows, look out on the water.

What to do
Horse show

An equine spectacle unmatched anywhere west of Vienna is 'The Dancing Horses of Andalusia', the show staged at the Las Cadenas Riding Theatre in Jerez, home of the Andalusian School of Equestrian Art, combining music, costume and perfectly-trained horses for an unforgettable hour's entertainment. Check with the Tourist Office for dates and times.

Water sports

All kinds within easy reach. In addition to beaches at Puerto de Santa María and Sanlúcar, there are equally good and large beaches at Rota (30 km) and Chipiona (33 km).

Fiestas
Horse Fair

The people of Jerez will tell you they are proud of three things: their wine, their horses and their women, in that order. They have a right to be proud of all three. Jerez is the foremost horse-breeding centre in the country. The biggest celebration of the year in Jerez is the Horse Fair, a moveable feast which takes place about three weeks after Easter. The fair officially lasts only six days, but, in fact, the festivities begin about ten days earlier and continue non-stop, with international riding competitions, car and motorcycle races, special flamenco shows, awards for show horses, contests for horse-drawn carriage teams, and a series of bullfights, at one of which a prize is awarded to the rancher with the best fighting bulls of the year.

To keep the party lively, clubs and bodegas set up *casetas* at the fairgrounds where there is music, wine and *tapas* all afternoon and most of the night, and the *caballeros* parade their señoritas sitting behind them on their lovely horses up and down the brightly decorated main street of the fair. Elaborate horse-drawn carriages, immaculately maintained and polished, some drawn by as many as six matched steeds, also circulate through the fairgrounds in the afternoon and evening.

Sherry harvest fiesta

This *fiesta*, held in September, usually around the 10th, celebrates the birth of the new wine. The four-day celebration includes an impressive ceremony in which newly-harvested grapes are pressed by dancing workmen. From these is made the first must, which is blessed immediately, in front of the Cathedral as 1,000 doves are released, each carrying a line or two of poetry about the new wine banded to one leg. The old Cathedral bell clangs and the town's orchestra blares out a musical tribute to the new wine. There are also bullfights, a parade and other events, plus a round of fabulous private parties given by the owners and managers of the major bodegas. The guests always include dignitaries from another city, country or region, since the harvest fair is dedicated each year to a different place. Among cities honoured in recent years have been Oporto, Berlin and London.

Flamenco Festival

Jerez is known as 'the cradle of flamenco'. Many of the greatest flamenco singers, dancers and guitarists have come from Jerez, and the festival in August is the place to see the established favourites as well as the newcomers in action.

Feria

Horse races on the beach, bullfights, flamenco, yacht races and other events at the end of August in Sanlúcar.

Carnival

Masquerade balls, *casetas*, flamenco and other events in Puerto de Santa María on the weekend before the beginning of Lent.

Holy Week

Processions of richly garbed and decorated holy images, borne by the brotherhoods of Jerez through the narrow streets, with spontaneous flamenco-music tributes from spectators and considerable pageantry.

Shopping

Wine, superior wine vinegar, and leather trappings for horses are good buys. Jerez market day is on Thursdays in the González-Hontoria Park, mostly food and clothing on sale.

Nightlife

Bahía de Cádiz Casino, Puerto de Santa María, offers various types of gambling, swimming pool, shops, disco and restaurant.

Joy Sherry, one of the most elegant discos anywhere, operates outdoors for most of the year in Puerto de Santa María, in the gardens of a real floodlit palace, reminiscent of Versailles.

Where to stay

With the notable exception of the Hotel Jerez, there are few hotels in Jerez worth recommending. This list includes hotels in Puerto de Santa María and Sanlúcar, which are covered under excursions from Jerez.

Top range

Jerez, Avenida Alvaro Domecq 35. Tel. (56) 330 600, telex 75059. A cosy hotel of moderate size that succeeds in giving you the impression that it is small and has to look after only you. Beautiful garden and pool, lively bar where winesellers and cattle dealers seal their bargains with a fino sherry and where bullfighters dress for the *corridas* in the small but important ring of Jerez. Marvellous breakfasts. The restaurant is good but overpriced. From 11,000 to 14,000 ptas.

Melia Caballo Blanco, N-IV, km 658 (Puerto de Santa María).

Tel. (956) 863 745, telex 76070. A hotel with various rooms grouped around a garden and pool amid lollipop pines, near Valdelagrana beach rather than the town centre. Air-conditioning, moderate restaurant. From 7,450 to 9,150 ptas.

Mid-range **Capele**, Calle Corredera 58. Tel. (956) 346 400. A small, comfortable residence hotel, central, with garage, bar and air-conditioning. From 5,775 to 7,500 ptas.

Aloha, Carretera Madrid-Cadiz, km 637. Tel. (956) 332 500. Roadside inn on the ring road on the north side of Jerez, with swimming pool, bar, air-conditioning and an economical restaurant. From 4,700 to 5,350 ptas.

Garage Centro, Calle Doña Blanca 10. Tel. (956) 332 450. Very elementary, central, garage. From 1,700 ptas (without private bath) to 2,700 ptas (with bath).

El Coloso, Calle Pedro Alonso 13. Tel. (956) 349 008. One-star official rating, clean. From 2,600 ptas (21 September to 19 March, without private bath) to 3,000 ptas (rest of the year, with bath).

Puertobahía, Avenida La Paz s/n. Tel. (956) 862 721, Valdelagrana (Puerto de Santa María). On the beach, with pool, children's pool, tennis, sauna, shops, and a moderate restaurant, but it caters for tour groups. From 4,100 ptas (21 September to March) to 5,000 ptas (rest of the year).

Guadalquivir, Calzada del Ejercito s/n (Sanlúcar de Barrameda). Tel. (956) 360 742. Close to the centre, bar, air-conditioning, economical restaurant – but the disco makes the whole hotel bounce. From 3,300 to 5,300 ptas.

Bottom range **Gover**, Calle Honsario 6. Tel. (956) 332 600. Central, garage. A modest hostel. From 1,400 ptas (October to March, without private bath) to 1,800 (rest of the year, with bath).

Where to eat The people of Jerez like their *perscaditos* – fresh small fish of several varieties – fried while you wait, to take home in a thick paper cone. One of the most popular spots to go for this take-away service is El Boquerón de Plata on the Plaza Santiago. Another characteristic of western Andalusia is the *venta*. A *venta* is a roadside inn which usually serves a menu limited to what is available locally. Way out in the country you might be offered fresh eggs, rabbit, vegetables from the garden and so forth. Most *ventas*, particularly those far from the cities, are pleasant, economical places to eat. As for restaurants, they have them too, and how!

Pricey **El Bosque**, Avenida Alvaro Domecq (Parque González Hontoria). Tel. (956) 303 333. Good food with careful service and an ample menu. The fino is ice-cold as it should be and the langoustines are the biggest, most impressive-looking in the market.

Venta Antonio, Carretera Jerez-Sanlúcar, km 5. Tel. (956) 330 535. Closed on Mondays in winter. The best place to eat a seafood dinner in Jerez. Always a good selection of the day's catch, and meat dishes too, for the occasional customer who orders them. Wide choice of sherries and Riojan wines.

Moderate

Don Peppone, Calle Cáceres 1, Valdelagrana (Puerto de Santa María). Tel. (956) 861 099. Closed on Sundays. Small, intimate, attentive service, good food, in a quiet residential area. Tables inside and on the terrace. The seafood kebab is a speciality. Varied wine list.

Bigote, Bajo de Guia (Sanlúcar de Barrameda). Tel. (956) 362 696. Closed on Sundays. There is a printed menu but the real one depends on the day's catch by fishermen living near this unpretentious little restaurant in an alley by the beach, which serves sublimely delicious langoustines and *acedías* (a small local variety of sole) from the Bay of Cádiz. Wash your meal down with the delicate manzanilla of Sanlúcar.

Arcos de la Frontera

Arcos (population 24,902), is 31 km east of Jerez on N-342. It is a white town with one long, stone-paved main street like a ramp, which leads up a steep hill to a square at the end, perched on a dizzyingly high cliff overlooking the River Guadalete and the green fields in its valley.

The town juts out into nothing, like the prow of a ship. Narrow, sinuous sidestreets and some of the houses that line them also look out over precipices. A stout stone balustrade lines one side of the square. The other three sides are occupied by a privately owned, and lived-in, castle, a Gothic church, the Town Hall and a parador.

When they run the bulls on Easter Sunday and for the *fiestas* of the town's patron, St Michael, on 29 September, girls as well as boys race down the hill in front of the horns. The streets are so narrow and twisting, there is not much room. The way some of the runners grab overhanging balconies and swing out of danger with a split second to spare is a show in itself; watched, of course, from the safety of a barred window or a balcony.

Where to stay:
top range

Parador Casa del Corregidor, Plaza del Cabildo s/n. Tel. (956) 700 500. The views alone are worth a stop, if only for a *tapa* in its moderate restaurant, and a *copa* of sherry. Contrary to appearances, it should not fall off the cliff, because it was recently closed for a year or more, precisely to reinforce the foundations. From 7,500 ptas (January to March) to 8,500 ptas (rest of the year).

El Bosque

This little white town (population 1,742), 28 km east of Arcos on C-344, is on the slope of a forested mountain. Its neat streets climb past window grilles bursting with dark pink, hanging geraniums. The southernmost trout fishing reserve in Europe is on its doorstep, and the Cortés de la Frontera National Hunting Reserve is nearby. The village of Benamahoma, 7 km to the east, holds a little-known *fiesta* on the first Sunday in August, re-enacting battles between Christians and Moors. Guess who wins.

Where to stay:
mid-range

Las Truchas, Avenida de la Diputación 1. Tel. (956) 723 086. Absolute quiet, forested mountain country for hiking, hunting and fishing. The name of the hotel tells you the speciality of its moderately-priced restaurant: freshly-caught trout. This is an eleven-room parador run by the provincial rather than the national administration, but it is being enlarged. From 3,400 to 4,000 ptas.

Grazalema

Grazalema (population 2,300), 30 km east of El Bosque on C-344, is one of the prettiest mountain towns in Spain. It is also the wettest, because it is close to the point on San Cristobal mountain with the highest annual rainfall in Spain, a paradox in this area which otherwise is one of the sunniest parts of the country. A little further up the slopes is a forest of Pinsapos, a type of conifer which grows nowhere else in Europe except here and on another mountaintop in Granada. Not surprisingly, the outstanding handicraft item in Grazalema is blankets. Some families from Jerez retreat to this cool town in the summer.

La Pileta cave

Near the village of Benaoján, 27 km to the east (C-344 east for 7 km past the point where it joins C-339, then right on a local road which passes through Montejaque), is La Pileta cave, which contains some still very visible Palaeolithic drawings of horses, deer and other animals.

Where to stay: mid-range

Grazalema, Carretera Comarcal de Aceso, km 344. Tel. (956) 111 342. Superb views, economical restaurant, garden. Only twelve rooms, but it is being enlarged. From 3,250 ptas (October to mid-March), to 3,920 ptas (high season).

Ubrique

Ubrique (population 16,327) is 27 km south-west of Grazalema on C-3331. It is the principal centre in all Spain for small handmade leather goods of all kinds. Townspeople work in their homes, turning out handbags, wallets, briefcases and many other items. They also make artistic tooled leather bindings for books and will produce specific items to order.

Where to stay

There is only one hotel in Ubrique, so book ahead. In the event that it is full, the hotel at El Bosque (see p. 161) is only 12 km to the north-west via a local road that crosses the River Tavizna (not the road you came on). Either hotel can tell you where to buy quality leather items at prices far below those of big-city shops.

Mid-range

Ocurris, Avenida Solís Pascual 49. Tel. (956) 110 973. A central leather merchants' hotel in the midst of lovely mountain scenery. You will be thankful for the central heating in the winter. From 2,600 ptas.

Algeciras

Algeciras (population 86,042) is 93 km south of Ubrique (C-3331 south to junction with N-340, then right on N-340 south-west around the bay); or 712 km south-west of Madrid via Málaga.

This is one of Spain's major ports but has little to offer tourists except excursions by ferry to the Spanish enclave of Ceuta, a duty-free port across the straits, or to other North African ports such as Tangier. The trip to Tangier takes two and a half to three hours. There is a hydrofoil, leaving on alternate days from Algeciras or Tarifa, which cuts down the time to less than one hour.

Algeciras is across the bay from Gibraltar. Lack of town planning has resulted in an urban hodge-podge, and the city's characteristic old centre, where most of the shops are, is screened by tall, nondescript buildings on the waterfront. Heavy industry has restricted good beach space to Getares at the mouth of the bay.

There are huge traffic jams in July and August when tens of thousands of Moroccans working in Europe go home for holidays by car or train and cross the straits by ferry. Algeciras is mobbed by whole families of North Africans, camping out on the streets beside or inside their overladen cars, whose budgets do not permit them to pay for a hotel. Ferry services cannot cope with the seasonal demand.

Where to stay:
top range

Reina Cristina, Paseo de la Conferencia. Tel. (956) 603 622, telex 78057. Far from the madding crowd, and never better said. On a hill overlooking the port, surrounded by great pines, this old-fashioned hotel shows that good service never goes out of fashion. Pool, tennis, shops, English breakfasts. From 9,900 ptas (October to mid-March) to 12,950 ptas (high season).

Mid-range

Las Yucas, Calle Agustín Bálsamo 2. Tel. (956) 663 250. A small, comfortable hotel near the railway station, with garden, bar and garage. From 4,500 ptas (January to May) to 5,500 ptas (rest of the year).

Octavio, Calle San Bernardo 1. Tel. (956) 652 461. Central, garage, bar. Adequate. From 6,100 ptas (January to June) to 6,500 ptas (rest of the year).

Alarde, Calle Alfonso XI 4. Tel. (956) 660 408. Central, garage, bar. From 4,450 ptas (16 September to 14 July) to 5,100 ptas (rest of the year).

Al-Mar, Avenida de la Marina 2. Tel. (956) 654 661. Central, garage, bar, economical restaurant. From 4,675 ptas (January to 14 July) to 5,425 ptas (rest of the year).

Where to eat:
pricey

Marea Baja, Calle Trafalgar 2. Tel. (956) 663 654. Closed on Sundays. Fine centrally located seafood restaurant with maritime décor.

Los Remos, Playa de Guadarranque (San Roque), 16 km east of Algeciras. Tel. (956) 760 812. Closed on Sunday evenings except in August. This restaurant on the beach, on the opposite side of the bay from Algeciras, is run by the same family as the preceding one; but this is the classic good seafood restaurant in the Algeciras Bay area, the standard by which others are measured. Nothing but the freshest of seafood, deliciously prepared.

Tarifa

Tarifa (population 8,295), 23 km south-west of Algeciras on N-340, has enjoyed a real economic revival since windsurfing became popular. The constant winds which funnel through the Straits of Gibraltar and whistle past the old pink Moorish castle in the Tarifa port always used to be a drawback, until windsurfing became all the rage. Aficionados of the sport say Tarifa is ideal because of the mild climate and reliable wind. Scuba divers also flock here because of the wide variety of sea creatures.

Here, Tarifa's Governor Alfonso Pérez de Guzmán made a costly stand against the Arabs when they besieged the city in 1292. They led his nine-year-old son, a prisoner, to a point outside the walls where Guzmán could see him; the Moorish leader told Guzmán to surrender the city or he would order the child's throat cut. Guzmán defiantly tossed his own knife out of a window, saying, 'Use this'. He then had to witness his own child's execution. The Spanish leader went down in history as 'Guzmán the Good'. In the castle, Calle Sancho IV El Bravo s/n (open Sunday to Wednesday, and all holidays, from 9.30 a.m. to 1.30 p.m.), you can see the window from which, it is said, Guzmán watched; it is bricked up.

What to do

About 12 km to the west, at a beach called Bolonia, are the ruins of a Roman city. There is also good underwater fishing at Bolonia.

Tarifa is the scene of a National Folk Music Festival in July.

Where to stay:
top range

Hurricane, Carretera de Cádiz, km 77. Tel. (956) 684 919. The windsurfers' hangout. Garden, pool, bar, moderate restaurant. From 6,250 ptas (October to 25 April) to 8,250 ptas (high season).

Mid-range

Balcón de España, Carretera de Cádiz, km 76. Tel. (956) 684 326. Closed November to March. Friendly service, moderate restaurant, bar, great views, garden, pool, children's pool. From 4,900 to 5,900 ptas.

Dos Mares, Carretera de Cádiz, km 78. Tel. (956) 684 035. Closed November to March. Garden, nice views, pool, moderate restaurant. From 5,000 to 5,500 ptas.

Mesón de Sancho, Carretera de Cádiz, km 94. Tel. (956) 684 900. Scenic views, garden, pool, tennis, bar, good, moderately-priced restaurant. From 3,700 ptas (mid-October to mid-June) to 4,250 ptas (rest of the year).

Where to eat:
moderate

Mesón de Sancho, address and telephone as above. Largely international cooking with some local dishes.

La Codorniz, Carretera de Cádiz, km 77. Tel. (956) 684 744. Closed in February. Seafood and small game.

La Tasca de Chan, Calle Batalla del Salado 57. Tel. (956) 684 223. Closed in November and every Wednesday. Fish, fried, baked or in sauce.

Zahara de los Atunes

Zahara (population 1,900) is 38 km west of Tarifa (N-340 to a local road past Tahivilla, with signpost indicating Zahara de los Atunes; left, or south, on this road, passing through La Zarzuela). Zahara's economy is based on tuna fish. Its fishermen capture the tuna in nets staked out to snare them as they run through the Straits of Gibraltar. Bars in town offer *tapas*, in season, of fresh tuna and baby shark.

Unlike Bolonia, Zahara's Atlantic beach is shielded from the wind. With beautiful fine white sand, Zahara offers you a beach all to yourself. Only a few German tourists, some of them bathing nude, seem to have discovered this area. There is a hotel and housing development in the hills at the eastern end of the beach, and many of the people who live there bathe in front of the hotel or on a sheltered beach below the estate, around a point from the vast Zahara beach. West of there, the empty beach stretches for many kilometres.

Where to stay: | **Atlanterra Palacio Sol**, Bahía de la Plata. Tel. (956) 432 608.
top range | Closed November to April. A self-contained holiday complex with opportunities for various sports, shops, and a pricey restaurant. From 11,000 to 15,400 ptas.

Mid-range | **Antonio**, Carretera de Atlanterra, km 1. Tel. (956) 431 214. Only eight rooms, so book ahead. Standing alone in its garden on the beach, this pleasant little inn with good food, good service and spacious rooms is great for a get-away-from-it-all holiday. Wonderful value for your money. From 3,200 ptas (October to May) to 4,500 ptas (rest of the year).

Castro, Calle Gobernador s/n (in the *pueblo* of Zahara). Tel. (956) 430 248. A plain hostel with an economical restaurant. Some rooms are in an annexe. Air-conditioning would be a big improvement. From 1,800 ptas (mid-October to March, without bath) to 3,250 ptas (rest of the year, with bath).

Where to eat: | **Antonio**, Carretera de Atlanterra, km 1. Telephone as above.
moderate | Closed in November. Complete menu dominated by the freshest seafood, cooked whole or in soups and stews. Good wine selection.

Barbate de Franco | This fishing town (population 20,849) is 13 km north-west of Zahara on a local road following the beach. There are several *chiringuitos*, simple restaurants in sheds on the beach, which serve mostly fish and salad.

About 13 km to the west, along a local road, is another excellent and scarcely used beach, Los Caños de Meca, near Cape Trafalgar, where Admiral Nelson defeated the French and Spanish fleets but was mortally wounded in 1805. A few kilometres further up the coast is yet another beautiful, almost deserted beach, that of El Palmar. At weekends, families from the nearby town of Vejer go down to the beaches at El Palmar and Los Caños de Meca.

Barbate is also the scene of a maritime procession, with all the fishing boats decked out in colourful pennants, in celebrations coinciding with the feastday of the Virgin of Carmen in mid-July. In mid-August there is a huge sardine festival on the beach.

Where to eat: | **Gadir**, Calle Padre Castrillón 15. Tel. (956) 430 800. Closed in
moderate | May and November, also every Tuesday. A touch of class in an unsophisticated town. International food with some Andalusian specialities.

Vejer | Vejer (population 8,119) is 10 km north-west of Barbate on C-343; a fascinating white *pueblo* on a mountaintop overlooking fertile fields and olive groves, it should not be missed. This pretty town is ideal for walking around and you can drop into its bars, like Esquinita, for a *tapa* of fried fish. Vejer's Divino Salvador Church was erected on the foundations of a mosque. The ruins of a Moorish castle brood over the town.

Vejer goes from one *fiesta* to another. On Easter Sunday a bull, whose horns are tipped with wooden balls, is turned loose in the streets. During the town's Spring Fair in April, several bulls, tied together with a long rope, are turned loose. Festivities in honour of the Virgin of the Olives take place on 7 May and 15–24 August, with *casetas* and plenty of live flamenco music. Thursday is market day.

Where to eat:
moderate

Antiguo Mesón de La Barca de Vejer, Carretera N-340, km 36 (at the foot of the mountain). Tel. (956) 450 369. Good service. Ten rooms are also available for travellers.

Conil

Conil (population 13,289), 21 km east of Vejer (N-340 east to Casa de Postas, then left), is a small fishing town with several holiday complexes used by summer visitors. Plenty of room on the long white sandy beaches. Flamenco festival on 25 July. Annual fair second week of September.

Where to stay:
mid-range

Flamenco, Calle Fuente del Gallo s/n. Tel. (956) 440 711. Closed November to March. Surrounded by individual houses and its own garden, with pool, tennis courts, moderate restaurant. From 4,150 to 6,500 ptas.

Where to eat:
moderate

La Gaviota, Playa de Nuestra Señora de Las Virtudes. Tel. (956) 440 836. International cooking.

Cádiz

Cádiz (population 157,766) is 27 km from Conil (local road north-east to junction with N-340, then left on N-340); or 656 km from Madrid on N-IV.

Cádiz has a history that goes back 3,000 or more years and was already an important place in Biblical times but, like many a *grande dame*, she does not look her age. The city was controlled by the Phoenicians from the ninth century BC. Then the Carthaginians took over and later the Romans. The Visigoths destroyed it and the Arabs conquered it, rebuilding the city in part. The Vikings raided it, and Alfonso X, The Wise, took it from the Moors. The English sacked Cádiz in 1596. So much battling did not leave many of the old buildings standing. Another reason why there are not many reminders of Cádiz's long past is that the city has apparently been sinking into the sea for the past few millenia. It is situated on a club-shaped peninsula, almost an island, and divers have discovered the outline of old buildings and walls under the sea at the end of the peninsula.

Main areas

Because of its size, which is limited in the peninsula, it is not too hard a place to find your way around in. Both approach roads, one by land and the other which crosses the Bay of Cádiz on a toll bridge, lead to the same entrance. From the Plaza de la Victoria, which is roughly where the wide part of the club begins, you can follow the road around the periphery of the city, mostly alongside the water, and make a complete circuit.

The railway station is at the Cádiz end of the isthmus, on the northeast side. The port is also on the north-east side, about where the head of the club is bulging. From there you can take ships to the Canary Islands, coastal passenger ships to Málaga, Valencia, the Canaries and Barcelona, and a local passenger-ferry to Puerto de Santa María. The Hotel Atlántico, the city's best, is by the park at the Atlantic end of the peninsula, called Parque Genovés.

Don't expect to see a lot of greenery for there is not much room to spare on this little spit of land.

Buses leave either from the Comes Station, which is on the Plaza de Independencia, near the customs offices in the commercial port, as opposed to the fishing port, or from Los Amarillos Station, which is on Avenida Ramón de Carranza, the road you take to make a circuit of the city. The Los Amarillos buses go to Sanlúcar, the Comes buses go to other destinations.

The Tourist Office (Tel. [956] 211 313) is just off that circular route, on the Calle Calderón de la Barca 1, a street which runs off the Alameda de Apodaca, which is the first street actually bordering the sea that you come to as you make the external circuit of the city. The nearest airport is in Jerez, about 40 km to the north via the A-4 motorway and N-IV.

What to see

Drago tree

There are two monumental drago trees which have been growing in the gardens by the Alameda de Apodaca for more than 500 years. The drago is a species related to the cactus and it is native to the Canary Islands. Nobody knows who planted them in Cádiz.

Cathedral

The eighteenth-century Baroque Cathedral does not look like much on the outside, perhaps because other buildings crowd so close to it that you cannot really stand back and look at it; but inside, through a side door, it is worth a look. In the church treasury they have two huge monstrances, one of them known as 'The Million', which is only taken out for the Corpus Christi ceremonies in June. There is also a painting by Murillo of the Immaculate Conception and an ivory crucifix by Alonso Cano.

Museums

Municipal Historic Museum (El Museo Histórico Municipal), Calle Santa Inés (open Tuesday to Friday from 9 a.m. to 1 p.m. and from 4 to 7 p.m., mornings only on Saturdays and Sundays; closed on holidays) contains an unusual model of the city from the eighteenth century, carved in teak and ebony.

Archaeological Museum (El Museo Arqueológico), Plaza Mina (open on weekdays from 10 a.m. to 2 p.m. and from 5.30 to 8 p.m. and from 10 a.m. to 2 p.m. on Saturdays; closed on Sundays and holidays), has collections of tools and instruments from the Neolithic and Palae-olithic periods and two stone coffins, called the 'Anthropoid Coffins', from the fifth century BC.

Excursions

The ferry trip to Puerto de Santa María and back makes a delightful mini-cruise for a summer's afternoon.

Fuente Amarga

The only spa in Cádiz, Fuente Amarga (Bitter Fountain) is 23 km to the south near Chiclana. It has individual Italian Carrara marble bathtubs, each cut from a single block of stone. The naturally chlorinated and carbonated waters are said to be good for people with respiratory ailments and skin problems.

Medina-Sidonia

This town, 46 km to the east via Chiclana, offers mountaintop views of Cádiz and the coast. The locals are crazy about a Christmas sweet they make there called the *alfajor*. If you are there in season, try some.

What to do

Cádiz is a good-time town. By day it gives the impression of being sleepy. When you've spent a night there you know why. They have taken advantage of every square metre of the limited land space to provide 'essential' urban amenities, like bars, discos, casinos, sea food restaurants and, just to keep the *Gaditanos* from getting that penned-in feeling, they knock off for a few days of *fiestas* several times a year.

Fiestas

The major *fiestas* are: the Carnival of Cádiz, riotous celebrations the week before Lent, complete with elaborate masquerade parades and balls, during which, by tradition, anything goes; Holy Week, with the pageantry which is typically Andalusian; Corpus Christi in June, accompanied by religious processions, dancing, bullfights and other special events. In August, which the people of Cádiz call 'The Big Month', there are bullfights, special theatrical performances, music and dance spectacles, regattas in the bay, and the most important summer football tournament in Spain. In January there is a *fiesta* dedicated to the lowly sea urchin, which is another excuse for residents to stuff themselves with the succulent shellfish of the bay. In addition, there are any number of local *fiestas*, which fit in among the major ones.

Discos

Most discos here seem to attract mixed crowds, young and old; the one in the Isecotel Hotel, called La Boite, on the Paseo Marítimo, is one such.

Beaches

Most popular is Victoria beach, currently spick-and-span, with showers, changing rooms and other facilities, recently remodelled.

Where to stay

There are more hotels on or near the Victoria beach than in any other part of town. This beach is on the ocean side of the isthmus, and therefore not close to the old part of town, where the better restaurants are.

Top range

Atlántico, Parque Genovés 9. Tel. (956) 212 301. The best hotel in Cádiz, in the park on the seafront, with ocean views, swimming pool, garden, garage and restaurant. This establishment is not an official parador, but it is affiliated to the chain. From 1,900 ptas (without private bath) to 8,500 ptas (with bath).

Mid-range   **Isecotel**, Paseo Marítimo s/n. Tel. (956) 255 401. Overlooking the Victoria beach, this modern hotel is very popular in summer. From 4,850 to 6,950 ptas.

Regio, Calle Ana de Viya 11. Tel. (956) 279 331. Near the entrance to the city and near Victoria beach. From 3,900 ptas (January to June) to 4,400 ptas (rest of the year).

Francia y París, Plaza Calvo Sotelo 2. Tel. (956) 222 348. A central residence hotel. From 4,200 ptas (October to March) to 4,500 ptas (rest of the year).

Regio II, Calle López Pinto 79. Tel. (956) 253 009. Parking, near the beach, newer than the other Regio. From 4,500 ptas (January to June) to 4,750 ptas (rest of the year).

San Remo, Paseo Marítimo 3. Tel. (956) 252 202. On the beach, nice views, bar, moderate restaurant. From 3,360 ptas (October to April) to 4,560 ptas (rest of the year).

Where to eat
Moderate   **El Faro**, Calle San Félix 15. Tel. (956) 212 501. One of Cádiz's finest restaurants, specializing in seafood.

El Anteojo, Alameda Apodaca 22. Tel. (956) 225 703. A fine restaurant serving Spanish food.

Curro el Cojo, Paseo Marítimo 2. Tel. (956) 253 186. Good, individual cooking. Wide selection of wines.

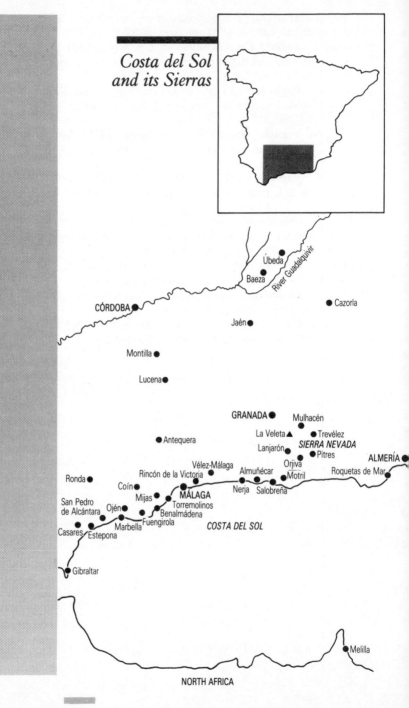

Costa del Sol
and its Sierras

Úbeda
Baeza
River Guadalquivir
CÓRDOBA
Cazorla
Jaén
Montilla
Lucena
GRANADA
Mulhacén
La Veleta
Trevélez
SIERRA NEVADA
Antequera
Lanjarón
Pitres
Vélez-Málaga
Orjiva
ALMERÍA
Rincón de la Victoria
Almuñécar
Motril
Roquetas de Mar
Ronda
Coín
Nerja
Salobreña
San Pedro
de Alcántara
Mijas
MÁLAGA
Torremolinos
Ojén
Benalmádena
Marbella
Fuengirola
COSTA DEL SOL
Casares
Estepona

Gibraltar

Melilla

NORTH AFRICA

Costa del Sol and its Sierras

Introduction

Less than a year before Columbus discovered America, the last Moorish king of Granada, Boabdil, was defeated by Ferdinand and Isabella. As he stood at what is to this day known as 'The Pass of the Sigh', on his way down to the coast and to exile beyond it, Boabdil turned to take one last look inland at the lovely kingdom he had lost, and he wept. Some say he would cry today if he looked the other way towards the coast. Like all generalities, that reflects only part of the truth: he could not possibly see Torremolinos from The Pass of the Sigh.

The Costa del Sol consists of about 300 km of Mediterranean coastline, stretching from Gibraltar to Almería, with huge beaches, hidden coves, impressive sea cliffs, package tourists, fugitives from British justice, Arab multimillionaires, a perfect climate and – despite overbuilding in some parts – many unforgettable beauty spots.

It is nothing if not cosmopolitan and always a trend-setter in music and style. It therefore comes as a surprise that just one or two rows of mountains beyond it, there lies another world, one of tranquillity, with sleepy, blindingly white towns where the people make their living by growing oranges, avocados and other fruits. That world is nevertheless intimately linked to the coast below it.

Málaga and Almería are the major ports and cities on this coast. Málaga is the catch-basin of the tourist tide that floods in. In the hinterland the lovely towers of the Alhambra and the mountains of Granada stand guard over the customs and music that have played such an important part in the long history of the people of Andalusia, Spain's largest and southernmost region. Beyond the mountains lies the long fertile valley of the Guadalquivir, a river that springs from the unspoilt forested mountains of Jaén to bathe the feet of a long and gracious Roman bridge in Córdoba, land of philosophers, passes through Seville (Sevilla), which it enriched by making that city a river port for the galleons bringing gold from the New World, and spills out into the marshes of the Coto Doñana, Europe's largest wildlife preserve, before losing itself in the sea near the Gulf of Cádiz.

This land is flamingly new in some parts, awe-inspiringly ancient in others. Of all the varied regions which make up the country, it is Andalusia that seems to say 'Spain' to most foreigners. Protected in the north by the rows of mountains where the orange and avocado groves stand, the Costa del Sol sees little rain and enjoys a climate in which even the coldest month of the year, January, has a mean temperature of 13.8°C (57°F) and when the temperature of the sea is 15.1°C (59°F). It is an ideal place for all kinds of water sports.

If you draw a line due north from Gibraltar on the map, you will see it cuts across the Guadalquivir Valley just west of Córdoba. This will be the western edge of the area I will consider along with the Costa del Sol. The northern border will be the valley itself, the heart of Andalusia, and the eastern edge will be a straight line drawn due north from Almería. The southern limit will be the coast.

Málaga

Málaga (population 503,251), is the capital of the Costa del Sol, but there is no need to stay here to see the coast. This is not to say that Málaga is without charm. It is a very pleasant city, which manages to retain an easy-going, friendly atmosphere. It is not growing very much, because most of the increasing number of permanent residents on the Costa del Sol prefer to live in smaller communities closer to the beach, the golf course or what have you; but there is much to see and do in Málaga, particularly in the area around the harbour. There you will find art galleries, the shopping district, the century-old bullring and Pablo Picasso's birthplace, on the Plaza de la Mercéd.

Ideally, you should stay not less than a week on the Costa del Sol, unless you plan to 'do' only Málaga, which is not recommended because you would miss more than half the fun. A stay of a week or more is particularly advisable if you plan to take in some of the sights beyond the coast such as a visit to Granada or Córdoba.

Getting there and transport

Daily flights from all over Europe land in Málaga throughout the year and air traffic is intense during the summer. Some flights to and from the Americas stop at Málaga. There is also a frequent daily service between Málaga and Madrid, Barcelona and other Spanish cities. Most Mediterranean cruises include Málaga as a port of call. There is a regular ferry service connecting Málaga with Tangiers and with Melilla, a Spanish enclave on the northern coast of Africa.

Málaga is the terminal of one of the country's main railway lines, which goes to Madrid and onwards. There is also a local train service that runs every half hour, covering the route between Málaga and Fuengirola. It stops at the airport.

Getting around by bus is easy. Local buses, which are frequent and cheap, run all along the coast. There are also buses to the towns beyond the coast, but in some cases it requires steady nerves to board these buses, which careen down narrow, twisting mountain roads and labour up the same slopes on the wrong side, with apparently little concern for what lies beyond the next crest or bend.

By car is the best way to travel around, though traffic is heavy on the main road along the coast during July and August.

You can reach the Costa del Sol via Gibraltar, but the runway there is short and the larger planes cannot use it. If you come in via Gibraltar and plan to hire a car, do so on the Spanish side of the gate. The reason is that cars rented in Gibraltar must be returned there whereas most Spanish car-hire companies will let you leave their car somewhere else in Spain if, for example, you want to fly home from Madrid.

There are over twenty yacht marinas and harbours with yacht facilities along the Costa del Sol; so it is easy to make your way along the coast by sea.

Main areas
The port is the centre of the city of Málaga; and a broad tree-lined boulevard, the Paseo del Parque, runs parallel to the main dock, the Muelle de Guadiaro. This avenue changes its name as it runs westward, to Alameda; it crosses the Tetuán Bridge and again changes its name to Ronda de Andalucía. It is the main street. On it, or very near it, are the bullring, the city hall, the provincial civil governor's office, the Málaga Palacio hotel, and – just south of it on the Calle Cuarteles – the railway station. The Cathedral, the stock market and the telephone exchange are just north of the Paseo del Parque.

So is the main shopping area. The central market is two short streets north of the Alameda. The airport is 9 km to the west of the Paseo de Guadiaro, on the road to Cádiz. In other words, the airport is on the same side of town as Torremolinos, Fuengirola and Marbella.

The Tourist Office is also quite central, at Marqués de Larios 5. Tel. (952) 231 445. There is another Tourist Office at the airport; Tel. (952) 312 044.

History
Málaga was a port of some importance in Roman times, but it obviously existed before that, though there is not much factual information about its distant past. The name, Málaga, is believed to come from a Phoenician word for 'salting place', which was probably a reference to its industry of preserving fish, a tradition carried on today by modern canning factories.

The Gibralfaro Castle on a high hill near the port, the remains of which stand next to the Gibralfaro parador, was built by the Moors on the foundations of a Phoenician fortress. The name, Gibralfaro, derives from a lighthouse (*faro*) there which served to guide ships to port and also formed part of an early-warning network of towers along the coast, from which pirates could be spotted in time to organize resistance, and from which bonfire signals could be relayed to warn of the danger.

King Ferdinand and Queen Isabella, known as the Catholic monarchs, captured this city, important for its maritime traffic, five years before Granada finally capitulated, but Málaga's Moorish defenders held out in the besieged Gibralfaro fortress for forty days before they were overcome.

One of Málaga's greatest periods of development was in the nineteenth century, when merchant vessels maintained a busy traffic between this city and ports in Africa and specially in the Americas. At the same time, a steel industry grew up in Málaga, thanks to the discovery of iron ore in the area.

With the loss of the Spanish colonies and the decline of the metalworking industry, Málaga once again fell on hard times, notwithstanding the production of fruit and vegetables in the fertile fields of the surrounding provinces. In the 1960s Málaga's fortunes began to improve, and they have continued to do so, because of the growth in international tourism.

What to see

Alcazaba

Calle Alcazabilla, near the Town Hall. Open daily from 10 a.m. to 1 p.m. and from 5 to 8 p.m. (summer) or 4 to 7 p.m. (winter). Closed on Sundays. An eleventh-century Moorish fortress, housing the **Provincial Archaeological Museum**, which has the same opening hours.

Gibralfaro Castle

Cerro de Gibralfaro. This hilltop fortress was probably originally built by the Phoenicians, but the present castle dates from the fourteenth century when it was built by the Emir of Granada, Yusuf I.

Roman theatre

Calle Alcazabilla, like the Alcazaba. Built between 27 and 14 BC, this theatre is as big as the one at Mérida in western Spain, but regrettably not as well preserved. The so-called House of Culture occupies what was the stage area.

Cathedral

Open daily from 10 a.m. to 1 p.m. and from 4 to 7 p.m. Known to the locals as 'La Manquita' (The Handless One) because one of its main towers was never finished, this Renaissance and Baroque temple was begun in 1528 and inaugurated in 1588. The work continued, off and on, until 1783, when it was left more or less as it is today. Take note of the wood-carving in the choir, with images of more than forty saints. The seats were carved by Luis Ortiz and José Micael in 1658; the saints are the work of Pedro de Mena.

Fine Arts Museum

Museo Provincial de Bellas Artes, Calle San Agustín 6. Open daily from 10 a.m. to 1.30 p.m. and from 5 to 8 p.m. (summer) or 4 to 7 p.m. (winter). Closed on Sundays and Mondays. A fine collection of Spanish paintings, including ones by Picasso, Zurbarán, Murillo and Alonso Cano.

Ethnological Museum

Museo de Artes Populares, Pasillo de Santa Isabel 10. Open daily from 10 a.m. to 1 p.m. and from 4 to 7 p.m. Closed from 14 August to 15 September and on Mondays. If you want to see how they lived in Spain in the not too distant past (or live even today in some of the more remote places) this is the place to go. You will find such things as wine-pressing troughs and homemade farming implements.

Excursions

Rincón de la Victoria

Cueva del Tesoro, 13 km east of Málaga on N-340. Open daily from 10 a.m. to 2 p.m. and from 4 to 7 p.m. Closed on Mondays in winter. A prehistoric cave with drawings and a *son et lumière* show.

Where to eat: pricey

Café de Paris, Calle Vélez-Málaga s/n. Tel. (952) 225 043. Closed on Tuesdays and for the last half of September. French cooking. Specialities include pheasant in cream sauce and fresh mackerel with spinach. Good service and wine cellar. A place the locals go to, to impress their guests.

Arroyo de la Miel

Arroyo de la Miel (population 3,645), 20 km west of Málaga, (turn off at Benalmádena), has a Tivoli World Amusement Park. All the rides plus restaurants, *tapa* bars, and daily and nightly shows in the outdoor auditorium during summer.

North Africa

For a real off-beat trip you can't beat **Melilla**, one of the two Spanish enclaves on the north coast of Africa, sovereignty over which is disputed by Morocco. You might say that they are Spain's 'Gibraltars'. Melilla, like the other enclave, Ceuta (opposite the Straits from Gibraltar), is a free port and a city with a strong military garrison. There are daily flights between Málaga and Melilla. There are ships that go to Melilla too, but they are not convenient because there are only three sailings a week in each direction (at 1.30 p.m. on Mondays, Wednesdays and Fridays to Melilla, and at 11.30 p.m. on Tuesdays, Thursdays and Saturdays to Málaga). The crossing takes seven hours.

Melilla has fine beaches, and the mixture of Spanish and Moroccan influence is evident everywhere. A Spanish city since the end of the fifteenth century, it consists of an old walled section, known simply as El Pueblo, on a rocky promontory, and the modern city, in a coastal vale. The municipal museum concentrates mainly on the military history of this territory, which began as a stronghold to counter pirate attacks on Mediterranean shipping. Prices of such goods as cameras, recorders and the like are cheap, but the customs officers are sharp-eyed when you return to mainland Spain.

Where to stay: mid-range

Parador Don Pedro de Estopiñán, Avenida Cándido Lobera. Tel. (952) 684 940. A small, modern inn, which offers the best lodging in Melilla. A quiet place with a swimming pool. November to June, 7,000 ptas; rest of the year, 7,500 ptas.

What to do in Málaga and on the coast

Málaga and the coast are in the leisure business in a big way. There is so much to do, the list would be endless. Apart from kilometres and kilometres of fine beaches, there are scores of golf courses. Yacht marinas are dotted all along the coast, and – never far from Málaga – horse-racing, regular bullfights in season, dog races, a water-based fun park and all kinds of participant and spectator sports, especially water sports. There is even good skiing at Solynieve, in the Sierra Nevada, which is 160 km from Málaga, 98 km from the coast at Motril, or 31 km from Granada. There is a train that runs from Granada to the ski resort as well as a frequent bus service.

Shopping

Typical products of the Costa del Sol and the sierras that lie behind it are straw rugs and mats (especially in Ronda and Antequera), wrought iron in traditional designs (Ronda), embroidery (in Mijas, a quaint but overly touristic village on the mountainside above Fuengirola), tin work, such as lamps, (in Vélez-Málaga, a town about 35 km east of Málaga) and pottery (at Coín, a farming town about 30 km from Málaga on the road from Málaga to Ronda. (There are weekly street markets in Fuengirola on Tuesdays and Marbella on Saturdays.)

Nightlife

There are more nightclubs, bars with music, discotheques and other nocturnal places and forms of entertainment along the Costa del Sol than you could ever visit in a lifetime. To find out what's good near where you are staying, get a copy of the excellent English-language monthly *Lookout*, published in Fuengirola, or other English-language publications such as the *Marbella Times*.

Casino Torrequebrada, Benalmádena, 20 km west of Málaga on the coastal road. Tel. (952) 442 545. All the usual games, like roulette and blackjack, plus a nightclub, two restaurants, disco, golf course and tennis and squash courts. Gambling rooms are open from 9 p.m. to 5 a.m. in summer, and from 8 p.m. to 4 a.m. in winter.

Where to stay in Málaga
Top range

Parador de Gibralfaro, Gibralfaro. Tel. (952) 221 902. This relatively modern building was built on the site of an old inn on the hilltop near the Gibralfaro fortress. On a clear day you can see Gibraltar, which is about 100 km to the west. Only twelve rooms so book way ahead. Double rooms: January to March, 6,500 ptas; rest of year, 8,000 ptas.

Málaga Palacio, Cortina del Muelle. Tel. (952) 215 185. A five-star hotel with a rooftop swimming pool right in the centre of the city, facing the port. From 7,900 to 10,000 ptas.

Mid-range

Don Curro, Sancha de Lara 7. Tel. (952) 227 200, telex 77366. A quiet, comfortable hotel in the centre with air-conditioning and other amenities. September to mid-July, 5,300 ptas; rest of year, 5,800 ptas.

Las Vegas, Paseo de Sancha 22. Tel. (952) 217 712. Frequent scene of conventions. Attractive swimming pool in the garden. Mid-October to the end of February, 4,400 ptas; March to mid-October, 4,950 ptas.

California, Paseo de Sancha 19. Tel. (952) 215 165. A small, central residence hotel. October to June, 2,950 ptas; rest of year, 3,650 ptas.

Lis, Calle Córdoba 7. Tel. (952) 227 300. A central residence hotel with bus service to and from the airport. From 2,560 ptas (October to the end of February) to 3,200 ptas (July to the end of September, and Holy Week).

Bottom range

Casanova, Calle Salitre 11. Tel. (952) 321 150. A small residence hotel, very centrally located and in lovely surroundings. Without bath, 2,100 ptas; with bath, 2,200 ptas.

Costa Rica, Calle Córdoba 5. Tel. (952) 213 577. A small, family-managed residence hotel in the centre of Málaga in attractive sur-

Where to eat
Pricey

Moderate

Economical

roundings. From 2,000 to 2,500 ptas.

La Alegría, Martín Grácia 10. Tel. (952) 224 143. Closed on Saturdays except when holidays fall on Saturdays. International and local cooking. Specialities include *ajo blanco*, a cold garlic soup.

El Figón de Bonilla, Calle Cervantes, Edificio Horizonte. Tel. (952) 223 223. Spanish food. Good *tapas*. Closed on Sundays and during the second half of February.

Antonio Martín, Paseo Marítimo s/n. Tel. (952) 222 113. Closed on Sunday evenings during the winter. Terrace overlooking the Mediterranean. Simple local cooking, mostly fish, fried, baked, or whatever.

Casa Pedro, Playa de El Palo, Paseo Marítimo. Tel. (952) 290 013. Closed on Monday evenings and during November. A favourite with tourists. Specialities, sardines and paellas.

West along the coast from Málaga

Torremolinos

Where to stay:
top range

Fuengirola

Where to stay:
top range

Where to eat:
economical

Marbella

The less said about this high-rise haven (population 20,484) of package-tourists the better except as a warning: check to see that the wind is not blowing from the east before you venture into the water. When it is, Málaga's sewage drifts inevitably towards Torremolinos.

The Tourist Office is at Edificio La Nogalera 517; Tel. (952) 381 578.

Parador del Golf; Tel. (952) 381 256. If you must stay in Torremolinos, this is the place to stay. Tucked away in your balconied room facing the pool and beside the beach, you are oblivious to the hubbub in the centre of over-developed Torremolinos town. There is an eighteen-hole golf course designed by Robert Trent Jones, tennis courts and an uncrowded beach: 7,500 to 9,000 ptas. Book well ahead.

Fuengirola (population 30,606) is neat, with a long and delightful broad beach, flanked by a flower-fringed road and wide pavement. It has been tastefully developed. About 8 km from Fuengirola is the touristy mountain village of Mijas, which offers wonderful views and respite from the noisy coastal resorts.

Las Palmeras, Paseo Marítimo. Tel. (952) 472 700, telex 77202. A very large hotel (537 rooms) on the beach, with good service and all facilities, including an extensive shopping gallery. Fuengirola's seafront is one of the most attractive on the coast. From 6,000 to 8,750 ptas.

El Abuelo, Avenida Boliches 11. Tel. (952) 474 672. Closed on Sundays and all of November and December. Castilian cooking, better than average in a holiday resort town; good service and personal attention.

Marbella (population 67,822, 56 km west of Málaga on the coastal highway) is the year-round venue for the European and Middle Eastern jet set. King Fahd of Saudi Arabia has a secluded mansion in the hills, as does wheeler-dealer Adnan Kashoggi. The coast's liveliest inhabitant is piano-playing promoter Don Jaime de Mora y Aragón, brother of Queen Fabiola of Belgium. Prince Alfonso von Hohenlohe is also one of Marbella's more distinguished residents.

It is the site of the coast's only mosque, beside the main road near Nueva Andalucía, which was built with a donation from King Fahd. The whole town is a perfect example of How to Do it Right. Marbella's old town, perfectly preserved and throbbing with life, is full of bright surprises and bursting with flowers at every turn of its narrow streets, most of which are wisely limited to pedestrians. The Tourist Office is at Miguel Cano 1; Tel. (952) 771 442.

What to do

Nueva Andalucía Casino (alongside Puerto Banús). Tel. (952) 780 800 or 780 804. All kinds of gambling, nightclub, restaurant, swimming pool. Games rooms open from 9 p.m. to 5 a.m. in summer and from 8 p.m.to 4 a.m. in winter.

Where to stay:
top range

Puente Romano, Carretera de Cádiz, km 184. Tel. (952) 770 100, telex 77399. This is the place to go if you fancy rubbing shoulders with people like Princess Caroline, Arab oil millionaires, Frank Sinatra or one of the high-living exiles from the Heathrow gold bullion robbery. Regine's discotheque is in the hotel. Apart from having everybody who is anybody, this place has everything as well: heated pool, tennis courts, solicitous service. From 20,000 to 26,000 ptas.

Mid-range

Refugio Nacional de Juanar, at Ojén. Tel. (952) 881 000. A hunting lodge, this establishment forms part of the state-run parador network, but its accommodation is more basic than most. There are only seventeen rooms, so it is not easy to get a booking. This lodge, with a pool, is deep in a pine forest in the Sierra Blanca (White Mountains) behind Marbella. A shady path leads about 150 m up the mountainside to a scenic viewpoint from which the coast is spread out before you, with Gibraltar looming close on your right.

Where to eat:
pricey

La Fonda, Calle Santo Cristo 9. Tel. (952) 772 512. Closed on Sundays. French, international cuisine. A superb restaurant in a town where competition is stiff and money is often no object. In an eighteenth-century house in the old town of Marbella, with furniture and decorations from that period, and with a flowery central patio for dining in summer, this restaurant looks as good as its food tastes. It should. It was founded by the son of Otto Horcher, whose restaurant in Madrid is world famous.

Estepona

Estepona (population 24, 261), 26 km south-west of Marbella or 82 km south-west of Málaga on the A-7, has survived the tourist boom reasonably well. Although six-storey buildings line the main road, blocking views of the beach, the original town is largely untouched, and still full of real Spaniards and authentic little Spanish shops and bars. Roman ruins nearby and a string of defensive towers recall tribulations of the past, like raids by Barbary Coast pirates.

The Tourist Office is at Paseo Marítimo, Pedro Manrique s/n; Tel. (952) 800 913.

Where to stay:
top range

Golf El Paraíso, Carretera de Cádiz, km 167. Tel. (952) 812 840, telex 77261. Heated pool, tennis, golf. On a ridge overlooking sea and countryside. From 8,000 ptas (January to June) to 9,000 ptas.

Where to eat:
pricey

El Libro Amarillo, Carretera de Cádiz, km 161. Tel. (952) 800 484. Closed during the first half of December, all of January and every Monday. International cooking with an American touch – but for the good. Specialities include cheese soufflé and, that rarity in Spain, good chocolate mousse.

The Hinterland

Whether you use Málaga or some other town on the coast as a base, there are many excursions you can make into the hinterland, and all of them will be rewarding. Unfortunately, most visitors get no farther from the beach than their hotel or some restaurant. The scenery in any case is superb, because one or more rows of mountains (depending on where you are) always lies close by. In many places they march right down to the sea. Such is the case with the Granada side of the coast. And, of course, anyone who has ever seen the mountains right behind Marbella realizes how lovely a backdrop even treeless hills can make. However, the mountains are for the most part wooded, there is more rainfall in the mountains than on the coast, and this makes for a happy combination – with water for the crops and sunshine for the tourists.

Ronda

This cliff-hanging market town (population 31,383), 122 km from Málaga), one of the most picturesque of western Andalusia, is 49 km by a good wide road from San Pedro de Alcántara, just west of Marbella. The road to Ronda is all uphill. There are regular buses between Marbella and Ronda. Ronda is perched 723 m high on the edge of a deep gorge, in the centre of a small range of mountains that bears its name.

The Tourist Office is in the Plaza de España 1; Tel. (952) 871 272.

History

A natural fortress whose walls encircle it in the form of a horseshoe, Ronda was founded by the Iberians and occupied by the Phoenicians, Carthaginians and Romans. A beautiful eighteenth-century bridge, with a tavern tucked handily under the roadway, spans the gorge and joins the two parts of the town. Far below, ruins of ancient canals can still be seen angling their way down the cliff faces to what were once Arab mills. The eighteenth-century bullring replaced an earlier one built in the sixteenth, and fights are scheduled regularly in the summer. The place where bullfighting on foot became accepted as an art,

Ronda is the scene of an annual fight in September in which the *toreros* and their teams dress as they did in the days when Goya painted the *corridas*.

What to see

The Collegiate Church of Santa María La Mayor is a former mosque, reconstructed in Gothic and Renaissance styles. The Arab baths, still very much intact, are in the lowest part of the town. About 12 km from Ronda is the site of the original town, with its Roman theatre.

Where to stay: mid-range

Reina Victoria, Calle Jerez 25. Tel. (952) 871 240. The garden ends at the edge of a precipice, with fabulous views. The building is as Victorian as its name and the service is as slow as one imagines it was in the age of horse-drawn carriages. January to mid-March, 6,600 ptas; rest of the year, 7,260 ptas. Book ahead as the hotel is popular.

Where to eat: moderate

Don Miguel, Calle Villa Nueva 4. Tel. (952) 871 090. Closed on Sundays in summer and Wednesdays in winter; also from 25 January to 10 February. Good solid Spanish cooking.

Casares

Casares (population 3,045) is 25 km up into the hills from Estepona, 82 km west of Málaga on the coastal road. It is one of the most beautiful white towns in Andalusia. Stuck on the top of a ridge at the foot of a decaying Moorish fortress, it looks like a film set. Perhaps because it is at the far western end of the Costa del Sol there are not many visitors.

East along the coast from Málaga

Nerja

Perched high above cliffs and rocky slopes with coves and beaches below, Nerja has a population of 12,012 and is 51 km east of Málaga on N-340. One of the prettiest villages on this coast, Nerja is rapidly developing, but still at the moment retaining its charm. It offers a lot to see, not the least of which are its extensive caves. The caves, which are 5 km from the town and full of beautiful stalactites and stalagmites, are open daily from 9 a.m. to 9 p.m. in summer and from 10 a.m. to 1.30 p.m. and 4 to 7 p.m. in winter. Ballet in the caves in a natural auditorium during the latter half of September. Occasional concerts as well, particularly during the summer. This cave complex, discovered in the 1950s, contained Bronze Age artefacts from about 1000 BC. Some of the finds are on display at a small archaeological museum on the site.

The Tourist Office is at Puerta del Mar 4; Tel. (952) 521 531.

Where to stay: top range

Parador de Nerja, El Tablazo s/n. Tel. (952) 520 050. A relatively modern building, with many rooms facing the sea, this parador offers all the usual comfort. A lift takes you down to the beach. The centre of town is close enough to be at hand, far enough to make it good exercise if you walk, which you should, in order not to miss the scenery. January to March, 8,500 ptas; rest of the year, 9,000 ptas.

Where to eat:
economical

Cueva de Nerja, Carretera de Almería, km 302. Tel. (952) 520 633. Andalusian food.

Almuñécar

Almuñécar (population 16,141), is a simple Spanish town that has miraculously managed to preserve its Andalusian architectural character, despite modern resort facilities being grafted on to it, and to avoid the destruction of its fascinating remnants of the past, which include Phoenician ruins, a Moorish castle and a graceful Roman aqueduct. The Tourist Office is at Puerta del Mar s/n; Tel. (958) 630 333.

Salobreña

Salobreña (population 8,119) marches up a steep hillside, its white houses jostling each other in narrow, twisting streets, led by a Moorish castle. From the summit you can see much of the coast and the Sierra Nevada.

Motril

Motril (population 39,784) lies on a coastal plain, planted in sugar cane and subtropical fruits and vegetables, like the *chirimoya* which, in case you never had one, looks like an artichoke, has the consistency of yoghurt and tastes like strawberries.

Where to stay:
mid-range

Costa Nevada, Calle Enrique Martín Cuevas s/n. Tel. (958) 600 500. A picturesquely-situated hotel with pool, tennis courts and restaurant. From 3,500 ptas (November to January) to 4,250 ptas.

Where to eat:
moderate

Tropical, Rodríguez Acosta 13. Tel. (958) 600 460. Closed every Sunday and for the whole of June and July. Spanish cooking.

Roquetas de Mar

Roquetas de Mar (population 19,006) is a small resort town 18 km from Almería at the far eastern end of the coast. Its distance from Málaga puts it somewhat off the beaten tourist track, though its major hotels pack in the package tours. There is a good yacht basin here. The beach is one of black gravel, not fine sand, but it is still pleasant.

Where to stay:
mid-range

Zoraida Park, Pez Espada s/n. Tel. (951) 320 750. Open April to October. Pleasant views, golf, tennis, pool. Very reasonable. From 2,600 to 4,500 ptas.

Bottom range

Hostal Aroma, Carretera Nacional 340. Tel. (951) 341 391. Good lodging for the money, with reasonably priced meals as well. From 1,475 ptas (without bath, low season) to 2,200 ptas (with bath, July to September).

Almería

Almería (population 140,946) is the capital of the province of the same name. It is a major southern Spanish port and it also has its own airport. There are beach resorts around it but, though Almería has its own beaches, this is not essentially a resort town. It is nevertheless very picturesque and its old quarter, shabbily attractive, climbs to the tenth-century Moorish Alcazaba high above the town.

Where to stay:
mid-range

Costasol, Paseo de Almería 58. Tel. (951) 234 011. A pleasant hotel, very central, relatively small, air-conditioned. From 4,450 ptas (October to mid-July) to 4,985 ptas (rest of the year).

Where to eat:
moderate

Club de Mar, Muelle 1. Tel. (951) 235 048. Seafood, Spanish and international cooking. Careful attention to detail makes meals especially good here. Terrace overlooking the sea.

Málaga – Antequera – Montilla – Córdoba

Córdoba is 187 km by road from Málaga and the road goes over some impressive mountains. The first part, from Málaga to Antequera, is wide, with gentle curves. The rest leaves something to be desired. To get to Córdoba by car, take the main road north from Málaga: the one marked Madrid and Antequera. There is a frequent daily train service, and Córdoba is a major railway junction.

Antequera

Antequera (population 41,608, 46 km uphill from Málaga) was founded by the Romans and is an agricultural market town. Stop off here if you have time. There is plenty to see in Antequera including a lover's leap, where legend says a Moorish governor's daughter and her hopeless lover, a captured Christian prince, jumped off hand in hand.

Where to stay: mid-range

Parador de Antequera, Calle García del Olmo s/n. Tel. (952) 840 061. This modern parador, in the white-walled regional style, is set in attractive surroundings. It is well furnished and the meals are quite acceptable. (Try the *sangría*.) From 5,500 to 7,000 ptas.

Montilla

About 90 km past Antequera you will see a sign indicating Montilla (population 21,400) to your right. This is another good place to stop if you have time. It is the area for the much appreciated Montilla-Moriles wines, which are similar to sherry.

Where to stay: mid-range

Don Gonzalo, Carretera Madrid-Málaga, km 447. Tel. (957) 650 658. Central, with bar and pool. Very good service. Double rooms, 4,200 ptas.

Where to eat: moderate

Las Camachas, Carretera de Málaga, km 446. Tel. (957) 650 004. Andalusian cooking, with specialities including angler fish and bull's tail soup. Some dishes are cooked in the good local wines.

To Córdoba

The view of Córdoba as you approach is striking. Its tawny old buildings lie on the other side of the River Guadalquivir, with the great reddish stone bridge built by the Romans in the foreground.

Córdoba

You will probably want to spend several days in Córdoba (population 284,737). It is a city which is full of monuments and was the cultural centre of Europe in the tenth century; the capital of Muslim Spain with a population more than twice as large as that of today, and the rival in the Arab world of Constantinople, Damascus and Baghdad. It is not, however, a place that offers many chances for excursions for it lies in a largely agricultural area of no special touristic interest. Córdoba is 182 km from Málaga.

Main areas

The most interesting part of Córdoba is, of course, the old section, which lies between the Roman Bridge in the south and the Plaza de Colón in the north. The famous Mezquita (Mosque), with its forest of columns, stands at the north end of the bridge, just behind the old bridge gate. The Episcopal Palace and the San Jacinto Church are across the street on the western side of the Mezquita. The Alcázar, of the Catholic Monarchs, is alongside the river just one street downstream from the Mezquita. In fact, just about all the historic buildings are in the area of narrow streets north and east of the Mezquita, an area bounded on the west by a broad, landscaped boulevard known in its various sections as the Avenida del Conde de Valladolid, Paseo de la Victoria and Avenida de Cervantes; on the north by the railway station, and with no real fixed boundary on the east, where it just peters out. The railway station is at the northern end of the broad boulevard.

The Tourist Office is at Calle Hermanos González Murga 13; Tel. (957) 478 721.

History

Córdoba's importance in pre-Roman and Roman times was as a crossroads and market town. Its privileged location, in the approximate centre of Andalusia, and mid-course along its principal river, contributed to its growth.

From the seventh to the ninth centuries, it was the capital of Muslim Spain and the court of the Caliphs of the west. It became a major centre of art, culture and science. Europe can thank Córdoba for preserving and developing the sciences of the ancients, and especially for translating writings on mathematics, astronomy and other such disciplines from the Arabic and Greek. At a time when kings in the north of Europe could not read or write, Córdoba's court boasted some of the greatest thinkers and artists.

In 1236 Córdoba was conquered by the Castilian King Ferdinand III, The Saint. Under the rule of the kings of Castile, Córdoba's bright star of destiny faded. The kings and queens of Castile spent long periods in Córdoba. It was in this city that Queen Isabella twice received Columbus when he was seeking financial support for his wild idea of finding a route to India by sailing west rather than east. During the second interview the Queen decided to invest in a long shot. So taken was she with Columbus' arguments that she sold her jewels to raise the necessary money.

Under the rulers of Christian Spain, with the centuries-long war against the Moors continuing, Córdoba was 'pacified'. The boulevard that lines the west side of the old city, as well as the Avenida del Gran Capitán and the Plaza de Colón, are the work of the Christian conquerors, who smashed thoroughfares through the maze of small streets in the oriental-style centre of the Moorish city. This was full of numerous blind alleys and only the natives could find their way in and out of something that resembled, and with good reason, the Casbah of Casablanca. The conquerors also made short shrift of ideas they considered dangerous and of people who did not think or dress the same way they did. Christian noblemen moved into the palaces, and Christian soldiers and immigrants, brought in by royal command from Navarra, León and Soria in Spain's north, settled in the city and its environs as the original inhabitants were driven out or subjugated.

It was not until the first part of this century that Córdoba's population, which had dwindled from 500,000 to 35,000 at the end of the Middle Ages and to 20,000 at the beginning of the nineteenth century, really began to recover.

Among those born in this province whose fame has spread afar are also a number of bullfighters, including the famous Manolete and Manuel Benítez, 'El Córdobes'.

What to see

Mezquita

It goes without saying that you must visit this famous monument, one of the most fascinating architectural legacies left to our times. It is open daily from 10.30 a.m. to 1.30 p.m. and from 3.30 to 6 p.m. The Mosque was begun in the eighth century on the orders of the Caliph, Abd-er-Rahman I. It was repeatedly added to as the city grew in size and importance, until it was completed in the tenth century under the reign of Al-mansur. It was built on the site of a Visigothic cathedral and some of the previous structure was incorporated. The final expansion and reforms under the Caliphs included the construction of the Mihrâb (prayer recess), with its beautiful dome and its incomparable mosaics, given to Caliph Al-Hakim II by the Emperor Constantine VII. The Mosque is full of surprises, with its patios and tinkling fountains and its string of tiny Christian chapels.

Cathedral

This is tucked away in the centre of the Mosque, and as such forms a part of it. It was begun in 1523 by Carlos V and was finished 243 years later. The various styles represented reflect the changes during the centuries the construction lasted.

Episcopal Palace

Opposite the western wall of the Mosque, this was once the residence of the Visigothic governors and later the fortified palace of the Caliphs. It was considerably altered in the fifteenth and seventeenth centuries.

Alcázar

A stone's throw away is the Alcázar of the Catholic Monarchs. It was built in the fourteenth century, and its great tiled hall is as beautiful today as it must have been when the royals inaugurated it 600 years ago, at a time when the world was smaller and truth was absolute.

Churches

There are many old churches in the cool narrow streets of the heart of Córdoba, but the prettiest ones are those built shortly after the Reconquest, when faith and enthusiasm were one. They typically combine Gothic, Romanesque and Mudéjar (Arab-Christian) styles, reflecting their origins and the times in which they were erected or transformed for use as Christian places of worship. Some of the more interesting churches are those of **San Pablo**, which houses a striking statue of the Virgin of Anguish by sculptor Juan de Mesa; **San Lorenzo**, Romanesque and Gothic; and the twelfth-century **San**

Provincial Archaeological Museum

Miguel with its Gothic-Mudéjar façade.

(Plaza de Jerónimo Páez) is one of the most complete in Spain, with art treasures by the Iberian, Roman, Visigothic and Arabic inhabitants of this city and its surrounding lands. Open daily from 10 a.m. to 2 p.m. and from 4 to 7 p.m.; closed on Mondays and Sunday and holiday afternoons. **The Provincial Fine Art Museum** (Plaza del Potro) has paintings by Murillo, Valdés Leal, Zurbarán, Ribera, Goya, Titian and Rubens. Open daily from 10 a.m. to 1.30 p.m. and from 5 to 7 p.m.; closed on Mondays.

The Museum of Cordoban Art and Bullfighting (Museo Municipal Taurino; Plaza de las Bulas, Casa de las Bulas) is what its name implies. The bullfight section is filled with curious mementoes of *toreros* like Manolete, including threadbare suits of lights, yellowing posters, fading capes and other items with just enough of an aura of decay to emphasize the respectability of bullfighting in Spain.

Excursion
Medina Azahara

About 12 km west of Córdoba, on a hillside overlooking the Guadalquivir, is the site of the remains of what the locals like to refer to as 'the Cordoban Versailles'. Archaeologists have dug out what is left of a magnificent tenth-century palace, spread out on three terraced esplanades on the wooded slopes of the Sierra Morena (Dark Mountains). The residence of Caliph Abd-er-Rahman III and his successors, it contained exquisitely devised furnishings of ceramic, wrought iron and wood. Open daily from 10 a.m. to midday and from 5.30 to 7 p.m. (3.30 to 5 p.m. in winter); closed on Tuesdays. Many of the items recovered from the excavation are on display at a museum on the site.

Also open are the reconstructed Salon of the Viziers and the Mosque. Excavations are still in progress at the site.

Shopping

Good buys include silver work, in which Córdoba's artisans have always excelled. The phrase Cordovan leather comes from the word Córdoba; the *Córdobanes*, or tanned, dyed, tooled, polychromed hides, make very elegant wall decorations today as they did centuries ago in the palaces of the merchants and nobles. Copper and brass objects, especially real or simulated oil lamps, are a speciality of **Lucena** (population 31,500) 73 km south of Córdoba on Route 331. **Hinojosa del Duque**, one of the northernmost villages of the province of Córdoba, is famous for its wrought iron, and they will make up pieces to your design or suggestion.

Nightlife

Tasca-hopping is a favourite nocturnal activity of Cordobans. It consists of going from one tavern to another, trying the *tapas*, the wine and the conversation in each, until you have had enough to call it a night. There are several good *tapa* bars in the vicinity of the Almodóvar gate.

At certain times of the year the best of the flamenco music performers can be seen in Córdoba. One such time is the fortnight in May of the Patio Festivals . . . when prizes are given for the most beautiful patios, the Montilla-Moriles wine flows abundantly and the haunting strains of flamenco ring from patios all over the city. Dates vary from year to year, so check in advance.

For those with modern tastes, Córdoba has few discos. They include Saint-Cyr, Calle Eduardo Lucena 4, big and booming; and Contactos at Calle Eduardo 8, better for couples than single men, despite the name.

Where to stay
Top range

Parador la Arruzafa, Avenida de la Arruzafa s/n. Tel. (957) 275 900. A modern building just 3 km from the centre of Córdoba, with flowery balconies off most of the rooms, broad terraces and spacious lounges. Good regional dishes, like almond *gazpacho*. Pool and tennis court. Book way ahead. January to March, 8,000 ptas; rest of the year, 9,000 ptas.

Husa Gran Capitán, Avenida América 3. Tel. (957) 479 250, telex 76662. A good, central, four-star hotel with garage, air-conditioning and other comforts. From 7,500 ptas (November to mid-March) to 8,500 ptas (rest of the year).

Meliá Córdoba, Jardines de la Victoria. Tel. (957) 298 066, telex 76591. Beautiful views of the old Jewish quarter, pool in lovely garden setting. From 9,500 ptas.

Mid-range

El Califa, Lope de Hoces 14. Tel. (957) 299 400. A small, very comfortable hotel right in the centre, with garage. From 7,000 ptas.

Selu, Eduardo Dato 7. Tel. (957) 476 500. Central, in a scenic location, with garage. From 3,700 ptas.

Where to eat
Moderate

El Caballo Rojo, Cardenal Herrero 28. Tel. (957) 475 375. The best place I know of in Córdoba. Andalusian cooking. Specialities include lamb with honey and white *gazpacho*.

Almudaina, Campo Santo de los Mártires 1. Tel. (957) 474 342. Closed on Sunday evenings. Andalusian and international cooking. The surroundings are great as the restaurant is in a fourteenth-century house in the old Jewish quarter, but the food is only average.

Ciro's, Paseo de la Victoria 19. Tel. (957) 290 006. Andalusian cooking, with bull's tail soup as a speciality.

Córdoba – Jaén – Baeza – Úbeda – Cazorla – Granada

Between Córdoba and Granada lies a very interesting and largely undiscovered part of Andalusia that you should visit if at all possible. You can go by local bus, but it is better if you can go by car.

Jaén

The first part of this route is 104 km long, and it takes you east from Córdoba on N-IV, a good major road, for about 10 km, where you should turn off to the right on N-324 in the direction of Jaén. You will drive through seemingly endless olive groves before reaching Jaén (population 98,000), capital of the province of the same name and an agricultural centre. The Santa Catalina Castle Parador here, perched on a razor-sharp ridge and surrounded on three sides by the town itself, is one of the most spectacular hotels in all Spain.

Where to stay:
top range

Parador Castillo de Santa Catalina. Tel. (953) 264 411. Marvellous views of the city and the countryside, but just forty-three rooms. The parador is built in the same austere stone style as the adjoining castle, which was rebuilt in the thirteenth century when Christian forces captured the town, but was actually constructed several centuries earlier. A bargain, with complete quiet at night, though bus tours stop during the day for lunch. January to March, 6,500 ptas; rest of the year, 8,000 ptas.

Where to eat:
moderate

Jockey Club, Avenida Generalísimo 16. Tel. (953) 211 018. Andalusian cooking.

El Mesón, Pasaje Nuyra. Tel. (953) 234 117. Closed on Sunday evenings in summer. Spanish cooking.

Baeza

When you leave Jaén, take route N-321 to Baeza, 50 km from the provincial capital. Baeza is a gold-mine of architectural beauty hidden away in the green fields of this little-visited fold of central Andalusia. It is a truly elegant little city with a population of less than 15,000. Many of its buildings, perfectly preserved and glowing in their yellow stone, date from Spain's Golden Age of the sixteenth century. These include the Gothic old Town Hall, the old university, the former courthouse (now the Tourist Office), the old prison and hall of justice which is the present Town Hall, the playhouse and many others. Both Baeza and Úbeda, further on, were designated 'exemplary cities' by the Council of Europe in 1975, the international year of architecture.

Where to stay:
bottom range

Juanito, Avenida Arca del Agua s/n. Tel. (953) 740 040. An unpretentious place, but clean, with central heating. From 2,600 ptas.

Where to eat:
economical

Juanito, Avenida Arca del Agua s/n. Tel. (953) 740 909. Andalusian cooking in a homely atmosphere with careful personal service and very good food.

Úbeda

Other pleasures lie ahead. Only 10 km further along the same road is Úbeda (population 28,717), another *señorial* town that looks like a film set, with its elegant Renaissance palaces and its solid stone public buildings with their intricately carved doorways.

If you cannot decide whether to stay in Úbeda, which is sometimes referred to as 'The Salamanca of Andalusia' because of its noble architecture, Úbeda makes it easy for you. They have already made your bed in one of those ancient palaces and there is stuffed partridge or baby lamb chops for dinner. It is the Condestable Dávalos parador.

Where to stay:
top range

Parador Condestable Dávalos, Plaza de Vázquez de Molina 1. Tel. (953) 750 345. This sixteenth-century palace has twenty-five rooms only, but since it is not in an area frequented by tourists, it is not hard to get a room, especially in winter. The old palace, the plaza it faces on to, and the town itself are beautiful. From 6,000 ptas (January to the end of March) to 8,000 ptas (rest of the year).

If such pleasures do not move you, move on, but make sure there are a couple of hours of daylight left. Next stop is the Parador del Adelantado, high in the Sierra Cazorla, where the rare Capra Hispanica mountain goat, ibex, deer and wild boar abound in a beautiful forest that hides the source of the Guadalquivir in the skirts of its wooded mountains.

Cazorla

The white town of Cazorla, population 10,006, clinging gamely to a hillside, is solitary and self-sufficient, doing very well off the pigs its people raise, the game they hunt and the fruits and vegetables they grow in gardens beside their simple homes. In the summer some families take in boarders.

Cazorla is about 45 km from Úbeda (104 km from Jaén if you drive direct, rather than through Baeza and Úbeda); and after you reach the *pueblo* you still have 28 km to go – all uphill and all on a twisting narrow road through thick forest.

Where to stay:
mid-range

Parador del Adelantado, 28 km south of Cazorla in the forest reserve (if you miss the signpost, ask anybody in Cazorla). Tel. (953) 721 075. The parador is of simple construction, white walls, red roof tiles and heavy wooden beams. It is what it looks like, a mountain lodge. It has thirty-three rooms, scenery, noisy animals at night, and a good heating system. The food is good and abundant with lots of game and garden-fresh vegetables. This is just as well, because there is nowhere else to eat without going down the mountain to Cazorla. There must be very few places in Europe so wild and beautiful. From 6,000 ptas (November to June) to 7,500 ptas (rest of the year and during Holy Week).

Granada

Who needs urging to go to Granada? Granada (population 262,182) is fully deserving of all the good reports you have heard about its incomparable scenery. Nestling at the foot of the spectacular Sierra Nevada mountains, on a fertile plain, with the unique Alhambra, the Generalife gardens, the Sacromonte gipsy caves (where some of the best flamenco music can be heard) and the charming Albaicín neighbourhood with its oriental aspect, Granada is a lovely city indeed.

Among the many things poets have written about this beautiful place, there are a few lines I cannot forget, penned by the Spanish poet Francisco de Icaza. They refer to a blind beggar: 'Give him alms, woman, for there is no greater misfortune in life than to be blind – in Granada.' Apart from its main business centre, which looks much like that of many other cities, Granada has a flavour of the *Arabian Nights*.

You will never forgive yourself if you visit this part of Spain and fail to see the incredibly beautiful Alhambra Palace. Of course, there is a lot more to see and do in Granada, but the Alhambra is a must. If possible, plan your visit for the cooler months. In spring and summer the crowds traipsing through this sensuous old structure are just too distracting for you to concentrate on the thousand and one details which catch your eye in what at first glance seems to be a very austere, blockish kind of architecture. But if you look closely you will notice that the cool, patterned tiles on the walls change design from panel to panel as you go around the rooms.

You can stay in Granada – if you can find a room – just sightseeing for several days, without becoming bored. In addition to the city, there are plenty of places to visit nearby, not the least of which is the Sierra Nevada. If you are there in winter, you may want to do some skiing. There is good snow until May. If you are there in summer, you will still want to go to the Sierra anyway. The twin peaks of La Veleta (3,398 m) and Mulhacen (3,482 m) are the highest in continental Spain, and you can stand on top of La Veleta on a clear day and see most of the Costa del Sol – and Africa as well. On a warm day in the spring you can even go snow skiing in the morning and drive down to the coast for some water skiing near Motril a few hours later.

One caution, however. Do not be deceived by Granada's sun at this time of year. Granada (altitude 685 m), like Madrid (altitude 655 m), is a very high city and even though it is in the south, it can get quite cold with winter temperatures often falling below freezing. You may need a sweater while touring the shady streets of El Albaicín, the gipsy quarter near the Alhambra, while down on the coast it is hot enough to stretch out on the beach.

Despite the crowds, an excellent time for music lovers to visit Granada is in June, during the annual music festival, though exact dates do vary. The festival performances take place in the Alhambra and the gardens of the Generalife, a setting that makes the occasion – which always features top musical talent – even more enjoyable.

● A few tips: Granada is a place where bookings should be made well ahead of the high season (summer), and don't even consider staying at the parador at the Alhambra Palace grounds unless you are making your plans more than one year in advance.

● To reach some of the more beautiful and remote towns and villages of the lofty Sierra Nevada (see p. 194), go by car. The local bus service takes too long, and it will not allow you to stop and get off at each lovely view. Also, do not try to cross the Sierra Nevada by any of a few local lanes that twist through the passes, such as the one which goes over the top from the high villages on the south side to Lacalahorra on the north side. I tried it once in June, and ran into a blinding snowstorm that both obliterated the narrow dirt track, which had no safety barriers or signs, and made it treacherously slippery.

Getting there

Granada has a small airport, with two daily flights to and from Madrid and one daily to and from Barcelona. Therefore, it can be reached from abroad by changing planes in Madrid or Barcelona, as an alternative to driving or taking the train up from Málaga. There is also a frequent express coach service between Málaga and Granada, but the129 km ride along these twisting mountain roads is not for the squeamish.

Main areas

Granada is not a very large city, but it is incredibly easy to get lost in, whether walking or travelling by car, since so many of its streets twist and end up in blind alleys. One-way streets, which help the traffic circulate faster and thus benefit the inhabitants, only make life more frustrating for those who do not know the city. If you have a car, perhaps the wisest thing to do is to park it outside the city and use the reasonably-priced taxis. The Tourist Office is at Pavoneras 19; Tel. (958) 221 022.

History

There were settlements occupying part of what is now Granada at least as far back as the fifth century BC, but Granada did not grow up to be the lovely city it is until the period of Moorish domination. In AD 1010 Zawi Ben Ziri, a Berber tribal chief living in the Iberian Peninsula, was awarded the fertile flatland of the River Genil for his loyal services to the new Caliph of Córdoba. The capital of the new emirate was Elvira, but Zawi Ben Ziri preferred Granada because it would be easier to defend.

He and his successors set about embellishing their capital, with the memory of the glories of Moorish Córdoba still fresh in their minds. Astute rulers managed to enlarge and enrich their emirate and, for centuries, to fend off the Christian warriors. From 1085 onwards they paid tribute to the kings of Castile, a tribute which amounted to an insurance policy.

When in 1236 the Christian forces took Córdoba, the jewel of the western Arab world, the refugees flocked to Granada, and they helped to enrich and beautify the city further, and to earn it a reputation which it retains even today, for being a city of poets. The luxury and refinement of Granada is all the more marvellous, considering that it was relatively small and sparsely populated.

Palace intrigues contributed to the fall of Granada. During the final decades of the fifteenth century, when the forces of Ferdinand and Isabella were methodically taking one objective after another, the Emir of Granada, Muley Hacén, was paying more attention to his mistress Zoraya (whose name before she crossed the lines was Isabel de Solís) than to the conduct of the war. Zoraya delighted in making Muley Hacén's son by his wife Aixa, Boabdil, a scapegoat for anything that went wrong.

When Muley lost the strongly fortified town of Alhama to the Christians, Boabdil and his mother Aixa seized the opportunity to lead an uprising against Muley Hacén; but fate did not reserve a hero's role for Boabdil. Leading his troops against the Christians, Boabdil was taken prisoner in Lucena and held for ransom. In 1483 he was released, and in 1485 his father formally abdicated; Boabdil found himself obliged to split his kingdom in two, giving half to his uncle Zagal. The Catholic monarchs wisely took advantage of the internal divisions of their enemy to advance. In 1485 Ronda fell. In 1487 the Christian forces took Málaga. Boabdil watched with dismay from the windows of the Alhambra as Christian raiders made forays into the Genil Valley at the very foot of his beloved Granada. In November 1491, he negotiated a surrender. On 1 January 1492, he and his entourage left the city with safe conduct assured to Málaga and from Málaga by ship to North Africa. To this day the bells in the Vela watchtower of the Alhambra chime incessantly from noon to nightfall every 1 January, ringing out the old era.

Even in his darkest moment, Boabdil had to endure the nagging words of his mother, whose intrigue was partially responsible for their mutual loss: 'You do well to weep like a woman for that which you were unable to defend like a man.'

What to see

Alhambra

Open daily from 9 a.m. to 7 p.m. in the summer and from 10 a.m. to 6 p.m. in the winter. The modest entrance fee also entitles you to visit the Generalife gardens. This storybook palace-fortress was begun in 1238, though the majority of the buildings date from the fourteenth century, on a green hillside in the foothills of the Sierra Nevada. Its architects made good use of the rushing streams that poured down the hillside, channelling them to supply fresh water for the palace, irrigate the gardens and fill the baths.

Inside the palace, known to its original occupants as 'The Red House', you will see the celebrated Patio of the Lions, the Patio of the Arrayanes (both with fountains), the romantic Queen's Dressing Room with its views of the Albaicín through windows that must have been designed by a sorcerer to retain their enchantment through the centuries. The baths, with their many star-shaped coloured skylights, give mute testimony to the delicate tastes of the people who inhabited this sensuously beautiful construction.

Just off the Ambassadors' Salon you will see a smaller room with a plaque, recalling that American author Washington Irving wrote his renowned *Tales of the Alhambra* here in 1829, when the palace was a noble ruin in which gipsies, thieves and story-tellers dwelt.

Carlos V's unfinished palace

A structure in the Italian Renaissance style is built within the grounds of the Alhambra, and attached to the Arabic palace. One of the talking points of Carlos' palace is the 'glory', a round room with ducts under the floor to carry smoke from fires below to heat it.

The **Fine Arts and Archaeological Museums** are in Carlos V's palace. The museums are closed on Mondays, Sunday afternoons and holidays. The Alhambra and its walls are illuminated on Saturdays, Sundays and holidays.

Alhambra complex   There is so much more to see in the Alhambra complex: the Martyrs' 'Carmen', a convent founded in 1573 by Spanish mystic St John of the Cross; the dungeons where Christian prisoners were kept; the house where composer Manuel de Falla lived, now a museum in his honour; the gate in the Tower of the Seven Floors, bricked up ever since Boabdil passed through it on his way out; the Alcazaba, a thirteenth-century fortress which is the oldest part of the complex, and the Vela watchtower, with its panoramic views of Granada.

Generalife   Beyond the walls of the Alhambra, on a nearby hillside, sits the Generalife palace and its gardens. The palace was used as a country house by the emirs and their families; but more important than the palace itself are its magnificent gardens.

Albaicín   This quarter deserves a walking visit. Its steep, twisting narrow streets and flower-filled balconies preserve all the flavour of an eastern city: and there are sudden marvellous views of the Alhambra lurking around every turn. Many of the houses in this quarter are occupied by gipsy families, whose ancestors moved into the houses abandoned by Moors.

Sacromonte   Although it is touristy, it is not altogether as artificial as you might think. The gipsies who live and dance in these cave homes make their living from visitors, but their dances and their music are authentic. Flamenco music is a living art, practised throughout Andalusia, and nobody takes it more seriously than the gipsies. Many of the caves are fitted with all mod. cons. and the Baroque decoration, featuring lots of brass pots and ceramic pieces, is the kind of decoration these people like to live with, whether the tourists come or not.

Cathedral   Begun in 1521 in a Gothic style, the building was taken over five years later by another architect, who superimposed Italian Renaissance style on the Gothic. It was finally finished in 1703. The entrance is on the Gran Vía de Colón. Open daily from 11 a.m. to 1 p.m. and from 3.30 (summer) or 4 (winter) to about 8 or 9 p.m. In the florid, Gothic Royal Chapel is the tomb that was designed for the Catholic monarchs, Ferdinand and Isabella, who were buried here in 1521.

Excursion   About 8 km north of the city on the road to Alfacar, Viznar is the
Viznar   burial place of much-admired modern Spanish poet Federico García Lorca, who was seized and killed by pro-Franco forces in 1936 in the early days of the Spanish Civil War. There is also a castle here, built only two centuries ago, with frescoes illustrating Cervantes' immortal tales of *Don Quixote*.

What to do   Holy Week (the week before Easter Sunday) is a good time to visit
Festival   most Andalusian cities, and especially so in Granada, where numerous processions of hooded penitents wend their way through the streets, carrying candles and huge crosses. Beautifully adorned statues on heavy platforms are borne on the shoulders of members of the *cofradías*, or brotherhoods of religious worship.

Shopping   Granada and the surrounding towns have maintained many typical crafts and cottage industries. A good place to buy their products is in the Albaicín in the Plaza Nueva and nearby streets. Typical are copper and tin utensils, highly decorative tin-plate lamps in the Arab style, woollen rugs from the Alpujarras, ceramic items, plus the inevitable mantillas (factory-produced in the vast majority of cases) and castanets, which at least have the virtue of being cheap!

Another place with a wide selection of souvenirs is the Alcaicería. It looks like an oriental bazaar with modern goods for sale, which is just what it is. This market complex dates from the time of the Moorish domination of Granada, and has been restored.

For those with a sweet tooth, the nuns at several convents make specialities that have not varied much from medieval times, and nor should they have done. At the Cistercian convent of San Bernardo, on the Carrera del Darro, they sell various types of cakes and sweets, depending on the time of year. The production reaches a mouth-watering climax at Christmas, when the nuns manage to turn out seventeen different varieties of traditional sweets simultaneously. Try their *glorias* (glories); they're worthy of the name. Also on the Carrera del Darro, the convent of Santa Catalina de Zafra bakes cakes to order, as well as their own almond-rich specials.

For good Spanish mountain hams, go to a shop called Sierra Nevada, Carrera Virgen 7, unless you have the opportunity to buy them on the spot at Trevélez.

Nightlife

Don't miss the Sacromonte caves and their gipsy music. Your hotel can advise you on prices. Remember that to hire a whole family of entertainers for a night is not cheap anywhere; so those without bulging wallets should stick to scheduled shows.

A simple evening stroll in Granada in the summer is a marvellous experience, particularly at a weekend, when the Alhambra is illuminated. You can stroll in the grounds of the Alhambra even during hours when the Palace itself is closed, since much of the walled area is always open, containing as it does a few hotels and some private houses.

Nightclubs

Peña Platería, Patio de los Aljives 13 (El Albaicín), closed on Saturdays. A private club, but temporary membership can be arranged at the door. Some of flamenco's most famous names drop in here to play to an audience of knowledgeable listeners.

El Patio, Calle Pedro Antonio de Alarcón (in the modern part of Granada), offers flamenco with *tapas*. There are various other lively taverns in the same area, which are frequented by students.

Where to stay
Top range

Parador de San Francisco, in the Alhambra grounds. Tel. (958) 221 440. Sixteenth-century convent built by the Catholic monarchs on the site of a mosque after their conquest of Granada. To get a room here, you should book more than a year ahead. The setting is priceless. The old convent is plain but attractive and there are a few parts where the more flamboyant original Arab architecture shows through. But the star here is not the parador itself but rather its position. January to March, 9,500 ptas; rest of the year 12,000 ptas.

Alhambra Palace, Peña Partida 2. Tel. (958) 221 468, telex 78400. Charming old hotel, built in the last century in the Moorish style. Within walking distance of the Alhambra. From 9,500 ptas.

Mid-range **Washington Irving**, Paseo del Generalife 2. Tel. (958) 227 550, telex 78519. Named after the author of *Tales of the Alhambra* and opened about a century ago, this hotel is full of local colour and ideally situated in the Alhambra grounds, but it is a little old-fashioned. Recommendable nevertheless. From 6,500 ptas.

Bottom range **Los Llanos**, Carretera de Motril s/n. Tel. (958) 597 001. This is 6 km south of Granada in Ogivares. No frills and out of town, but just right for the budget travellers visiting Granada. From 1,000 ptas (without bath) to 2,000 ptas (with bath).

Where to eat
Moderate **Cunini**, Calle Capuchina 14. Tel. (958) 263 701. Closed on Sunday evenings. Spanish cooking, with emphasis on seafood. Preparation for the most part is simple and the fish are very fresh.

Sevilla, Calle Oficios 12. Tel. (958) 224 665. A restaurant with more than a half a century behind it, whose main clientele is composed of tourists, but which nevertheless continues to produce good food. Regional cooking with specialities including the Sacromonte omelette, hake in Seville sauce and stuffed sweet peppers.

La Alcaicería, Calle Oficios 6. Tel. (958) 224 341 or 226 970. A great location near the Cathedral. Serves Cordoban specialities like gazpacho and, for dessert, nuts with cream and honey. You probably can't pronounce the name of this place, but just show it in writing to any taxi driver and he'll take you there. The food makes a more pleasant mouthful than the name.

Sierra Nevada Winter or summer, this should not be missed. The ski resort here is just 31 km from Granada. The road is twisty, steep, not as wide as you would like, and from November until March it is often icy. There are buses that make the trip several times daily. While most of the hotels are closed in summer, the Sierra Nevada parador is open all year and it also serves meals. In summer you can drive all the way up to within a stone's throw from the peak of La Veleta. This is the highest road in Europe. In winter, there is usually plenty of snow at this, Europe's southernmost winter-sports resort. In summer, the very high and wild mountains offer wonderful opportunities for hiking and mountain climbing. Near the top of La Veleta, a signposted turn-off leads to a fabulous and totally unspoilt mountain lake, known as the Laguna de la Yegua (Mare's Lagoon). Bars and cafés are conveniently located beside parking areas at sites with panoramic views on the road up from Granada.

What to do Depending on the season, winter sports or hiking, mountain climbing, and hang-gliding (with or without skis). Mountain refuge cabins, stocked with essentials for stranded climbers, dot the peaks.

There are two cable-cars, four chair-lifts and ten ski tows. The longest run is 8 km, descending from the top of La Veleta to the hotel area in the valley; its gentle slopes make it suitable for skiers of medium skill. There are numerous other runs, of greater or lesser difficulty. The combined capacity of the various lifts is about 11,000 skiers per hour, more than that of any other single ski resort in Spain. Also available at the resort are facilities for swimming (heated pool), tennis, miniature golf, clay-pigeon shooting and bowling. Sports equipment is available for hire or purchase.

Where to stay:
mid-range

Parador Sierra Nevada, Carretera de Sierra Nevada, km 35. Tel. (958) 480 400. A comfortable skiers' hotel in winter, a cool holiday hotel in the lofty Sierra Nevada in summer, but it has only thirty-two rooms. Skiers should note that this hotel is 7 km from the ski resort proper. However, so far as skiing is concerned there is no problem, since a ski-lift connects with a cable-car which goes to the tops of the main runs. From 6,000 to 7,000 ptas.

Alpujarras

These are the zones of picturesque villages on the slopes of the Sierra Nevada, one of the most scenic parts of Spain and one which fascinated the late Irish author, Gerald Brennan. The best way to make a tour of them by car, starting from Granada, is to take the road to Motril and the coast (N-323), but turn off it to the left 27 km from Granada, onto a road (C-332) which leads to **Lanjarón** (population 4,800), a famous spa. You will find bottled water from Lanjarón all over Spain and particularly in the south; it is a good brand to stick to.

Lanjarón is lovely and peaceful, situated at the foot of the Bordaila ridge. It has a fine trout river and beautiful wooded surroundings.

Where to stay:
mid-range

Miramar, Calle Generalísimo Franco 10. Tel. (958) 770 161. A place to relax in a superb mountain setting. From 3,600 ptas.

From Lanjarón, go to Orjiva, and then take the road to **Pampaneira** (population 834) and **Bubión** (population 700), two villages which look like they have been tacked up there on the side of the mountains. Bubión enjoys the distinction of being the birthplace of a Spanish boy, Osel Iza Torres, who in 1987, at the age of twenty-three months, was declared by lamas from a monastery in Nepal to be a reincarnation of one of their most revered teachers. The boy, accompanied by his parents, went to the Himalayan lamasery, where he was ceremoniously invested and began what is expected to be a long training as a Buddhist monk.

Return to Pampaneira and take the road to **Pitres** (population 1,100), **Pórtugos** (population 660) and **Trevélez** (population 1,663), a town justly famous for its delicious hams.

Where to stay:
bottom range

Pampaneira, José Antonio 1, Pampaneira. Tel. (958) 763 002. A tiny residence hotel with superb views. From 2,000 ptas (January to June) to 2,500 ptas.

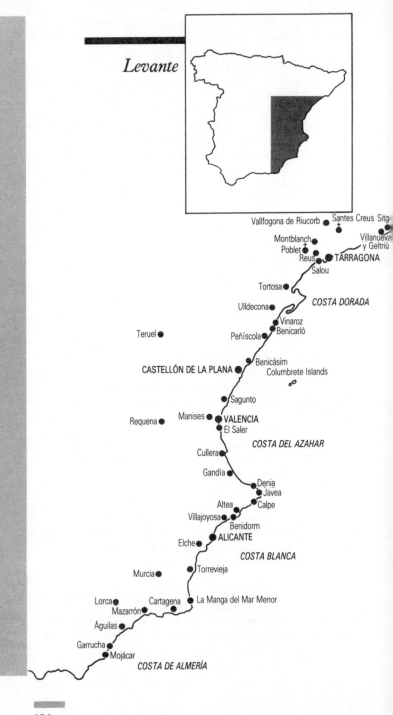

Levante

Vallfogona de Riucorb
Santes Creus Sitg
Montblanch
Villanueva y Geltrú
Poblet
Reus
TÁRRAGONA
Salou
Tortosa
COSTA DORADA
Ulldecona
Vinaroz
Benicarló
Teruel
Peñíscola
Benicásim
CASTELLÓN DE LA PLANA
Columbrete Islands
Sagunto
Requena
Manises
VALENCIA
El Saler
COSTA DEL AZAHAR
Cullera
Gandía
Denia
Jávea
Altea
Calpe
Villajoyosa
Benidorm
Elche
ALICANTE
COSTA BLANCA
Murcia
Torrevieja
Lorca
Cartagena
La Manga del Mar Menor
Mazarrón
Águilas
Garrucha
Mojácar
COSTA DE ALMERÍA

Levante

Introduction

Spain's long east coast, south of Barcelona, encompasses a great variety of scenery: some spectacular, some dull and some ordinary, but often changing character without warning. It is a mix of sprawling ribbon resort developments, suburban-style holiday estates of villas and apartments, traditional fishing villages and undistinguished towns. Many beaches, particularly along the Costa Blanca, are first class.

The climate, from Barcelona down to Cabo de Gata, on the southeastern tip of the province of Almería, is generally mild, with little or relatively little rainfall; but there are many subtle differences in scenery, and some really noticeable ones in climate and cuisine as you go down the coast. Barcelona and Tarragona wear their long history well but the further south you go, the more you get the impression that history for the locals began only a few centuries ago, with the Reconquest. As for food, fish is a staple all down the coast, but the many variations on the *paella* theme do not come into their own until you get to Valencia and Alicante, and they fade out again further south. One thing these coastal areas do have in common, however – unlike the rocky Costa Brava, north of Barcelona – is that the beaches tend to be long and open, rather than tucked away in coves.

This coast is known as the Levante, and it can be divided roughly into four parts: the 160-km **Costa Dorada** (Golden Coast), one of the busiest holiday coasts, which includes Barcelona and the province of Tarragona and a handful of cut-price, uninspiring holiday resorts to the north. Just south of the province of Tarragona lies Castellón, which together with Valencia, constitutes the **Costa del Azahar** (Orange Blossom Coast). It takes its name from the garden-like valleys of citrus groves marching down to the coast, perfuming the air with the aroma of orange and lemon blossoms.

Then there is the **Costa Blanca** (White Coast), which is undoubtedly the best known part of Spain's eastern shoreline. It takes in the provinces of Alicante (where Benidorm is) and Murcia. Charming towns nestle in its forested mountains, and some of Spain's more famous wines come from this area.

At the bottom end of the east coast is the province of **Almería**, much of it arid, craggily mountainous and uninhabited, with towns few and far between. It has such convincing deserts that much of the film *Lawrence of Arabia* was shot there. At the same time it is a centre of advanced solar power technology. Its constant sunshine, with rain a distinct rarity in some parts, led to its being chosen as the site for several experimental solar power stations, under the joint sponsorship of the European Community, the Spanish and the West German governments.

The major cities on the east coast, from north to south, are: Tarragona, which boasts a wealth of Roman structures; Castellón de la Plana, with its added attraction of the Columbrete Islands, a paradise for both deep-sea and underwater fishermen (and fisherwomen); Valencia, a city which hardly needs any introduction, the home of the *paella* and the scene of what is probably the world's greatest fireworks show, the *Fallas*, every March; Alicante, a busy port and, surprisingly, a winter resort for many Spaniards as well as a summer one for foreigners; Murcia, an inland city; and Cartagena, a large port and naval base.

Costa Dorada

Castelldefels

This town (population 24,559) is 20 km south of Barcelona. A sprawling holiday resort where many people who work in Barcelona live. It has 5 km of fine sandy beach, much of it lined by pine trees, a castle and several medieval towers. It is of limited interest except possibly as a beachside base for exploring Barcelona.

Where to stay:
top range

Gran Hotel Rey Don Jaime, Avenida del Hotel s/n. Tel. (93) 665 1300. On the beach in a scenic location with its own pool. From 10,000 ptas (November to February) to 12,000 ptas (rest of the year).

Where to eat:
moderate

La Bonne Table, Avenida de la Constitución 390. Tel. (93) 665 3755. Closed on Mondays and all of November. A small, good French restaurant.

Sitges

Sitges (population 11,850), 40 km south of Barcelona, was an old-established resort long before Benidorm or Torremolinos were twinkles in the holiday developers' eyes. Although commercialized, it retains a real Spanish flavour; a sort of animated Spanish Bournemouth, highly popular but not brash and with a maturity that places it apart from newer resorts. It has a big, busy beach with the old town above, capped by a magnificent church. Lively and now regaining popularity with package holiday-makers.

Where to stay:
top range
Villanueva y Geltriú

Calipolis, Paseo Marítimo. Tel. (93) 894 1500, telex 53067. On the beach, scenic location. From 5,475 to 8,650 ptas.

A cultural centre (population 43,560, 45 km south of Barcelona), in its own right, with two medieval neighbourhoods and an art museum in a tenth-century castle.

Bernard et Marguerite, Calle Ramón Llull 4. Tel. (93) 815 5604. An outstanding French restaurant.

Tarragona

The Romans knew they had found something good when they settled in Tarragona (population 111,689). In the first century AD the poet Martial, thought to be a native of Tarragona, told his friend Liciano to visit: 'the sun-warmed coast of Tarraco when the snow falls and the hoarse voice of the north wind howls through the land'. Today Tarragona is a busy industrial and commercial centre, noisy, traffic cluttered and very Spanish. It is a good base for excursions to surrounding resorts, though unabashed townies might prefer the urban atmosphere of a real working Spanish town. Sea breezes keep Tarragona comfortable in the summer, and winter temperatures remain mild. Snow is out of the question except occasionally in the mountains behind the city. The steady sunshine gives the wines from Priorato, in those mountains, a sugar content so great that they naturally develop up to 18 degrees of alcohol. The *Tarraconenses* will not forgo their freshly caught fish. The small fishing craft return to port every day, and their catch is auctioned off at a dockside market known as *la lonja*.

The city of Tarragona stands on a hill overlooking the sea and its own port area. The old part of the city is now surrounded by a modern one, but the old walls have been kept intact. Interestingly, it is a Roman wall, though actually built on a previous wall from the Megalithic period.

Getting there   While Tarragona, like all the major cities along the east coast mentioned in this section, has its own airport, passengers arriving from abroad land at Barcelona (98 km to the north), the destination of most of the international traffic in this part of Spain.

Many visitors to the east coast arrive by car. There is a fine motorway (with toll stations about every 100 km or less) from France, crossing the border into Spain at La Junquera, and continuing through Gerona and Barcelona and on down the coast as far as Alicante, except for a brief stretch of ordinary motorway south of Valencia. Tarragona is 253 km north of Valencia.

Trains, of course, also link the major coastal cities with Madrid and Barcelona, and there is a frequent daily service from Barcelona. For yachtsmen, there is a marina at Salou.

Main areas   Most of the historic monuments lie in the old part of Tarragona, on the high ground overlooking the sea. A park skirts nearly three whole sides of the old city, and between the park and the monumental quarter itself are the remains of the old walls. A good point of reference is

the Balcón del Mediterráneo, overlooking the sea at the wide boulevard known as the Rambla del Generalísimo. Below you are the ruins
of an amphitheatre built under the Emperor Augustus. Turn and walk
to your left. After you cross another tree-lined street, the Rambla de
San Carlos, you will see a large building on your left, the Archaeological Museum. Immediately after that, on your left, is a building known
as the Praetorium, because it was used as a guard house in Roman
days. Successive rebuilding has changed its appearance considerably.
Augustus lived there from 28 to 26 BC, and in the Middle Ages the
princes of Tarragona and Aragón lived there.

Take a street leading off from the side of the Praetorium, called
Nao, walk three short streets and turn right on the Calle Mayor. You
will see the fascinating Cathedral two streets ahead of you. Other
structures in the old centre of the town include the nineteenth-
century seminary, the thirteenth-century church of St Paul, and the
Roman Forum. A graceful Roman aqueduct, which is known as 'The
Devil's Bridge', stands 4 km outside the city on the road to Lérida.

The railway station is at Rambla Vella 14; Tel. (997) 235 012. The
provincial Tourist Office is at Plaza Imperial Tarraco 1; Tel. (997)
232 614. The city Tourist Office is at Fortuny 4; Tel. (997) 233 415.
The regional Tourist Office is at Rambla Nova 26; Tel. (997) 233 034.

History The Romans took over in Tarragona some time before 218 BC. In 45
BC, Julius Caesar designated Tarragona a province of the Roman
Empire and continued to use it as a base for Roman expansion
throughout the Iberian Peninsula. Natives of Tarragona say St Paul
preached in their city, which was quickly converted to Christianity.

The Visigothic King Eurico destroyed the city and later the Muslim
invaders levelled it again. In the twelfth and thirteenth centuries, the
Bishops of Vich and Barcelona started its reconstruction. Their job
was completed by yet another conqueror of the city, Ramón
Berenguer IV, Count of Barcelona.

What to see ● **Walled city** In reality, all of the ancient part of Tarragona is a
living museum. Even many places outside the walled city are simply
reeking with historical significance. The present port was built largely
with stones from the ruins of Roman buildings that were destroyed in
the successive invasions. Apart from the sights mentioned in main
areas above, you should try to take in the following, all of them in or
near Tarragona.

● **Cathedral** Apart from its own architectural merits, the Cathedral is fascinating because it was built on the site of a mosque which,
in turn, had been built on the site of a temple dedicated to Jupiter. The
Cathedral was begun in the second half of the twelfth century and
consecrated in 1331, so it is not surprising to see such a fortress-like
nave, unadorned and solid-looking. However, the fact that it took several centuries to finish it is clear from the successive Romanesque,
Gothic, Plateresque and Churrigueresque influences.

● **Archaeological Museum** Plaza del Rey s/n. This has a good collection of ancient coins. It is open daily from 10 a.m. to 1 p.m. and 4.30 to 8 p.m. and from 10 a.m. to 1 p.m. on Sundays and holidays in summer; from 10 a.m. to 1.30 p.m. and 4 to 7 p.m. in winter. Closed on Mondays throughout the year.

● **Mausoleum of the Centelles** About 5 km from the city, near the village of Constantí. This fourth-century funeral monument shows the penetration of Christianity into the Roman Empire. Mosaics inside depict Biblical scenes, such as Daniel in the lions' den, Jonah and the whale and the three Maccabeans in the Babylonian furnace.

● **El Medol Quarry** Some 6 km from Tarragona on the road to Barcelona. This is the source of the stone from which many of the local Roman buildings were made. A column in the centre of the quarry is known as L'Águlla del Medol (The Medol Needle).

● **Bará Arch** (Arc de Bará) One of the most remarkable Roman arches in Spain. It spans the Vía Augusta, just off the road to Barcelona, 20 km from Tarragona. Dating from the second century AD, it consists of two massive blocks of stone joined together by a semi-circular arch. Both sides are decorated by simulated fluted columns with Corinthian capitals.

What to do in and around Tarragona

There are over 200 km of coastline on the Costa Dorada, with facilities for yachting, fishing, snorkelling and swimming (fresh and salt water, including heated pools in winter). Fishing is not restricted to the sea; Tarragona's rivers contain freshwater crabs, eel, carp, pike, trout and black bass.

In July and August, the Festivals of Spain, featuring leading performers in music, dance and theatre, are staged in the Roman amphitheatre at Tarragona. Every Sunday from March to May the townspeople of Ulldecona, 133 km south of Tarragona near Tortosa, perform a Passion Play.

Street market In Tarragona's Plaza Corsini, Tuesdays and Thursdays; Bonavista Quarter on Sundays.

Where to stay
Top range

Imperial Tarraco, Rambla Vella 2. Tel. (997) 233 040, telex 56441. Splendid views, very central, courteous service, garage, pool, tennis court and air-conditioning. From 8,250 ptas.

Mid-range

Lauria, Calle Lauria 4. Tel. (997) 236 712. Near the beach, swimming pool. From 3,900 ptas (mid-September to June) to 4,500 ptas (high season).

Paris, Calle Maragall 4. Tel. (997) 236 012. Pleasant views. From 3,300 ptas (October to June) to 3,800 ptas (high season).

Sant Jordi, Vía Augusta s/n. Tel. (997) 237 212. Situated on the beach, good view. From 2,900 ptas (October to May) to 3,350 ptas (high season).

Marina, Vía Augusta 151. Tel. (997) 233 027. Closed October to April. Scenic location. From 1,100 ptas (without bath) to 3,200 ptas (with bath).

España, Rambla Nueva 49. Tel. (997) 232 712. Attractive location. No frills. From 2,800 ptas (October to June) to 3,400 ptas (high season).

Anterman, Vía Augusta 221. Tel. (997) 235 701. Closed November to April. Centrally located hostel. From 2,400 to 2,600 ptas.

Where to eat
Pricey

Sol-Ric, Vía Augusta 227. Tel. (997) 236 829. Closed 15 December to 15 January. Probably the best restaurant in the city, specializing in Catalan food. Very full wine list.

Mesón del Mar, Playa Larga. Tel. (997) 239 401. Closed 1 November to Palm Sunday. Primarily a seafood restaurant, managed by the same family that runs the Sol-Ric but slightly less expensive. On the seafront, with lovely views. Try the codfish fritters.

La Galera, Rambla Nova 16. Tel. (997) 236 143. Closed on Sunday evenings and all day Wednesdays. Yet another restaurant of the Tomás family, like the two above, and also very good. Simple cooking, with seafood specialities, such as hake with fennel and roast sea bass.

Moderate

Club de Ténis, Carretera de Barcelona s/n. Tel. (997) 201 887. International cooking.

Around Tarragona

Monasteries of Santes Creus and Poblet

The two most important monasteries, for historic and artistic reasons, are the Cistercian Abbey of Santes Creus, about 30 km from Tarragona, built between the twelfth and fourteenth centuries, where the rulers of Aragón are buried, and the Monastery of Poblet, founded in 1149 and probably built on the site of a Roman village. Poblet is near Montblanch, on Route 240, leading north-west from Tarragona, and part of this town has been declared a national monument because of its historic old buildings. Regular guided bus tours go to these monasteries several times a week, making the round trip from Tarragona in one day.

Where to stay:
mid-range

Grau, Calle San Pedro III 3, Santes Creus. Tel. (997) 602 458. Nothing fancy, but air-conditioned. From 1,400 ptas (without bath, mid-September to mid-July) to 2,500 ptas (with bath, high season).

Ducal, Calle Diputación 11, Montblanch. Tel. (997) 860 025. A modest hostel. Central, scenic and comfortable. From 2,350 ptas (January to June) to 2,550 ptas (high season).

Bottom range

Fonoll, Calle Ramón Berenguer IV 2, Poblet. Tel. (997) 870 333. Only seventeen rooms, minimal service, but the scenery is superb. A one-star hostel. From 1,300 ptas (without bath) to 1,500 ptas (with bath).

Vallfogona de Riucorb

Vallfogona (population 128), 69 km north from Tarragona, is an important spa. If you are health or weight conscious, this beautiful, tiny mountain village would be an excellent place to stay a few days, and a good base for visits to the monasteries of Santes Creus and Poblet. To reach it from Tarragona by car, take Route 240 north to Montblanch, then Route 241 north-east to Santa Coloma de Queralt, then turn left on a local road signposted to Vallfogona de Riucorb. The season lasts from April to November.

Where to stay:
mid-range

Hotel Balneario, Carretera del Balneario s/n. Tel. (997) 880 025. Medicinal baths, bar, chapel. This hotel is open all year. From 3,955 ptas (end of September to the end of June) to 4,615 ptas (high season).

Reus

This city (population 80,710) just 12 km from Tarragona, lays claim to the title of 'Dried Fruit Capital' of the world because it exports so much dried fruit from the orchards of the area. Catalonia's flamboyant turn-of-the-century architect, Gaudí (1852–1926), who designed the unfinished Holy Family Cathedral in Barcelona, was born in Reus, as was the painter Fortuny (1838–74). There is a street market: Lonja del Mercado Agrícola, Plaza Prim, on Mondays and Saturdays. Go there to watch more than to buy. This is the market for dried fruits and cooking oil.

Where to stay:
mid-range

Gaudí, Calle Arrabal Robuster 49. Tel. (997) 305 545. A hostel with a bar, centrally located. From 3,250 ptas (September to June) to 3,740 ptas (rest of the year).

Bodega visit

Unión Agraria Cooperativa, Arrabal San Pedro 5. Tel. (997) 304 847. Producers of Tarragonan red wines, exported to Britain and Canada. Weekday visits without prior arrangement from 9 a.m. to 1 p.m. and from 3 to 6 p.m.

Salou

This town (population 2,103, 12 km south of Tarragona) is a pur-pose-built holiday resort spread out along a coast of sandy beaches and small rock and sand bays in a hilly, pineshaded setting. A fairly conventional, though not unattractive resort, buses operate twice hourly from Tarragona. Neighbouring Cambrils is transforming itself into a resort, though it's still at heart a small fishing village with typic-ally Spanish bars round the harbour. You might like to stop in this area for a night or two on your way south. If so, book ahead, especially if you are coming in July or August or during the week before Easter. There is a street market at Vía Roma, on Mondays.

Where to stay:
mid-range

Carabela Roc, Calle Pau Casáls 108. Tel. (997) 370 166, telex 56709. Residence hotel, good value for money, on the seafront. Closed 1 November to 14 April. From 3,950 to 4,950 ptas.

Negresco, Playa Dorada. Tel. (977) 380 392, telex 56499. Closed 1 October to the end of March. Picturesque setting, pool. From 4,000 to 7,000 ptas.

Tortosa

Tortosa (population 31,445), 84 km from Tarragona, is further south, and is a good base for taking in the River Ebro delta. Tortosa has a fourteenth-century Gothic cathedral and an original monument to those who died in one of the bitterest battles of the Civil War, the Battle of the Ebro. This is a modern creation built on the only pylon that was left standing after a bridge there was blown up. There is a street market at Paseo del Ebro on Mondays. Buses from Tortosa will take you to beaches in the Ebro delta, including the 6 km-long Enveija beach. Check bus routes and times at your hotel or at the municipal Tourist Office, Calle de la Rosa 10; Tel. (997) 441 923.

Where to stay:
mid-range

Parador Castillo de la Zuda. Tel. (997) 444 450. Fabulous location high above the town. Spacious rooms, simply furnished, in a beautifully rebuilt old Moorish castle. Swimming pool and garden. The dining room opens for supper at 8 p.m., a detail which travellers from north of the Pyrenees will appreciate. From 6,000 to 7,000 ptas.

Berenguer IV, Calle Cervantes 23. Tel. (997) 440 816. Central, and a very complete hotel for the price. From 3,000 ptas.

Costa del Azahar

This takes in the area from Vinaroz, in the northern part of the province of Castellón de la Plana, to Gandía, in the southern part of the province of Valencia. The principal city is Valencia. From north to south, the better-known places are Vinaroz, Benicarló, Peñíscola, Benicásim, Castellón, Sagunto, Valencia, El Saler, Sueca and Gandía.

Province of Castellón de la Plana

Along the 112-km coast of the province of Castellón de la Plana, a number of minor rivers flow into the Mediterranean. The interior is mountainous. Most of Castellón's coast is favoured by sandy beaches, but it is less developed, from a touristic point of view, than stretches of beach farther north or south. Camping grounds dot the coastline. White villages in the sierras are stuck on peaks like eagles' eyries. As well as the orange and lemon trees whose perfume gives its name to this coast, the rich earth and mild climate favour the cultivation of other fruits and vegetables. The oil from olives grown in this province is prized highly, and there are some greatly respected vineyards in the interior.

Winters are mild in the coastal towns where orange trees, burdened down by the bright fruits at Christmastime, line the main streets. The same is not true of the mountain towns, where winters are cold and snow is no rarity. Few of the coastal towns near Castellón see many tourists, and some of the picturesque mountain towns receive virtually none, which makes them all the more fascinating for the visitor.

Vinaroz

Vinaroz (population 17,564), 78 km from Castellón, 141 km north of Valencia, is a fishing port with good beaches.

Where to stay:
mid-range

Miramar, Paseo de Blanco Ibañez. Tel. (964) 451 400. On the beach and at the same time central. A hostel rather than a hotel but good value for money. From 2,950 ptas.

Benicarló

This town (population 16,587) is 73 km from Castellón, 136 km north of Valencia. Attractive seaside promenades, a good harbour and pleasant beaches.

Where to stay:
mid-range

Parador Costa del Azahar, N-340, km 145. Tel. (964) 470 100. Right on the beach and in the heart of the citrus-growing country. Good, long beach, pretty gardens. From 6,000 to 7,500 ptas.

Where to eat:
moderate

Bélgica, Avenida Ferrandiz s/n. Tel. (964) 300 035. Closed on Wednesdays and from 7–31 January. International cooking with a Belgian twist, including the inevitable chips, which are, however, very good.

Peñíscola

Peñíscola (population 3,077), 71 km from Castellon, 134 km north of Valencia. Peñíscola probably existed even before the Phoenicians settled there. The impressive fortress, with its castle dominating the white town, was the refuge of 'Pope Luna', Pedro Martínez de Luna, who under the name of Benedict XIII, was one of the three people simultaneously claiming to be pope at the time of the Council of Constanza in the early fifteenth century. The castle is open for visits. Summer: from 9 a.m. to 1.30 p.m. and from 4.30 to 8 p.m. Winter: from 10 a.m. to 1 p.m. and from 3.30 to 6 p.m. Tourist Office: Paseo Marítimo. Tel. (964) 480 208.

On 7–9 September, celebrations in honour of the town's patron saint, the Virgin of the Hermitage, include traditional dances that reflect an Arab influence, followed by mock battles between armies of Christians and Moors; they fight for two days, and each day a different side wins.

Where to stay:
top range

Hosteria del Mar, Carretera Benicarlo-Peñíscola, km 6 (exit 43 from the motorway). Tel. (964) 480 600, telex 65750. Medieval dinner on Saturday nights. Situated on the seafront, good restaurant, air-conditioned, pool. From 5,500 to 9,000 ptas.

Where to eat:
moderate

Sol d'Or, Carretera C-500, km 2.7. Tel. (964) 400 653. Closed 16 September to 30 March. Supper is served from 8.30 p.m. Levante cooking. In the hills but not far from the coast.

Benicásim

With a population of 4,705, Benicásim is 13 km from Castellón, 76 km north of Valencia, situated by a beautiful bay. This is a popular resort with Spaniards. Large summer houses line the beach. The Desert of the Palms is 7 km away; it is not really a desert, but rather an area sprinkled with pines and cypresses. The Desert of the Palms is the site of a Carmelite monastery where the faithful go for spiritual 'retreats'. The 729-m high Bartolo Peak offers sweeping views of the surrounding countryside.

Where to stay:
mid-range

Azor, Paseo Marítimo s/n. Tel. (964) 300 350, telex 65503. Closed October to March. Sea views, riding, tennis, miniature golf. From 4,100 to 4,500 ptas.

Castellón de la Plana
Getting there

Castellón (population 126,464), 192 km south of Tarragona, 63 km north of Valencia, is surrounded by flatlands.

You can reach Castellón easily by train (it is on a main line running north and south along the coast) or by road, since the motorway, which runs from France past Barcelona, sticks close to the coast as it crosses the province of Castellón, continuing on to Valencia.

Castellón is not a large city and all the main points of interest, like the Cathedral, the Town Hall and the bullring, are close to each other.

Castellón does not have an airport. The railway station for lines running north and south is at the Plaza de España. Tel. (964) 226 234 or 203 240. The Tourist Office is at Plaza de María Agustina 5; Tel. (964) 221 000. The yacht club is at Escollera Poniente, El Grao. Tel. (964) 222 764.

History

The origins of Castellón are unknown, but it was originally a Roman or Greek colony called Castalia, on the La Magdalena hill which is part of today's town; in any case the first reliably recorded date in its history is AD 1233, the year when Christian warriors drove out the Moors.

What to see

Cathedral This is a real curiosity, because it was totally destroyed in the Civil War, and totally rebuilt – complete with copies of its original fourteenth and sixteenth century Gothic and Renaissance features – in our time.

Provincial Museum of Fine Arts and Archaeology (Museo Provincial de Bellas Artes y Arqueología), Calle Caballeros 25. Open daily from 10 a.m. to 2 p.m.; closed on Sundays and holidays. The best part of the collection is the ceramics, though there are also statues and nineteenth-century paintings.

Where to eat: moderate

Rafael, Calle Churruca 26, El Grao. Tel. (964) 222 088. Closed on Sundays and holidays, during the first half of September and from 24 December to 7 January. Reserve a table or you won't have a chance. Regional specialities, which means lots of fresh fish and variations on the culinary theme of the coast, the *paella*.

Sagunto

This town (population 54,759) is 21 km from Valencia. Sagunto, which was apparently a very old Greek colony, earned its place in history because of its inhabitants' heroic resistance when Hannibal besieged their city during the Punic Wars. Steelworkers in this coastal town compared their struggle against reconversion measures in the 1980s to the town's earlier holdout. Sagunto is notable for its well preserved Roman amphitheatre and ancient fortifications. Good beaches are 5 km from town.

Where to stay: mid-range

Azahar, Avenida País Valenciá 8. Tel. (96) 266 3368. Centrally located, with parking area. Not fancy, but then neither is the price. From 2,900 ptas.

Valencia

Some 259 km south of Tarragona, Valencia has a population of 751,734. Valencia is the third largest city in Spain, with a correspondingly large centre, and a lot to see. So put on some good walking shoes and don't hesitate to take a taxi for they aren't expensive.

Getting there   Valencia is accessible by air, road, rail and sea. The Manises Airport, just 12 km from the city, is the destination of numerous international flights, mostly from European capitals, as well as frequent national ones. Its passenger volume is well over one million per year and still growing.

A major seaport, Valencia is the point of departure for the Balearic Islands as well as a port of call for passenger ships both on coastal lines and heading for the Canary Islands.

The railway station is at Plaza de Alfonso el Magnánimo 2; Tel. (96) 321 3004. The airport number is (96) 370 9500. The offices of Aucona, the Spanish shipping line, are at Manuel Soto Ingeniero 15; Tel. (96) 367 0704. The fine motorway from the French–Spanish border makes car trips from the north-east quick and relatively painless. There are local buses which head north and south from Valencia, stopping at every coastal town and village. Other buses cover inland routes. Ask at the Tourist Office for timetables.

Main areas   The centre of the town is bounded on the north by a branch of the River Turia; on the south by the Gran Vía Ramón y Cajal and the Gran Vía Germanias; on the west by the Calle Guillém de Castro; and on the east by the Calle de Colón, which goes from the bullring to the Civil War Memorial Arch.

Some hotels are in this area, but by no means all. The main railway station, the North Station, is next to the bullring. The Manises Airport is reached via the road leading westward to Madrid.

Inside the area are dozens of monumental buildings. Some of the most important are the Cathedral, on the Plaza de la Reina, almost in the middle of the central area; the Archbishop's Palace across the street, and the Royal Basilica, on the Plaza de la Virgen, very close to the Cathedral. The municipal Tourist Office (Tel. [96] 321 0417) is in the City Hall, on the Plaza del País Valenciano, which is a large triangular plaza, the apex of which intersects with the Calle de San Vicente, the street which runs right up the middle of the town centre.

The Provincial Museum of Fine Arts lies just outside the area defined above. It is on the opposite side of the river, on the Calle San Pio V, between the Puente Trinidad (Trinity Bridge) and the Puente del Real (Royal Bridge).

History   The most ancient peoples of the Mediterranean colonized the Iberian Levante, the east coast; and there are towns with a clearly substantiated Phoenician, Greek or Carthaginian origin. Valencia was probably founded by the Romans, having previously been settled by the Greeks, but it did not achieve importance until the Arabs took it over in AD 714. The region's irrigation system is thought to have been laid out by the Romans, but improved by the Arabs; and even today, outside the Cathedral's Door of the Apostles, at noon every Thursday, the 'Water Court' holds session. It is a tribunal that deals only with disputes about irrigation; its judgements are delivered orally, with no records, and there is no chance for appeal; punishments usually involve the privation of water for the fields of anyone who has abused the system.

El Cid, Spain's folk hero of the Reconquest of the country from the Arabs, took Valencia in 1094, but his wife Doña Ximena lost it to the Moors again after his death in 1099. From 1099 Valencia was the capital of an independent Emirate, until it was reconquered by Jaime I of Aragón in 1238.

In 1808 Valencia rose up against Napoleon's forces and established its own government. In 1812, the French Marshal Suchet overcame a British and Spanish division of defenders, and the French occupied the city until 5 June 1813. Valencia was the last capital of the Spanish Republic in the Civil War.

What to see

Cathedral

Situated in the centre of the old town, this is a good place to start a brief walking tour. Its eight-sided tower, known to the locals as the Miguelete, was never finished. The name Miguelete comes from the fact that the great bell was inaugurated on St Michael's Day 1418. You can climb to the top of it and survey the surrounding countryside, perhaps even try to count the 300 belfries Victor Hugo said he saw from here. The Cathedral was originally a Roman temple dedicated to the worship of Diana, goddess of the hunt; it was transformed into a church under the Visigoths, into a mosque under the Moors, and finally into a church again after Jaime I's victory. Owing to the long period of reconstruction, this Cathedral is a mixture of Romanesque, Gothic and Baroque styles. The locals claim a chalice here is the genuine Holy Grail as used by Christ at the Last Supper.

Medieval granary

In a nearby street, known as Almudín, stands a medieval granary, which is now a Palaeontological Museum. Open daily from 10 a.m. to 1 p.m. and 4 to 6.30 p.m. and from 10 a.m. to 1 p.m. on Saturdays and Sundays. Closed on Mondays.

Convent

A good example of well-preserved Gothic architecture is the Santo Domingo Convent on the Plaza de Tetuán. The interior is fourteenth and fifteenth century; the porch is sixteenth century.

Bridges

The three bridges over the River Turia with ogival arches, the Real, the Trinidad and the Serranos, are beautiful. The towers and archway of the Serranos Bridge combine the splendour of an arch of triumph with the solidity of a fortress. The twin towers of Quart, on the western edge of the old section, on the Calle Guillém de Castro, were built in 1441 as part of the city wall.

Museums

Valencia's many museums include the **Provincial Museum of Fine Arts** (Museo de Bellas Artes) on the Calle San Pio V on the north side of the river (open daily from 10 a.m. to 2 p.m. and from 4 to 6 p.m. Closed on Mondays and on holiday afternoons) with paintings by Hieronymus Bosch, Ribera, Van Dyck, El Greco, Goya and a self-portrait by Velázquez. There is also the **National Museum of Pottery and Handicraft** in the Marqués de Dos Aguas mansion. (The

Baroque façade of this fifteenth-century building is incredible; and, perhaps understandably, its designer, Hipólito Rovira, went crazy after he did it.)

What to do
Fiestas

All along this coast they take their merrymaking seriously, with the result that the *fiestas* tend to be long and delightfully exhausting. One of the most famous celebrations in the world is the annual pyromaniac spree of the Valencians known as the *Fallas*, which goes on for a fortnight, accompanied by bullfights, parades, and other events that culminate in the deafening *cremá*, or burning, on the night of 19 March, the feastday of St Joseph, when scores of satirical statue groups made of wood and *papier-mâché*, some of them several storeys high, are put to the torch. Why Valencia has never burned down I cannot say. Enough gunpowder is touched off in fireworks to blow any ordinary town off the map.

Sports

In the sea and in rivers, from a boat or underwater, fishing is a favourite activity all along the coast. Boats, yachts and equipment are for hire in most major coastal towns. There are yacht basins and ports for small vessels all along the coast, including the towns of Benicasím, Valencia, Cullera, and Gandía. Duck-shooting in season and bird-watching are popular pastimes at the Albufera (see page 212). Water-skiing is, of course, possible all along the coast. There are many golf courses and horse races in season at the track at El Saler.

Shopping

The Plaza del País Valenciano where the City Hall is, is the centre of the major shopping area of the city of Valencia, and the place where most hotels and restaurants are concentrated. Products to take back home are pottery and ceramic work in general from Manises, and hand-painted fans, whose ribs are delicately carved from wood or bone (avoid the plastic ones!) and whose cloth is painted in minute detail, usually with seventeenth-century themes. Valencia, you might be interested to know, exports fans and rice to Japan. There is an artisans' and antique dealers' market every Sunday morning at the Plaza de Nápoles y Sicilia.

Nightlife

The opera season is in May. Valencia is musically minded, with its own symphony orchestra, its own choral society, a group known as Friends of the Guitar and other musical organizations. Check at your hotel or at the Tourist Office for concert details.

Casino Montepicayo, 14 km from Valencia on the A-7 motorway, offers not only gambling, but also horseback riding, tennis, a swimming pool, occasional bullfight festivals at its own small ring, and a discotheque.

Pachá, Calle Emilio Baro 71, por la Carretera de Alboraya. Closed on Mondays, Tuesdays and Wednesdays. One of a chain of very popular discos in Spain. This one has frequent live rock performances and is usually crowded, despite its size.

Xuquer Palace, Plaza Xuquer 7. Nightclub frequented by a more mature crowd.

Where to stay
Top range

Astoria Palace, Plaza Rodrigo Botet 5. Tel. (96) 352 6737, telex 62733. Central and comfortable. From 10,200 to 11,500 ptas.

Dimar, Gran Vía Marqués del Turia 80. Tel. (96) 334 1807, telex 62952. Air-conditioned, centrally located. From 8,000 to 10,000 ptas.

Mid-range

Inglés, Calle Marqués de Dos Aguas 6. Tel. (96) 351 6426. Like a rose that is past its bloom, but clean and central. From 6,000 ptas.

Llar, Colón 46. Tel. (96) 352 8460. Parking, right in the centre. A bargain at 4,650 ptas.

Metropol, Calle Játiva 23. Tel. (96) 351 2612, telex 64773. Near the railway station and the bullring, air-conditioned. A bit old-fashioned but pleasant. From 5,400 ptas.

Oltra, Plaza del País Valenciano 4. Tel. (96) 352 0612. In the heart of the heart of Valencia, with a ringside seat at its windows for the *Fallas* and other celebrations in the city's main square. Air-conditioned. From 5,775 ptas.

La Marcelina, Playa de Levante 72. Tel. (96) 371 3151. Closed December and first half of January. On the beach. From 2,900 ptas.

Where to eat
Pricey

La Hacienda, Avenida Navarro Reverter 12. Tel. (96) 373 1859. Closed on Saturdays at midday and all day every Sunday. International cuisine. A fine restaurant. Specialities include fisherman's soup and rib steak.

El Condestable, Calle Artes Gráficas 15. Tel. (96) 369 9250. Closed on Sundays. Good international cooking. Seafood specialities.

Les Graelles, Arquitecto Mora 2. Tel. (96) 360 4700. Closed on Saturday evenings, all day on Sundays and during August. Regional cuisine, which means rice and seafood.

Moderate

Ma Cuina, Gran Vía Germanías 19. Tel. (96) 341 7799. Valencian rice dishes, fresh fish and Basque dishes. A reminder on the menu says, 'Good cooking takes time. Please allow us the time.' It is especially true that a good Valencian rice dish cannot be kept on the steam table and must be cooked to order and, certainly, the rice here is worth waiting for.

Two towns inland from Valencia

Requena

Requena (population 18,512), on N-322, is 100 km from Valencia. This is not touristy but a market town, with an old Moorish castle, medieval walls and the house of El Cid, which is open to visitors. A colourfully named spa, **Fuente Podrida** (Rotten Spring), is 33 km from Requena; but the fountain that the locals really enjoy is the one in Requena that spouts wine at the end of August to celebrate the grape harvest. The wine flows free for anyone who cares to drink it.

Bodega visit

Ibervino SL, Aldea de Roma, Requena. Tel. (96) 230 0855. Utiel-Requena red and rosé wines exported to the UK and to Costa Rica.

Where to stay:
mid-range

Telephone Francisco López Cervera to arrange a visit.

Avenida, San Agustín 10. Tel. (96) 230 0480. From 2,250 ptas (September to May) to 2,650 ptas (high season).

Balneario Fuente Podrida. Tel. (96) 377 4954. Closed from 20 September to 30 June. The hotel at this spa, Fuente Podrida, is charming, complete with swimming pool, in beautiful surroundings that invite long walks, but should you tire of walking to the waters, there is a bar. Chapel too. From 2,420 ptas (without bath) to 3,355 ptas (with bath).

Teruel

This town deserves to be known better. Teruel (population 28,225) is 145 km north-west of Valencia via Sagunto. There are some spots that stand back from the bustling coast, aloof and self-sufficient, and there are places which are caught in little eddies of time, scarcely affected by the rushing current of the centuries. Teruel is such a place. Teruel is a link between the coast and Old Castile, lying on the ancient road from Valencia to Soria and Burgos. It was already a city long before Madrid underwent its transformation from a dusty village on the banks of a stream called the Manzanares into a full-blown capital.

Teruel is not in Valencia. It is a part of Aragón. However, it is in the southernmost part of that region, a mountainous area which, traditionally, has been oriented towards the coast. Teruel is a beautiful city in a remote part of the country which lives proudly with some of the finest examples of Mudéjar architecture, that which makes the transition from Arabic to Christian culture as expressed in brick and mortar, on the Iberian Peninsula.

What to see

It is a city for lovers, cherishing for itself one of the most romantic pages of Spanish history. In a chapel near San Pedro's Church, each of two marble sarcophagi sculpted by Juan de Avalos is topped by a reclining figure, one a young man, the other a young woman, reaching out to touch each other's hands. In this chapel also rest the mummified bodies of the Lovers of Teruel.

Tradition has it that in the thirteenth century Diego de Marcilla and Isabel de Segura fell in love, but her parents refused to approve the match because Diego had no fortune and, as a second son, he would not inherit one either. Undaunted, Diego asked Isabel to wait for him for five years while he went off to the wars to win fame and fortune.

When the five years were about to run out, Isabel's family found a more suitable suitor, from their point of view; the brother of the powerful lord of nearby Albarracín; and – so the story goes – Isabel was betrothed against her wishes on the very day the five years were up.

Diego, of course, returned. He burst into the bridal suite and begged Isabel to come with him, now that he had returned with honours and possessions; but she refused to give him even a kiss, pointing out sadly that she was now a married woman. It was too much for Diego, who had braved all and done the impossible to be near his beloved Isabel; and he dropped dead of a broken heart.

The next day, as the funeral was taking place at the Church of San Pedro, a slim, veiled woman, dressed in black from head to toe, walked hesitantly up to the coffin, then threw her arms around Diego's cold body – and fell down dead. It was Isabel, giving her lover the kiss she had refused him in life.

The church and chapel are open daily from 9 to 11 a.m. and from 8 to 9 p.m., except in winter, when they are open from 9 to 11 a.m. and from 7 to 8 p.m.

Where to stay:
mid-range

Parador de Teruel. This is 2 km north of Teruel on N-234. Tel. (974) 601 800. A plain, modern building with sixty rooms, usually not hard to book into, offering golf and tennis. From 6,500 ptas (November to June) to 7,500 ptas (high season).

South from Valencia

There are quite a few places worth stopping at along this section of the coast.

El Saler

La Albufera, a big freshwater lake with marshlands next to the sea, is a popular excursion from Valencia. The town on the lake is El Saler, 16 km south of Valencia. Daily bus excursions leave from principal hotels. Local buses also cover this route. La Albufera is a birdwatchers' paradise. Many species of migratory birds arrive on schedule as if by clockwork. People who live on the edge of this lake make their living by fishing from rowing boats and other small craft. Between the Albufera and the sea there is an eighteen-hole golf course, a parador, a racecourse; and along the coast are several kilometres of wide, golden sandy beaches. Rowing boats can be hired on the lake.

Where to stay:
top range

Parador Luis Vives, Carretera del Saler, km 16. Tel. (96) 323 6850. A recent building in a pine grove on the beach with pool, golf course, tennis court and air-conditioning. From 9,000 ptas.

Where to eat:
moderate

Devesa Gardens, Carretera del Saler, km 15. Tel. (96) 367 0676. Closed on Sunday evenings and, in winter, all day Mondays. A large restaurant in the middle of a sports complex that somehow manages to keep serving acceptable food, primarily Valencian specialities. But don't go on a Sunday, because that is when every family in Valencia descends on the place with all their children.

Cullera

A busy holiday resort (population 20,245), 41 km south of Valencia, with good beaches and a yacht harbour. The town is at the foot of a hill on which stands what is left of a twelfth-century castle. Cullera is uncomfortably crowded in summer, when thousands of holiday flats are occupied.

Where to stay:
mid-range

Sicania, Playa del Raco. Tel. (96) 152 0143, telex 64774. A fairly big hotel on the beach with a balcony off every room; air-conditioning. From 4,800 ptas (November and December) to 5,300 ptas (high season).

Gandía

Gandía (population 48,494) is 69 km south of Valencia. Highly tourist-oriented, in a pretty area, surrounded by citrus groves. Good long beach and yacht club. King Ferdinand ceded this town, as the seat of a duchy, to the infamous Borgia family. St Francis of Borgia, the 'white sheep' of the family, was born here. Townspeople act out the Way of the Cross (Christ's Passion) on Palm Sunday and there are colourful religious processions during Holy Week. There are some great old buildings but you have to look hard to find them among the snack bars.

Costa Blanca and Almería

The Costa Blanca, or White Coast, takes in the seaboard south of Gandía, all the way down to the fishing port of Águilas. South of there, and on down to the Cabo de Gata, which is the cape that marks the south-east corner of Spain, is the Almería coast. The latter part is less populated and less developed. The principal city on the Costa Blanca is Alicante and the main resort on this coast is Benidorm, a household name for package holidays. Another city, Murcia, also has an airport which is the destination of some international flights, but Alicante and its airport are the main points of entry for this section. Starting at the northernmost part of the Costa Blanca and working southwards, the towns are as follows:

Denia

This resort (population 22,162), 94 km north of Alicante, has sheltered beaches and a port, and outcrops of holiday estates. The name is believed to come from a temple dedicated to Diana by the Ancient Greeks, who lived there. There is a regular passenger service between Denia and San Antonio, on the island of Ibiza.

Between Denia and Alicante, the coast is marked by a proliferation of villa and apartment developments; foreign colonies inhabited mainly by northern Europeans seeking sun, a cheaper cost of living and, in some cases, retirement homes. It is not inspiring for anyone wishing to get to grips with Spanish Spain. Well south of Alicante, however, you are off the main tourist trails.

Where to stay:
mid-range

Costa Blanca, Pintor Llorens 3. Tel. (965) 780 336. Simple but adequate, in the centre. From 2,500 to 3,800 ptas.

Jávea

This town (population 10,964), 85 km north of Alicante, lies on a rocky part of the coast, and has a pleasant harbour and seafront, and scattered holiday estates. Jávea has a number of caves in the coastal rocks, some of which are accessible only from the sea.

Where to stay:
top range

Parador Costa Blanca, Playa del Arenal 2. Tel. (965) 790 200. An undistinguished modern building, but the rooms are spacious and comfortable, with lovely views. Sea breezes cool the covered terrace, the beach is handy and the food is good. From 7,500 ptas (November to June) to 9,500 ptas (rest of the year).

Where to eat:
moderate

Villa Selina, Partida Puchol 96, Carretera del Puerto. Tel. (965) 790 698. Closed on Wednesdays and from mid-November to mid-December. International cooking with good meat.

Calpe

Calpe (population 8,000), 60 km from Alicante, is a growing resort and fishing town, in the shadow of the impressive Peñón de Ifach, a 327-m-high rock jutting out from the coast, which has been compared to Gibraltar. The resort is mainly purpose built without much character, but the beaches are good and the background setting of terraced hills and mountains is pleasing.

Where to stay:
mid-range

Venta la Chata, Carretera Valencia-Alicante, km 145. Tel. (965) 830 308. Closed November and December. Homely atmosphere with only seventeen rooms and a restaurant, which features simple dishes with garden-fresh vegetables and flipping fresh fish. From 4,500 ptas, not including meals.

Where to eat:
pricey

Capri, Playa del Arenal. Tel. (965) 830 614. A Spanish and regional restaurant that is more crowded in the evening than at lunchtime.

Altea

This resort (population 11,108), 51 km north of Alicante, is more fashionable than the next town along the coast, Benidorm, perhaps because its pebble beach did not draw the package tour crowds until after Benidorm began to become overcrowded.

Where to stay:
top range

Cap Negret, Carretera Valencia-Alicante, km 132. Tel. (965) 841 200. Scenic location, pool, tennis. From 5,500 (April and May) to 7,500 ptas.

Benidorm

Benidorm (population 25,544), 43 km north of Alicante, is known as 'Blackpool on the Med'. It is arguably Spain's most successful resort and, like it or hate it, it offers what many people want from a holiday. A high-rise, concrete jungle on two superb, clean beaches. Every possible kind of entertainment. Good quality accommodation, which is cheapish offseason; it could make a base for a day or two while exploring the hinterland. The population swells to several hundred thousand in high season and the fresh water supply is sometimes inadequate. Tourist Office: Avenida Martínez Alejos 16; Tel. (965) 853 224.

Mini-cruises

A boat leaves several times a day from the port in Benidorm to the island in the bay. This is an uninhabited, sparsely vegetated rock, with a bar at the landing and lots of birds. Skin-divers like it.

Also departing from the port of Benidorm, on weekday afternoons from July to September, is a sightseeing boat that makes a coastal tour as far north as Peñón de Ifach and back, stopping at Altea. Check with the Tourist Office for times, which are variable.

Villajoyosa

Villajoyosa (population 20,638), 33 km north of Alicante, has preserved much of its personality despite the massive influx of tourists. It still has some of its old walls, and there is an ancient fortress-church tucked away somewhere among the shops selling sun-tan lotion and inflatable mattresses. Each year Villajoyosa stages a 'remake' of a medieval battle between Moors and Christians. This, taking into account its preparations and practice sessions, goes on for a fortnight or more. The people of Villajoyosa belong to twenty-two specific 'military' units with names like the Pirates, the Bedouins or the King's Guard. The battles take place to the deafening roar of blank cartridges and fireworks, and participants wear elaborate costumes while there is a host of bare bellied, be-veiled señoritas. Even foreigners are invited to join the fun, by enrolling in the *Piojosos* (the Louse-Ridden-Ones), a rag-tag band of mercenaries. It costs nothing – but a lot of stamina on the battlefield, at the table and at the bar.

Where to stay: top range

El Montiboli, Partida Montiboli s/n. Tel. (965) 890 250, telex 68288. More than a hotel, this exclusive self-contained holiday residence complex is in a beautiful section of the coast, with its own private beach and wooded areas with lovely sea views. From 11,000 ptas (September to June) to 14,000 ptas.

Where to eat: pricey

El Montiboli. Address as above. Tel. (965) 890 250. This hotel restaurant is the exception that proves the rule. No cardboard crumpets or shoe leather steaks here. This restaurant, like the hotel it forms a part of, is very good. The only problem is the price, but then, Villajoyosa is one of the few culinary oases on this part of the coast.

Alicante

Getting there

Alicante (population 251,387) is 245 km south of Valencia by road. A major Spanish port as well as a summer and winter holiday resort, it is a port of call for regularly scheduled passenger ships bound to and from other Spanish mainland ports, the Balearics, the Canaries, France and North Africa.

Scheduled flights connect its El Altet Airport with other Spanish cities as well as major cities around the world. It is on two important railway lines, one connecting it to Madrid and the other running north and south along the coast. Train services are frequent on both lines.

Main areas

Alicante looks out to the sea as it always has. The centre of activity is along the long waterfront, and the better hotels and restaurants are mostly close to the port. The Santa Bárbara Castle, which rises high above the city on a steep hill to the right of where the road from Valencia enters Alicante, makes a good landmark. If you continue along that road, you are following the waterfront. Past the castle is the old quarter, with its crooked, narrow streets.

If you get the chance to look down on the old quarter from the castle, you will see it retains a Middle Eastern look. Continue along this street; there is a charming *paseo* along the waterfront, shaded by palm trees, the pavement imaginatively tiled in bright colours, with pavement cafés, and you will see the port on your left. On your right you will see a broad boulevard, its central reservation blooming with flowers, which intersects with the *paseo*. This boulevard is the Avenida Doctor Gadea, one of the principal thoroughfares of Alicante. Walk up this boulevard about eight short streets (past the Calvo Sotelo square on your right) and you come to a landscaped roundabout. The main street that intersects with the boulevard here is Avenida de Alfonso el Santo. Three streets to your left is Alicante's Madrid railway station.

The Tourist Office is at Esplanada de España 2 (near the port, along the *paseo*). Tel. (965) 200 000. The El Altet Airport is south of the city along the road which leads to Murcia.

History   The origins of many of the towns along the Spanish Levante are lost in prehistoric times. Cave paintings found in Alcoy, Játiva and Gandía give evidence of a relatively advanced culture in the middle Palaeolithic period, probably before 10,000 BC.

The Phoenicians, followed by the Greeks and Carthaginians, and then the Romans, settled on this sunny coast centuries before Christ was born. Then came the Goths and the Visigoths. The Moorish invasion of the Iberian Peninsula next brought a long period of relative peace. For more than 500 years Alicante and the lands surrounding it remained under Moorish control. Agriculture, with Arab irrigation methods, began to prosper, with the introduction of the orange tree. In the eighth or ninth century AD the Levante region and its main port become known as Alekant. A form of Latin influenced by local tongues began to be the dominant language in the tenth century, even under Moorish rule.

In 1492, the year the last of the Moors were expelled, the Jews were also forced to leave all Spain. Then, in the early sixteenth century, the expulsion of the Moriscos (Arab Christians) brought economic chaos to the Levante, forcing the departure of nearly one-third of the population, whose ancestors had lived there for centuries.

In modern times, Alicante was the last pocket of resistance in the Civil War. The war ended on 1 April 1939, one day after Franco's forces marched into Alicante. In 1968 Julio Iglesias, then a young football player in Madrid, won the first Benidorm song festival.

What to see   *Santa Bárbara Castle*   This is on the Benicantil summit. The best way to reach it is by a lift, which can be boarded at the Paseo de Gomis (where the Valencia road joins the street bordering the port). The castle is open daily from June to September from 9 a.m. to 1.30 p.m. and 4.30 to 9 p.m. and from 9 a.m. to 9 p.m. on Sundays and holidays. From October to May it is open daily from 9 a.m. to 7 p.m. Great views. It can be reached by road as well, but is hardly worth the traffic hassle when you can take the lift.

An amusing **museum** in the castle (open daily from 10 a.m. to 1 p.m. and from 4 to 6 p.m.; closed on Mondays), contains a collection of all the *ninots* (satirical figures which form part of the statue groups that are burned in annual spring *fiestas*), which have been 'pardoned' from fiery destruction each year for the past fifty years. One is saved from the flames every year.

Archaeological Museum

This is on General Mola 6. Open daily from 9 a.m. to 2 p.m. and from 11 a.m. to 1 p.m. on Sundays and holidays. Closed on Mondays. An interesting collection of artefacts found in the area, displayed in a neo-Renaissance building. Stone Age, Carthaginian and Roman objects.

Asegurada Museum

On the Calle Villavieja. Open daily from 10 a.m. to 1 p.m. and from 5 to 8 p.m. Closed on Mondays and on Sunday afternoons. An extensive collection of outstanding contemporary art, including paintings and sketches by Dalí, Picasso, Tápies, Juan Gris, Joan Miró, F. Zobel, Saura and Genovés, and sculptures by Pablo Serrano, Pablo Chillida and others.

Excursions

The area well south of Alicante is off the beaten tourist track and is well worth exploring.

'Lemon Train'

On a little narrow-gauge railway, this runs up and down the coast between Alicante and Denia several times a day, stopping at every town on the way. It is a 'fun' way to see the coast. Take a picnic lunch.

There is also a regular boat to the little island of Tabarca, 11 km off the coast.

Mountains

There are various possibilities, if you have a car, to drive up into the mountains behind the coast. There are lots of caves in the mountains; among the most interesting are La Cueva de la Vieja and La Cueva del Queso, which have prehistoric paintings of animals and human figures, discovered in 1910. Visits are by prior arrangement only. Contact the Mayor of Alpera (near Almansa), or ask help from the Tourist Office. To drive to Alpera, take the N-330 to Almansa (97 km from Valencia), then 13 km more, past the Almansa reservoir (built, incidentally, by the Arabs) on N-430 – in the direction of Albacete. Soon after passing the reservoir you will see a small road to your right; Alpera is 9 km up that road. An old Moorish legend says the mountains are all hollow in this part of the country, and in their depths rests a golden goddess.

What to do

Water sports predominate among activities along this coast. Water-skiing: in addition to the normal system of being towed behind a boat, water-skiers can use the mechanically-towed course at Rincón de Loix, at the far north-east end of the Benidorm beaches. It consists of a cable strung from a series of towers, similar to a snow-ski tow, which takes the skier on a fast quadrangular course. There are rental agencies in all principal towns on this coast that can provide yachts and launches with or without crew for fishing, excursions, water skiing and so on. Underwater fishing all along the coast, particularly in Villajoyosa. Windsurf boards are for hire or sale in all the main coastal towns. There are plenty of golf courses. Many hotels have tennis courts and most towns have municipal ones.

Fiestas

The Hogueras de San Juan (St John's day bonfires) take place on 24 June in Alicante and also in many other coastal towns; they burn *fallas*, similar to those in Valencia.

Shopping

● **Ibi** (38 km from Alicante on the road to Alcoy) is a major toy-making centre and some of the factories welcome visitors, selling their wares at wholesale prices.

● **Gata** (about 80 km north of Alicante) is dedicated almost exclusively to making cane furniture and rush-matting.

● **Guadalest** (about 12 km from Benidorm and 55 km from Alicante via Benidorm) is known for its handmade lace. Prices are not much higher than you would pay for the machine-made variety.

Nightlife

The Costa Blanca is as alive by night as it is by day. Every town and village has its nightclubs, late-night eateries, pavement cafés and other establishments for after-dark entertainment.

Where to stay
Top range

Meliá Alicante, Playa de Postiguet s/n. Tel. (965) 205 000, telex 66131. On the breakwater, beside the beach, very central, with all facilities, but rather impersonal because it is so big (547 rooms). From 8,890 to 9,940 ptas.

Gran Sol, Avenida Méndez Núñez 3. Tel. (965) 203 000. Good service, central, air-conditioned, panoramic view from the bar on the thirty-second floor. From 7,200 ptas (mid-September to the end of July) to 9,000 ptas.

Mid-range

Adoc, Finca Adoc, bloque 17. Tel. (965) 265 900. On the Albufereta beach 3 km north-east of the centre of the city. A residence hotel with heated pool, tennis courts, air-conditioning and pleasant views. From 4,000 to 5,000 ptas. Closed October to March.

Palas, Calle Cervantes 5. Tel. (965) 209 310. Right on the waterfront. An old palace converted into a forty-nine-room hotel. Satisfactory and quaint but not luxurious and definitely old-fashioned. From 4,380 ptas (January to June) to 5,500 ptas (high season).

Palas, Plaza del Ayuntamiento 6 (another one by the same name and run by the same management, the difference being that this is classified as a residence hotel and the other one as an ordinary hotel). Rates similar to the previous one, except that the top rate here is 50 ptas more.

Leuka, Calle Segura 23. Tel. (965) 202 744, telex 66272. In the upper part of the city, not within easy walking distance of the beach or the port, but very comfortable for the price. Air-conditioned. From 4,340 to 5,100 ptas.

Where to eat
Pricey

El Delfín, Esplanada de España 12. Tel. (965) 214 911. Simply the best food in Alicante. The restaurant is upstairs, the bar-café is on the

218

ground floor, facing the *paseo* in front of the port. Fish, of any kind, is superb.

Dársena, Muelle del Puerto. Tel. (965) 207 589. Closed all day Mondays (except when Monday falls on a holiday) and on Sunday evening. This is the place to order a *paella* or the rice *abanda*.

Moderate   **La Goleta**, Esplanada de España 6. Tel. (965) 200 338. Closed Wednesdays. An old-fashioned but quite good restaurant, especially for fish, facing the port. Attentive service.

South along the coast from Alicante

Elche   Elche (population 162,873), 23 km south of Alicante, is the scene of the curious 'Mystery of Elche', a medieval miracle play which is performed every year, on 14–15 August. The chief thing to see in Elche is the palm grove, which is unique in Europe, with more than 100,000 trees. First known to be cultivated by the Carthaginians 300 years before Christ, this same grove was tended by the Romans and the Arabs who improved its irrigation system.

Where to stay: **Huerto del Cura**, Calle Federico García Sanchiz 14. Tel. (965)
top range   458 040, telex 66814. This establishment, a regional rather than a state-run parador, is relaxing and delightful. More like a motel in the American style than a hotel, it has individual guest bungalows in the garden. There is a pool, a disco and a tennis court. From 7,500 to 8,500 ptas.

Torrevieja   Torrevieja (population 12,314), 48 km from Alicante, has grown too fast yet it still has charm. It stands blindingly white beside extensive salt pans, a relic of pre-Christian and later industry.

Where to stay: **Berlin**, Torre del Moro s/n. Tel. (965) 711 537. On the beach, sce-
top range   nic views, golf, pool, discotheque, but noisy. From 6,000 to 8,000 ptas.
La Manga del   La Manga (population 1,780), 145 km from Alicante, is on a long
Mar Menor   spit of land which separates the Mediterranean from a shallow inland sea, the Mar Menor, where the salt concentration is much higher than the Med; this surprisingly results in sweeter-tasting fish. Gastronomically apart, however, La Manga is a featureless resort dominated by a long line of high-rise hotels; a kind of scruffy, package holiday outpost. You won't miss much by giving it a detour. It should not be confused with nearby La Manga holiday village, an up-market, self-contained holiday development with an unusually wide range of sporting facilities, including golf, tennis, water sports and even cricket.

Where to stay: **Galua-Sol**, Hacienda Dos Mares. Tel. (968) 563 200. Near the golf
mid-range   course and also very near the town of Torre-Pacheco, which is justly

famous for its melons. Try them. Bathing in the hotel pool or the inland sea or the Med. All water sports. A good hotel for the price. From 4,800 ptas (mid-September to June) to 7,500 ptas (high season).

Where to eat:
economical

El Mosqui, Carretera del Faro, Cabo de Palos. Tel. (968) 563 006. Typical regional dishes, with sea views and congenial service. The menu includes lamb and other meats, but the fish is what you want. Ask for *estero* fish, raised in fenced-off areas of the Mar Menor, with a distinctive flavour.

Cartagena
and
Mazarrón

Cartagena (population 172,751), 126 km from Alicante, is a major naval port and the site of naval shipyards. It is typically Spanish and worth a coffee stop at least. At Plaza Heroes de Cavite you can see the original submarine invented in 1888 by Isaac Peral. **Mazarrón** (population 10,262), 133 km from Alicante, has grown into a resort rather gracefully, with lots of apartment blocks but few hotels.

Águilas

Águilas (population 20,595), 178 km from Alicante, is a bit off the beaten track but increasingly popular notwithstanding its limited beach space. This fishing town made world headlines in 1967 when the United States lost a nuclear bomb in the sea off Palomares as the result of a mid-air collision. It took thousands of American airmen, soldiers and sailors, equipped with the most advanced gadgetry, three months to find it; and when they did, it turned out to be in the very part of the sea in which an Águilas fishing-boat captain, known to this day as 'Paco, el de la bomba' ('Paco, the bomb man'), had told them to look, right from the beginning. He saw it fall, but American officials had relied more on their technology than on an eye-witness.

Almería coast

Garrucha

Garrucha (population 3,258), 213 km from Alicante, is a fishing town next door to the small farming village of Palomares. Garrucha has a good beach that is anything but crowded.

Mojácar

Mojácar (population 1,581), 222 km from Alicante, is a dramatic hill village, gleaming white, rising among bare rocks from a dried-up, sunbaked landscape, and overlooking the sea. From a distance it looks like a white frosted cake. It is a perfect Moorish town, though now totally geared to holidays, mainly packaged. Carefully restored, it is full of atmosphere; all that is lacking is the indigenous population, though it's not hard to peel back the centuries. The main, and practically only, street winds round and round the hill until it reaches a square at the top. There is a reasonable nearby beach where tourist development is gathering pace. A local legend tells that Walt Disney was born in Mojácar, a poor Spanish boy; a statement not confirmed by the Walt Disney Organization. Hotels and pleasant *pensiones* are on the beach as well as up in the town.

Where to stay:
mid-range

El Puntazo, El Cantal s/n. Tel. (951) 478 229. A very pleasant and clean hostel on the beach and away from it all, with only twenty-one rooms, some of which have balconies overlooking the sea. The restaurant is good and reasonable too. This place is not, however, for those who want to be in the town of Mojácar, which is much too far to walk. From 2,145 ptas (October to May) to 2,400 ptas (high season).

Parador Reyes Católicos, Playa s/n. Tel. (951) 478 250. On the beach, a modern building which blends in well with the landscape, poolside buffet. From 6,000 ptas (November to June) to 8,000 ptas (high season).

Two towns inland from Alicante

Two places worth visiting inland from Alicante are Murcia and Lorca.

Murcia

Murcia (population 288,631) is 78 km south of Alicante. See the Santa Clara Convent, Calle Alfonso X El Sabio 1, founded in 1248 by King Alfonso X's wife, Queen Violane, with a Gothic cloister and a Mudéjar patio; also the eighteenth-century San Nicolás Church.

Where to stay:
top-range

Rincón de Pepe, Calle Apóstoles 34. Tel. (968) 212 239, telex 67116. The main reason for staying at this central residence hotel is the food, which is great. From 7,200 to 8,250 ptas, not including food.

Where to eat:
pricey

Rincón de Pepe. Tel. (968) 212 249. A family business founded more than sixty years ago by the uncle of the present owner-manager, Rincón de Pepe is a gourmet's landmark in south-east Spain.

Lorca

This town (population 60,627), 131 km south of Alicante, has a wealth of medieval architecture which the tourists have bypassed. Even a flood that killed 6,000 people in 1802 did not wash away the splendid stones. A column on the little San Vicente Plaza marks the Vía Heraklea; it was placed there by the Roman Emperor Augustus; the devout later topped it with a bust of their local boy made good, St Vicente Ferrer. The main square, where the Church of St Patrick (Colegiata de San Patricio) and the Town Hall stand, dates largely from the sixteenth and seventeenth centuries.

Lorca produces hand-woven woollen rugs, bedspreads and wall-hangings in traditional colourful patterns.

Where to stay:
mid-range

Alameda, Calle Musso Valiente 8. Tel. (968) 467 500. Central, air-conditioned, garage, bar. From 3,100 ptas (January and February) to 3,325 ptas.

Where to eat:
moderate

Los Naranjos, Calle Jeronimo Santa Fé 43. Tel. (968) 469 322. Regional specialities.

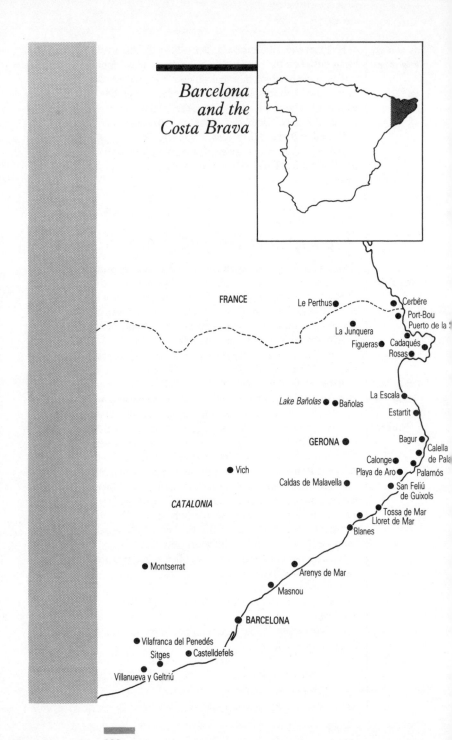

*Barcelona
and the
Costa Brava*

FRANCE

Le Perthus

Cerbère
Port-Bou
Puerto de la ¿

La Junquera

Figueras

Cadaqués

Rosas

La Escala

Lake Bañolas   Bañolas

Estartit

GERONA

Bagur

Calella
de Palai

Calonge

Playa de Aro

Palamós

Vich

Caldas de Malavella

San Feliú
de Guixols

CATALONIA

Tossa de Mar
Lloret de Mar

Blanes

Montserrat

Arenys de Mar

Masnou

BARCELONA

Vilafranca del Penedés

Sitges   Castelldefels

Villanueva y Geltriú

Barcelona and the Costa Brava

Introduction

This section deals with most of Catalonia, the proud, busy, autonomous north-eastern corner of Spain that includes the big, lively Mediterranean port of Barcelona and the well-known Costa Brava. The only parts of Catalonia that will not be touched on here are the Pyrenees and Tarragona, the southernmost province of the region, which are described in other sections of this book (see pp. 239 to 265 and 199 to 204).

Catalonia is made up of four provinces: Barcelona, where the regional capital of the same name lies; Gerona, whose seaboard makes up the Costa Brava; Tarragona; and landlocked Lérida. Barcelona has the most industry. Farming and livestock-raising are important activities throughout the region, and fishermen in small boats work the coastal waters. The rugged Costa Brava, with its mild climate and its scenic coves and villages, is primarily engaged in catering for tourists. The Barcelona coast is also very touristy, but the proportion of Spaniards on its beaches is higher, mainly because of its proximity to the city. The lovely and varied countryside of the interior is little visited by foreigners, and there are far fewer facilities there for the visitor, except in the ski resorts of the Pyrenees.

The Catalan language is phonetically closer to what is spoken in the part of France just north of the border. However, Catalans also speak Castilian, the Spanish you would study if learning it at school, and – particularly in the areas popular with holiday-makers – many of them speak English and other languages.

Barcelona

Barcelona is the most important place in this area for many reasons, and not just because of its size. It is a very ancient city, it is one of the major ports of the Mediterranean, a centuries-old centre of culture and industry, and at the same time a modern, forward-looking metropolis offering enough to see and do to keep any visitor busy for as long as he wants to stay. It is also one of the principal points of entry into Spain by air and sea.

Barcelona's official population is 1,752,617, but that figure is deceptive. The city has grown so much that towns which formerly surrounded it are now a generally indistinguishable part of the urban area. Greater Barcelona's population is over three million.

Getting there
There are regular scheduled flights to and from major European cities and destinations world wide. Barcelona is an almost obligatory port of call for Mediterranean cruises, and some of them begin there. Passenger ships sail regularly to Italy, North Africa, the Balearic and Canary Islands and Spanish mainland ports.

If you come by car, it could not be simpler. Just enter Spain via Le Perthus in France and you are on the Spanish coastal motorway (A-7) (which, I should point out, does not follow the coast in the province of Gerona). If you are looking for something along the northern end of the Costa Brava, you would do better to cross the border at Cerbère in France, Port-Bou in Spain. This road (C-252) is no motorway, but it twists and turns through some terrific views. If you want to continue to follow the coast, you have to turn off at Llansa and take a similar road in the direction of Cadaqués. If you enter Spain by road via the Hendaye-Irún border crossing, at the opposite end of the Pyrenees, take route N-121 to Pamplona, then take the A-68 motorway to Barcelona. From Madrid take the road to Saragossa (Zaragoza), N-II, then pick up the motorway to Barcelona. Madrid is 620 km from Barcelona.

There are hourly or half-hourly flights between Madrid and Barcelona throughout most of the day, every day. There is a rail link between the airport and the central Sants Railway Station in Barcelona with trains running about every twenty minutes. Frequent trains link Barcelona with other European cities. There is a daily Talgo (a streamlined luxury train) to and from Geneva. Sants is the main railway station, but check your tickets to see if they are for arrival or departure at Sants or at the Estación de Francia. The latter is also in the city, and actually closer to the main sights. There is also a regular bus service between Barcelona and many other European cities.

Main areas
Although Barcelona is a large city, most of the places you will want to see are concentrated in a fairly compact central area. It is generally a modern city, with broad boulevards and streets laid out with almost mathematical precision. This cannot be said, however, of the old part of the city near the port, whose streets were traced by the ancients well before cars were even dreamed of.

A central landmark is the Plaza de Cataluña, a square with a large clock in a flower bed, at the upper end of one long street with a broad tree-lined pavement between the two vehicular traffic lanes. This street, known as the Ramblas, because each of its sections is the Rambla of Something or Other, stretches from the Plaza down to the port. On this street, or just off it, are dozens of places of interest, including good restaurants, museums, the main red-light district, the old Gothic Quarter, the Town Hall, the Catalan Regional Government and the Cathedral.

This is not to say, however, that everything worth seeing or doing in Barcelona is there. The main Olympic complex, for the 1992 games, is taking shape on the Montjuich hill; this is also the neighbourhood of Barcelona's extensive fairgrounds, which are always occupied by some kind of commercial, industrial or cultural fair of national or international importance. The Miró Museum is also at Montjuich. There is also an amusement park on the mountainside. You can get to the amusement park by cable-car from the port area, but it runs only at weekends and on holidays. The best way to see all the attractions in this areas is to take a taxi.

Some department stores face the Plaza de Cataluña. Parallel to the Ramblas, and on the opposite side of the Plaza is the Paseo de Gracia. Walk up this street (uphill) and you will find many of Barcelona's most elegant and exclusive shops. Further up the Paseo de Gracia, you will see several buildings designed by the famous Catalan architect of the turn of the century, Gaudí.

Barcelona has an underground railway system, which does not cover all parts of the city, but is useful in the centre and is cheap. Maps at every station help you orient yourself.

The airport, at Prat de Llobregat, is 14 km south-west of Barcelona; Tel. (93) 317 0112. The Estación de Sants (railway station) is on the south-west side of the city's centre, not far from the fairgrounds. The Estación de Francia, the other important railway station, is close to the waterfront and to the Ciudadela Park, where the Regional Parliament meets. Iberia Airlines has its principal Barcelona office on the Plaza de España, which is at the entrance to the fairgrounds, near Montjuich. The Tourist Office is at Gran Vía de Les Corts Catalanes 10. Tel. (93) 301 7443.

History

Roman ruins in the old part of Barcelona testify to the antiquity of the city, though it was actually founded in 218 BC by the Carthaginians and there were settlements in the area as far back as 5000 BC. Some of the ruins, like those alongside the Cathedral, have been left uncovered and treated like a park. The layout of the old part of Barcelona tells something of the city in times past, when narrow winding streets were fine for people and animals.

Barcelona is used to being conquered, and to conquering its conquerors. That is why to this day the region of Catalonia retains its own language and its distinctive customs and also why it remains in the forefront of creativity. Barcelona was conquered by the Romans in

133 BC, levelled by the Franks in the third century AD, taken by the Moors in c. 718, conquered by Charlemagne's forces in 801 and sacked by Moorish raiders in 985. In the eleventh century Barcelona gained its *usatges*, the Catalan equivalent of *fueros* (privileges) of Aragón and the Basque Country. In the thirteenth and fourteenth centuries Barcelona was a major power in the Mediterranean area. Catalonia included the Balearics, Sardinia, the French Rosellón region and most of Spain's east coast. At the end of the fifteenth century, however, Barcelona was brought under the Castilian rule of Ferdinand and Isabella.

On 11 September 1714, Barcelona fell to the forces of Philip V, the first Spanish Bourbon king, and it lost its *usatges*. But its people's fight for independence has never been forgotten. The Catalan national holiday is on 11 September. This must be the only place in the world where the national day celebrates a defeat rather than a victory.

What to see   There is really so much to see and do in Barcelona, one of the liveliest, most historic, and delightful cities in Spain, that you should budget your time carefully in order not to miss anything.

Barrio Gótico   Don't miss the medieval Gothic Quarter, the *Barrio Gótico*, with the museums and other features it contains. As you go down the Ramblas from the Plaza de Cataluña, the Gothic Quarter is on your left, reaching from the Ramblas to the Vía Layetana, which parallels them, a surprisingly straight old Roman street that has somehow managed to keep its name for a couple of millennia.

Cathedral   In this quarter, you will find the marvellous Gothic Cathedral, finished in 1480 after nearly two centuries of work. But the result was worth waiting for. What other cathedral has a shady patio in the middle with ducks swimming in a pond graced by tall palm trees?

Plaza de San Jaume   Other highlights of the quarter are two buildings facing each other on the stone-paved Plaza de San Jaume, the Generalitat, or Catalan Government, and the Barcelona City Hall. Moços de Escuadra, Catalan policemen in red and blue fancy-dress uniforms, stand guard at the door to the Generalitat. Look up one of the side streets and you'll see a wonderful Gothic arch and enclosed passageway over the street, connecting it with the fourteenth-century 'House of the Priests', today a part of the Generalitat complex. The stairway in the Generalitat – you can go inside and see – is a symphony in stone, and one of the most photographed stairways I know of. Across the plaza, the City Hall, built only a century ago, communicates with the past via one of its façades, on the Calle Ciutat, which was left standing from the fourteenth century and was incorporated into the relatively more recent building.

Federico Marés Museum   Next to the Cathedral, on the Calle Condes de Barcelona, is the Federico Marés Museum, containing an intriguing collection of ancient items for everyday use, like instruments for mending and sewing, ladies' make-up kits and articles of personal adornment, in

BARCELONA STREET MAP

Plaza de la Glorias

Diagonal

Avinguda

8

Ciudadela Park

11

Paseo de Gracia

Gran Via de les Corts Catalanes

1

6

7

3

Via Layetana

2 Plaza de San Jaume

4 5

Calle Ciutat

Plaza de Cataluña

Ramblas

MEDITERRANEAN SEA

PLACES OF INTEREST

1 Tourist Office
2 Cathedral
3 *Barrio Gótico*
4 Generalitat
5 City Hall
6 Federico Marés Musuem
7 Picasso Museum
8 Holy Family Cathedral
9 Montjuich Castle and Amusement Park
10 Joan Miró Foundation Museum

RAILWAY STATIONS

11 Francia
12 Sants

12

10

Montjuich

9

addition to many old statues from Roman, Arabic and later times which give an insight into habits of dress. It is open daily from 9 a.m. to 1.45 p.m. and from 4 to 7 p.m.

Picasso Museum

Part of the Barrio Gótico spills over to the other side of the Vía Layetana in this area. Cross the Vía Layetana and ask the way to Calle Montcada 15, which is more or less parallel to the Vía Layetana near the port. This is the Picasso Museum, open daily from 9.30 a.m. to 1.30 p.m. and from 4.30 to 8 p.m.; Sundays and holidays from 10 a.m. to 2 p.m.; closed on Monday mornings. You will not see many of the paintings you are accustomed to associating with the great Spanish artist of our times, but rather an enlightening collection of his early work. For the snipers, it will show that he did, in fact, know how to paint things that looked like something recognizable. Perhaps the most delightful item in this little museum, however, is the Picasso porn on the top floor – his collection of drawings of ladies in various states of *déshabillé*, but with gentle florid touches.

Gaudí

The Holy Family Cathedral (Templo de la Sagrada Familia), the unfinished masterpiece of the flamboyant architect Antonio Gaudí (1852–1926), to which he dedicated forty years of his life. Even if you aren't much of a cathedral-gazer, you will certainly find this one different and worth the visit.

Antonio Gaudí, born in 1852 in the Catalan town of Reus, is Catalonia's greatest architectural genius of modern times, and clearly among the world's greatest of his day. He did not belong to a school of architecture; if anything, he created a one-man school of his own. Gaudí had a vision of the world which he managed to transmit in such tough materials as iron and stone that incorporated curves, flowers and decorative features. He stood alone, struggling against a formidable tide of his time which stripped every adornment from building in the name of functionalism, and which spurned every curve and caprice. He died in Barcelona in 1926 after being hit by a tram.

The list of museums is much too long to deal with here but the Tourist Office will supply you with a complete list. They include not only museums of art of many periods and types, but also a museum of perfumes, a footwear museum, a theatrical museum, a museum of music and a museum of decorative arts. There is a small Gaudí museum in a house which he designed in the Guell Park. Open daily from 11 a.m. to 1.30 p.m. and from 4.30 to 7 p.m.; closed on Saturdays. Perhaps the most notable feature of the park is the Hall of One Hundred Columns and the terrace which it supports. The columns tilt at crazy angles and the benches bordering the big terrace are covered in colourful tiled designs.

Excursions

Barcelona is an excellent base for excursions to places like Montserrat, the monastery in the saw-toothed mountains of the same name, which is the spiritual heart of Catalonia; Vich, a town which sided with the Carthaginians against the Romans in the Punic Wars;

and Vilafranca del Penedés, where most of Spain's sparkling wine comes from.

Tibidabo

Ask at your hotel or a taxi driver where to find the Plaza Tibidabo, where you can catch the *Tranvía Azul* (Blue Tram). Take the funicular to the top, where there are panoramic views of the city and some of the surrounding countryside. There is an old-fashioned amusement park on top, which has a curious museum housing old, mechanically-animated figures.

Montjuich

This is another place from which to get a good view of the city, but there is less to see here than on Tibidabo. Nevertheless it is pleasant to go to the top of Montjuich, preferably by taxi, and stop for a leisurely lunch in the restaurant perched on the walls of the old fort. From the windows of the restaurant you can get a clear idea of the geometric precision with which most of Barcelona is laid out.

If you are a modern art fan you will want to see the **Joan Miró Foundation's Museum** on Montjuich. Open daily from 11 a.m. to 8 p.m. and from 11 a.m. to 2.30 p.m. on Sundays and holidays. Closed on Mondays.

On your way down, you will get good views of the principal Olympic Stadium, being prepared for use in 1992.

Vilafranca del Penedés

Vilafranca (population 25,020), 48 km south of Barcelona, inland, and **San Sadurní de Noya** (8 km from Vilafranca), are wine towns in the area that produces more wine than any other part of Catalonia and most of Spain's sparkling wine. The wine museum at Vilafranca (Plaza Jaime I, open daily from 10 a.m. to 2 p.m. and from 4 to 6 p.m.) is the best of its kind in Spain, with displays that demonstrate the evolution of the wine-making process. While you are here, you can include a tour of the bodegas, but you should arrange it by telephone first. In Vilafranca, an excellent bodega in every respect is that of Miguel Torres (Calle Comercio 22; Tel. [93] 890 0100), which produces some of Spain's finest wines. Guided tours are conducted, by prior appointment, from Monday to Friday between 9 a.m. and midday and 3 and 5 p.m. Call Alberto Fornós to arrange it. Several members of the Torres staff speak English.

For the bubbly, you can visit the cellars of Freixenet, Spain's largest exporter of *Cava*, as the sparkling wine is called when made by the same process as Champagne. Freixenet is at Calle Joan Sala 2, San Sadurní de Noya. Tel. (93) 891 0700. It is just off the motorway, 8 km away from Vilafranca. Guided tours are between 10 a.m. and midday and 4 and 6 p.m., Monday to Friday. Contact Mercedes Argany to arrange your visit.

Montserrat

There are bus tours to Montserrat (population 189), 55 km west of Barcelona, inland; check at the Tourist Office for details. You can also get a train to Monistrol, which is at the foot of the mountain of Montserrat, and from there you can get a bus to the monastery. Trains leave frequently throughout the day from the station of the

Ferrocariles de la Generalitat at the Plaza de España in Barcelona. An eleventh-century monastery, which inspired Wagner's setting for *Parsifal*, it contains one of the most revered images of the Virgin Mary in Spain, popularly known as La Moreneta, because the face and hands are black. The Romanesque wooden statue dates from the twelfth century. The famous Escolanía boys' choir, which was founded in the thirteenth century, is one of Spain's foremost musical groups of its type. The choir sings daily at 1 p.m. and 7 p.m. There is also a museum with a collection of Spanish and Flemish art; open daily from 10 a.m. to 2 p.m. and from 3.30 to 6 p.m. There is a suspended cable-car which goes from the monastery to a mountaintop grotto, operating daily approximately every twenty minutes between 10 a.m. and 2 p.m. and 3 to 6 p.m.

Vich   An industrial town (population 30,057), 69 km north of Barcelona on N-152, inland. In pre-Roman times, Vich was the capital of an important kingdom. Among its monuments are the ruins of a second-century Roman temple, a neo-classical Cathedral and the fifteenth-century Town Hall with a seventeenth-century addition. The Episcopal Museum (Museo Episcopal), Plaza del Bisbe Oliva, contains polychromed Romanesque paintings and cloths from the tenth to the thirteenth centuries. There is a parador here (Tel. [93] 888 7211), overlooking a lake, about 14 km east of Vich.

What to do   Barcelona is so full of things to do, you could not possibly take it all in unless you decided to live there. As for the coast, there are plenty of opportunities for sports activities, especially water sports. Briefly, these are some of the things you can do in Barcelona:

Stroll down the Ramblas and through the Gothic Quarter, and through the red-light district as well, which is at the foot of the Ramblas and mostly off to the right. This part of the city really comes alive at night. Watch out for pickpockets. Men should beware particularly of a modern technique, in which a girl, a perfect stranger, rushes up and hugs you while her accomplice deftly lifts your wallet.

Spectator sports   Barcelona has two big-league football clubs, and there is at least one important game per week in season. The Montjuich race-track is the scene of frequent car and motorcycle races.

Sports   For those who like to participate, the opportunities are extensive in this sports-minded city. Horse riding can be practised in a number of places; for details contact the Federación Catalana de Hípica. Tel. (93) 230 9053. There are six golf courses in and around Barcelona, not counting those further up and down the coast. Swimmers who prefer pools to the sea will find that many hotels in Barcelona and along the coast have pools, both indoor and outdoor. In addition, there are many pools open to the general public. Among those, the better ones in the Barcelona area include Club Natación Barcelona, Escullera Levant s/n. Tel. (93) 319 4600; and Real Club Marítimo, Moll d'Espanya s/n. Tel. (93) 315 0017.

Yachting enthusiasts will find ports or yacht marinas with facilities for small private craft in the Barcelona port area; Real Club Marítimo de Barcelona, Tel. (93) 315 0007; or Real Club Naútico de Barcelona, Tel. (93) 315 1161. Numerous other facilities are available for yachts up and down the coast. Either of the two clubs mentioned can furnish full details.

Tennis players will find that some hotels have their own courts. In addition, information on courts in the area to which you wish to go can be obtained at the Club de Tenis Barcino, Pasaje Forasté 33, Tel. (93) 417 0805, or Real Club de Tenis Barcelona, Avenida Diagonal s/n, Tel. (93) 240 9244 or (93) 249 4354.

Shopping

Barcelona is a style leader. Its design studios lead the rest of the country and take their place beside the famous design houses of Europe. Its architects, like Gaudí in the past and Bofill today, are also trend-setters. For general shopping, the big department stores in the vicinity of the Plaza de Cataluña and the Vía Layetana are ideal. For more expensive items, particularly clothing and jewellery, try the Paseo de Gracia. For just about anything and with bargains in low-priced goods, there is a **Flea Market** on Monday, Wednesday, Friday and Saturday in and around the Plaza de las Glorias, near where the new Olympic City is being built. A tip: you are expected to haggle over prices at this market. There is a stamp and coin market at the Plaza Real (just off the Ramblas, to the left, as you go down, opposite an intersecting street known as Nou de la Rambla) on Sunday mornings.

Nightlife

There is nightlife for everybody in Barcelona. It is the Spanish city most connected with opera, and, of course, Barcelonans adore their local Catalan girl made good, Montserrat Caballé. Operas are performed at the Liceo on the Ramblas. Concerts are frequent all year round, and the most important ones are booked into the Palau de la Música, a theatre in the modernistic style and one of the most individual concert halls in the world, with excellent acoustics.

For one of the best music-hall shows in Europe, go to **La Scala**, Paseo de San Juan 47; Tel. (93) 232 6363. It is a Lido-type spectacle in all its glory, and you can dine there too, with show and meal for a reasonable all-in price. Closed on Mondays. Other top music halls include **Belle Epoque**, Calle Muntaner 246, and **El Molino** (old-fashioned), Calle Vial 99. There are plenty more.

Discotheques abound. 'In' at present is **Up and Down**, Calle Numancia 179, the discotheque with the most; that is, the most affluent and youthful clientele, the most decibels and the most palatable disco food. You can escape from the thunder to the upper two floors, where drinks and food are served. Warning: you can dress wildly but you must (would you believe it?) wear a tie. Theoretically, it is a private club, but it is easy to get in as a visitor.

Where to stay
Top range

Princesa Sofia, Plaza Papa Pio XII 4. Tel. (93) 330 7111, telex 51032, 505 rooms. Barcelona's biggest and best, with good service,

231

spacious rooms, swimming pool and all the extras you expect in a five-star hotel but don't get in some others of the same category in Barcelona. From 18,600 ptas.

Colón, Avenida de la Catedral 7. Tel. (93) 301 1404. This comfortable, pleasant, old-fashioned hotel faces the main façade of the Cathedral and is in the most scenic part of the city. Service is good, and there is a garage. Cheap at the price: 9,175 ptas.

Ritz, Gran Vía 668. Tel. (93) 318 5200, telex 52739. A bit stuffy, but with a good kitchen, centrally located, very good service. From 25,000 ptas.

Mid-range
Astoria, Calle Paris 203. Tel. (93) 209 8311, telex 94429. Central, not too noisy, good views of the city from top-floor rooms. Television, bar, baby-sitters available. From 6,550 ptas.

Gran Vía, Gran Vía Corts Catalanes 642. Tel. (93) 318 1900. This is a gem in its price range, in a nineteenth-century mansion with a fabulous art nouveau staircase and a mirrored breakfast room. From 5,450 ptas (November to May) to 5,850 ptas (high season).

Regina, Calle Vergara 2. Tel. (93) 301 3232, telex 59380. Family atmosphere, refrigerator in each room, near the Ramblas but on a quiet street. From 6,500 ptas.

Europark, Calle Aragón 325. Tel. (93) 257 9205. A residence hotel, centrally located, with garage. From 7,800 ptas.

Condado, Calle Aribau 201. Tel. (93) 200 2311, telex 54546. Central, with its own restaurant. From 6,800 ptas.

Bottom range
Mont Thabor, Ramblas 86. Tel. (93) 317 9404. Central and, above all, cheap. From 1,000 ptas (without bath) to 1,500 ptas (with bath).

Clavel, Calle Clavel 4. Tel. (93) 214 6009. From 1,450 ptas (without bath) to 1,850 ptas (with bath).

Where to eat
People who like good food will find more places than they can count, where the food is just scrumptious. To mention only a few of my favourites:

Pricey
Vía Veneto, Calle Ganduxer 10. Tel. (93) 200 7244. Very elegant with exquisite food in the international style and flawless service. Specialities include small fillet steaks in mustard sauce and grilled fish.

Hostal Sant Jordi, Travesera del Dalt 123. Tel. (93) 213 1037. Closed on Sunday evenings and during August. Catalan food, made with the freshest ingredients. Specialities include 'Costa Brava fish soup' and game, depending on the season.

Moderate
Los Caracoles, Calle Escudellers 14. Tel. (93) 302 3185. Situated in the Gothic Quarter. This is a typical Catalan restaurant with great traditional character. The entrance is through the kitchen, so you get a close look at how the food is prepared. Specialities include mushrooms, *butifarra* sausage and fish soup.

Antigua Casa Solé, Calle San Carlos 4. Tel. (93) 319 5012. Closed for the first two weeks both of February and September. A fish restaurant that has been pleasing Barcelona's tastebuds for over eighty years.

Aitor, Calle Carbonell 5. Tel. (93) 319 9488. Closed on Sundays and from mid-August to mid-September. Basque cooking. Specialities include hake fillets in baby squid sauce and, for dessert, 'fried milk' with anise liqueur.

La Barceloneta. This is the name of a district of the city, rather than a place to eat. There are quite a few popular restaurants in this area near the port, where the emphasis is on fresh fish and Catalan cooking at popular prices. The décor of the restaurants is plain as a rule, and the crowds often make the service a little slow, but the proof of the value of such places is their staying power. **Casa Costa**, for instance, has been serving Barcelonans for more than fifty years.

Casa Costa, Calle Baluarte 124. Tel. (93) 319 5028. Closed on Sunday evenings. The most traditional of the popular fish restaurants. Try the *zarzuela* (shellfish salad) or the mixed grill of fish and shellfish. There is parking space here.

Economical   **Can Culleretes**, Calle Quintana 5. Tel. (93) 317 6485. Closed on Sunday evenings, all day Monday, and during July. Strictly Catalan; but if you do not understand the menu, you will not go wrong by blindly ordering the menu of the day. Highly recommended. Catalans have been eating here for more than two centuries.

Vegetariano, Calle Santa Ana 11. The name means exactly what you think. If you are vegetarian or just curious to see the many ways vegetables can be served deliciously, try it. If you think a meal is not complete without fish or meat, let them show you otherwise. Self-service.

North from Barcelona and the Costa Brava

The immediate coast north of Barcelona is part of the Costa Dorada, which also extends south beyond Tarragona and is covered on pp. 198 to 202. However, the northward stretch of coast between Barcelona and Tossa de Mar can be safely ignored. It consists of a hotch potch of package holiday resorts without character or charm and that often have the main railway cutting off the towns near the beaches. Only Blanes (population 20,178), 64 km north of Barcelona, has any real claims to being a Spanish fishing town as well as a resort.

Although the first of the holiday costas, and still popular, the Costa Brava is far less developed than the Costas Blanca or del Sol. It's also far more attractive, a rugged coast of rocky inlets and sandy coves, with cork and pine trees growing down to the water's edge. Some beaches shelve steeply and are of pebbles or coarse sand. Most resorts are little more than enlarged fishing villages, cheerful, informal and still retaining the atmosphere of pre-mass tourism days.

Lloret de Mar

The Costa Brava begins at Lloret, a resort with lots of everything except charm. Lloret (population 10,480), 70 km north of Barcelona, probably has more hotel beds and tourist apartments than any other town on the Costa Brava and it also has the liveliest nightlife on this coast. If you don't want this, head further north.

Tossa de Mar

Tossa (population 2,969), 83 km north of Barcelona, the first package holiday resort in Spain, still retains some character: narrow streets and medieval fortifications. This is where the most scenic stretch of the Costa Brava really gets going and continues spectacularly to the French border.

Where to stay: top range

Gran Hotel Reymar, Playa Mar Menuda. Tel. (972) 340 312, telex 57094. Central and scenically located, with bar and pool. Closed from November to April. From 7,200 to 8,800 ptas.

San Feliú de Guixols

San Feliú (population 12,006) is 105 km north of Barcelona. Full of authentic Spanish atmosphere, this is a bustling commercial town rather than a beach resort. With an attractive esplanade and venerable buildings, it has a fine bay in one of the most beautiful parts of the Costa Brava, because the cliffs in this area are the highest on the coast. Memorable views from the Hermitage of Sant Elm, 3 km from the centre. The beach at San Pol, 3 km from San Feliú, is better than the one at the port. The S'Agaro beach is also good for water sports. S'Agaro itself is an exclusive suburb of San Feliú, with an exclusive hotel, **de la Gavina**.

Where to stay: mid-range

Montjoi, Sant Elm s/n. Tel. (972) 320 300, telex 94442. Garage, swimming pool, scenic location. Closed from November to March. From 3,000 to 4,600 ptas.

Where to eat: pricey

El Dorado Petit, Rambla Vidal 11. Tel. (972) 321 818. Catalan cooking with an international influence. This restaurant is even better than the good one by the same name in Barcelona.

Gerona

Gerona (population 87,648) is 99 km north of Barcelona and 59 km from the French border. If you come by plane, you may arrive in Gerona, if your ultimate destination is the northern part of the Costa Brava. If you come by car, you may want to stop here to rest on your way further south. In either case Gerona deserves a visit of at least a day. The ancient part of the city is one of the best preserved in Catalonia.

What to see

Your visit should include a look at the following.

● The **Arab Baths** (open daily from 10 a.m. to 2 p.m. and from 4 to 7 p.m., except in winter, when they are open only from 10 a.m. to 1 p.m.), which were rebuilt in 1294.

● **Roman walls** in the centre of the town.

● **Archaeological Museum**, notable for the twelfth-century monastery in which it is housed and for its prehistoric artefacts and its statues from the eleventh to the fourteenth centuries. There is an out-door market every Tuesday and Saturday in the Paseo de la Dehesa.

Excursion to Bañolas

Bañolas (population 12,348) is 18 km from Gerona. It is on the edge of a natural lake fed by underground rivers and grew up around a ninth-century Benedictine monastery. The present **Sant Esteve Monastery** building dates from the sixteenth and seventeenth centuries. The **Darder Municipal Museum** at Bañolas, Plaza Estudios 2, is a sight to see with a macabre collection of stuffed and mounted 'monsters' and of human skulls. Lake Bañolas is a centre for small-craft sailing, motorboating and windsurfing. The best spots tend to get crowded at weekends in good weather.

Where to stay in Gerona: mid-range

Costabella, Avenida de Francia 61. Tel. (972) 202 524. A small hotel, with garage. From 3,870 ptas (November to April) to 4,450 ptas (high season).

Ultonia, Avenida Jaime I 22. Tel. (972) 203 850. Centrally located, garage. From 5,060 ptas (January and February) to 5,700 ptas.

Europa, Carrer Juli Garreta 23. Tel. (972) 202 750. Small, central. From 3,200 ptas.

Spa

The **Caldas de Malavella** spa, used since Roman times to allevi-ate the symptoms of rheumatism and respiratory and circulatory complaints, is 20 km south of Gerona, via N-II, then left on a local road for the last 5 km or so. Spain's most appreciated mineral water, Vichy Catalán, comes from these springs.

Where to stay: mid-range

Balneario Prats, Plaza Sant Esteve 7. Tel. (972) 470 051. Scenic and central location at Caldas de Malavella. Bar, garage and restaurant. From 2,000 to 4,100 ptas.

Playa de Aro

A major tourist centre (population 1,391), 111 km north of Barce-lona, with nightlife that draws tourists from other towns up and down the coast. Long sandy beach.

Where to stay: top range

Columbus, Paseo del Mar s/n. Tel. (972) 817 166, telex 57162. On the beach, with golf courses, heated pool, scenic views. From 5,450 to 11,000 ptas.

Hostal de la Gavina, Plaza de la Rosaleda, S'Agaro. Tel. (972) 321 000, telex 57132. Closed November to March. The highest-priced hotel on the Costa Brava. What price exclusiveness? From 15,500 to 22,500 ptas.

Where to eat: pricey

Mas Nou, Urbanización Mas Nou. Tel. (972) 827 853. Closed 10 January to 10 February and every Wednesday in winter except holi-days. International cooking with a French touch. Terrace.

Calonge

Calonge (population 4,362) and its port, San Antonio de Calonge, 115 km north of Barcelona, has mushroomed with the increasing tourist trade in recent years. Calonge has a medieval quarter around its castle. San Antonio is 3 km from the centre of Palamós.

Palamós

Palamós (population 12,178), 118 km north of Barcelona, has an excellent harbour, and is a centre for yachting, water-skiing and so on. The nearby cliffs make this a scenic place. Nearly 1 km of beaches.

Where to stay:
mid-range

Trias, Paseo del Mar s/n. Tel. (972) 314 100. Closed mid-October to 1 March. Central location with lovely views, garage, bar, swimming pool, facilities for the handicapped. From 5,000 to 7,000 ptas.

Where to eat:
moderate

María de Cadaqués, Calle Notaries 39. Tel. (972) 314 009. Closed on Mondays and from 15 December to 15 January. The cooking is uncomplicated and the fish is very fresh. Hard to get into without a reservation. Good selection of Catalan white wines to go with the seafood.

Calella de Palafrugell

A town (population 424), 130 km north of Barcelona, which still looks pretty much like a fishing village, and has a string of small beaches. It is picturesque, quiet and relatively unspoilt and more attractive than its next-door neighbour, Llanfranch.

Bagur

Bagur (population 2,277), 134 km north of Barcelona, with the centre huddling around its castle on a hill, and neat, white-washed walls in the narrow streets. Great view from the top. Various coves in the area, each one more beautiful than the other, embrace small sandy beaches. The Aiguablava parador (see below) is in one of those coves.

Where to stay:
top range

Parador Costa Brava, Playa de Aiguablava. Tel. (972) 622 162. Perched on a cliff above the sea, this inn is in one of the most scenic locations on the Costa Brava. Its restaurant specializes in Catalan food and is well rated. There is a swimming pool, plus air-conditioning, a sauna, facilities for water sports and hunting. From 7,500 to 8,500 ptas.

Estartit and La Escala

Estartit (population 687) is 135 km north of Barcelona; its fishing quarter has virtually disappeared, but it has a good marina. Its biggest asset is its beach, which is one of the best on the Costa Brava. Its 2 km beach faces the little Medas Isles, where the Spanish Government has established a marine wildlife reserve. **La Escala** (population 4,048), 160 km north of Barcelona, is an authentic fishing townlet rather than a resort. There is an excellent beach ten minutes' walk away at Ampurias, where you can wander among the remains of Greek and Roman civilizations. Nearby is a sprawling holiday development.

Figueras

Figueras (population 30,227), 220 km north of Barcelona, where Salvador Dalí lives now, in a palace with high walls and huge eggs on the turrets. The **Dalí Museum** is here too, with an old Cadillac mounted on a column as a centrepiece. Open daily from 10.30 a.m. to 12.30 p.m. and from 3.30 to 7.30 p.m.; closed on Mondays in winter. Not on the coast, Figueras is an important centre of commerce.

Where to stay:
mid-range

Ampurdán, Carretera General Madrid-Francia, km 763. Tel. (972) 500 562. Centrally located, with garage and a good restaurant. From 5,200 to 6,400 ptas.

Where to eat:
pricey

Ampurdán, Address as above. Catalan cooking. Fish dishes predominate.

Rosas

Rosas (population 8,101), 188 km north of Barcelona, is a fair-sized fishing port and the most important tourist centre in the northern part of the Costa Brava. It is at one end of an immense bay, with mountains rising dramatically behind and 4 km of sandy beaches. Views from the heights are panoramic and especially beautiful at sunset. Yacht marina, medieval buildings and archaeological remains make it a worth-while stop, regardless of the fact that it is very touristy. Big holiday hotels have been built along the beach.

Where to stay:
mid-range

Almadraba Park, Playa Almadraba s/n. Tel. (972) 256 550, telex 57032. Pool, lovely scenery, sauna. Closed 20 October to 10 April. From 5,700 to 7,200 ptas.

Where to eat:
pricey

Hacienda El Bulli, Cala Montjoi. Tel. (972) 257 651. Closed on Mondays and on Tuesdays at midday as well in the low season. Also closed 15 January to 15 March. French and international cooking.

Cadaqués

This fishing town (population 1,547), 198 km north of Barcelona, retains its charm and resists the changes wrought by tourism elsewhere since access is by a tortuous mountain road or by sea and the mass of tourists are kept at bay. The former home of Salvador Dalí and of distinguished writers and poets, Cadaqués continues to inspire artists and lovers. Its tiny beaches are proof of the saying, 'Good things come in small packages'.

Where to stay:
mid-range

Llane Petit, Playa Llane Petit s/n. Tel. (972) 258 050. Closed from October until March. A small hotel with garaging in a lovely setting. From 3,500 to 6,500 ptas.

Where to eat:
moderate

La Galiota, Calle Narcís Monturiol 9. Tel. (972) 258 187. Open daily all summer; in winter only open on Saturdays, Sundays and holidays. A small, often crowded place.

Puerto de la Selva and Port-Bou

Puerto de la Selva is a peaceful fishing port in a tranquil setting of craggy hills; the big, natural harbour is encircled by hills and headlands. **Port-Bou** marks the end of the Costa Brava. It is a small, drab frontier town wedged in a deep cleft among bare hills. It is the arrival point of trains from France; otherwise, it has little to recommend it.

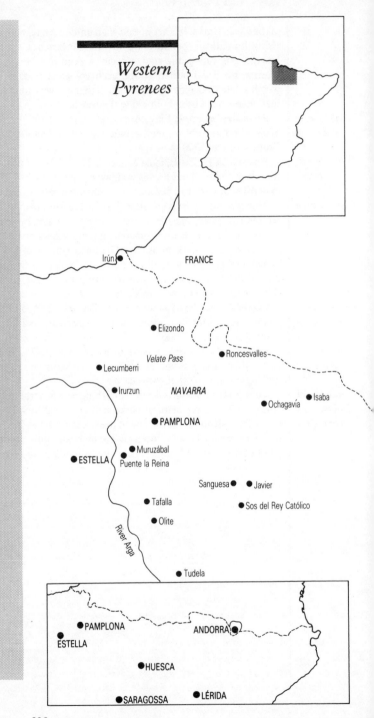

Western
Pyrenees

Irún

FRANCE

Elizondo

Velate Pass

Roncesvalles

Lecumberri

Irurzun

NAVARRA

Ochagavía

Isaba

PAMPLONA

Muruzábal

ESTELLA

Puente la Reina

Sanguesa

Javier

Tafalla

Sos del Rey Católico

Olite

River Arga

Tudela

PAMPLONA

ANDORRA

ESTELLA

HUESCA

SARAGOSSA

LÉRIDA

Pyrenees

Introduction

The formidable mountain barrier of the Pyrenees, with many peaks over 3,000 m high, has long served to isolate Spain from the rest of Europe and preserve its exotic character. In much the same way, high mountain ranges within Spain limited cultural and commercial exchange and thus tended to preserve local traditions and languages. In this age of satellite television, global marketing of mass-produced goods and a growing international travel industry, the differences in customs, which intrigue all of us and which are often a major factor in influencing a choice of holiday destination, are becoming fewer all the time. The Pyrenees are, however, an exception. They are slower to change than many other parts of the world; even in this age their topography continues to keep the region isolated and for this reason they are a good choice for the traveller who wants to know more about the world he lives in.

Most of this very extensive mountain range actually lies on the Spanish side of the border. It constitutes an especially beautiful part of the country, ideal for mountain climbing and winter sports, and a perfect area for admirers of Romanesque architecture. It is also an area with abundant wildlife, because of its relative inaccessibility and because of the many parks and wildlife preserves that have been created there. The rural population, for the most part, is dedicated to farming. Because of the good skiing, the tourist season in most towns is in the winter.

The major Spanish cities related to the Pyrenees by reason of trade routes, markets, history or language and culture, from west to east, are Pamplona, Huesca and Lérida. Saragossa (Zaragoza) is important too because it is, and has been through the ages, the capital of Aragón, the region in which the most impassable peaks lie. There is a considerable amount of industry in both Pamplona and Saragossa.

Barcelona is a starting point for visitors going to the eastern end of the Pyrenees and to the postage-stamp-sized country of Andorra, an independent co-principality, ruled, according to a medieval pact, by the King (now by the President) of France and the Archbishop of the Spanish town of Seo de Urgel. There are other national curiosities in the Pyrenees, such as the enclave of Llivia, a Spanish town completely surrounded by France. Then there is the appropriately-named village of Plan, whose bachelors put it on the map one long winter's night in 1985, when they were playing cards in the only bar and hankering for some female company. It dawned on them that there were few girls of marriageable age in the whole valley because they were all being lured away by the bright lights of the cities.

Although Plan, they reasoned, was not a bad village, being pleasant, reasonably attractive and modestly prosperous, it was boring. And it was growing more boring all the time, what with a lack of pretty faces and the cries of children. So they came up with a plan for Plan. They chipped in to put an advertisement in a newspaper in the nearest city, Saragossa, about 200 km away, inviting marriage-minded young women to phone the bar. They received hundreds of calls, some surprisingly from as far away as Tokyo and London. So they organized a *fiesta* such as the town had never seen before. They turned the main square into a brightly decorated disco and dining area. They made preparations to roast whole calves and sheep. They coaxed the rest of the townspeople into making bedrooms available for their guests.

When all was ready, and the spring thaw had definitely set in, they wrote to all the girls who answered their advertisement, about 300 of them, and chartered buses to bring them from Saragossa and Barcelona. Some couples hit it off right away; and, before a year had gone by, the first Plan-plan wedding had taken place. The first child of a couple who married after meeting at the bachelors' ball was born less than two years after that first party. It was so successful that the bachelors have repeated it every year since.

Plan has no hotels, so any lady readers who would like to check it out for themselves should ask the Saragossa Tourist Office for the dates of the annual match-making *fiesta*, a moveable and moving feast.

You cannot travel from one end of the Pyrenees to the other without going down into the relatively flat country below because the terrain is too rough. Therefore I will consider this area in three parts: the western Pyrenees, reachable from Pamplona; the central part, reachable from Saragossa or Huesca, and the eastern part, reachable from Barcelona or Lérida.

The Western Pyrenees: Pamplona

Pamplona (population 183,126), is 98 km from the border-crossing at Irún, 159 km from Bilbao and 175 km from Saragossa. This is where the San Fermín bullrunning festival that was popularized by Hemingway takes place every year, on 6–14 July. This is not a particularly swinging town for the rest of the year, when they practically roll up the pavements at night; but it does have some good restaurants and it makes a good base for taking in the scenery, while stopping off on your way to or from the mountains. Pamplona is cold and rainy in the winter but mild the rest of the year.

Getting there

Pamplona and Navarra, the ancient kingdom (and now an autonomous region) of which it is the capital, should ideally be seen by car, but you can reach them by train. A major railway line passes through the city, running to Madrid and beyond from France. There are plenty of trains in either direction throughout the day. The railway station (Tel. [948] 250 246) is 2 km from the town centre on the road to San Sebastián; the railway ticket office is at Calle Estella 8 (Tel. [948] 222 429). The bus station is on Avenida Conde Oliveto 2 (Tel. [948] 111 531), one street west of the Plaza Principe de Viana, near the Citadel.

Pamplona does have an airport at nearby Noaín (Tel. [948] 318 202), though scheduled international flights do not normally land there.

Main areas

The old fortress-city of Pamplona is the most delightful part of the town, and the young people gather there to talk and to take refreshment in the bars in its narrow streets at night. The Plaza del Castillo, rectangular and green, is at the centre of the old town. The bullring lies at its southern edge and the Cathedral, begun at the end of the fourteenth century, stands on the ramparts of the east side. The Navarra Museum is on the northern edge, and the star-shaped Citadel perches high above gardens in the south-west corner of the old town.

Most of the better restaurants and hotels are in the area surrounding the Plaza del Castillo. The Tourist Office is at Calle Duque de Ahumada 3; Tel. (948) 220 748.

History

Pamplona, on the banks of the River Arga, lays claim to 2,000 years of history. It fell to the Moors more than once in the eighth century AD. In 778 Basque troops expelled the Moors and asked for Charlemagne's protection. He took advantage of the opportunity to topple the walls just in case the city should try to reject his rule. The Pamplonans were so annoyed that they wiped out Charlemagne's rearguard at Roncesvalles (Roncevaux) in a battle immortalized in the *Song of Roland*. Nevertheless, Navarra fell under the rule of French kings for nearly three centuries, as a result of marriages between royal families, until it was formally annexed by Aragón and later by Castile in the early sixteenth century, retaining a degree of home rule, which it lost in 1841 after the first Carlist War.

Later it recovered some of its *fueros*, or privileges. As the names of Navarra's towns indicate, much of its population is or originally was Basque and Pamplona is often referred to by its Basque name of Iruña. However, it does not officially form part of the Basque Country according to the present regional boundary lines.

What to see

The **'San Fermínes'** are celebrations in honour of the patron saint of Pamplona, St Fermín. The principal events are the daily early morning races along a route of city streets leading from the Town Hall to the bullring, in which young men run with the same fierce fighting bulls which are to be fought later that day in the bullring. Any able-bodied man or woman is entitled to run if he or she chooses, whether or not they are from Pamplona.

It looks dangerous and it is. The bulls are fast; they weigh half a ton each; their horns can gouge and hook with accuracy and strength, powered by great neck muscles; and they are bred to attack. To compound the risk, there are so many people taking part that some runners find it hard to escape from a bull's horn because of the mob blocking their way at the crucial moment. Every year there are gorings; occasionally some of the revellers die.

When they are not running in front of the bulls, the young men spend their time at the bullring for the daily fight featuring top-class *matadores*, dancing a *jota* in mass formation in the streets and drinking red wine from wineskins. Although some girls now run along with the men, the nature of this death-defying ritual makes it one of the last and greatest of the world's great macho parties, fittingly popularized by Hemingway. The author of *The Sun Also Rises* is commemorated by a bust outside the bullring.

If you are thinking of visiting Pamplona during the San Fermín *fiestas* in July, you had better book at least one year ahead. The hotel capacity is limited; and many San Fermín regulars have a standing order for their rooms. During the *fiestas* even a mattress on the floor is a good find. Many Pamplona people take in boarders for the period. Some young people even sleep outside in the squares, having run with the bulls in the morning and having partied all night. Some are happy to see the 'San Fermines' just once, but there are others who can't quit and keep coming back. In any case, there is something contagious and exhilarating about the event.

Cathedral   Outside the *fiesta* period, take in the fourteenth-century Gothic Cathedral, with its neoclassical façade by Ventura Rodríguez, added in the late eighteenth. The Cathedral is open daily from 8 a.m. to 1.30 p.m. and 4 to 10 p.m. in summer, and from 8 a.m. to 12.30 p.m. and 6 to 8 p.m. in winter.

Other places   Also look at: the **Town Hall**, with its Baroque façade, from a
worthy of note   balcony of which the mayor sets off the *chupinazo*, the first small rocket that signals the start of the San Fermín *fiestas*; the thirteenth-century Gothic fortress-church of **San Cernín**; and the **Citadel** (Ciudadela), a sixteenth-century fort set in lovely gardens, which is now used for art exhibitions and concerts. The **Navarra Museum** (Museo de Navarra), Calle Santo Domingo s/n, is in a building originally used as a hospital with a mid-sixteenth-century Plateresque doorway. The outside is all you can see. The museum has been closed for renovation since 1985.

What to do   Mountain-climbing is practised throughout the area, though, of

Sports | course, it should not be attempted without proper training and equipment. For the less ambitious, there are plenty of lanes and paths for walking and hiking. Hunting and fishing are also popular activities, particularly around Higa de Monreal, Ulzama, Aéxcoa and Salazar; the sierras of Alaiz, Leyre, Urbaza, Andía and Santiago de Lóquiz, and the Valleys of Roncal and Larraún. Hunting and fishing licences are required, and closed seasons and bag limits must be respected. Arrange licences beforehand if possible, through an official Spanish tourist office abroad. If you bring your own guns you should obviously inquire first for regulations concerning arms.

There is skiing at Isaba and other towns, but Navarra does not have any organized ski resorts as such. These are to be found further east.

Shopping | Spain's most famous wineskins (*botas*) are produced in Pamplona under the brand name of ZZZ (Tres Zetas). Buy them at Calle Comedias 7. There are various ways to 'cure' your *bota*, that is, to make it suitable for drinking wine from. Here is one:

Fill it first with dry aniseed liqueur and let it hang by its cord for a few days. Empty it and fill it immediately with red wine of reasonably good quality. After a day or two pour out this wine and fill it again with some more reasonably good red. It is now ready for use. Initially, wine from a *bota* tastes of leather but eventually that taste goes away. Keep the top on it, never use it for any other liquid, drink frequently from it and never let your *bota* go dry, or it will be ruined.

Interesting buys in the mountain villages are wooden pitchers and shoes and similar handicraft. Small carved wooden statues are also good items to take back home. In Isaba, the Roncal cheese is a must.

Nightlife | There is not much nightlife in Pamplona and even less in the mountains. Just about the only evening entertainment that draws any kind of crowd is eating and drinking. The bars in the streets around the Plaza del Castillo tend to fill up after dark with young men (and relatively few young women) who talk endlessly and sometimes sing. In good weather they form groups in the street outside the bars. The thing to drink is Pacharán, a slightly sweet red liqueur of the region. Drink it chilled, and sparingly.

Where to stay | Most of Pamplona's hotels can be found in the old part of the town, around the Plaza del Castillo, or in the vicinity of the Town Hall or the Cathedral. All hotels charge at top rate during the San Fermines.

Top range | **Tres Reyes**, Jardines de la Taconera s/n. Tel. (948) 226 600, telex 37720. This is Pamplona's best, a medium-sized hotel with good service, air-conditioning and television in the rooms. From 10,000 to 22,000 ptas.

Nuevo Hotel Maisonnave, Calle Nueva 20. Tel. (948) 222 600. In the old quarter. Television in the rooms. Parking. From 5,400 to 11,000 ptas.

Ciudad de Pamplona, Iturrama 21. Tel. (948) 266 011, telex 37913. A relatively new, very functional hotel near the University of

Navarra in the modern part of town. Comfortable and businesslike, but the rooms could be a trifle larger. From 5,800 to 11,000 ptas.

Mid-range   **Amezcoa**, Calle Iturralde y Suit 1. Tel. (948) 235 043. A simple hostel with no frills and no private baths. From 1,800 to 4,000 ptas.

Bearán, Calle San Nicolás 25. Tel. (948) 223 428. A basic residence hostel with only fifteen rooms. From 1,100 ptas (without bath, low season) to 2,600 ptas (with bath, May to September).

Ibarra, Calle Estafeta 85. Tel. (948) 220 606. Simple, no private baths, just twelve rooms. Right on the street where the bulls run. From 1,400 to 4,000 ptas.

Velate Monastery, Travesia de Velate 2. Tel. (948) 253 054. Ten unadorned rooms. From 2,000 ptas (without private bath, October to June) to 7,000 ptas (with bath during the San Fermínes).

Bottom range   **Casa García**, Calle San Gregorio 12. Tel. (948) 223 893. Central, small and plain. From 1,150 ptas (no private baths).

Where to eat   The western end of the Pyrenees is an area in which people are proud of their local customs and take eating very seriously. As a result it is a land of good restaurants, but not cheap ones. Nearly all of them stick to traditional Navarrese cooking. If all you want is a snack, go to the nearest bar and ask for a *tapa*; but if you have the time and inclination to savour some really good dishes that you will not easily find elsewhere, then do stop at one of the following places.

Pricey   **Las Pocholas**, Paseo de Sarasate 6. Tel. (948) 222 214. Closed on Sunday evenings and from 15 July to 15 August. A superb restaurant that is a real institution in Navarra, featuring Basque cooking, run by three sisters, known as The Sweethearts (*Las Pocholas*), who look after every smallest detail. Specialities: *ajo arriero* (a kind of scrambled eggs with garlic) and lamb.

Josetxo, Plaza Príncipe de Viana 1. Tel. (948) 222 097. Closed on Sundays and all of August. Another place where you cannot go wrong. Very central. Private dining rooms are available. Navarrese cooking. Specialities include lamb, and sirloin in truffle sauce. Excellent wine list.

Hartza, Calle Juan de Labrit 19. Tel. (948) 224 568. Closed on Mondays, also 15 June to 10 August and 24 December to 5 January. Another restaurant run by three sisters, and very well they do so too. Good Spanish cooking and a good wine list. Specialities include baked fish and garden-fresh vegetable dishes.

Don Pablo, Calle Navas de Tolosa 19. Tel. (948) 225 299. Closed on Sunday evenings and all of August. Navarrese cooking, with the emphasis on fresh vegetables.

Moderate   **Shanti**, Castillo de Mayor 39. Tel. (948) 231 004. Closed on Sunday and Monday evenings and throughout July. Go through the bar and have a *tapa* on your way, but leave room for the restaurant's specialities which include delicacies such as roast pig's feet and clams with rice. Good local wines at reasonable prices.

Towns and villages around Pamplona

A warning: there is not much accommodation in some of the villages in this part of the Pyrenees, so it is advisable to map out your route and make reservations in advance if only by a day. Many of the roads are narrow and twisting, frequently blocked by livestock, with roller-coaster dips, are not easy to negotiate at night and are downright dangerous in winter after dark. It pays not to risk getting stuck on them with no place to stay.

The following towns, in the order listed, make up an itinerary that circles Pamplona, taking in most of the spots worth stopping at in this part of the Pyrenees and the foothills. To cover the whole route would take four days or more. You may want to do just a part of it. For that reason, the distance from Pamplona is included in each case, as well as the distance from the previous town mentioned.

Elizondo

Elizondo (population 2,516), 58 km north of Pamplona via the N-121. On the way, you cross the Velate Pass, which is lined with old inns. In the town many of the ancient houses have coats of arms engraved in stone on them. Livestock market every other Saturday at the Parque del Mercado. Fabulous view from the Baztán viewpoint.

Where to stay: mid-range

Baztán, Carretera de Pamplona a Francia, km 52. Tel. (948) 580 050. Scenic location, pool, restaurant, choice of organized excursions using this hotel as a base. From 4,650 ptas (September to June) to 4,950 ptas (July and August).

Lecumberri

Lecumberri (population 683) is 57 km south-west of Elizondo via Santesteban, Ezcurra and Leiza, along a twisty road with scenery that doesn't relent (or 33 km north-west of Pamplona on route N-240). A popular summer resort and principal town of the lovely Larraún Valley. Mountain climbing, hiking, hunting – with wild boar and quail among the possibilities – and fishing for salmon and trout. A road leads from here to the San Miguel in Excelsis Sanctuary, built in the Romanesque style, with a well preserved enamelled *reredos*.

Estella

This town (population 13,086) is well worth a visit and is 82 km from Lecumberri via Irurzun, where you should turn right, and Echarri-Aranaz, where you should turn left. It is 44 km south-west of Pamplona on N-111. Estella was once a regular stop on the medieval pilgrims' route to the shrine of St James at Santiago de Compostela. Later, in the nineteenth century, Estella was the court of the Carlist monarchs. Part of the centre, where the old **Royal Palace** and several admirable Romanesque and Gothic churches stand, has been officially designated a 'monumental zone'. **San Pedro de la Rua**, which dominates the town, dates from the twelfth century; there are many other churches to visit in the town.

Bullrunning, Pamplona-style, takes place during the annual *fiestas* on the first weekend in August. Market: every Thursday at Plaza San Juan. Some 2 km from Estella, on the road to Logroño, is the twelfth-century **Irache Monastery**, with a Plateresque cloister from the fourteenth.

Where to stay: **Irache**, Carretera de Logroño, km 43. Tel. (948) 551 150. This is 4
mid-range km outside Estella. From 5,320 to 5,600 ptas.

Puente Puente la Reina (population 2,002), 29 km east of Estella on
la Reina N-111 (24 km from Pamplona), is named after its eleventh-century bridge over the Arga, still standing solidly, which was a landmark for medieval pilgrims on their way to Santiago de Compostela. Bullrunning in the streets and bullfights the last week of July. Market on Saturdays at the Plaza de Mena. In Muruzábal, 6 km to the east, there is the unusual octagonal medieval church of Santa María at Eunate.

Bodega visit Navarra produces some fine wines. The Bodega de Sarriá SA in Puente la Reina (Tel. [948] 267 562) is one of the better known. Bottled under the label of Señorío de Sarriá, its wines are sold not only throughout Spain, but are also exported to Europe, North America and the Far East. The rosé is especially good. Telephone ahead if you would like to visit the bodega.

Tafalla This town (population 9,863), 24 km south-east of Puente la Reina via Artajona (35 km south of Pamplona on route N-121), attracts art lovers because of the fascinating Renaissance wooden altarpiece carved by Juan de Ancheta in the Church of Santa María.

Where to stay: **Hostal Tafalla**, Carretera Pamplona-Zaragoza, km 38. Tel. (948)
mid-range 700 300. Bar, restaurant. From 3,500 ptas.

Olite Olite (population 2,829), 7 km south of Tafalla on N-121 (42 km south of Pamplona), is proud of its castle of the kings of Navarra, begun in the early fifteenth century. Now a parador, its looks as if it has come straight out of a fairy tale. Bullrunning and bullfights for four days in mid-September.

Where to stay: **Parador Príncipe de Viana**, Plaza de los Teobaldos 2. Tel. (948)
mid-range 740 000. From behind the battlements of your castle, you look out onto rolling forested countryside. Large iron chandeliers and a suit of armour in the reading room complete the décor. Great value for the money. From 6,000 ptas (November to June) to 7,500 ptas (high season).

Tudela Navarra's second city, Tudela has a population of 24,629 and is 52 km south of Olite (94 km south-east of Pamplona). Its Cathedral, built in the twelfth and thirteenth centuries, and its narrow, twisting streets are the city's major attractions. Particularly noteworthy is the 'Judgement Door' of the Cathedral. Bullrunning and bullfights, last week of July. Tourist Office: Plaza de los Fueros s/n. Tel. (948) 821 539.

Where to stay: **Hostal de Tudela**, Carretera de Zaragoza s/n. Tel. (948) 820 558.
mid-range Parking area. Restaurant with modest prices. From 3,100 ptas

(November to April) to 3,500 ptas (high season).

Where to eat: pricey

Choko, Plaza de los Fueros 5. Tel. (948) 821 019. Closed on Mondays. On the attractive main square, this restaurant specializes in Navarrese cooking.

Javier

Javier, or Xavier (population 171) is 93 km north of Tudela via Tafalla, where you should turn right, passing through Aibar and Sanguesa (52 km from Pamplona). Javier is the birthplace of the great missionary St Francis Xavier. Only a few kilometres from Javier, near Yesa, is the eleventh-century San Salvador de Leyre Monastery. There is a Tourist Office at Yesa on the Pamplona road; Tel. (948) 884 040.

Sos del Rey Católico

Some 18 km south of Javier on C-127 (53 km south-east of Pamplona), this town (population 1,120) was the birthplace, as its name suggests, of King Ferdinand, who with Isabella unified Spain. There is a parador at Sos, which is in a relatively new building, but which is in harmony with the nearby remains of the Sada Castle where Ferdinand was born.

Where to stay: mid-range

Parador Fernando de Aragón, Calle Sainz de Vicuña 1. Tel. (976) 888 011. Centrally and scenically located, with views of King Ferdinand's castle, which is being restored. From 5,500 ptas.

Isaba

Isaba (population 558), 70 km north of Sos on C-137 (94 km east of Pamplona via N-240 and C-137), is a winter sports centre for locals but it does not have any mechanical ski lifts or other such facilities that would make it a fully-fledged resort. On 13 July, at the Stone of St Martin near Isaba, the mayors of the towns in the Roncal Valley turn out in full regalia, just as they have done since 1375, to receive the Tribute of the Three Cows from the inhabitants of the French Valley of Baretous, just over the border. It is the occasion for a joint *fiesta* with their French neighbours.

Where to stay: mid-range

Isaba, Carretera de Pamplona s/n. Tel. (948) 893 030. This beautifully-located, small modern hotel has a restaurant, pool and sauna. From 3,850 to 5,300 ptas.

Ochagavía

One of the prettiest spots in the Salazar Valley, Ochagavía (population 577), 29 km west of Isaba (85 km from Pamplona), is a favourite spot for mountain climbers.

Roncesvalles

This tiny village (population 42), 40 km west of Ochagavía (47 km north-east of Pamplona), is where Charlemagne was trounced (see p. 241). Also called Roncesvaux, it is the site of several twelfth- and thirteenth-century churches and hostels where the physical and spiritual needs of pilgrims on their way to Santiago were attended to. The early thirteenth-century Gothic abbey here was restored in the 1940s. Its cloister and church are particularly beautiful. King Sancho the Strong, the founder of the abbey, is buried in the church, and is represented there by a life-size statue, 2.25 m tall. They say that this was really his height. Opposite the abbey is the Chapel of Spiritus Sancti, and *Itzandegula*, an ancient church which is now a hay-barn.

The Central Pyrenees

The central, or Aragonese, Pyrenees include the tallest peaks. Valleys are steep and narrow for the most part, and there are quite a few large lakes. Ice and snow make communications difficult in the winter. The nature of the terrain makes for an endless series of hairpin bends, many of which are quite narrow. Most of the roads, like the valleys, run roughly north and south. Thus, to get from one place to another in an easterly or westerly direction, it is often necessary to travel a considerable distance, down towards the plain then back up into the high mountains on another road.

Notwithstanding all that, a railway line does cross the central Pyrenees, and there is an international station at Canfranc, near the ski resorts of Somport and Candanchú, close to the border with Navarra, the westernmost region of the Pyrenees. The railway line goes southward, passing close to Jaca and on to Saragossa, a major junction. A loop of the same line links Huesca with Saragossa and Jaca.

Saragossa is the capital and principal city of the ancient kingdom of Aragón, which is now an autonomous region. It stands on the banks of the Ebro, one of Spain's five main rivers. Huesca, a city midway between Saragossa and the French border, is a crossroads of the central Pyrenees. The most important Aragonese town close to the high peaks is Jaca. Because of its national and international communications links, Saragossa is a good place to start your tour of the central Pyrenees.

Saragossa (Zaragoza)

This city is worth seeing, even if you intend to head off quickly for the towns high in the hills. Saragossa (population 590,750) is 175 km from Pamplona, 296 km from Barcelona and 325 km from Madrid. The region it dominates is extremely varied, containing vast plains, a desert (Los Monegros), and towering peaks along its northern edge. Saragossa is an industrial city and at the same time an important market and supply town. It is a major canning centre. It is the site of an American military base, which is strongly opposed by some of Saragossa's political leaders and many of its people. In Saragossa stands the shrine of the celestial patroness of Spain, the Virgin of Pilar. She is represented by an ancient, black wooden statue, covered in gilded bronze, which – according to legend – remained on the spot where the Virgin appeared to St James on 2 January AD 40, standing on a marble column.

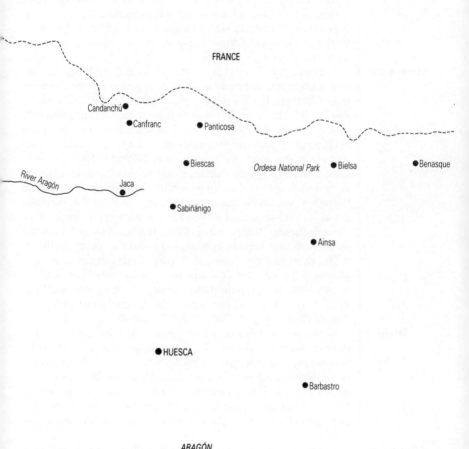

Central Pyrenees

Getting there Saragossa has its own airport, but few international flights land there. There are daily domestic flights, however, which connect the city with Madrid or Barcelona. The train service from Barcelona, Madrid and other Spanish cities is frequent. The road from Barcelona is a proper motorway; but, unfortunately, the road from Madrid is quite ordinary. If you come from France by car, you can reach Saragossa via Irún and Pamplona; via Puigcerdá (at the border near Andorra) and Lérida; or via La Junquera (Le Pérthus on the French side), Barcelona and Lérida. These are the best crossing points but there are others.

Main areas The inner part of town lies on the south bank of the Ebro, and most of the landmarks are close to the river near the Puente de Piedra (Stone Bridge). It is in this neighbourhood that you will find the Basilica del Pilar, a late seventeenth-century construction apparently built on the site of an older church. Here you will also find: the Town Hall; the provincial civil governor's office; La Lonja; and the Cathedral of the Seo, which was built between 1119 and 1550.

Six streets south of the Puente de Piedra, on the Calle Don Jaime I, there is an intersection with a main street, Calle Coso. One street to the right is the central Plaza de España and, leading off it, the broad Paseo de la Independencia. Most major hotels are in the vicinity of the Plaza de España. There are two railway stations: El Sepulcro, on the west side of town near the bullring; and El Arrabal, on the north side of the river near the Puente de Piedra. Trains depart from both stations to just about all destinations, so the best way to know which station to go to for a specific train is to call RENFE information: (976) 211 166. The airport is 10 km west of the city on the road to Madrid. Tourist Office: Plaza de Sas 7. Tel. (976) 230 027.

History Known as 'The Mistress of Four Civilizations', Saragossa began as the Iberian city of Salduba. The Roman Emperor Augustus founded the town anew in 24 BC, giving it his name, Cesaraugusta, and inviting retired legionnaires to settle down there. Under the Moors, who conquered it in AD 713 and called it Sarakusta, the town prospered. In 1118 it became the capital of a Christian kingdom and later became part of Spain when the country was united by Ferdinand and Isabella.

What to see
Churches The seventeenth-century **Basilica del Pilar** (Plaza Catedrales), the main spiritual attraction, is where the richly robed Virgin of Pilar statue is kept. **San Pablo Church** (Calle San Pablo), a thirteenth-century building with a fourteenth-century Mudéjar tower. The **Cathedral of the Seo or San Salvador** (Plaza La Seo) is a fascinating building. It started life as a mosque and was subsequently altered during various periods. As a result, it is a curious mixture of Arabic, Gothic, Plateresque and Mudéjar styles. Also worth seeing is **Santa Engracia Church** (Plaza Santa Engracia), with its unusual collection of relics of numerous martyrs.

Aula Dei Carthusian Monastery

In the Barrio de la Montaña, this monastery contains Goya frescoes. No women are allowed because the monks still live a secluded life and, understandably, pretty girls would be likely to distract them.

Best museums

Pablo Gargallo, Plaza San Felipe. Open daily from 10 a.m. to 1 p.m. and from 5 to 7 p.m.; Sundays and holidays, from 11 a.m. to 2 p.m.; closed on Tuesdays. Modern sculpture. **Provincial Museum**, Plaza de Jose Antonio. Closed on Mondays and holidays, but not on Sundays: antiquities of the area plus a few Goyas. Open daily from 10 a.m. to 2 p.m.; closed on Mondays and holidays (not Sundays).

Old stones

Aljafería Palace, Aljafería. Open daily from 9 a.m. to 1 p.m. Eleventh-century Hispano-Arabic architecture, very unusual. **Roman walls** – what is left of them – Plaza Lanuza s/n. Third century. **Puerta del Carmen**, Avenida Cesaraugusta 1. Neoclassical gate built in 1789 in the outer of two rings of walls.

What to do

Saragossa has only one golf course (La Penaza, km 307 on the Madrid–Barcelona Road). It has no such novelty as an aquapark or a racetrack. The city does have frequent trade fairs. Generally, however, the average Saragossan's idea of fun is to march on the nearby base used by the US Air Force. A famous theatre, the Principal, has recently been refurbished, and a series of cultural events have been booked for it, but they are the exception rather than the rule.

About the only time the place comes alive is for about ten days around 12 October, when they celebrate the *fiestas* of the Virgin of Pilar, the advocation of Spain's patron, the Virgin Mary, whose ancient statue is revered in the Basilica del Pilar. In addition to religious ceremonies, the Pilar *fiestas* include bullfights, street-dancing and many other events.

For the rest of the year, citizens of Saragossa looking for something to do generally look elsewhere, and the visitor would be well advised to do the same. North of Saragossa, in the mountains, there are plenty of activities. Hiking, hunting and mountain climbing are especially popular. Detailed information is available from the Tourist Office. Ski resorts in the central Pyrenees that have information offices in Saragossa, and, in one case, Barcelona, are as follows: Estación Invernal del Valle de Astún, Plaza Independencia 19, Saragossa. Tel. (976) 217 677. Panticosa Turística SA, Gran Vía 3, Saragossa. Tel. (976) 213 748. Estación de Esquí de Cerler SA, Calle Marco Aurelio 8, Barcelona. Tel. (93) 209 5900.

Shopping

The main shopping area in Saragossa is along and around the Paseo de la Independencia and the Gran Vía. Good buys include pottery and ceramic wares. Some of the best come from Teruel, typically in shades of green and violet, and from Muel, typically in blue or blue and white. There is a flea market on Sundays and Wednesdays around La Romareda stadium and painters peddle their 'masterpieces' in the Plaza de Santa Cruz on Sunday mornings.

251

Nightlife   It probably goes without saying that outside of Saragossa there is very little nightlife, except for *après-ski* in the winter resorts. Saragossa itself, however, is reasonably lively, with several areas where *tapa* bars, discos, and other such establishments are found.

Tapas   Around the Plaza San Miguel. Or, if you prefer your tapas from the sea, try some of the bars and *marisquerias* off the Calle Don Jaime I, near the Plaza de España. On a more unusual note, drop in at El Monaguillo (The Altar Boy), Calle Refugio 8, where the recorded music is mostly Gregorian chant and religious symphonies. Nibble on *bocadillos* (filled rolls) here while you sip your wine.

Discos   **Pachá**, Calle Sevilla 6; young and late crowds, moderate prices, up-to-date music.

Yuppies, Calle San Ignacio de Loyola 23. This draws the kind of crowd its name suggests, best at weekends.

Casino   **Monteblancos**, Carretera N-II, km 343 (at Alfajarín, outside Saragossa); Tel. (976) 100 004. Open from 5 p.m. to 4 a.m. All kinds of opportunities to lose money – blackjack, roulette and so on. The complex includes a restaurant and a discotheque. No tie or jacket required for the men, though jeans are taboo.

Where to stay   Saragossa is not a city much patronized by foreign tourists, though quite a few Spaniards visit it, either because of the trade and agricultural fairs or because it is the 'home' of the patron Virgin of Spain, the Virgin of Pilar. Its hotels are quite adequate and comfortable and generally good value for the money. Most of the main hotels are in the vicinity of the Plaza de España and the Avenida de la Constitución.

Top range   **Gran Hotel**, Calle Costa 5. Tel. (976) 221 901, telex 58010. An old but remodelled five-star hotel with a quite decent restaurant. Air-conditioning, mini-bars in rooms, television, parking. From 9,500 to 11,500 ptas.

Mid-range   **Don Yo**, Calle Bruil 4. Tel. (976) 226 741, telex 58768. Air-conditioned, modern, television and mini-bars in rooms. From 8,000 ptas.

Goya, Calle Cinco de Marzo 5. Tel. (976) 229 331, telex 58680. Good location for shopping. From 5,500 to 7,200 ptas.

Rey Alfonso I, Calle Coso 17. Tel. (976) 218 290, telex 58226. Central, air-conditioned, garage, with a pleasant restaurant. From 8,000 ptas.

Oriente, Calle Coso 11. Tel. (976) 221 960. Central, air-conditioned. From 5,800 ptas.

Where to eat
Pricey   **Costa Vasca**, Teniente Colonel Valenzuela 13. Tel. (976) 217 329. An old restaurant that is always up to date with international culinary trends. Try the sole in dillweed sauce and the sirloin in red wine sauce.

Gurrea, San Ignacio de Loyola 14. Tel. (976) 233 161. Closed on Sundays and during August. International cuisine, good service, parking.

Horno Asador Goyesco, Calle Manuel Lasala 44. Tel. (976) 356 870. Closed on Sundays and the first two weeks of August. Aragonese cooking with a French touch. Specialities include fish with Pernod sauce, langoustines in cider and tenderloin with prunes in brandy sauce.

From Saragossa to the French Border

Do not assume that you can take in more than a few of the high Pyrenees towns – especially in the winter – unless you have plenty of time and you love hard driving. The towns are listed in an order that allows you to go from one to another directly, roughly from east to west, and return to Saragossa, the regional capital with road, air and rail links to the rest of the world, any time you like.

Visit to a bodega

Villanueva de Gallego, 13 km north of Saragossa on the Huesca road. Aragón's best-known wines come from the Cariñena district, in which this town is situated. Bodegas Palafox (Tel. [976] 115 172) produce the hearty red wine that is characteristic of these parts. The bodega, which is on the main road of the town, is open for visits Monday to Friday from 8 a.m. to 2 p.m. and from 4 to 7 p.m. It is best to telephone ahead.

Huesca

Huesca (population 47,372), 69 km north of Saragossa on N-330, is the capital of the province of the same name, which contains the highest summits in the Pyrenees, including Aneto (3,404 m) and Las Tres Sorores (3,353 m), and some of Spain's best ski resorts. The old quarter of this small city is very attractive. Huesca's Gothic Cathedral and the old university are certainly worth a visit. Tourist Office: Calle Coso Alto 23; Tel. (974) 225 778.

Where to stay: mid-range

Pedro I de Aragón, Avenida del Parque 34. Tel. (974) 220 300, telex 58626. Very central, parking. From 5,450 ptas.

Sabiñánigo

Sabiñánigo (population 9,538), 124 km north of Saragossa and 55 km north of Huesca on N-330, is the most important industrial town in this part of the Pyrenees. The churches in the villages surrounding it, however, in what is known as the Serrablo district, such as those at Lárrede, Satue, Isún, Oros-Bajo and Susín, are prime examples of Mozarabic art. (The Mozarabs were Christians ruled by the Moors but allowed to practise their own religion.)

Where to stay: mid-range

La Pardina, Calle Santa Orosia 36. Tel. (974) 480 975. Parking area and swimming pool. On the outskirts of town. From 4,100 ptas except 1–20 August, when the price rises to 4,500 ptas.

Jaca

Once the residence of the kings of Navarra, Jaca (population 13,771) is 141 km north of Saragossa and 17 km west of Sabiñánigo on N-330. Nowadays its location on the road to several popular ski resorts makes it a far more international place than other towns in this remote corner of Spain.

What to see

Noteworthy are: its Romanesque Cathedral; the Town Hall in the Plateresque style; the Benedictine Convent with fine Romanesque details; the Citadel which was begun in 1592; ancient bridges over the River Aragón in various styles; and the outstanding Diocesan Museum of Romanesque Painting. It is open daily from 11.30 a.m. to 1.30 p.m. and from 4.30 to 6.30 p.m. Tourist Office: Plaza Calvo Sotelo s/n. Tel. (974) 360 098.

Where to stay:
mid-range

Gran Hotel, Paseo del General Franco 1. Tel. (974) 360 900. Swimming pool, parking area and attractive garden. From 4,500 to 6,000 ptas.

Where to eat:
moderate

La Cocina Aragonesa, Cervantes 5. Tel. (974) 361 054. Closed on Tuesdays in summer. Aragonese cooking in a charming atmosphere. Specialities include venison, lamb and fresh vegetable dishes.

Candanchú

Unlike most of the other high resorts, Candanchú (population 202), 170 km north of Saragossa and 29 km north of Jaca on N-330, is on a main road. The road runs over the mountains to Pau in France, 90 km away. A railway line runs through the same pass (Somport). The international rail station at Canfranc brings passengers to within a short distance of the ski runs of Candanchú, one of Spain's oldest and best equipped winter resorts. Some of its nineteen ski lifts or tows reach the top of the 1,986-m peak of El Tobazo. There is a children's area, which is permanently supervised, and there are also skiing lessons for children. Twelve hotels in the Candanchú–Canfranc area, not to mention the numerous apartments, assure ample lodging, provided you book one or two months ahead in winter. The Spanish Army's ski school is nearby, and the ski troopers use the same runs as the civilians. **Astún**, another ski resort, with nine lifts or tows, is just 3 km from Candanchú. Mountain climbers practise there in summer.

Where to stay:
mid-range

Edelweiss, Carretera Zaragoza-Francia, km 189.4. Tel. (974) 373 200. Closed all of May, first two weeks of June, second two weeks of September, all of October and November. From 3,000 to 3,200 ptas (summer) and 6,700 ptas (winter).

El Formigal

El Formigal, 168 km north of Saragossa on Route C-136 via Sabiñánigo, or 67 km from Candanchú via Jaca (taking the turn-off to the left to C-136 just before reaching Sabiñánigo), is considered part of the town of Sallent de Gallego (population 1,142), 5 km further north on the same road. El Formigal is just 70 km from Pau, France, via the Portalet Pass; but the road is closed in winter. One of El Formigal's ski runs is 7 km long. There are eighteen lifts, tows or other devices to get skiers up the slopes, capable of carrying 12,527 passengers an hour. When there is not enough snow left for skiing, the hunters move in, looking for wild boar and deer.

Where to stay:
top range

Formigal, Urbanización de Formigal s/n, Sallent de Gallego. Tel. (974) 488 000, telex 58885. Closed in May, June, September, October and November. Disco, restaurant, scenic location. From 5,200 to 5,950 ptas (summer) and 8,950 ptas (winter).

Panticosa

Panticosa (population 749) is 168 km north of Saragossa on C-136 via Sabiñánigo, turning right on a local road at Escarilla; or 8 km from El Formigal. Skiing, hunting, fishing, mountain climbing and even a cure for rheumatism can be found here. This resort, complete with five lifts, capable of handling 3,200 passengers an hour, and with runs suitable for every category of skier from novice to professional, is just 7 km from the beautiful spa of the same name, 1,636 m up in the mountains – nearly 400 m above the town. The many possibilities make this a year-round resort. Hunters will find roebuck, wild boar and game birds. Anglers go for trout. Hikers will discover icy mountain lakes even in summer.

Spa-visitors take the waters, which are said to be good for those suffering from skin trouble, problems with the digestive system and rheumatism. The hot springs have been in use since Roman times. In 1915 and 1917, avalanches demolished a hotel and a casino. But rest easy; so far as anyone can predict, the existing hotels are not in any such danger. When the snow has gone, there are guided walking tours to nearby lakes and peaks. In case the Panticosa water does not do the trick for your rheumatism, there are also weekly bus trips to the French shrine of Lourdes, just 110 km away. Tourist Office: Calle San Miguel 27. Tel. (974) 488 125.

Where to stay:
mid-range

Escalar, Calle La Cruz s/n. Tel. (974) 487 008. At the ski resort rather than the nearby spa. Scenic views, heated pool, restaurant with reasonable prices. From 2,400 ptas (summer) to 2,800 ptas (winter).

Gran Hotel, at the spa. Tel. (974) 487 161. Closed 10 September to 25 June. Recently renovated but with all the flavour of a leisurely past. Pool, tennis court, garden, sauna, handball court. You can drink the curing water, shower or bathe in it, or even jump into a swimming pool full of it. From 3,800 ptas.

Ainsa

Ainsa (population 1,209), 188 km north-east of Saragossa on C-138 via Huesca and Barbastro, or 86 km south-east of Panticosa on C-140 via Biescas, is a town of solid medieval appearance in some of the loveliest mountain country you can find anywhere in the world. The approach road is a corkscrew, if you come from Panticosa. Do it by day. That way you will not only be safer, you will also not miss the scenery. In the town itself, have a look at the Church of Santa María, with its tall, twelfth-century Romanesque tower and its five-sided cloister from the thirteenth century, and at the arcaded main square. Ainsa is the gateway to the Ordesa National Park.

Ordesa
National
Park

The Park can be entered from several points along the local road that leads northward up the River Cinca valley from Ainsa to Bielsa and Monte Perdido. This park, with an area of more than 15,000 hectares, is in the wildest part of the Pyrenees, and wildlife abounds. The Ordesa Valley is the last natural habitat of the Pyrenean mountain goat. There are numerous waterfalls and thick forests of Scots pine, black pine, beech and fir. Impressive gorges and canyons can be seen along the courses of the Rivers Yago and Aso.

There is a small parador near **Bielsa** (population 429), which is 220 km north-east of Saragossa on C-138 via Huesca and Barbastro, or 32 km north of Ainsa. The hotel, patronized mostly by hunters, overlooks the Horse's Tail Falls.

Plan

Plan, the village from which bachelors sent out their SOS to marriageable maidens (see p. 240), is also in the vicinity. You can get to the village from Bielsa by taking the road back towards Ainsa and turning left at Salinas de Sin, 7 km south of Bielsa. Plan is 12 km along this road, up the Cinqueta Valley. Early autumn is a lovely time to visit this area. Bear in mind that roads are a challenge, even in summer.

Where to stay: mid-range

Parador Monte Perdido, Valle de Pineta de Bielsa, 14 km west of Bielsa. Tel. (974) 501 011, telex 46865. This very comfortable little inn sits at the end of a road high on a mountain, dominating wilderness landscapes of the Ordesa Park. Its restaurant serves regional specialities. From 6,000 ptas (November to June) to 7,500 ptas (rest of the year).

Benasque

Benasque (population 983) is 223 km north-east of Saragossa on C-139 via Huesca and Barbastro (turn right onto C-139 to cross the River Cinca 20 km past Barbastro). It is 66 km north-east of Ainsa (take C-140 eastward from Ainsa, then turn left on C-139 at the T-junction 30 km past Ainsa). The village stands at the head of the steepest valley in the Pyrenees. Many of its houses, still in perfect condition, were built in the twelfth and thirteenth centuries. The Cerler winter resort, 5 km to the south, is visible from Benasque.

Cerler

Cerler (population 111) is 227 km north-east of Saragossa via Huesca, Barbastro and Benasque; or 5 km south-east of Benasque; it offers skiers an overall drop, measured vertically, of 1,000 m. The difficulty of getting to this place is compensated for by its tempting, sheltered slopes and its seven Olympic-class runs. There are nine ski-lifts or tows, with a capacity of 4,330 skiers an hour. The complex lies at the foot of the Montes Malditos (Damned Mountains), so called by shepherds because they are almost bare of pasture.

Where to stay: top range

Monte Alba, Estación de Esquí s/n. Tel. (974) 551 136. Closed May, October and November. At the foot of one of the runs, and in town at the same time. Impressive scenery, tennis court, indoor pool, sauna. From 4,200 ptas (June to September) to 8,500 ptas (December to April).

The Eastern Pyrenees

The eastern Pyrenees can be reached directly by road from France, or with relative ease from either Barcelona or Lérida. They have a greater number of ski resorts than any other section of the Pyrenees or, for that matter, than any other region of Spain. They also have more spas and more lakes. Full of beauty spots, old monasteries and mountain paradors for skiers and hunters, the eastern Pyrenees offer the added attraction of proximity to the tiny independent country of Andorra, perched on a handful of mountain tops between France and Spain. Andorra has long lived on its tax-free shopping, its winter and summer mountain resorts and, like the rest of the high Pyrenees on both sides of the French–Spanish border, on smuggling.

Lérida (Lleida)

Lérida (population 109,573), 140 km from Saragossa and 156 km from Barcelona, is not actually a mountain town. It is only 155 m above sea level. Yet it is the market and metropolis for the eastern Pyrenees because of its good communications with the mountain towns and villages. It is the capital of the province of the same name, the only landlocked province of Catalonia. It is the one with the most contact with Aragón, and it shares certain human and geographical affinities with that region.

Lérida is a pleasant, clean town, the sort of place you could enjoy staying in for a few days to soak up some of its flavour. But don't go there if you are looking for an active nightlife. In Lérida, the only way to get that is to create it yourself. Even as a base for excursions, it is not particularly enticing, since the distances to the peaks, where the resorts and most of the prettiest places are, are considerable and the roads are challenging to say the least. Rather than a base for excursions, Lérida should be considered as a starting and/or finishing point for a visit to the high altitude towns of the eastern Pyrenees.

Getting there   Getting to the eastern Pyrenees is a fairly simple matter. Major, or at least good, roads cross the mountains at or near Viella, Seo de Urgel, Puigcerdá, Camprodón and La Junquera to enter Spain. However, the only one of those roads which is almost certain to remain open all winter is the one that enters via La Junquera.

Therefore, if you come by road, you may decide to enter at either end of the Pyrenees, where the crossings are less dependent on the weather. Assuming you wish to visit the eastern Pyrenees from west to east, Lérida is the logical starting point. The best way to reach Lérida is by car or train, since Lérida's small airport does not normally receive international flights. Trains, however, are fast and frequent, since Lérida is a major stop on the line between Madrid and Barcelona. There is also a regular bus service from Barcelona, Saragossa and other large towns.

Main areas   In Lérida, just about everything you would want to find or see is

Eastern Pyrenees

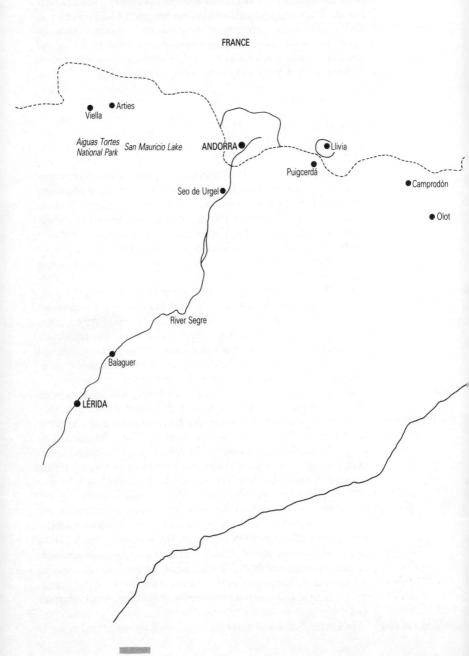

either in the Citadel or at the bottom of the hill surrounding it, near the River Segre. The old part of the city lies along the river, mostly to the south-west of the Citadel. It is in this part that you will encounter not only historic and artistic monuments, but also the Tourist Office, government offices, banks, shops and some hotels. The main street of this section is the Rambla Fernando, which changes its name successively, as it runs generally from east to west, to Avenida Francesc Meliá, Avenida de Blondel (briefly), Avenida de Madrid and Avenida Alcalde Areny. The western half of this many-named street runs alongside the river.

The railway station is at the north-eastern end of the Rambla Fernando. The bus station is at the corner of Avenida de Madrid and the Plaza de Espanya. The regional Tourist Office is at Avenida Blondel 1, near the municipal Tourist Office, at Arco del Puente s/n; Tel. (973) 248 120. The Town Hall, built in the thirteenth century, is only one street away at Plaza de la Pahería 1. Within easy walking distance are various other intriguing old palaces, churches and fortifications.

History

Lérida is so old, it has forgotten its exact age. Iberian chiefs like Mandonio, who resisted first Carthaginian and then Roman rule, and was executed for it, are remembered in street names. The Romans and, later, the Arabs, had a great architectural and cultural influence on the town's development and many place names in this area have an obvious Arabic origin.

What to see
Citadel

Called La Zuda, on a hilltop overlooking the river, the Citadel contains the ruins of an old Arab castle – just one nave remains standing – and the Old Cathedral (Catedral Viejo), built in a progression from Romanesque to Gothic styles between the twelfth and the fifteenth centuries, with a lovely cloister. The Old Cathedral, or Seo, is open daily from 10 a.m. to 2 p.m. and from 4 to 8 p.m.

New Cathedral

Reputedly the first neoclassical structure in Catalonia, it dates from the eighteenth century and has an interesting collection of tapestries.

Town Hall or Palacio de la Pahería

A thirteenth-century building with a beautiful façade and a Romanesque patio. Open on weekdays from 10 a.m. to 2 p.m. and from 6 to 8 p.m. It houses a small archaeological museum containing artefacts found during restoration of the building itself. In another part of the Town Hall, a Catalan code of laws from the eleventh century is on display.

Old St Mary's Hospital

Now the Institute of Leridan studies, this is an impressive fifteenth- and sixteenth-century Gothic structure which now houses some collections relating to the history of the region.

Diocesan Museum

This is in the Episcopal Palace, Plaza Bisbe Pino 1. Ancient and medieval Leridan sculptures, Gothic paintings and so on.

Excursion
Balaguer

This town (population 12,432), 30 km north-east of Lérida, boasts several historic monuments, including the beautiful fourteenth-century cloister of the Santo Domingo Monastery, and the Santa María Church in the centre of town.

Where to stay.
mid-range

Conde Jaime de Urgel, Calle Urgel 2. Tel. (973) 445 604. Although the hotel is not owned by the state it is affiliated to the parador chain. It offers all comforts. Scenic views, pool, bar, restaurant, central location. From 4,500 ptas (January to March) to 4,900 ptas (rest of the year).

What to do

The principal tourist attraction of the area is winter sports in the various mountain resorts. Baqueira-Beret (see also p. 262), for example, in the Arán Valley, is King Juan Carlos' favourite place to take the royal family skiing. When he does, security measures are extreme. Even so, Basque terrorists managed to place a bomb in the hotel where his bodyguards were staying in the winter of 1986–87. No one was hurt, and the King and his family stayed for the rest of their holiday as if nothing had happened.

Summer visitors come here for the prospects of hunting, fishing, hiking and generally enjoying the scenery and the fresh air. Spas are the destinations of many visitors. The current trend for healthy living leads many people to spend a few days from time to time at one of these 'magic' springs. Crowds are also drawn by the living folklore of the Pyrenees and every town and village holds a *fiesta* in honour of its patron saint. Such *fiestas* always include traditional dancing and singing, while some include sports competitions, parades and other events. The Tourist Office can tell you where and when to find them.

The place to look for nightlife worthy of the name is in the ski resorts, where the *après-ski* discotheques soak up the energies that holidaymakers have failed to expend on the runs. Nevertheless, there are a few 'in' spots in Lérida where the young people congregate, such as:

Wonderful, Carretera de Zaragoza, km 461. Reasonable prices, lively atmosphere. A real barn of a place, with bars everywhere and two video screens.

Where to stay

Generally speaking, hotels in Lérida are good value. In fact, you will pay more for similar or inferior accommodation in the mountain towns. Most of Lérida's hotels are in two areas: in the old city at the foot of the citadel, or in the newer part to the north of it, along the axis of the east–west street called Avenida Prat de la Riva.

Mid-range

Sansi Park, Avenida Alcalde Porqueres 4. Tel. (973) 244 000. Central, air-conditioned, garage, television, only twenty-six rooms. From 4,900 ptas.

Principal, Plaza Pahería 8. Tel. (973) 240 900. Central. From 3,000 ptas.

Condes de Urgel II, Avenida de Barcelona 17. Tel. (973) 202 300. Modern, comfortable, air-conditioned, television in rooms, on the outskirts. From 5,600 ptas.

Bottom range

Rexi, Avenida Blondel 56. Tel. (973) 270 700. Small, centrally located residence hotel. From 1,550 ptas (without private bath) to 1,749 ptas (with bath).

Caribe, Anselmo Calve 20. Tel. (973) 243 584. A very basic pensión that also offers cheap meals. From 1,100 ptas (without private bath) to 1,749 ptas (with bath).

Where to eat
Moderate

Forn del Nastasi, Calle Salmerón 10. Tel. (973) 234 510. Closed on Sunday evenings, all day Monday, and for the first two weeks of August. Catalan cooking. Air-conditioned. Specialities include snails and duck.

Sheyton, Avenida Prat de la Riva 39. Tel. (973) 240 033. Closed the first two weeks of August. Catalan and international food, pub-like atmosphere. Air-conditioned.

El Pati, Plaza Noguerola 5. Tel. (973) 237 432. Closed on Sundays and during August. In an elegant old home. Local cuisine.

Into the mountains from Lérida

Viella

About 14 km before you get to Viella (population 1,356), 164 km north of Lérida on N-230, you go through a narrow, dripping tunnel 6 km long. At either end of the tunnel you are likely to be stalled by huge herds of sheep. The countryside around here is spectacular. This ancient capital of the beautiful Arán Valley is a mecca for fishermen and hunters. Four-wheel-drive vehicles can be hired to take you deep into the rugged country.

The thirteenth-century Romanesque **San Miguel** church has a charming octagonal tower; inside there is a carved head and upper torso of Christ, dating from the twelfth century. Colourful *fiestas*, with typical dances and a pilgrimage to the mountain shrine on 8 September for the birthday of the Virgin Mary. There is also a pilgrimage and distribution of bread, cheese, and brandy mixed with spring water on 22 May in honour of the locally revered St Quitería.

Where to stay: mid-range

Parador Valle de Arán, Carretera del Tunel s/n. Tel. (973) 640 100. This attractive modern building has unbeatable views of several villages and snow-capped mountains. The food is also good. Tour buses often stop here for meals. From 7,000 ptas.

Arties

Arties (population 242) is 170 km from Lérida, 6 km east of Viella. The reason there are so many ski resort towns so close together in this area is the ruggedness of the terrain. The Tuca-Betrén resort lies just south of the road between Viella and Arties. Its total descent, measured vertically, amounts to 1,150 m, and there are nine ski lifts with a capacity of 3,990 passengers an hour. In the other direction lies Baqueira-Beret, only 5 km away, an even more important skiers' venue. There are also eight refuge cabins in the area for the use of mountain climbers, who move in after the skiers have left.

Where to stay: mid-range

Parador Don Gaspar de Portola. Tel. (973) 640 801. This has only forty rooms, compared with the one at Viella, which has one hundred and thirty five. Skiers have special lockers for their skis and boots. Many rooms have a view of the town, with its granite houses and slate roofs. Food served at this parador is Catalan with a French touch. The basement garage is useful for wintertime travellers.

Baqueira-Beret

This is 172 km from Lérida and 9 km from Arties. A resort frequented by the beautiful people, including the King and Queen of Spain. Technically, it is part of the town of Salardú (population 208). The twenty-five runs at this resort, with fifteen lifts or tows and a capacity of 7,800 skiers per hour, offer skiers a choice they seldom, if ever, have at other resorts.

There are runs for beginners, as well as for accomplished skiers, and a slalom stadium, complete with flags and personnel to do the timing. Three of the runs start at the summit of Cap de Baqueira (2,500 m) and end up at the base (1,500 m high). There is also a nursery. Hunters seek chamois, wild boar and grouse after the snow has sufficiently melted. There are plenty of trout in the scores of mostly natural lakes of the region. There are also facilities for hang-gliding.

Where to stay:
top range

Montarto. Tel. (973) 645 075. Closed from September to November and during June and July. At the foot of the runs. Restaurant, garage, tennis court, pool, disco. From 5,400 ptas (August) to 11,000 ptas (rest of year).

Where to eat:
pricey

Borda Lobato, Carretera Viella – Port Bonaigua s/n. Tel. (973) 645 075. Closed May to November. Catalan cuisine.

Espot

With a population of 212, Espot is 169 km from Lérida via Balaguer and C-147, taking the turn-off to the left 12 km past the Llavorsi tunnel; or 43 km south-east of Baqueira-Beret via C-147 and the Bonaigua Pass, taking the turn-off to the right 3 km past La Guinqueta. Note that this latter route, from Baqueira-Beret, is not feasible in winter when the Bonaigua Pass is closed, owing to frequent snow slides on the north side.

Espot is much more than just a skiers' rallying point. It dominates the lovely Espot Valley, a wonderland of natural lakes and rushing rills. The Aiguas Tortes and San Mauricio Lake National Park is reachable from Espot. Covering an area of over 22,000 hectares, this natural park is the country's second largest, beaten only by Coto Doñana in south-west Spain. The San Mauricio Lake and the huge Els Encantats peak (2,747 m), which is reflected in the lake, dominate the landscape. Wildlife includes chamois, wild boar, the rare snow partridge and ermine. The Super Espot ski resort, 2 km above Espot, is popular with weekend trippers from Barcelona, 270 km to the east. Mountain climbers find this area particularly challenging, but a word of warning: only experienced climbers should try the ascent of Els Encantats. Tourist information: Pirineos Espot SA, Avenida Generalísimo Franco 614, Barcelona; Tel. (93) 322 1053.

About 45 km south of Espot, near Rialp, is another ski resort, Llessui, with 30 km of runs and nine ski lifts.

Where to stay:
mid-range

San Mauricio, Calle San Mauricio s/n. Tel. (973) 626 125. Central, garage, scenic views, very simple accommodation. Open all year. From 1,650 to 2,750 ptas.

Saurat, Calle San Martin s/n. Tel. (973) 635 063. Closed 20 October to 31 March. More comfortable than the San Mauricio, with restaurant, nightclub, children's playground and scenic views. From 2,700 to 3,300 ptas.

Seo de Urgel

Seo de Urgel (population 10,681) is 133 km north-east of Lérida on C-1313; or 88 km east of Espot via C-147, turning left at Sort on a local road, which leads to Adrall and the junction with C-1313, 6 km south of Seo. The latter route is highly scenic, so you should drive by day. Again, it is not recommended in the dead of winter because of snow on the road, particularly between Sort and Adrall.

Seo de Urgel (literally, Cathedral of Urgel) has been the seat of a diocese since AD 527. The present cathedral, a Romanesque structure in the centre of town, built in the eleventh and twelfth centuries, is open daily for visits from 9 a.m. to 2 p.m. and from 4 to 8 p.m. but not on holiday afternoons. By reason of a seven-centuries-old treaty, Seo's archbishop is the co-prince of Andorra, which is just 10 km up the road. He and the other co-prince, the President of France, are represented in Andorra by their respective delegates, or Sindics. Seo shares a quiet little airport with Andorra.

The principal town in a dairy farming area, Seo is the scene of a country fair on 3–4 November and a cattle show on 1 May. On the outskirts is an old Roman fortress, the Castellciutat. Near Parroquia de Orto, about 9 km south, stand some ancient dolmens. Tourist Office: Calle Estudios 4. Tel. (973) 350 010.

Where to stay:
mid-range

Parador de Seo de Urgel, Calle Santo Domingo s/n. Tel. (973) 352 000. A modern building near the Cathedral. Garage, indoor pool, good restaurant serving Catalan specialities. From 5,500 ptas.

Where to eat:
pricey

El Castell, Carretera Lérida-Puigcerdá km 129. Tel. (973) 350 704. Closed for lunch on Mondays and from 15 January to 15 February. Local fish, game, and farm products, Catalan style. Specialities also include grilled meats.

Llivia

Llivia (population 921) is 187 km north-east of Lérida via Seo de Urgell and Puigcerdá on C-1313; it is 6 km inside France from Puigcerdá; follow signs at the French border. The town is 56 km east of Seo de Urgell.

This ancient farming town, with its pasture and woodlands, is a historical curiosity, a 12.9-square-kilometre Spanish enclave in France. When diplomats, representing the Spanish and French monarchs, were discussing the terms of the Treaty of the Pyrenees in the seventeenth century, Llivia was exempted from French annexation because, unlike most other settlements in the Cerdanya district, it had long been officially recorded as a town and not merely a settlement or village. The treaty, signed in 1659, recognized Spanish sovereignty in

Llivia, and accorded its inhabitants the right in perpetuity to pass freely through French territory to and from their town. Subsequent agreements ironed out the details, and guaranteed Llivians the right to transport whatever they wanted from Spain without duty. There have been a few hiccups, such as the time when Napoleon did not want to recognize the old pact, but Llivia managed to survive.

This town, with pre-Roman ruins, boasts the oldest pharmacy in Europe, established in 1415. You can visit it along with the Municipal Museum, Calle Forns 4, from 10 a.m. to 1 p.m. and from 3.30 to 7 p.m. The market (mostly local produce) is on Saturdays in the Plaza Mayor. Catalan is the local language.

Where to stay:
mid-range

Llivia, Carretera de Puigcerdá s/n. Tel. (972) 896 000. On the edge of town, it has sixty-three rooms and is the only hotel. Restaurant, pool, garage and tennis court. Since more curiosity seekers come to visit in summer, rates are lower in winter. From 3,000 ptas (mid-September to mid-July) and 4,500 ptas (rest of the year).

Where to eat:
economical

Can Ventura, Plaza Mayor 1. Tel. (972) 896 178. Closed all of October and every Tuesday except holidays. Catalan cooking: trout, Catalan-style snails and stewed tongue. Selection of Spanish wines.

La Molina

La Molina (population 353) is 200 km north-east of Lérida via Puigcerdá, on N-152; or 25 km south of Llivía via Puigcerdá. This town is the centre of a group of ski resorts, including Supermolina and Masella, all within a few kilometres of each other and all within easy reach of Barcelona. A railway which crosses the Pyrenees near Puigcerdá brings skiers from Barcelona and from France; there is a station at La Molina. By road, La Molina is only 155 km from Barcelona. There is even an airport, suitable for light aircraft only, which some skiers, who own or can afford to hire private planes, use, at Alp, just 8 km away. Such accessibility results in crowded runs on winter weekends. The area is popular in warm weather too, when hunters, mountain climbers and hikers move in. Nevertheless there is enough wide open country to keep it from feeling crowded. Tourist information: Turismo y Montaña SA, Calle Rosellón 237, Barcelona; Tel. (93) 212 796.

Where to stay:
mid-range

Adsera, at the foot of La Molina runs. Tel. (972) 892 001. Garage, pool, scenic views, disco. From 4,400 to 5,400 ptas.

Palace, Supermolina. Tel. (972) 892 016. Higher up than the Adsera, with a bus service to the town (though this is definitely no metropolis). From 5,600 to 6,700 ptas.

Our Lady of
Nuria
Monastery

Nuria (population 15), 224 km north-east of Lérida; 24 km east of La Molina. While you are in the area, winter or summer, do not miss the opportunity to take the cog railway at Ribas de Freser (24 km east of La Molina on N-152) up to Our Lady of Nuria Monastery on the slopes of the 2,913-m Puigmal mountain. This is the site, according to legend, where St Gil hid his eleventh-century carving of the Virgin Mary in a cave when he was being pursued by the wicked Gothic King

Witza. The statue is still venerated in the sanctuary today. The Ribas Valley is extraordinarily beautiful, especially in spring and autumn. Skiing on natural runs in winter, with five ski lifts. Tourist information: FF.CC. de Montaña a Grandes Pendientes, Paseo de Gracia 26, Barcelona. Tel. (93) 301 9777.

Where to stay:
mid-range

Nuria, the sanctuary itself. Tel. (972) 730 326. Chapel (of course), bar, restaurant with reasonable prices, scenic views in abundance, forests full of noisy birds and animals, skiing seven months out of the year, and, in warmer weather, rowing on a mountain lake. From 2,800 to 3,300 ptas.

Olot

Olot (population 24,892) is 270 km north-east of Lérida on C-150, via Puigcerdá and Ripoll; or 46 km east of Ribas de Freser via Ripoll. An industrial town in a unique landscape of extinct volcanoes, some of which, known as Els Butadors, 'breathe out' currents of fresh air.

On the second Sunday of July, Olot is the scene of the Aplec de la Sardana, a folklore *fiesta* in which about 5,000 dancers take part, as groups from all over Catalonia gather to show off their many local versions of the Sardana, the characteristic dance of the region. During the week of 8 September there are processions and dancing by figures representing giants, dwarfs and historic personalities, plus religious ceremonies to celebrate the feastday of The Mother of God of Tura. Tourist Office: Calle Mulleras 33. Tel. (972) 260 141.

Castelfullit de la Roca, 7 km north on a local road, is a picturesque town perched on top of a huge outcropping of rock.

Where to stay:
mid-range

Montsacopa, Calle Mulleras s/n. Tel. (972) 260 762. Central, simple, with a reasonably priced restaurant. From 3,455 ptas.

The
Basque
Country and
The Rioja

FRAN

SAN SEBASTIÁN
Fuenterrabía
Hendaye
Behobia

Bermeo

Guernica

BILBAO

River Nervión

Amorebieta

Cestona

Loyola ✝ Azpeitia

VITORIA

River Ebro

HARO

RIOJA

LOGROÑO

Sto Domingo de la Calzada

Nájera

Navarrete

Anguiano

Alfaro

CORUNNA

SANTIAGO
DE COMPOSTELA

OVIEDO

SANTANDER

BILBAO

SAN
SEBASTÍAN

VITORIA

PONTEVEDRA

LEÓN

ORENSE

HARO

LOGROÑO

VIGO

Green Spain

Introduction

Spain is a dry country, a land of parched plains and endless Mediterranean beaches with a clockwork sun that never fails, a place where water can be so scarce it is often cheaper to drink wine. Right? Wrong. At least, not all Spain is like that. There is a broad, green strip that runs across the top of the map, and within that verdant belt lie some of the most enticing, delightful and historic places in the whole country. Places like Covadonga, where the 800-year-long fight by Christian warriors to reclaim the Iberian Peninsula from Muslim rule began; and Santiago de Compostela, which was one of the greatest tourist attractions of the Middle Ages. To this city thousands and thousands of penitents, adventurers, religious-minded men and women, and opportunists from all over Europe walked for hundreds of kilometres to seek blessings at the shrine where tradition says St James the Apostle is buried. There are also the Altamira caves near Santander, with their amazingly preserved wall paintings by the cave-man ancestors of modern Europeans; and there is the Basque Country, a land of fierce nationalist sentiment and of the oldest language in Europe.

Green Spain stretches all the way from the mouth of the River Bidasoa near San Sebastián on the French border, westward through the Basque Country, the region of Cantabria, the Principality of Asturias to Galicia; a direct distance of about 500 km. It extends for more than 100 km south, as the crow flies, to The Rioja, the district which produces Spain's best known table wine. It also takes in the wild and lovely Picos de Europa (Peaks of Europe) mountains, so beloved by its inhabitants that one contemporary Spanish philologist wrote a book to prove that the area was the site of the original Garden of Eden.

It is both industrial and rural. In the Basque Country heavy industry exists side by side with busy fishing ports and farms. There are major shipping ports all along the north and north-west coasts, including those of Bilbao, Santander, Gijón, Avilés, and Corunna (La Coruña). Dairy-farming is important in Santander, while Asturias is Spain's principal coal-mining region. The province of León, part of which is covered in this chapter, is largely agricultural, though it too has a significant mining industry. The region of Galicia has important industrial centres like Vigo, but fishing and agriculture are also mainstays of its economy. In fact, fishing is a prime activity all along this coast, on which are situated the home ports of half of Spain's fishing fleet, which is the largest in the European community.

The climate varies throughout this area, but it does have one common factor: there is enough rainfall to keep the countryside always green. The climate of the northern coastal regions is milder than that of the central tableland. There are sheltered valleys where it stays so warm that citrus and other semi-tropical fruits are able to grow. Fierce storms lash the north-west coast occasionally, and, less frequently, the northern coast as well. Snow is unusual in Bilbao, almost unheard of in Santander and Corunna, and virtually impossible in Vigo; but it does block the mountain passes which lead down to the north coast from the high land for days at a time every winter.

Three different languages are widely spoken in Green Spain, and there is a fourth that is still not quite dead. The language that everyone understands is Castilian Spanish, the kind non-Spaniards are more or less familiar with. Many Basques, however, prefer to speak their own language, Euskera, which is so ancient it is not even a member of the Indo-European family of languages. Most Galicians also speak their own lilting language, called Galego or Galician, which is at least as similar to Portuguese as it is to Castilian. In remote parts of Asturias, some people still speak Bable, one of the Romance languages (the linguistic family which descends from Latin). But there is no need to feel daunted because here, as elsewhere, many people and especially those involved in the travel business are able to speak at least some English.

Since Green Spain takes in several Spanish regions with markedly different characteristics, this section is divided into three parts: the Basque Country and The Rioja; the north central coast and the Peaks of Europe; and, lastly, Galicia. The towns are listed in such a sequence that the visitor who has the time and inclination can follow a route that will take him or her all the way across the north, from east to west. Visitors with less time can pick up the route at any point they are especially interested in. The starting point for each of the three parts is a major city; these are San Sebastián, Santander and Corunna.

The Basque Country and The Rioja

The Basque Country actually straddles the Pyrenees at its western end, though the larger part does lie inside Spain. Various Basque political movements, and not just the violent ones like ETA, whose initials stand for Basque Homeland and Liberty, confess to the long-term aim of uniting these two parts of their land. In this section, however, the term 'Basque Country', clearly, refers only to the Basque region of Spain.

Mountains stand close behind the coast in most of the Basque Country. The round green hills, many of them wooded, march right down to the sea, and colourful fishing ports nestle in the coves. Big, blockish, whitewashed stone farmhouses with shady wooden balconies, known as *caserías*, dot the hillsides. In the valleys, tall chimneys pour out grey smoke. Motorways link the three main cities of the region, Vitoria (the Basque capital, also known by its name in Euskera, Gasteiz), San Sebastián (Donostia) and Bilbao (Bilbo). The other roads in the region tend to be relatively narrow and twisting, but the lovely countryside frequently compensates for this.

Basque cooking is famous in both Spain and France. Curiously, the men take at least as much interest as the women in good cooking. In a number of Basque cities and towns there are private clubs for men only, dedicated to a single activity: preparing and enjoying good food. Each member takes a turn at cooking a meal and each tries to outdo the other. It goes without saying that you can expect to eat well in a region where the locals attach so much importance to food.

San Sebastián (Donostia)

Elegant San Sebastián (population 175,576) was for many years, before the Spanish Civil War and during the years of the Franco dictatorship, the summer capital of Spain. The whole government and the entire accredited diplomatic corps would pack up and move there from Madrid for the summer months. And no wonder. The symmetrical semi-circular Concha beach there is not only large, clean, beautiful, well manicured and of fine golden sand; it also has the advantages of lying in a protected cove and of having a backdrop of stately buildings. San Sebastián ceased to be the summer capital after General Franco's death in 1975.

Since the Basque Country is one of Spain's smallest regions, distances are relatively short, and San Sebastián makes a good base for excursions. You could spend a week here without running out of places to see and things to do. It lies only 18 km from the French border.

Getting there

If you come to Spain by car, the main point of entry at the western end of the Pyrenees is on a motorway, the A-8, which crosses the frontier at Behobia. A national highway, the N-I, also crosses the border close to there, at Hendaye (or Hendaya in Spanish). Both these roads lead to San Sebastián and the Basque Country.

If you come by air, you can fly to San Sebastián via Madrid or Barcelona. Bear in mind, though, that San Sebastián's airport handles very little traffic; there are only two flights daily to/from Madrid and only one to/from Barcelona. An alternative would be to use Bilbao's airport, which handles more traffic and does have some international flights. However, the Bilbao airport is about 120 km from San Sebastián. A main railway line crosses the border near Hendaye, and there is frequent and good service. All trains stop at San Sebastián, even fast trains like the Paris–Madrid Talgo, which makes the run daily.

Main areas San Sebastián looks north towards the Bay of Biscay. Its lovely bay is protected by a hill on each side: to the west, Mount Igueldo, where there is an amusement park, and to the east, Mount Urgull, topped by the Santa Cruz de la Mota Castle. Much of the city also lies on the west bank of the River Urumea, which empties into the sea just east of Mount Urgull.

The best hotels are on or near the Paseo de la Concha, which runs along the beach. The station for national and international trains is on the east bank of the river, between the María Cristina and Santa Catalina Bridges. Narrow-gauge local trains leave from the Basque Railway Station, on the opposite side of the river, alongside the Alava Park. The airport is at Fuenterrabía, near Hendaya, 18 km to the east. There is a small port for fishing boats, at the foot of Mount Urgull near the Concha beach. San Sebastián's main port, Pasajes, which handles a lot of freight but no long-distance scheduled passenger ships, is 4 km east of the city at the mouth of the River Oyarzún.

The Tourist Office is at Miramar (at the east end of the Paseo de la Concha), on the corner of the Calle Andía; Tel. (943) 426 282. There are also tourist offices at the Santiago Bridge in Irún (at the border) and at the Behobia border crossing point.

History It is not certain how old San Sebastián is, but in AD 1200 its people agreed to swap their allegiance from the kings of Navarra to the rule of King Alfonso VIII, The Noble, of Castile, after he promised to respect their special rights and privileges. Such pacts between Basque cities and the kings of what was to become Spain were repeated in succeeding centuries. The Basques lost their special privileges in the nineteenth century, but have regained a considerable degree of home rule under the 1978 constitution.

The city was besieged many times by French troops and in 1709 the Duke of Berwick took the city of San Sebastián, but only after laying siege to it for two months. While San Sebastián was again under siege in 1813 by the British, a disastrous fire destroyed much of the city, but it was quickly and attractively rebuilt.

What to see
View from Mount Igueldo Don't miss this because the city itself is a lovely sight, curving around the beautiful bay with the island of Santa Clara in the middle. You can take the funicular up the mountain from the end of the Avenida de Satrústegui at the west end of the Concha beach.

Old Quarter   This is the most distinctive area of San Sebastián. A stroll through its streets and a close look at the neat little fishing port are a must. Landmarks include the San Vicente Church, which is the city's oldest, built in 1507, and the Santa María Basilica, rebuilt with a Churrigueresque façade in 1764. A path leads from the basilica up the mountainside to La Mota Castle, a military museum. Don't bother with this museum, but do take in the views from the broad terrace at the top. The park is open daily from 7 a.m. until one hour after sunset.

San Telmo Museum   This is in the Plaza Ignacio Zuloaga and is open daily from 10 a.m. to 1.30 p.m. and from 3.30 to 5.30 p.m.; closed on Sunday afternoons and Monday mornings. The museum is a potpourri, with a little bit of everything and not enough of anything: El Grecos and Flemish painters, artefacts representing Basque history and modern paintings. The best part of it is the museum building itself, which is a lovely sixteenth-century convent with a Renaissance cloister.

What to do

Fiestas   For one week on and around 15 August there are numerous celebrations in connection with the religious feastday of the Assumption of the Virgin Mary, including bullfights, folkdances and processions.

●   A word of warning about *fiestas* in the Basque cities: in recent years, there have been numerous clashes between police and celebrators as a result of incidents involving Basque sympathizers. In such scuffles it has not been uncommon for many people to be injured.

Jai Alai or Pelota   This fast-action game, which has a number of different versions, is played with wicker scoops, paddles or with a hand, which is only partially gloved, and is native to the Basque Country. There are matches almost every day at the Carmela Balda Frontón in the Anoeta sports complex in the southern part of town, or at the Galarreta Frontón in Hernani (11 km south). Basque fans bet on players and results, but the betting is as fast-paced as the game, and it is conducted in sign language; so don't rub your nose or scratch your head while watching; you might wind up owing a fortune.

Other Basque sports   These are well worth seeing and are to be found at most local *fiestas*. They include log-chopping, in which each contender stands on top of the huge trunk he is to cut through, and the chips fly so fast you wonder how it is possible any of them survive past the age of sixteen with all their toes. Another typically Basque activity is rock-lifting. Some of these broad-shouldered types in the flat berets are capable of hoisting rocks weighing hundreds of kilos onto their shoulders. Then there are the races of teams of oxen dragging immense boulders. Ask the nearest Spanish Tourist Office abroad, before you arrive, which towns will be celebrating their annual *fiestas* during your stay in the Basque Country.

Sculling races   The most important rowing races of the year in this part of the country take place in the San Sebastián bay on the first and second Sundays of September.

Shopping   The ideal thing to buy, or order for taking or sending home, in this part of the country is wine. But it is best to order it direct from the bodegas in the Rioja district, which are described on p. 278. For a souvenir of the Basque country, you may want to take back the typical black beret, which you can buy in any department store or hat shop here or, better, in Bilbao. Do not buy a red beret, because it could involve you in an unwanted argument; it is the symbol of the Carlists, who support the installation of a king from another line on the Spanish throne.

Shops around the Hotel de Londres y de Inglaterra offer a selection of the most fashionable clothes, particularly for women.

Nightlife
Old Quarter

There are many *tapa* bars in the old quarter, which is usually teeming with people until well past midnight. Nearly all these traditional bars are good. Among the best are **Alcalde**, Calle Mayor 19, and **Kabutzia**, in the Yacht Club, on the waterfront next to the City Hall, with a sweeping view of the bay.

Casino

The **New Kursaal Casino**, Calle Zubieta 2, in the same building as the Hotel de Londres y de Inglaterra, offers French- and American-style roulette, blackjack and others. It also has a bar and restaurant.

Discos,
terrace bars

There are several of each along the long pedestrian-only promenade known as the Paseo de la Concha and, further west, Miraconcha and Avenida de Satrústegui.

Where to stay

Most of the best hotels are on or near the Paseo de la Concha, overlooking the bay. There are some less expensive *pensiones* in the old quarter.

Top range

De Londres y de Inglaterra, Calle Zubieta 2. Tel. (943) 426 989, telex 36378. Central, on the beach, with all comforts and good service, and superb views. The restaurant is good too, though expensive. From 8,200 to 9,900 ptas.

María Cristina, Paseo de la República Argentina s/n. Tel. (943) 426 770. Luxury in the grand style, recently refurbished. Central, garage. Restaurant even pricier than that of the hotel above. From 15,000 ptas (January to June) to 22,000 ptas (rest of the year).

Costa Vasca, Avenida Pio Baroja 15. Tel. (943) 211 011, telex 36551. Pool, tennis, quiet area, garage, shops. From 9,500 ptas.

Mid-range

San Sebastián, Avenida de Zumalcárregui 20. Tel. (943) 214 400, telex 36302. Near the beach, own pool, garden, garage. From 8,000 ptas.

Niza, Calle Zubieta 56. Tel. (943) 426 663. On the beach, central, scenic views, bar. Only forty-one rooms. From 4,950 to 6,250 ptas.

Arana, Calle Vergara 7. Tel. (943) 426 946. A respectable, centrally-located residence hotel. From 3,200 ptas (without private bath) to 5,300 ptas (with bath).

Avenida, Subida a Igueldo. Tel. (943) 212 022. Closed October to March. Residence hotel with great views, pool, garage, bar. From 4,500 ptas (April to June) to 5,500 ptas.

Codina, Avenida de Zumalcárregui 21. Tel. (943) 212 200. On the beach. From 3,250 to 5,250 ptas.

Where to eat

Some of Spain's best restaurants are in the Basque Country. In addition to the famous ones, you will find that even smaller out-of-the-way ones often serve very good food. The Rioja district similarly enjoys a well earned reputation for good cooking.

Pricey

Arzak, Alto de Miracruz 21. Tel. (943) 285 593. Closed for two weeks in June and for three weeks in November; also Sunday evenings and all day Monday. Original and superior variations on Basque dishes at this justly-praised restaurant. Very good selection of wines. Menu varies but seafood is a speciality.

Akelarre, Barrio de Igueldo. Tel. (943) 212 052. Closed during first half of June and for two weeks in December; also Sunday evenings. This place has won several gastronomic awards, which will not surprise you if you decide to dine here. Lovely view of the San Sebastián bay too. International *haute cuisine* with a Basque touch. Excellent wine cellar.

Moderate

Casa Paco, Calle 31 de Agosto 28. Tel. (943) 422 816. Closed in August, Holy Week, all Sundays and holidays, and Mondays for lunch. Non-Spaniards will be gratified to know that this place opens early (by Spanish standards) for supper, at 8.30 p.m. Basque cooking. Grilled fish and meats a speciality. Good wine selection.

Aita Mary, Calle del Puerto 23. Tel. (943) 425 726. Closed on Sundays in winter. Basque cuisine, with fresh fish and vegetable dishes a speciality.

Around San Sebastián

There are many interesting towns you can visit, using San Sebastián as a base. Here are a few that offer you the choice of returning to San Sebastián to sleep or staying overnight.

Fuenterrabía

Fuenterrabía (population 11,276), 20 km from San Sebastián via the A-8 motorway, taking the turn-off to the airport. An ancient walled town, Fuenterrabía (Hondarribía in Basque, as the name appears on some signposts) was the scene of many battles. On 8 September, the feastday of the Virgin of Guadalupe, the whole town turns out for a celebration, keeping a vow their ancestors made to commemorate the end of a terrible sixty-four-day siege by French forces 350 years ago. The old town is right out of a history book, and some of the walls still bear battle scars. There is a good beach, and just across the mouth of the river you can see France.

Where to stay: top range

Parador el Emperador, Plaza de Armas del Castillo. Tel. (943) 642 140. Only sixteen rooms in this tenth-century fortress-turned-hotel, originally built by King Sancho of Navarra, so book well ahead.

Look out of a window, through walls 2 to 3 m thick, and you will understand why this place has withstood so many battles. From 6,000 to 8,500 ptas.

Cestona   Attractive Cestona (population 3,778) is 44 km from San Sebastián via the motorway that leads to Bilbao, turning off at exit N-9 to road C-6317 southbound. The local bus services between San Sebastián and Azpeitia, a little further south, stops here. Basque *fiestas* 8–15 August with regional games and contests. This is one of the only two spas in the Basque provinces. Waters from the two springs here are said to be helpful to sufferers from liver disorders. About 1 km up the hillside is the entrance to the Ekain Cave, which contains prehistoric wall paintings.

Where to stay: **Gran Hotel Balneario Cestona**, Paseo de San Juan s/n. Tel.
mid-range   (943) 867 140. Open only July to October. In the centre of Cestona. Pool, tennis court, restaurant, bar, garage, gym, sauna. From 4,400 to 5,400 ptas.

Azpeitia   Azpeitia (population 12,958) is 8 km south of Cestona on C-6317, or 52 km from San Sebastián via Cestona. The principal attraction of this furniture-manufacturing town is the shrine and birthplace of St Ignatius Loyola, founder of the Jesuits. The shrine, at the end of a broad avenue 1.5 km from the centre, is overwhelmingly sumptuous, in Italian Renaissance style, and the house where he lived in his youth is surrounded by the temple complex that was finished in 1783.

Vitoria – Logroño – Haro – Bilbao

The following towns are arranged in route form. The shortest direct road distance from San Sebastián is shown in each case, as well as the distance from the previously mentioned town. This route is far from exhaustive, but it will show you a small selection of the more interesting places.

Vitoria   The capital of the Basque region (population 192,773) is 118 km
(Gastéiz)   south-west of San Sebastián on the N-I highway. Vitoria is an industrial town on a high plain, fortified and given a city charter in 1181, with a beautiful, well-preserved old quarter on a central hill. The Duke of Wellington defeated Marshal Jourdan's troops here in 1813, and the victory is commemorated by a monument in the Plaza de la Virgen Blanca.

Vitoria has its own airport, Foronda, 8 km to the east on the road to Pamplona, with a daily service to Madrid and less frequent flights to other Spanish cities. The Tourist Office is at Parque de la Florida s/n; Tel. (945) 247 766 – in front of the Canciller Ayala Hotel – in the south-west part of the city. The railway station is at the end of Calle Eduardo Dato in the southern part of the city; Tel. (945) 212 386. The bus station is on Calle Calvo Sotelo 34.

What to see   All of the old part is well worth visiting on foot. Several noble old buildings other than those mentioned below are open for visits. The ten principal streets of this part of town, most of them limited to pedestrians, are unusual for being concentric with the old Cathedral at one end, at the highest point, and the Town Hall at the other.

Of special interest

● **Arms Museum** (La Armería) has a fascinating collection of weapons from all ages and is at the Basque government headquarters, the Ajuria-Enea Palace, Calle Fray Francisco de Victoria 3. It is open daily from 11 a.m. to 2 p.m. and from 5 to 7 p.m., except Saturdays, Sundays and holidays, when it is open only from 11 a.m. to 2 p.m.; closed on Mondays.

● **Fine Arts Museum** (Museo de Bellas Artes) in the Agustí Palace, Plaza Fray Francisco 8. The hours are the same as for the Arms Museum. Most interesting are the works of religious art and the collection of playing cards from the fifteenth to the twentieth centuries.

● **Santa María Cathedral** (Old Cathedral), Plaza de Santa María. The early fourteenth-century main doorway is full of charming statues in successive archways.

Fiestas   The biggest annual *fiestas* in this city take place on or around 5 August, the religious feastday of the White Virgin. This *fiesta* kicks off with the descent on a cable in front of the Town Hall of a doll representing a legendary merrymaker, Celedonio. Events over the next few days after that are similar to those that characterize the *fiestas* of other Basque cities.

Where to stay: top range   **Gastéiz**, Avenida de Gastéiz 19. Tel. (945) 228 100, telex 35451. Elegant, with the usual amenities. From 8,500 ptas.

Mid-range   **Parador de Argomaniz**, 15 km east of Vitoria via N-I (turn right about 8 km outside of Vitoria). Tel. (945) 282 200. Absolute peace and quiet in this stately, seventeenth-century palace, with lovely views. The restaurant serves typical regional dishes like hake in white wine and kidney bean stew. From 5,500 ptas.

Canciller Ayala, Calle Ramon y Cajal 5. Tel. (945) 130 000, telex 35441. This is the classic good hotel in Vitoria. Centrally located, facing the Florida park, it has a garage, and television in the rooms. From 7,800 ptas.

General Alava, Avenida de Gastéiz 53. Tel. (945) 222 200, telex 35468. Garage, airport bus service, bar. From 5,750 ptas.

Where to eat: pricey   **Dos Hermanas**, Calle Madre Vedruna 10. Tel. (945) 243 696. Closed on Sundays and 4 August to 10 September. Still going strong after a century of good cooking, Basque style. Great Spanish wine selection.

Ikea, Calle Paraguay 8. Tel. (945) 224 199. Closed every Monday, Holy Week and 10 August to 10 September. Fish dishes a speciality.

The restaurant has a good wine list to choose from.

Zaldiarán, Avenida Gastéiz 17. Tel. (945) 248 112. Closed on Tuesdays and Sunday evenings. Vitoria-style Basque cooking. Attractive décor. Try the *kokotxas* (hake jowls) fried in batter.

El Portalón, Calle Correría 151. Tel. (945) 224 989. Closed every Sunday, Christmas season and for most of August. In a handsome, sixteenth-century building. Basque food, including sole with mushrooms and anglerfish in Rioja wine sauce.

Logroño

Logroño (population 110,980) is 86 km south-east of Vitoria via N-I and A-68; or 169 km south of San Sebastián via Alsásua and Echarri-Aranaz. This is the capital of the Rioja region, where many of Spain's best wines originate. The Rioja wine district actually reaches into parts of the neighbouring provinces of Alava, Burgos and Navarra, and it does not take in all of the region known as La Rioja.

Useful addresses

The Tourist Office is on the Calle Miguel Villanueva 10, facing the Espolón. Tel. (941) 215 497. The railway station is at the Plaza de Europa, in the south-east corner of the city about six streets from the Espolón. Tel. (941) 213 856. The bus station is at the corner of the Avenida de Pio XII and Avenida de España, near the train station.

What to see

Logroño is a pleasant city, the monumental part of which is concentrated in an area just south of the two bridges – an ancient one of stone which is still in use and a more modern one of steel – which cross the River Ebro. Four churches in this part of town are worth mentioning: **Santa María del Palacio** (eleventh century), founded by the Emperor Constantine, has a 146 m pyramidal tower; **Santiago el Real** (sixteenth century) has an ornate Renaissance altarpiece; **San Bartolomé** (thirteenth century) has the best display of Gothic sculpture in the region, in its main doorway; and the **Santa María la Redonda** Cathedral (fifteenth century) has handsome twin Baroque towers.

Just south of this area, if you follow the Calle Sagasta (the one which crosses the steel bridge), you will arrive at the lovely **Plaza Espolón**, the real centre of the city. It has a large esplanade and a bandstand, which is the scene of concerts and other events, such as ceremonies to celebrate the wine grape harvest, 20–27 September. An equestrian statue on this square gave rise to the earthy Spanish saying: 'to have more than Espartero's horse' which is said of any person showing unusual bravery. Observe the horse closely and you will understand.

Fiestas

Several towns near Logroño have unusual *fiestas*. In San Vicente de la Sonsierra (32 km west of Logroño via N-232) hooded penitents make small puncture wounds in each others' backs with bits of broken glass, then they flagellate themselves as they march in Holy Week processions with blood streaming down their backs. In Anguiano (45 km south-west of Logroño via Navarrete and Nájera, turning south on C-113 at Nájera) men, wearing traditional skirts, perform a frenzied and death-defying dance on stilts on the steep, twisting, stone-paved streets and stairs of the town; 21–23 July. At Alfaro (78 km east of Logroño on N-232) youths run through the streets with the bulls, Pamplona-style; 15–18 August.

Where to stay: **Los Bracos**, Calle Bretón de los Herreros 29. Tel. (941) 226 608,
top range telex 37126. Near the Plaza Espolón. Garage, air-conditioning, television in rooms. From 8,100 ptas.

Mid-range **Gran Hotel**, Calle General Vara del Rey 5. Tel. (941) 252 100. On the Espolón, in a charming turn-of-the-century mansion. This is the bullfighters' favourite hotel in Logroño, with a pleasant terrace off the café in summer. Garage. From 3,960 ptas (16 October to 1 May) to 4,180 ptas (rest of the year).

Carlton Rioja, Gran Vía D. Juan Carlos I 5. Tel. (941) 242 100. The café is a popular local meeting place. Central location, garage, television in rooms. From 6,500 ptas (26 October to end of May) to 7,000 ptas (rest of the year).

Murrieta, Calle Marqués de Murrieta 1. Tel. (941) 224 150. Central, on the western edge of the old quarter, with garage. From 4,025 ptas (16 October to May) to 4,250 ptas (rest of the year).

Abadía de Valvanera, Monasterio de Valvanera, 17 km southwest of Anguiano. Tel. (941) 377 044. A working monastery with twenty-nine rooms for rent in an historic building with mountain views. Restaurant with simple cooking. Naturally, the monks brew their own Benedictine liqueur and it is for sale. From 3,000 ptas.

Where to eat: **La Mercéd**, Calle Mayor 109. Tel. (941) 221 166. Closed on Sundays and first two weeks of August. Riojan cooking and a vast selection of Riojan wines. Elegant décor.

Machadao, Portales 49. Tel. (941) 248 456. Closed on Sundays and all of August. Luxurious setting, delicious food, Riojan-style, served with wines of the region.

Moderate **El Cachetero**, Calle Laurel 3. Tel. (941) 228 463. Closed on Sundays, Wednesday evenings, and 15 July to 15 August. Riojan cooking, good value for money. Specialities: roast kid, codfish and scrambled eggs with garlic (*ajoarriero*).

Haro This town (population 8,581) is 44 km west of Logroño via N-232; or 160 km from San Sebastián via Vitoria. This is the principal town in the best part of the Rioja wine district. In times past, there was so much wine and so little water that builders sometimes mixed wine with their mortar.

On 29 June, the young men and women take part in an annual wine battle, squirting, splashing, pouring and dousing each other with an estimated 50,000 litres of the liquid. The day starts with a hike up the nearby Bilibio hill to the shrine of Haro's patron saint, San Felice, for Mass, followed by the collective wine bath. Calves are then turned loose in the streets to liven things up. Dancing and huge quantities of Rioja's good food round off the day.

Santo Domingo de la Calzada, a town full of lovely medieval buildings, with a parador in a beautiful twelfth-century hospital, is just 16 km south of Haro, and is a delightful place for an excursion.

Visits to bodegas

Since this is Spain's most important district for the production of table wines, it would be skimping to list just one winery, or bodega. Here then are a few from which you can choose one for a visit – or visit them all, but do not plan to drive afterwards.

Bodegas Muga SA, Barrio de la Estación s/n. Tel. (941) 311 825. This bodega exports a large proportion of its fine red wines to Europe and North America. Visits, by prior arrangement, Monday to Friday, from 10 a.m. to midday and from 4 to 5 p.m. Call Señor Crespo for an appointment. Wines can be bought there.

Compañía Vinícola del Norte De Espana (CVNE), Avenida Costa del Vino 21. Tel. (941) 310 650. This company exports good white, red and rosé wines to the United States, Britain and West Germany. Visits Monday to Friday, from 8 a.m. to 1 p.m. and from 3 to 6 p.m., except in August. Call Rafael Chacón to arrange a day and a time. Wine sales at the bodega.

Federico Paternina SA, Avenida Santo Domingo 11. Tel. (941) 310 550. Exporter of highly-praised white, red and rosé wines to countries all over the world. Visits Monday to Friday, from 8.30 a.m. to 1 p.m. and from 3.30 to 6 p.m. No retail sales here, but this bodega's products are available in shops all over the country.

Where to stay: mid-range

Higinia, Calle Vega 31. Tel. (941) 310 100. Centrally located, with a fairly cheap restaurant. From 1,780 ptas (without private bath) to 2,790 ptas (with bath).

Parador de Santo Domingo de la Calzada, Plaza del Santo, Santo Domingo de la Calzada (16 km south of Haro). Tel. (941) 340 300. Only twenty-seven rooms, so book ahead. This parador serves good Riojan specialities, such as stuffed sweet peppers. Inside the nearby cathedral there is a cage containing a rooster and a hen, reminders of the legend of how two roast chickens came to life and flew off the dinner plate of the town magistrate. This unexpected event was confirmation that St Dominic had saved the life of a young man, a pilgrim on his way to Santiago, who had been unjustly sentenced to be hanged for theft, on the false testimony of a woman he had spurned. From 6,500 ptas (November to June) to 7,500 ptas.

Where to eat: pricey

La Kika, Calle Santo Tomás 9. Tel. (941) 311 447. Open for lunch only. Closed in October. A small place with excellent cooking and a limited menu. You will be advised what dishes there are on the day you dine. Riojan cooking, with fine vegetable dishes as well as meats and fish. The house wine is a palatable Rioja.

Terete, Calle Lucrecia Arana 17. Tel. (941) 310 023. Closed every Monday, Sunday and holiday evenings and all of October. A real institution, that has been offering roast lamb and other dishes for well over a century. Good Riojan house wine at a low, low price.

Bilbao (Bilbo)

With a population of 433,030, Bilbao is 90 km north of Haro via A-68; or 99 km west of San Sebastián via A-8. The capital of Vizcaya, one of the Basque provinces, and one of Spain's major industrial centres, Bilbao straddles the River Nervión, which is lined with gantry cranes. The new Bilbao superport gives it a capacity and facilities for becoming one of Europe's busiest ports. This city, however, is still struggling to recover from a long recession, aggravated by the assassinations, extortions, kidnappings and other crimes perpetrated by the outlawed secessionist organization ETA, which have put a damper on investment.

Main areas   The modern part of the city is surrounded on three sides by a loop of the river. The main east–west street is the Gran Vía de Don Diego López de Haro. Many official buildings, including the local headquarters of the Basque regional government, are on or near this street. The Gran Vía is also a principal shopping street. Three other important streets, the Alameda de Recalde, Calle Ercilla and Calle Elcano, intersect with the Gran Vía like rays of a star, at the central Plaza de Federico de Moyua. Railway stations for local and long-distance trains are beside the river at the eastern end of this street. The Tourist Office is at Alameda Mazarredo s/n. Tel. (94) 423 6430. This is a street which traces an arc across the northern part of the modern city on the left bank. The Sondica Airport is 8 km north of the city.

What to see   Although it was founded in 1300, Bilbao does not have many noteworthy old buildings; but the **old quarter**, most of which lies on the right bank of the river opposite the Santander Railway Station in the eastern part of the city, does have a certain charm, particularly because of the backdrop of the steep hills which crowd close to the river bank. Many restaurants and *tapa* bars are located in this area.

● **Santiago Cathedral**, built in the fourteenth century and restored in 1571 after a fire, preserves its Gothic cloister, which was finished in 1404; the façade, however, was rebuilt in 1885.

● **Fine Arts Museum** (Museo de Bellas Artes), Parque de Doña Casilda Iturriza. Open daily from 10 a.m. to 1.30 p.m. and 4.30 to 7.30 p.m. and from 11 a.m. to 2 p.m. on Sundays; closed on Mondays. It contains a good collection of old and modern works of art. The modern section is dominated by the Basque sculptor Chillida's *Monument to Iron*. Old masters represented in this museum include El Greco, Goya and Velázquez.

Fiestas   Bilbao's principal *fiestas* take place during the 'Big Week', which begins on the first Saturday after the feast of the Virgin of Begonia on 15 August. These *fiestas* feature major bullfights, street dancing and processions. A number of races between *traineras*, which are long rowing boats, take place on the River Nervión in August and September.

Where to stay
Top range

Bilbao's principal hotels are all within a few streets of the Plaza de Federico Moyua, into which the Gran Vía runs.

Ercilla, Calle Ercilla 37. Tel. (94) 443 8800, telex 33449. This central hotel is a favourite with journalists because of its good communications, good service and excellent restaurant. Its bar is usually lively, and its café is the ideal place for a snack. From 12,000 ptas.

Villa de Bilbao, Gran Vía 87. Tel. (94) 441 6000, telex 32164. Bilbao's only hotel to get a five-star rating from the tourist authorities, the Villa de Bilbao is patronized to a considerable extent by politicians. It is the newest of the major hotels and is very much in the centre of things. Spacious rooms, heated swimming pool, tennis court. From 13,560 ptas.

Mid-range

Avenida, Avenida Zumalcárregui 40. Tel. (94) 412 4300, telex 31040. On a hill near the Begonia Basilica, this is not in the centre, but it is still within easy taxi distance of it. Live music at dinner on Fridays. From 6,400 ptas.

Conde Duque, Paseo de Campo Volantín 22. Tel. (94) 445 6000, telex 31260. On the opposite side of the river from the modern city centre and in a rundown neighbourhood but clean and satisfactory. From 6,500 to 6,800 ptas.

Nervión, Paseo de Campo Volantín 11. Tel. (94) 445 4700, telex 31040. Near the above hotel and close to the Town Hall. Primarily a hotel geared to tour groups and conventions. From 6,400 ptas.

Where to eat

Bilbao is a great place to eat. Apart from the restaurants I've mentioned here, there are literally scores of places where you can eat extremely well, provided you stick to Basque food.

Pricey

Bermeo, Calle Ercilla 37 (in the Hotel Ercilla). Tel. (94) 443 8800. Closed on Sunday evenings. A very fine restaurant serving Basque specialities. Attentive service and attractive décor. Comprehensive wine list.

Guria, Gran Vía 66. Tel. (94) 441 0543. Closed on Sundays. One of Bilbao's most famous eateries, formerly located in the old quarter. Basque cooking at its best. Specialities: cod, various styles, and different vegetable pastries and puddings.

Moderate

Machimbenta, Calle Ledesma 26. Tel. (94) 424 8495. Closed on Sundays. Primarily patronized by businessmen, this central restaurant has been serving Bilbao for more than a quarter of a century, and serving it well. Strictly Basque cooking, but you will not be disappointed, even if you do not understand the menu. Try the *piperada*, an original version of the French *ratatouille*, and the fresh tuna fish in tomato sauce.

Kirol, Calle Ercilla 28. Tel. (94) 443 7011. Closed on Sundays, holidays and all of August. A very small basement dining room but the food is excellent. Basque cooking, of course. Special dishes depend on what is available at the market, but a regular is sweet peppers stuffed with either meat or fish.

Guernica – Bermeo

Guernica

Guernica (population 17,836) is 47 km north-east of Bilbao via Bermeo; or 97 km west of San Sebastián via A-8, turning north on C-6313 at Amorebieta. This is the town where, for centuries, kings swore to respect the special rights and privileges of the Basques. When King Juan Carlos went there to address the Basque Parliament in 1978, he was heckled by nationalist members of the regional parliament.

The old oak tree under which King Ferdinand swore in 1476 to respect the privileges of the Señorío de Vizcaya no longer stands, but a seedling of a seedling of that tree does stand on the spot, and it is sacred to the Basques. A museum in the same building as the Vizcaya Casa de Juntas (Assembly House) displays a piece of the original tree.

General Franco understood the importance of Guernica as a symbol of the Basque cause. Perhaps for that reason, in order to crush Basque hopes for home rule or independence from the start, he chose Guernica in the Spanish Civil War as the testing ground for the world's first massive air raid on a civilian target. It was carried out on 26 April 1937, by Hitler's *Luftwaffe* on his behalf. Although today the tools of war are infinitely more lethal, the shock waves of that attack reverberated around the world. Spanish painter Pablo Picasso immortalized it in his huge canvas *Guernica*, which today hangs in an annexe of the Prado Museum.

Bermeo

On the way from Bilbao to Guernica on C-6313 you pass through Bermeo, one of the most charming of Basque fishing ports and if the fleet is in you will see a rainbow of fishing vessels, each in a different bright colour.

Where to eat:
pricey

El Faisán de Oro, Calle Adolfo Urioste 4. Tel. (94) 685 1001. Closed on Wednesday and Tuesday evenings, some of November and December. Basque version of *nouvelle cuisine*.

North Central Coast and the Peaks of Europe

This section includes the regions of Cantabria (Cantabrica) and Asturias and the province of León, which belongs to the region of Castille and León. It is largely mountainous, and, to judge by the objects and paintings found in caves such as the famous Altamira Caves at Santillana, it has been inhabited from the very earliest days.

The scenery is consistently beautiful thanks to the combination of mountains, sea and the climate, which keeps everything green and does not have the extreme variations in temperature as, for example,

North Central Coast and
the Peaks of Europe

Madrid. There are zones of surprisingly mild microclimates in sheltered valleys. The average minimum temperature in Santander in January, the coldest month, is 6.8°C (43°F) and the average maximum in August, the hottest month, is 22.3°C (72°F). Stay as long as you like, but to try to 'do' this whole area in less than two weeks would be exhausting and unsatisfactory. The best thing is to pick and choose among the places and activities available.

Santander

The easiest starting point, and centre for excursions, in this area is Santander (population 180,328), which has retained an air of elegance acquired early this century, when it became a fashionable watering place for prominent Spanish families, who followed the lead of their Royals. At the same time many buildings are new, much of the city having been rebuilt after a disastrous fire in 1941.

Getting there
You can reach Santander by car, ferry, train or plane, but, generally, its communications links with the world – and for that matter, with the rest of Spain – leave something to be desired. The ferries that ply between Santander and Plymouth several times a week (but less frequently in winter) are, however, an alternative for those from the UK coming by car, but who do not wish to drive across France.

By road, Santander is 146 km west of Guernica via Bilbao on the N-634 road, and 264 km west of Irún, on the French border. Those distances will be shorter, and the journey will be quicker, once the long-awaited coastal motorway is completed. The road from Madrid to Santander crosses the formidable Escudo Pass before heading downhill to the coast. This pass, with its steep, twisting road, only wide enough for one vehicle in each direction, is one to take cautiously at any time of year. But, in winter, snow and ice often make it impassable.

Travellers arriving from the north of Europe will not find it very convenient to come by train as there is no standard Spanish-gauge railway running along the northern coast, but only a local, narrow-gauge line. To reach the north and west of Spain from abroad, you must almost invariably pass through Madrid, from where the main lines radiate like spokes of a wheel.

Santander's airport, 7 km south of the city, offers flights to and from Madrid twice daily, and once a day to and from Barcelona and Pamplona; but there are no international flights. Travellers flying from abroad must therefore change in Madrid or Barcelona.

Getting around the region
It may be hard to get to, but Santander, and the area to which it gives access, is certainly worth the effort. Once you arrive, there are local buses which go to just about every village on the map, and which

link Santander with other principal towns and cities, where further local buses are available. However, in spite of this, the rugged nature of the terrain and the distances involved may make it worth considering hiring a car.

Main areas   Santander is spread out along the seafront with its port actually facing south towards the sheltered Bay of Santander. The main road that leads from one end of the city to the other is the Paseo del General Davila, which runs behind and above the town.

However, because getting down into the lower part of the city from this road by car is complicated in some places, it is best to use one of the smaller east–west streets if you wish to go into the town centre. If you are driving from Bilbao, you will find yourself on the Calle del Marqués de la Hermida, in the port area. At the end of this street lies the Customs House, where you can continue by turning half-left onto the Calle Antonio López. This leads, after a few streets, to the ferry dock (behind a fence on your right). You are now in the town centre; parking is not very easy. To go west from here, you should take the Calle Castilla, which parallels and is one street north of Marqués de la Hermida.

The Plaza Porticada, a colonnaded square, is right in the middle of the city. You can see it from the park on your left, just past the ferry dock. The Tourist Office (Plaza de Velarde 1; Tel. [942] 211 417), Post Office, and Cathedral are all on or adjacent to the Plaza. The railway station is three streets from the Plaza along the Calle de Cádiz, which runs alongside the Cathedral. The better hotels are mostly at the east end of the city, near the Sardinero, the best of Santander's twelve beaches. There are numerous restaurants and some hotels in the vicinity of the Plaza Porticada. The Santander Summer University is housed in the lovely Magdalena Palace, on a small peninsula at the eastern end of the city.

History   Santander itself is not particularly interesting from an historical point of view. From at least the thirteenth century it has been the main port of Castile. It prospered especially during the nineteenth century, and in the early part of this century became a stylish resort when the Spanish Royal Family decided to spend its summers in Santander.

What to see   There is a lot to see in this area, but little in Santander itself. All the same, you might want to see the **Provincial Museum of Prehistory and Archaeology**, Calle Casimiro Sainz 4. Open daily from 9 a.m. to 2 p.m.; closed on Mondays. One of the most complete collections of Stone Age implements and artefacts in Europe, most of which have come from caves and sites in the area.

Excursions   There are a number of interesting coastal towns, each of which has its own particular character.

Santoña, 48 km east of Santander, is defended by two fortresses in its snug bay, with two good beaches.

Suances, 31 km west of Santander, is at the mouth of the Rivers Saja and Besaya. The town is on high ground overlooking the fishing port and the extensive beaches.

Comillas, 48 km west of Santander, is sometimes called 'The Archbishop's Village', because of its stately old buildings and luxurious mansions. There is also a pretty beach and fishing port.

What to do

Water sports

Between Cantabria and Asturias, there are about a hundred good beaches, many of them totally undeveloped. The waters are full of many kinds of fish, but you need a licence to fish, whether in the sea or in rivers and lakes; contact the Tourist Office for details. Santander's Yacht Club, on the Paseo de Pereda east of the Plaza Porticada, will advise you if you wish to do some sailing.

Hunting

A licence is required if you wish to hunt game here, which includes wild boar, deer and mountain goat. Contact the Tourist Office for details.

Hiking and mountain climbing

There are facilities for these activities throughout the Peaks of Europe, including a number of high-altitude refuges for climbers. Tourist Offices will tell you their exact locations. These are spectacular mountains, rising up to 2,600 m and with vertical faces as high as 2,000 m and here, as elsewhere, climbing should not be practised in isolated areas by amateurs except in the company of experienced climbers. Spain has a number of climbing accidents each year. The Cantabrian Mountain Climbing Federation has offices at Calle Fernández de la Isla 11, Santander. Tel. (942) 313 023.

Skiing

There are five ski resorts in the Peaks of Europe. All of them have ski lifts of one kind or another and all have hotels reasonably close to the runs. None of them is normally as crowded as those in the Pyrenees; but it is also fair to say that they are not as developed and not all of them are as good. Rocks, for instance, represent a danger on the upper slopes of the Picos de Europa resort. For details, see 'ski resorts' on pp. 286–7.

Shopping

Picón cheese from Tresviso is a good buy. But for the star of the cheese world in this part of the country, you will have to wait until you get to Oviedo, where you can buy the genuine Cabrales cheese. *Sobaos* and *quesadas* are typical Cantabrian cakes.

Nightlife

Casino

Gran Casino del Sardinero, Plaza de Italia. Tel. (942) 276 054, open from 7 p.m. to 4 a.m. All kinds of gambling. Happy hour at the bar from 9 to 10 p.m.

Bars

This is a lively city at night, especially in the summer. The better-class establishments are mostly near the Sardinero beach and there are plenty of them. Bar and disco prices are almost invariably quite reasonable.

Festival

The International Festival of Music and Dance in August in the Plaza Porticada features top performers.

Where to stay

Businessmen's hotels tend to be near the Plaza Porticada. Tourist hotels tend to be near the Sardinero beach. Cheaper lodgings are scattered throughout the centre, but mostly back from the seafront.

Top range

Real, Paseo de Pérez Galdós 28. Tel. (942) 272 550. A beautiful old building, well maintained. Open only July to mid-September. Near the Summer University and close to the beaches. Has an expensive restaurant. From 12,420 to 15,525 ptas.

Bahía, Calle Alfonso XIII 6. Tel. (942) 221 700, telex 35859. Central, close to the ferry port. Shops, bar. From 5,500 ptas (mid-September to mid-June) to 8,500 ptas (summer).

Mid-range

Sardinero, Plaza de Italia 1. Tel. (942) 271 100, telex 35795. A lovely building overlooking the beach, with spacious rooms. From 4,300 ptas (October to June) to 6,350 ptas (rest of the year).

Rex, Avenida Calvo Sotelo 9. Tel. (942) 210 200. Very central, close to the ferry port. From 4,500 to 7,000 ptas.

María Isabel, Avenida de García Lago s/n. Tel. (942) 271 850. At the north end of the Sardinero, with terrific views. Pool, disco, garage. From 3,900 ptas (October to June) to 6,350 ptas (rest of the year).

Rhin, Avenida Reina Victoria 155. Tel. (942) 274 300. A residence hotel on the Magdalena beach. From 4,225 ptas (October to mid-June) to 6,025 ptas (rest of the year).

México, Calle Méndez Núñez 2. Tel. (942) 212 450. Residence hotel. From 3,300 ptas (mid-September to June) to 4,300 ptas (rest of the year).

Where to eat
Pricey

Bar del Puerto, Calle Hernán Cortés 63. Tel. (942) 213 001. Fish, fish, fish. For forty years, they have been serving fish, and it is a great success. Classic Spanish recipes.

Moderate

La Gaviota, Calle Marqués de la Ensenada 32, right in the fishermen's quarter. Tel. (942) 221 006. Grilled fish, simple cooking.

Colasa, Calle Antonio López 11, Comillas (50 km west of Santander). Tel. (942) 720 001. Closed October to May. Unusually good home-style Cantabrian cooking.

Ski resorts

These are not listed in any route order, since the road network doesn't make this practical.

Alto
Campóo

Some 99 km south-west of Santander via N-611, turning right onto C-628 (westbound) at Reinosa. Popular with climbers and hikers too once the snow begins to melt. Additional information: Cantursa, Calle Juan de la Cosa 1, Santander. Tel. (942) 215 050.

Where to stay:
mid-range

Vejo, Avenida Cantabria 15, Reinosa (75 km from Alto Campóo). Tel. (942) 751 700. Garage. From 4,200 ptas (31 August to 6 July) to 5,150 ptas (rest of the year).

Picos de Europa

This is 133 km south-west of Santander via N-634 westbound, then south on N-621 through Potes to Fuente Dé.

Where to stay:
mid-range

Parador Rio Deva, Fuente Dé (at the resort, 3.5 km from Espinama). Tel. (942) 730 001. A modern, comfortable building, open all year. Restaurant. Scenic views. A cable-car takes you from the parador to the 1,850-m Hoyo de Lloroza, 750 m higher, in three and a half minutes. From 5,500 to 7,000 ptas.

Picos de Valdecoro, Calle Roscabado s/n, Potes (20 km from Picos de Europa resort). Tel. (942) 730 025. Scenic views, bar. From 3,630 ptas (October to June) to 3,850 ptas (rest of the year).

Valgrande-Pajares

The resort is 268 km south-west of Santander by road, at the Pajares Pass on N-630, via Oviedo. Hotels in the vicinity are open all year round. Additional information at Sociedad Deportiva Astur-Leonesa de Pajares, Calle Fuela 187, Oviedo. Tel. (985) 215 506.

Where to stay: mid-range

Asturias, Calle Fernando Merino s/n, La Pola de Gordón (33 km from resort). Tel. No. 5 of San Emiliano, province of León (manual, not dialable). Scenic views. Economical restaurant. From 1,800 ptas (without bath) to 2,200 ptas (with bath).

San Isidro

San Isidro is 277 km south-west of Santander via Oviedo, where you take N-630 southbound, Santa Cruz, where you take C-631 eastbound, and Cabañaquinta, where you take a local road eastbound for about 30 km to the San Isidro Pass and ski resort. Lodging in the area is extremely limited. Additional information: Estación Invernal del Puerto de San Isidro, Plaza San Marcelo 6, León. Tel. (987) 213 500.

Where to stay: bottom range

Pico Agujas, Puebla de Lillo (at the resort). Tel. (987) 735 025, extn 40. Only seventeen rooms. Very simple.

Santander–Santillana del Mar–Covadonga–Oviedo

There are two routes you could take from Santander to Oviedo. The first more or less follows the coast and passes through Santillana del Mar and Covadonga. The second is the more mountainous inland road via Cervera de Pisuerga and León.

Santillana del Mar

This was a town (population 3,884), 26 km west of Santander via N-634 and C-6316, of prosperous noblemen in the Middle Ages, and its architecture attests to that. The entire town has been officially declared an historic monument. Set in a fertile plain near the sea, Santillana was once the capital of eastern Asturias. One of the most attractive old towns in Spain, it has perfectly preserved its original character but with one exception: the cars which rumble through the narrow stone-paved streets and park everywhere, blocking pavements and spoiling the view for your camera. The Tourist Office is at Plaza Ramón Pelayo. Tel. (942) 818 251.

What to see

You can see the Rovolgo meadows, an old duelling ground where *caballeros* (Spanish knights) once settled their differences with swords, and many old stone houses, each bearing the coat of arms, carved in stone, of the family which inhabited it. A fine collection of religious art is on display at the cloister of the Regina Coeli Convent, founded in 1599. The warm yellow stone of the Collegiate Church (Colegiata) of

Saint Juliana, patron saint of the town, adds to the beauty of this twelfth-century gem among Romanesque churches.

Altamira Caves

The Altamira Caves, which have been described by some as the 'Sistine Chapel of Cave Paintings', are just outside Santillana. They used to be open to the public, but in order to limit further deterioration of the red, ochre and black wall paintings and carvings, some of which are nearly 15,000 years old, the caves are now opened only by special request. If you are interested in prehistoric cave art, however, there are many other caves open to the general public in this area. One, La Cueva de las Aguas, is only 9 km from Santillana.

The whole area is riddled with caves, though not all of them are of archaeological interest. When the new parador, opened in 1987, was being built at Santillana on the site of the old annexe, architects and engineers were set special problems by one such cave when they realized that the ground on which they were building was hollow. The new parador, incidentally, has been designed to blend in completely with the rest of the town. It complements the previous one, in an old palace (see below).

Where to stay:
top range

Parador Gil Blas, Plaza Ramón Pelayo 11. Tel. (942) 818 000. Both the old and the new sections are equally comfortable. Parking area, garden, pricey but good restaurant serving regional specialities. From 7,500 to 9,500 ptas.

Mid-range

Los Infantes, Avenida Le Dorat 1. Tel. (942) 818 000. An old palatial home recently converted into a hotel. Parking area, garden, small disco, moderately-priced restaurant. From 3,700 ptas (October to March) to 6,100 ptas.

Altamira, Calle Cantón 1. Tel. (942) 818 025. An old stone house with a flowery interior patio. Parking area, restaurant. From 3,700 to 4,200 ptas.

Where to eat:
pricey

Los Blasones, Plaza de la Gandara. Tel. (942) 818 070. Closed November to March and Sunday evenings in spring and autumn. Cantabrian cooking.

Asturias

Going west from Santillana you pass into the principality of Asturias, which is mountainous right down to the coast, with a mild climate at lower altitudes. Its landscapes are ones of rolling green hills, pleasant coves and snowy peaks. Perhaps influenced by Cantabria's claim to be the original Garden of Eden, officials in Oviedo have adopted the slogan, 'Asturias, Paradise on Earth'. If so, the thin sour cider they drink all over this region must be a punishment for Adam and Eve's messing around with the apple. The principality is Spain's main coal-mining region, and its economy also relies heavily on fishing and dairy farming. Steel-making and shipbuilding activities have been on the decline for the past few years.

Covadonga

To reach Covadonga, turn south off the N-634 just before Arriondas, which is 157 km west of Santander, onto the C-637 towards Cangas de Onis. Here, turn left onto the eastbound C-6312 before turning right after 4 km onto a local road to Covadonga, which is 7 km further on.

This is where the Christian warlord Don Pelayo began the Reconquest nearly 1,300 years ago. Europe's history would have been very different had he not persevered. Here are the grottoes where he probably hid from the Emir of Córdoba's hit men, the statue of the Virgin he probably venerated and the sweeping views of a country too beautiful for him to give up. Don Pelayo and his 300 men succeeded in ambushing the Emir's powerful army by causing a landslide, which buried the troops. From that time on, the Christian movement began to regain control of the Iberian Peninsula, gradually growing in force over the next seven centuries and finally ousting the last of the Moorish kings in 1492.

From Covadonga, Oviedo is 120 km direct to the north on A-66 and N-630.

Santander–Cervera de Pisuerga– León–Oviedo

The second route to Oviedo starts by going inland to Cervera de Pisuerga.

Cervera de Pisuerga

Cervera (population 2,963) is 131 km south of Santander via N-611 to Aguilar de Campóo, where you turn off west onto a local road. On the way from Santander you pass through the industrial town of Reinosa, before reaching high mountain country. Aguilar, famous for its biscuit factories, lies in a tranquil farming valley. Cervera is surrounded by tall mountains and is just 3 km from the Fuentes Carrionas hunting reserve, where small and large game, including the brown bear, live in the forests and meadows. A chain of lakes adds to the attraction of this town as a base for hiking, camping and hunting.

Where to stay: mid-range

Parador Fuentes Carrionas, on a hill 2 km above Cervera de Pisuerga. Tel. (988) 870 085. This parador, opened in 1975, overlooks the large Ruesga Lake and the wooded and snow-capped mountains beyond. Each of the large rooms has a balcony with good views. The parador's restaurant serves regional dishes and game. In summer, you will see dozens of tents and caravans along the shores of the lake, though there is no formal camping ground.

One fine summer morning in 1986 guests at the hotel looked out over the lake from their balconies to discover that all the campers had suddenly disappeared as if by magic. The 'magic' turned out to be a bear who had wandered down the slopes, probably in search of food, and had clawed open one of the tents.

From here you can walk along some lovely country lanes that lead up to tiny mountaintop *pueblos* (villages). The scenery is spectacular.

León   This city (population 131,134) is 170 km south-west from Cervera; or 332 km from Santander via Oviedo. The road to León takes you through high and lovely country, frequently changing between high plains and snow or tree-covered peaks. About 31 km north of Cistierna, which is roughly halfway between Cervera and León, lie the ruins of Riaño, a stock-breeding town of about 900 inhabitants in an incredibly beautiful valley that violently but futilely resisted being drowned by the waters of a dam project. Riaño's townspeople made their last stand against the Civil Guard police and the construction machinery in the spring and summer of 1987; several were injured; one Riaño man committed suicide rather than leave his home and his valley. To make sure the townspeople would not come back before the waters poured in, practically the whole town was bulldozed to rubble.

History   The medieval kingdom of León united with Castile briefly several times but the final link was not made until the thirteenth century with the marriage of León's King Ferdinand to Queen Isabella of Castile; that union was the foundation of modern Spain.

What to see   León's **Cathedral** (Santa María de Regla), begun in 1205, is one of the most graceful of Spain's Gothic monuments and is particularly famous for its stained glass windows. Nearby is the remarkable Church of **San Isidoro**, which contains the Panteón de los Reyes, the mausoleum of the early kings of León and Castile. This is decorated with well-preserved Romanesque frescoes, painted in about 1160, which are still fresh and full of life.

In June, the *fiesta* of 'Las Cantaderas' is celebrated in the cloister of San Isidoro to commemorate the abolition of the tribute of one hundred damsels demanded annually by Moorish rulers.

Tourist Office: Plaza de la Regla 4 (in front of the Cathedral). Tel. (987) 237 082.

Where to stay: **San Marcos**, Plaza de San Marcos. Tel. (987) 237 300, telex
top range   89089. For all those who have ever wanted to stay in a museum, this is undoubtedly one of the world's great hotels. Originally a monastery of the Knights of Santiago, later a hospital for pilgrims on their way to Santiago, today, carefully restored and maintained, it offers hospitality to travellers as one of the smartest paradors in all Spain. Construction began on its magnificent, ornate stone façade in 1530. The broad main staircase and the cloister also date from the sixteenth century. One wing is a large medieval church, still used for religious services. Inside the hotel, antique rugs, tapestries, statuary and ancient carved wooden ceilings make a stay here a unique experience. In every other respect, it is, of course, totally modern, with air-conditioning, television, disco and a good restaurant. From 9,600 ptas (November to June) to 10,700 ptas.

Mid-range   **Conde Luna**, Calle Independencia 7. Tel. (987) 206 512, telex

89888. Central, garage, heated pool, shops, sauna. From 6,400 ptas (October to March) to 7,100 ptas (rest of year).

Quindos, Avenida José Antonio 24. Tel. (987) 236 200. Central, television in rooms. From 4,200 ptas.

Riosol, Avenida de Palencia 3. Tel. (987) 223 650. Central, bar. From 3,850 ptas (November to mid-March) to 4,200 ptas (rest of the year).

Where to eat: pricey

Casa Pozo, Plaza de San Marcelo 15. Tel. (987) 223 039. Closed first two weeks of July and from Christmas Eve until 7 January; also every Sunday. Leonese cooking. Trout and salmon fishermen go to this restaurant to eat fish, so it must be good.

Moderate

Adonias, Calle Santa Nonia 16. Tel. (987) 206 768. Closed on Sundays. Typical Leonese cooking, which means lots of sausages, pork and stews.

Patricio, Condesa de Sagasta 24. Tel. (987) 241 651. Closed on Mondays and Sunday evenings. Regional cooking; short menu which varies according to availability.

El Racimo de Oro, Calle Caño Vadillo 2. Tel. (987) 257 575. Closed on Tuesdays and Sunday evenings. Historic house, comfortable atmosphere. Charcoal grill. Leonese cooking.

Oviedo

Oviedo (population 190,123) is 220 km west of Santander; or 119 km north of León via A-66 and N-630. This is the capital of the principality of Asturias.

Useful addresses

The station for long-distance trains is at the north-western end of the Calle de Uria. The airport is 47 km to the north, near Avilés; only domestic flights land there. The Tourist Office is at the Plaza de la Catedral 6. Tel. (985) 213 385.

What to see

Among sights to see is the Cathedral, with its filigreed-stone Gothic tower built in the sixteenth century. It would be even prettier if they would wash the grime off the stone. Another is the lovely Santa María del Naranco Church, 4 km out of town to the north-west. Others are the sixteenth-century university and the seventeenth-century Town Hall and court house. The old part of the town lies one or two streets east of the large, central Parque de San Francisco.

Where to stay: top range

Hotel de la Reconquista, Calle Gil de Jaz 16. Tel. (985) 241 100, telex 843280. An impressive red-stone building, erected in the eighteenth century as a hospital, tastefully converted into a modern hotel with glassed-in cloister and a charming chapel. (The manager has the key.) In addition to the surroundings, customers benefit from garage, air-conditioning, television in rooms, sauna and restaurant. My only complaint is that you have to be an engineer to understand how the shower works. From 10,000 ptas (January to mid-March) to 12,000 ptas (high season).

Mid-range

La Jirafa, Calle Pelayo 6. Tel. (985) 222 244, telex 89951. A hotel on the top floors of a tall building; garage. From 7,975 ptas.

Ramiro I, Calle Calvo Sotelo 13. Tel. (985) 232 850, telex 84042.

Not quite central but close. Garage, bar. From 5,550 ptas (October to June) to 6,700 ptas (rest of the year).

Regente, Calle Jovellanos 31. Tel. (985) 222 343, telex 84310. Centrally located, garage, television in rooms. Good views of the old quarter from upper floors. From 7,295 ptas.

Where to eat: **Trascorrales**, Plaza Trascorrales 19. Tel. (985) 222 441. Closed
pricey mid-August to mid-September, Christmas season, Holy Week and every Sunday. A traditional Asturian restaurant in a classic old building, offering new variations on old themes. Speciality: entrecôte with Cabrales cheese.

Casa Fermín, Calle San Francisco 8. Tel. (985) 216 452. Closed on Sunday evenings. *Nouvelle cuisine*, Asturian style.

Moderate **Casa Conrado**, Calle Arguelles 1. Tel. (985) 223 919. Closed all of August and every Sunday. Asturian cooking, including Asturian stew and home made cottage cheese.

Principado, Calle San Francisco 6. Tel. (985) 217 792. Asturian cooking. Closed on Tuesdays and Sunday evenings. Historic house, comfortable atmosphere. Charcoal grill. Leonese cooking.

Excursion One of Asturias' most colourful *fiestas* is the Wedding of the *Vaqueiros*, celebrated every August on a mountaintop at Aristébano, near the coastal town of Luarca, 89 km from Oviedo. Although nomadic livestock herding is now a thing of the past, the festival celebrates old customs among descendants of the families who used to spend their summers on the grassy highlands and their winters in the valleys with their cattle and sheep. Until this century, the *Vaqueiros* suffered from discrimination, perhaps because they lived apart from the rest of society. Every year at least one couple is married at the *fiesta*. In 1987 there were two couples. The veiled bride and groom, in their *Vaqueiro* finest, arrived on horseback. An oxcart brought the bridal bed in procession behind them as the bagpipes wailed. Girls, in white blouses and red and green skirts, and boys, in simple black suits and cloth footgear, wearing a kind of stocking cap, danced. No cathedral could offer a more beautiful setting.

Shopping Best buy is the really ripe and stinky Cabrales cheese wrapped in vine leaves; Asturians say it is at its peak when it has worms in it, but, fortunately, the wormless variety seems to prevail.

Nightlife Oviedo is not a city famous for its nightlife, but the action, what action there is, is in the bars around the university, some of which have live music.

Galicia

You might say the Galicians invented tourism. What else would you call the unique flow of visitors from all over Europe to see the tomb of

Galicia

Vivero

El Ferrol

CORUNNA

Betanzos

Lugo

bo Finisterre

SANTIAGO DE COMPOSTELA

Noya

La Estrada

GALICIA

Villagarcía de Arosa

Cambados

La Toja

PONTEVEDRA

Carballino

Ons Island

Sangenjo

ORENSE

Ribadavia

Cies Islands

VIGO

Nigrán

Puenteareas

Bayona

Tuy

St James the Apostle in Santiago in the late Middle Ages? It was not all down-market tourism either. Pilgrims to Santiago included the jet-set of the time: rulers of Portugal, France, England and Spain, bishops, priests, monks, scholars and prominent nobles from as far away as the Urals. Among the visitors were St Francis of Assisi, who later founded the Order of the Franciscans, and St Domingo de Guzmán, who founded that of the Dominicans. The first chain of establishments catering to tourists was undoubtedly the string of monasteries, hostels and hospitals set up by the Benedictine monks along the Way to Santiago.

Tourism in this lushly green north-western corner of Spain has fallen off a bit since then. Nowadays, relatively few visitors from abroad go to Galicia, and more's the pity, because it is a place full of Celtic charm and great natural beauty. The Galicians themselves travel around their region a great deal, for pleasure as well as business; and the people who do visit Galicia from abroad include a large percentage of Galician emigrants or their descendants. So many people have emigrated from here, particularly to the New World, that Galician communities have been a great social and cultural influence in many Latin American countries.

Galicia's attractions include: its many beautiful and bountiful *rías*, or long bays; its gentle climate; its great natural ports; its good food; its wealth of historic monuments; and even its *meigas* or witches. Do witches exist in twentieth-century Spain? Galicians have an answer for that in their own lilting language, Galego, which is more widely spoken in its home region than any other of Spain's regional languages. That answer is a stock phrase, which unfortunately loses all its music in translation, but none of its respect for the unfathomable: '*Meigas?* I don't believe in them, but if you ask me if they exist, they do.'

Four provinces make up the region: Corunna (La Coruña in Castilian, A Cruña in Galego), Lugo, Pontevedra and Orense; and the capital city of each bears the same name as its province. The regional capital is the truly monumental city of Santiago de Compostela. All the provinces except Orense border the Atlantic.

Corunna (La Coruña)

Corunna (population 232,356), 340 km from Oviedo or 547 km from Santander via N-634 and N-VI, is an ideal place to start your visit. It is a good base for excursions to the north coast, to Lugo, to the historic town of Betanzos and to General Franco's birthplace of El Ferrol. It is Galicia's most populated area. It has an excellent port and an airport, and it is at the beginning of a motorway which, though only partially completed at present, will eventually reach 200 km south to Tuy, on the border with Portugal. Stay in Corunna a week, sallying out to the countryside and the *rías*, and you will not regret it, even if it rains, which it often does. Ideally, you need two to three weeks if you intend to visit other parts of Galicia.

Getting to and around Galicia

The road from Santander to Corunna is one hard day's journey and though there are lovely views at every turn, there are too many turns. There are twelve trains daily between Madrid and Corunna (some of which will take cars). The *Rías Altas* is a good choice because it provides sleeper compartments and a restaurant for a pleasant overnight journey. Fast day trains from Madrid, like the Talgo, take about nine hours.

Visitors planning to fly to Galicia can choose between Corunna, Santiago or Vigo. Santiago offers the greatest selection of flights by far, and has the only airport in Galicia with a certain amount of international traffic. The flight from Madrid lasts about forty-five minutes.

There are yacht marinas and ports for small craft all along the Galician coast, and its many bays offer good shelter for small vessels. If you do have a yacht of your own, you will be able to visit as many of the little ports on the numerous bays of this region as you like. International cruise liners stop at Galician ports, but ocean liners, as a form of transport, are pretty much a thing of the past.

Buses

Once in Galicia, there are local buses which go everywhere. Galicia is, however, a land of countless tiny villages; there is a confusing array of place names and the buses never stop stopping. In some remote areas, there is even a compartment on the bus to take your cow, for this is a land of small-holdings, and every rural Galician family owns one. The buses are a great way to discover the intimate secrets of this land, but they require more time than the average holiday-maker can spare.

Main areas

Corunna occupies a small peninsula and the adjoining land. It can be conveniently divided into three parts: the old town, which lies mostly on the peninsula; the isthmus, which contains a busy commercial and shipping centre, and the Ensanche, where most residential areas and some industries are located. The city has two harbours, one facing north-west and the other south-east. The latter one is the port; the other has a lengthy beach of fine sand, whose two sections are known as Riazor and Orzán.

The port looks out on a bay, the Ría de Coruña, and local ferries cross this bay to three different destinations on the opposite side. Santa Cristina and Perillo are the nearest and, in fact, they form a part of greater Corunna, also linked to the city by a bridge.

Old quarter

The part that comes alive at night is the old quarter, with the Plaza de María Pita, where the Town Hall is at its centre. By day, the street that traces an arc along the seafront of the port, which changes its name several times along the way from one end to another, offers a beautiful perspective of the city. It is lined by a park on one side leading down to the docks, and on the other by the many-windowed galleries which earned Corunna its name of 'The Crystal City'. Early morning is a good time to see this to good effect, when the sun reflects off the thousands of windowpanes, and the brightly coloured fishing boats, lashed to each other, bobbing up and down on the waters.

The long-distance railway passenger terminal is the Estación Cristobal, at Ronda de Estaciones, just off the main road to Madrid, the Avenida Alcalde Alfonso Molina. There are at least four different bus stations; once you know your destination, ask the Tourist Office where the appropriate bus station is. The Alvedro Airport is 9 km south of the city. There are many restaurants in the old quarter, around the Plaza María Pita, and along the waterfront of the port. Most of the better hotels look out onto either of the two harbours. The Tourist Office is at Dársena de la Marina (facing the port). Tel. (981) 221 822.

History

Tin mines in the area put this town, originally populated by Celts and Iberians, on the Phoenicians' trade route. Later the Romans enlarged it and gave it a city charter. In 1588 it was the gathering point for Spain's ill-fated Invincible Armada. The following year, Drake sacked the port but he could not take the city, thanks to the bravery of a local heroine, María Pita, after whom the main square is named.

What to see
Sir John Moore's tomb

This is in the tiny San Carlos Garden, behind a spike-topped iron fence, on a hilltop just past the Dársena, the little and most sheltered area of the port, where small craft huddle together on stormy days. Views from here are lovely. The general died in 1809 while defending the city against the French during the Peninsular War; his funeral was described in the famous poem by Charles Wolfe.

The Tower of Hercules

Open daily from 10 a.m. to 1.30 p.m. and from 4 to 7.30 p.m. There are 242 steps to the top. This structure at the northern end of the peninsula on which the old city is located is probably the oldest working lighthouse in the world. Legend has it that there was an earlier tower, but the Romans built the present one in the second century. Some 1,600 years later it was refaced with stone.

Provincial museum

(Museo Provincial de Bellas Artes) In the Plaza Pintor Sotomayor, the museum is open daily from 10 a.m. to 2 p.m. and also from 4 to 6 p.m. in summer. Goya's bullfight sketches are the best exhibits.

What to do in Corunna and Galicia

● **Fishing** This is a major industry as well as a sport for non-professional fishermen. All over Galicia, you will see the people with their baskets or buckets and their spades, when the tide is out, digging in the estuaries for clams. You will see an endless array of boats, motor-powered, sail-powered or man-powered, carrying people seeking the harvest of these *rías* so rich in marine life. In town after town you can attend the auctions of fresh seafood right off the boats. Join the crowd.

● **Sailing, yachting** The opportunities are endless. Details from the Real Club Naútico, at the Dársena in the port area. Tel. (981) 222 716.

● **Golf** In Corunna, contact the Club de Golf, Calle Cantón Grande 9. Tel. (981) 225 540.

● **Tennis** Club de Tennis, Calle Cantón Grande 6. Tel. (981) 226 530.

● **Swimming** Galicia has hundreds of kilometres of coastline and countless beaches. Some are more famous than others, some are less safe than others. Generally, beaches inside the *rías* are safe from treacherous currents. Beaches open to the sea are less so, depending on the weather.

● **Fiestas** Every town in the region has one or more big *fiesta* a year, some lasting for several days at a time. Some of the more exciting, colourful or entertaining ones are the following: The Ribeiro Wine Festival at Ribadavia, province of Orense, 28 April to 1 May, Galicia's most important wine event. Corpus Christi, in June, when the people of Puenteareas, province of Pontevedra, cover the streets with carpets of flowers in intricate designs.

A Rapa das Bestas, wild horse round-up and *fiestas*, 3–5 July at San Lorenzo de Sabucedo, near La Estrada, province of Pontevedra; also 4 July at Vivero, province of Lugo. Sardinada, sardine festival, 25 July at Cambados, Pontevedra, with free food for all. Albariño wine *fiestas* also in Cambados, first Sunday in August.

Octopus *fiesta*, 14–15 August, at Carballino, Orense, in honour of the town's patron saint, San Cipriano, with all the octopus you can eat, fireworks and folk dances.

Shopping   The people of Galicia still produce quite a few handicraft items. Particularly prized are: laces from Camariñas, Corunna; ceramics from Sargadelos, Corunna; gold and silverware from Santiago; wickerware from Padrón, Corunna; hand-woven linen from Fonsagrada, Lugo; and bagpipes, tambourines and drums from Piedrafita del Cebreiro, Lugo. Some of these items you will find in shops in the cities, particularly those near the villages where they are made; others you will probably not see unless you go to the place of origin.

Nightlife   The old quarter and the area facing the port is quite lively at night. Pavement cafés are open most of the year in the port area, and the numerous bars around the Plaza María Pita are crowded most summer evenings and at weekends. Some have live music. The Clangor discotheque on the Riazor beach packs them in in summer.

One place where nobody seems to go to sleep in summer, and, for that matter, on pleasant weekends during the rest of the year, is the Santa Cristina zone, where the beaches are uncrowded, albeit not so good as others nearby, and there are a fair number of houses and flats for rent to holiday-makers. Technically outside the city, it is just across the *ría* in the south-east corner of the city via the Pasaje Bridge. Music booms from bars, cafés and discos throughout this area, and people tend to congregate in the streets at night.

Where to stay

Since the old quarter is on a peninsula, central Corunna is surrounded on practically all sides by water. This can easily cause confusion to newcomers. The best thing to do is forget about where the water is and to fix your attention on other features. The long park in front of the port is a good orientation point. If you can see it, it means you are on the south side of the isthmus. There are several hotels in this area. Stand in the middle of the park, face away from the water and you will be facing north-west. You cannot see it, but the other side of the isthmus is then about six streets straight ahead of you. There are hotels near the water on that side too.

Mid-range

Rias Altas, Playa de Santa Cristina s/n, Perillo. Tel. (981) 635 300. On the beach, rooms recently redecorated, satisfactory restaurant with good service, pleasant views, sauna, heated pool, bar. From 5,200 ptas (16 September to 14 July) to 6,400 ptas (rest of the year).

Finisterre, Paseo del Parrote s/n. Tel. (981) 205 400, telex 86086. Scenic views, in the old part of the city, pool, tennis court, sauna, restaurant, good breakfasts. From 6,000 ptas (16 September to 14 July) to 8,000 ptas (rest of the year).

Atlántico, Jardines Méndez Nuñez 2. Tel. (981) 226 500, telex 86034. Very central, harbour views, on a park, bar. From 5,500 ptas (16 September to 14 July) to 7,500 ptas (rest of the year).

Riazor, Avenida Barrie de la Maza s/n. Tel. (981) 253 400. On the beach, near the football stadium (an advantage only for out-of-town fans), garage, television in rooms. From 3,700 ptas (October to June) to 5,000 ptas (rest of the year).

España, Juan de la Vega 7. Tel. (981) 224 506. Very central, near the port and in the shopping district. From 3,200 to 4,200 ptas.

Where to eat

Pricey

La Yebolina, Calle Capitán Troncoso 18. Tel. (981) 205 044. Seafood only, and especially shellfish – served with the distinctive rosé wine of Cigales, ice-cold. Plain wooden tables and benches, but five-star service.

Duna 2, Calle Estrella 2. Tel. (981) 227 023. Closed Sundays; except in summer and over Christmas. *Nouvelle cuisine* with the emphasis on seafood.

El Rápido, Calle Estrella 7. Tel. (981) 224 221. Closed on Sundays except in August and September. Speciality: superior shellfish.

Moderate

Coral, Calle Estrella 5. Tel. (981) 221 082. Closed on Sundays except in summer. Seafood.

Around Corunna

If you can stay a week in the Corunna area, and still allow another week or two to see the rest of Galicia, you will want to see some of the nearby sights, which you could do in a day, if necessary.

El Ferrol

This town has a population of 91,764 and is 69 km north-east of Corunna, via Betanzos. This is General Franco's birthplace; it used to be called El Ferrol del Caudillo (of the leader) in his honour. After he died, they dropped the 'del Caudillo'. It is the site of Spain's largest naval base and has important shipyards. There are some pleasant beaches nearby.

Where to stay:
mid-range

Parador de El Ferrol, Calle Almirante Vierna s/n. Tel. (981) 356 720. Typical regional architecture, with a gallery containing many tiny windowpanes. Garage, bar, central location. From 6,500 ptas (January to March) to 7,000 ptas (rest of the year).

Almirante, Calle Frutos Saavedra 2. Tel. (981) 325 311. Garage, central location. From 4,400 ptas (September to June) to 4,900 ptas (rest of the year).

Where to eat:
moderate

Pataquina, Calle Dolores 35. Tel. (981) 352 311. Closed on Sunday evenings. Spanish and especially Galician cooking.

Betanzos

Betanzos (population 11,385) is 40 km south of El Ferrol; or 23 km east of Corunna on N-VI. This is the original Roman port, silted up through the ages until it ceased to be usable. Elegant old palaces attest to its importance in the past. Steep, narrow streets add to its charming aspect. Unusual assortment of medieval churches in and near this town.

Where to stay:
mid-range

Los Angeles, Calle Los Angeles 11. Tel. (981) 711 511. Very modest, with restaurant. From 2,350 ptas (mid-September to mid-July) to 3,100 ptas (rest of the year).

Where to eat:
moderate

Edreira, Calle Linares Rivas 8. Tel. (981) 770 803. Closed on Mondays and for the last three weeks of September. Simple Galician food. Spanish tortilla (potato omelette) is a speciality.

Corunna–Santiago–Noya

This series of towns, arranged in route form, is intended to whet your appetite for Galicia, so you can discover more of its little known delights for yourself. If you have time to see only one town, the one you should not miss is Santiago.

Santiago de Compostela

Santiago has a population of 93,695 and is 64 km from Corunna on the A-9 motorway. As you approach this city, the beauty of its old stone is clearly visible. Its Cathedral is one of the most praised artistic monuments in the Christian world. Since the Middle Ages, the Vatican has conferred the status of Holy City on Santiago, a privilege enjoyed by only two other cities in the world, Jerusalem and Rome.

Santiago became a mecca for Europe's medieval pilgrims after the discovery near there in the ninth century of what was said to be the tomb of St James the Apostle who – according to tradition – died in the Middle East but whose body was taken to Galicia by Christians fleeing persecution.

Useful addresses

The railway station is at Avenida General Franco; Tel. (981) 596 050. The airport is at Labacolla, 12 km east of the city on the Santiago–Lugo road. The Tourist Office is at Rúa del Villar 43. Tel. (981) 583 087.

What to see

The Cathedral, begun in 1075 on the site of an earlier church, reflects the importance of medieval Santiago. Its three façades open onto three different squares, and its huge proportions leave no doubt that it was intended to serve large numbers of the faithful. The main façade is the Obradoiro, a Gothic work, and recessed in it is the main entrance, of earlier construction, the twelfth-century Portico of Glory, which experts consider to be the best example of its period of a complex carving incorporating religious statuary. Inside, beneath the main altar, is the crypt of the apostle. The most disparate styles, from Romanesque to Plateresque, vie for viewers' attention inside, yet somehow make up a harmonious whole.

As you enter the main door of the Cathedral you will see a central post. Put your fingers in the crevices between the carved stone vines like the pilgrims of old did, seeking indulgences. The stone has been worn smooth from so many worshippers' hands.

The best time to see Santiago is on 24 July, the eve of the saint's feastday. The fireworks in the plaza in front of the Cathedral make you wonder why the place has not burned down yet after so many centuries of celebrations. The Galician National Day is on 25 July as well as the feastday of Santiago (St James).

The High Mass in the Cathedral on 25 July is the occasion for bringing out the *botafumeiro* (literally, 'smoke barrel'), a tubby yard-high silver incensory strung from a stout rope attached to a hook high in the central dome. When it has started smoking well, a red-robed team of hefty monks tugs on the other end of the rope until they get lift-off. Then, pulling together on a guide-rope with the co-ordination of a rowing team, they get the thing swinging in ever-greater arcs along the transept back and forth across the nave, trailing smoke above the heads of the churchgoers. You can actually hear it whoosh by. In the Middle Ages, among all those unwashed indulgence-seekers, a jumbo-sized incense dispenser was just the thing; today it is a curiosity that inspires a great deal of respect, especially if you happen to be beneath it as it goes steaming by.

According to an unconfirmed story told in Corunna, it happened once that when some members of the Invincible Armada were receiving their final blessing before departure at the Santiago Cathedral, the *botafumeiro* broke loose from its moorings as it swung across the church and came crashing down, bringing a few of the devout closer to their Maker, somewhat earlier than they had expected. Some considered it a bad omen, rightly so as it turned out, but the ships set out regardless. The moral is : Don't be around when the *botafumeiro* comes down.

Here is a date to note in your diary: 31 December 1992. This is the day when a sealed door, used only for such occasions, will be opened to celebrate the beginning of the next Holy Year in Santiago, 1993.

Other buildings of interest

Every old building here is a gem, but there is one that really stands out: the Romanesque church of **Santa María la Real Del Sar**, in a grassy field on the outskirts. It is the only one you will ever see in which the walls slant inwards at the base. Inside this solid twelfth-century stone church you can see how the columns lean outward and the side walls are actually farther apart at roof level than at the base. The experts cannot make up their minds whether the architect designed it that way, or whether it shrank at the bottom because of inadequate foundations.

The prominence of the Cathedral makes it easy to find your way around Santiago. It stands on the large Plaza del Obradoiro, opposite the Rajoy Palace, now the seat of the Galician Regional Government and the Santiago Town Hall. On the left, as you face the cathedral, is the Hostal de los Reyes Católicos, the Catholic Monarchs' Hotel, begun in the fifteenth century and finished in the seventeenth.

The San Jerónimo College, a fifteenth-century building which today is the Rectorate of the University of Santiago, is on your right, as you face the cathedral. Behind it is another medieval building with a lovely cloister, Colegio de Fonseca, which now houses the university library and the Galician Regional Parliament. There are dozens of other magnificent old homes and churches in the city, and many are open to the public.

What to do

There are plenty of cultural activities in this university town. The chapel of the Hostal de los Reyes Católicos is used for concerts and recitals. Its elegance and tranquillity also attract many congresses and conventions. Every Thursday there is a livestock market, the principal one in Galicia.

Where to stay

Except for the Hostal de Los Reyes Católicos, the larger hotels are mostly on the outskirts or in the modern part of the city, close to the road to the airport. There are, however, a number of smaller, more modest places right in the centre.

Top range

Hostal de los Reyes Católicos, Plaza del Obradoiro. Tel. (981) 582 222, telex 86004. Live like a king in this palace which was begun in the fifteenth century by Ferdinand and Isabella as a hostelry. Duly restored and modernised, it is still serving its original purpose as a part of the state's parador chain. There are four interior courtyards, each from a different period, all of them stately. The various halls and public areas retain a regal air. From 12,000 ptas (November to June) to 14,000 ptas (rest of the year). A few rooms with shower only are cheaper.

Araguaney, Calle Alfredo Brañas 5. Tel. (981) 595 900, telex 86108. New, luxurious, in the modern part of town, with heated pool, sauna, shops, garage and bar. From 9,300 ptas (November to March) to 11,500 ptas (rest of the year).

Mid-range   **Peregrino**, Avenida Rosalía de Castro s/n. Tel. (981) 591 850, telex 82352. Recently remodelled, on the southern edge of town, with heated pool, moderately priced restaurant and bar. From 5,200 ptas (November to March) to 6,500 ptas (rest of the year).

Compostela, Calle General Franco 1. Tel. (981) 585 700, telex 82387. Central, comfortable. From 4,600 ptas (November to 12 April) to 6,200 ptas (rest of the year).

Where to eat   **Don Gaiferos**, Rua Nova 23. Tel. (981) 583 894. Closed on Sundays and all of January. International and Galician cooking, Galician wines.

Moderate   **Alameda**, Puerta Fajara 15. Tel. (981) 584 796. Closed Christmas Eve to 5 January. Galician food, including delicious *empañadas*.

La Tacita de Oro, Avenida del General Franco 31. Tel. (981) 562 041. Galician and some international dishes.

Noya   On your way to Pontevedra from Santiago there is a delightful detour you can make to the town of Noya (population 13,867). One of the most attractive fishing ports in the area, it is 37 km south-west of Santiago. This town has one of Galicia's few bullrings. *Fiestas* 24–28 August, with regattas, cooking competitions and folk dancing.

Where to stay: **Hostal Ceboleiro**, Calle General Franco 15. Tel. (981) 820 531.
bottom range   Clean, comfortable, meals served too. From 1,400 ptas.

Cabo   If you were to drive farther west and then north along the coastal
Finisterre   road, you would come to Cabo Finisterre, Spain's westernmost cape which, literally, was 'The End of the Earth' so far as Europe was concerned, until Columbus demonstrated the contrary.

Noya–Pontevedra–Vigo

From Noya you can rejoin the N-550 at Padrón from where Pontevedra is 36 km further south.

Pontevedra   Pontevedra (population 65,137), 56 km south of Santiago on N-550; or 120 km south of Corunna, has a melancholy charm about it, but the real reason it should be on your tourist map is its surroundings. It is the major city of the part of Galicia known as the Rías Bajas (Lower Bays), a part blessed by a delightfully mild climate, good harbours, lots of fish and fertile soil. Some towns along the Rías Bajas double or triple in population in the summer, and practically all the holiday-makers are Galicians, though quite a few French people go there too. Attractions nearby include the following.

Around Pontevedra

Sword dances: **Carril**, 22 km north-west of Pontevedra via Villagarcía de Arosa, includes sword dances as part of its annual *fiestas* in August. There is a Tourist Office at Villagarcía, at Plaza de la Ravella 1. Tel. (986) 501 008.

Bodega visit: **Cambados**, 15 km south of Carril on the Ría de Arosa, is the home of the delicate white wine so prized in Galicia, Albariño (which is also the name of the principal grape variety used in making it). One of the bodegas you can visit in Cambados, by prior appointment, is Bodegas del Palacio de Fefiñanes SA (Tel. [986] 542 204), which produces a very good Albariño, dry and golden yellow. You can buy wine at the bodega, in the seventeenth-century Fefiñanes Palace.

Spa: **La Toja**, 15 km west of Cambados is linked to the El Grove Peninsula by a bridge. Renowned for its lush beauty, this pine-forested island has many expensive houses and a famous spa with a hotel and a casino. People bathe in, breathe in the vapour of, cover themselves with mud made with, and drink the waters from the springs here, in the hope of curing skin disorders and rheumatism.

Beach resort: **Sangenjo**, 25 km south-east of La Toja on the Ría de Pontevedra. Magnificent beaches – some not far from town – are completely deserted.

Robinson Crusoe Islands: Well, almost. At **Portonovo**, a fishing port less than 2 km west of Sanjenjo, you can board the excursion boat to Ons Island, at the ocean end of the Ría de Pontevedra. You can camp if you want to stay overnight, or come back in the evening as nearly everybody else does. There are lovely beaches, good fishing, and three simple restaurants near the quay, where you can eat fish and salads.

Where to stay in and around Pontevedra
Top range

Gran Hotel de la Toja, Isla de la Toja (31 km from Pontevedra). Tel. (986) 730 025, telex 88042. Turn-of-the-century elegance in a charming watering place amid a beautiful natural setting with splendid views. The hotel is self-contained, with restaurant, shops, golf, tennis, sauna, mud baths, disco. From 6,800 to 13,650 ptas.

Mid-range

Parador Casa del Barón, Calle Maceda s/n. Tel. (986) 855 800. A sixteenth-century nobleman's palace with a grand stone staircase. From 6,000 ptas (November to June) to 7,500 ptas (rest of the year).

Rías Bajas, Calle Daniel de la Sota 7. Tel. (986) 855 100, telex 88068. Central, functional. From 4,200 to 5,700 ptas.

Virgen del Camino, Calle Virgen del Camino 55. Tel. (986) 855 904. Central, television in rooms. From 4,200 to 5,700 ptas.

Parador del Alvariño, Paseo Cervantes s/n, Cambados (26 km from Pontevedra). Tel. (986) 542 250. A modern building in the Galician regional style, with a central patio and fountain. Pleasant bar and garden. From 6,000 ptas (November to June) to 7,500 ptas (rest of the year).

Panadeira, Playa de la Panadeira, Sanjenjo (17 km from Pontevedra). Tel. (986) 723 728. A delightful little family-style hotel with its own private beach in the heart of town. Good cooking, good service. Only thirteen rooms. From 2,000 to 4,000 ptas.

Where to eat: pricey

Doña Antonia, Soportales de la Herrería 9. Tel. (986) 847 274. Seafood with a *nouvelle cuisine* touch.

Moderate

Calixto, Calle Benito Corbal 14. Tel. (986) 856 252. Closed on Tuesdays and Christmas holidays. Galician cooking.

Vigo

Vigo (population 258,724) is 34 km south of Pontevedra on the A-9 motorway; or 154 km south of Corunna. Now a major port and Galicia's most important industrial city, producing cars and ships. Vigo was a Celtic settlement in the pre-Christian era. Like Pontevedra, its surroundings offer fascinating possibilities:

More Robinson Crusoe: the **Cies Islands** make an ideal excursion. They lie at the mouth of the Vigo estuary, offering steep climbs, fine beaches and peaceful fishing. Check at Vigo's Tourist Office, Jardines de Elduayen. Tel. (986) 430 577, for schedules of boats from Vigo.

Sunken treasure: A number of galleons, with cargoes of wood and gold, were scuttled in the deep **Rande Straits** in the Ría de Vigo during a battle in the early eighteenth century to keep them from falling into English hands. So far as anyone knows, the gold is still down there. The Castro, a venerable fortress at the highest part of the city, is a good place from which to get a view of the Straits.

The best ocean beach (as opposed to a beach on an estuary) in the whole region is: Playa de América, at **Nigrán**, 21 km south-west of Vigo on C-550. The wide beach is several kilometres long, sheltered and the water deepens very gradually; it is teeming with ocean life. Roads leading to this area become congested on Sundays in good weather as Vigo's citizens go out for a day at the beach. About 5 km to the south-west stands Bayona, the first European city to learn the news of the discovery of the New World.

Portuguese handicraft: every Thursday at **Tuy**, 51 km south-east of Playa de América via Vigo, or 30 km south of Vigo, there is a joint Spanish–Portuguese market and many shops have some Portuguese items for sale.

Where to stay: top range

Ciudad de Vigo, Calle Concepción Arenal 4. Tel. (986) 227 820, telex 83307. The best place to stay in Vigo. Good service, central, with scenic views and a garage. From 6,900 to 8,200 ptas.

Bahía de Vigo, Cánovas del Castillo 5. Tel. (986) 226 700. Attentive service. From 8,000 to 10,000 ptas.

Parador Conde de Gondomar, Monterreal, Bayona (23 km from Vigo). Tel. (986) 355 000. This modern parador, opened in 1966 on the site of a fortress where the Spanish tribal chief Viriato defeated Roman invaders, is super. Hidden behind 3 km of crumbling stone

H. V. Morton, *A Stranger in Spain.* Somewhat old-fashioned, but this book manages to present the contrasts of Spain in a sympathetic way.

George Orwell, *Homage to Catalonia.* A first-hand account of the frustrating internal divisions on the Republican side, which facilitated General Franco's victory.

Walter Starkie, *Spanish Raggle Taggle.* Starkie found a nobility in the gipsies which Spaniards themselves often fail to see.

Hugh Thomas, *The Spanish Civil War.* Still the most objective book on a conflict that was a prelude to the Second World War.

James Yates, *Mississippi to Madrid.* The simply told story of a black American's baptism by fire in the Spanish Civil War.

Golf Clubs

Golf Almerimar, Golf Hotel Almerimar, El Ejido, Almería. Tel. (951) 480 950. Open all year. Eighteen holes.

Aloha Golf, Nueva Andalusía, 29600 Marbella, Málaga. Tel. (952) 782 388. Open all year. Eighteen holes.

Atalaya Park, Ctra. de Banahavís, km 7, 29680 Estepona, Málaga. Tel. (952) 781 894. Open all year. Eighteen holes.

Centro Deportivo Barberan, Apartado 46.263, 28043 Cuatro Vientos, Madrid. Tel. (91) 218 8505 or 218 9869. Open all year. Nine holes.

Club Deportivo La Barganiza, Apartado 277, 33080 Oviedo. Open all year. Nine holes.

Club de Golf Bellavista, Carretera de Huelva-Aljaraque, km 6, 21110 Aljaraque, Huelva. Tel. (955) 318 083. Open all year. Nine holes.

Club de Campo La Bilbaína, 48100 Laukariz-Munguía, Vizcaya. Tel. (94) 674 0858 and 674 0462. Open all year. Eighteen holes.

Club de Golf Las Brisas, Apartado 2, Nueva Andalusía, 29660 Marbella, Málaga. Tel. (952) 780 300 – 785 544. Open all year. Eighteen holes.

Club El Candado, Urbanización El Candado, 29018 El Palo, Málaga. Tel. (952) 294 666, 290 845 or 294 816. Open all year. Nine holes.

Club de Golf de Castiello, Apartado 161, 33080 Gijón, Asturias. Tel. (985) 366 313 or 372 387. Open all year. Eighteen holes.

Real Club de Golf de Cerdaña, Apartado 63, 17080 Puigcerdá, Gerona. Tel. (972) 881 338. Open all year. Eighteen holes.

Club de Campo Villa de Madrid, Carretera de Castilla km 2, 28040 Madrid. Tel. (91) 207 0395 or 449 0726. Open all year. Twenty-seven holes.

Cortijo Grande Club de Golf, Cortijo Grande, 04639 Turre, Almería. Tel. (951) 479 176. Open all year. Eighteen holes.

Club de Golf de La Coruña, Apartado 737, 15080 Corunna. Tel. (981) 285 200 or 284 786. Open all year. Eighteen holes.

Club de Golf Costa de Azahar, Carretera Grao-Benicásim s/n, 12100 Grao de Castellón, Castellón. Tel. (964) 227 064 or 220 408. Open all year. Nine holes.

Club de Golf Costa Brava, 'La Masía', 17246 Santa Cristina de Aro, Gerona. Tel. (972) 837 150/52. Open all year. Eighteen holes.

Club de Golf Costa Dorada, Apartado 600, 43080 Tarragona. Tel. (977) 655 416. Open all day. Closed on Monday. Nine holes.

Club de Golf Don Cayo, Conde Altea 49, 03590 Altea, Alicante. Tel. (965) 840 950 or 840 716. Open all year. Nine holes.

Las Encinas de Boadilla, Carretera de Boadilla – Pozuelo km 1.400, 28660 Boadilla del Monte, Madrid. Tel. (91) 633 1100. Open all year. Closed on Mondays. Nine holes.

Club de Golf Escorpion, Apartado 1, 46180 Bétera, Valencia. Tel. (96) 160 1211. Open all year. Eighteen holes.

Golf Guadalmina, Guadalmina Alta, 29670 San Pedro de Alcántara, Málaga. Tel. (952) 781 317. Open all year. Thirty-six holes.

Herreria Club de Golf, 28200 San Lorenzo del Escorial, Madrid. Tel. (91) 890 5905, 890 5111 or 890 5244. Open all year. Eighteen holes.

Club de Golf Ifach, Carretera Moraira-Calpe km 3, 03720 Urbanización San Jaime, Benisa, Alicante. Open all year. Nine holes.

Club de Golf Javea, Carretera Jávea-Benitachell km 4.500, 03730 Jávea, Alicante. Tel. (965) 792 584. Open all year. Nine holes.

Real Club de Golf Lomas-Bosque, Urbanización El Bosque, Villaviciosa de Odón, Madrid. Tel. (91) 616 2382 or 616 2170. Open all year. Eighteen holes.

Club Golf Llanvaneras, 08392 San Andrés de Llanvaneras, Barcelona. Tel. (93) 792 6050. Open all year. Closed on Mondays. Nine holes.

Club de Campo de Málaga, Apartado 324, 29080 Málaga. Tel. (952) 381 120 or 381 255. Open all year. Eighteen holes.

La Manga Campo de Golf, La Manga Club, 30385 Los Belones, Catagena, Murcia. Tel. (968) 569 111. Open all year. Thirty-six holes.

Club de Campo del Mediterraneo, Urbanización La Coma s/n, 12190 Borriol, Castellón. Tel. (964) 321 227. Open all year. Eighteen holes.

Club de Golf de Mijas, Apartado 138, 29080 Fuengirola, Málaga. Tel. (952) 476 843. Open all year. Eighteen holes.

Golf La Moraleja, Marquesa Viuda de Aldama 50, 28409 La Moraleja, Madrid. Tel. (91) 650 0700. Open all year. Eighteen holes.

Real Sociedad de Golf de Neguri, Apartado 9, 48980 Algorta, Vizcaya. Tel. (94) 469 0200 or 469 0208. Open all year. Eighteen holes.

Club de Golf Nerja, Apartado 154, 29080 Nerja, Málaga. Tel. (952) 520 208. Open all year. Nine holes.

Nuevo Club de Golf de Madrid, Carretera de La Coruña km 26, 28290 Las Matas, Madrid. Tel. (91) 630 0820. Eighteen holes.

Nueva Andalucía (Los Naranjos), Apartado 2, 29080 Nueva Andalucía, Marbella, Málaga. Tel. (952) 787 200 or 780 300. Open all year. Eighteen holes.

Club de Golf de Pals, Playa de Pals, 17256 Pals, Gerona. Tel. (972) 636 006. Open all year. Closed on Tuesdays. Eighteen holes.

Golf El Paraiso, Carretera Cadiz-Málaga km 167, 29080 Estepona, Málaga. Tel. (952) 783 000. Open all year. Eighteen holes.

Real Golf de Pedreña, Apartado 233, 39080 Santander. Tel. (942) 500 001 or 500 266. Open all year. Eighteen holes.

Club de Golf La Peñaza, Apartado 3.039, 50080 Saragossa. Tel. (976) 342 800. Open all year. Eighteen holes.

Club Pineda de Sevilla, Apartado 796, 41080 Seville. Tel. (954) 611 400 or 613 399. Open all year. Nine holes.

Golf Playa Granada, Urbanización Playa de Granada, 18006 Motril, Granada. Tel. (958) 600 412. Open all year. Nine holes.

Golf Playa Serena, Urbanización Playa Serena, 04740 Roquetas de Mar, Almería. Tel. (951) 322 055. Open all year. Eighteen holes.

Club de Golf Pozoblanco, San Gregorio 2, 14400 Pozoblanco, Córdoba. Tel. (957) 100 006. Open all year. Nine holes.

Real Club de Golf 'El Prat', Apartado 10, 08080 El Prat de Llobregat, Barcelona. Tel. (93) 379 0278. Open all year. Twenty-seven holes.

Real Club de la Puerta de Hierro, 28035 Madrid. Tel. (91) 216 1745. Open all year. Thirty-six holes.

Real Automóvil Club de España, José Abascal 10, 28003 Madrid. Tel. (91) 625 2600 or 447 3200. Open all year. Eighteen holes.

Golf Rio Real, Apartado 82, 29080 Marbella, Málaga. Tel. (952) 773 776. Open all year. Eighteen holes.

Club de Golf Roca Llisa, Apartado 200, 07080 Ibiza. Tel. (971) 304 060 or 304 437. Open all year. Nine holes.

Campo de Golf El Saler, Parador Nacional Luis Vives, Campo de Golf El Saler, El Saler, Valencia. Tel. (96) 161 1186. Open all year. Eighteen holes.

Golf San Andrés, Carretera Cadiz-Málaga km 14, 11130 Chiclana, Cádiz. Tel. (956) 855 667. Open all year. Nine holes.

Club de Golf de San Cugat, 08302 San Cugat del Vallés, Barcelona. Tel. (93) 674 3908 or 674 3958. Open all year. Closed on Mondays. Eighteen holes.

Real Golf Club de San Sebastián, Apartado 6, 20080 Fuenterrabía, Guipúzcoa. Tel. (943) 616 845 or 616 846. Open all year. Eighteen holes.

Golf Santa Ponsa, 07080 Santa Ponsa, Mallorca. Tel. (971) 690 211, 690 800 or 690 750. Open all year. Eighteen holes.

Real Aero Club de Santiago, General Pardiñas 34, 15701 Santiago de Compostela, Corunna. Tel. (981) 592 400, 592 394 or 562 060. Open all year. Nine holes.

Club de Golf Severiano Ballesteros, Apartado 760, 39080 Santander. Tel. (942) 311 741. Nine holes.

Campo de Golf de Somosaguas, Somosaguas, 28011 Madrid. Tel.

(91) 212 1647. Open all year. Nine holes.

Club de Golf Sotogrande, Apartado 14, 11080 Sotogrande, Cádiz. Tel. (956) 792 050. Open all year. Eighteen holes.

Golf La Toja, 36991 Isla de La Toja, Pontevedra. Tel. (968) 730 726 or 730 818. Nine holes.

Club de Golf Terramar, Apartado 6, 08080 Sitges, Barcelona. Tel. (93) 894 0580, 894 2043 or 894 2266. Open all year. Eighteen holes.

Golf Torrequebrada, Apartado 67, 29680 Benalmádena-Costa, Málaga. Tel. (952) 442 742. Open all year. Eighteen holes.

Club de Golf de Ulzama, 31799 Guerendiain, Navarra. Tel. (948) 305 162. Open all year. Nine holes.

Club de Golf Vallromanas, Apartado 43, 08080 Montornés del Vallés, Barcelona. Tel. (93) 568 0362. Open all year. Closed on Tuesdays. Eighteen holes.

Aero Club de Vigo, Reconquista 7, 36201 Vigo. Tel. (986) 221 160, 223 215 or 272 493. Open all year. Nine holes.

Campo de Golf Villamartin, Apartado 35, 03080 Torrevieja, Alicante. Tel. (965) 320 350. Open all year. Eighteen holes.

Club Valdelaguila, Apartado 9, 28080 Alcalá de Henares, Madrid. Tel. (91) 885 9659. Nine holes.

Club de Golf Valderrama, Apartado 1, 11080 Sotogrande, Cádiz. Tel. (956) 792 775. Open all year. Eighteen holes.

Club de Golf Los Villares, Ronda de los Tejares 1-2°, 14080 Córdoba. Tel. (957) 474 102 or 350 208. Open all year. Eighteen holes.

Vista Hermosa Club de Golf, Apartado 77, 11500 Puerto de Santa María, Cádiz. Tel. (956) 850 011. Open all year. Nine holes.

Real Aero Club de Zaragoza, Sección de Golf, Coso 34, 50004 Saragossa. Tel. (976) 214 378. Nine holes.

Real Golf de Zarauz, Apartado 82, 20080 Zarauz, Guipúzcoa. Tel. (943) 830 145 or 831 396. Open all year. Nine holes.

Index

in Itálica 151
in Mérida 137
in Segóbriga 126
in Segovia 103
in Vich 230
Romans, in Spain 12–13, 147,
    166, 173, 179, 182, 207,
    208, 216, 225, 236, 259, 296
  in Numancia 121–2
  in Tarragona 199, 200
Roman theatres 137, 174, 206
Roncal 243
Roncesvalles 241, 247
Ronda 75, 176, 179–80, 191
Roquetas de Mar 181
Rosas 236–7
Rovolgo meadows 287
Rubens, Sir Peter Paul 185
Rueda, wine from 57

Sabiñánigo 253
Sachetti, Juan Bautista 92
saffron 60
Sagunto 206
Salamanca 110–14
  accommodation 113–14
  Casa de las Conchas 111
  Cathedrals 112
  churches 111, 112
  Convent of the Agustinos 111
  history 111
  main areas 110–11
  nightlife 113
  restaurants 114
  shopping 113
  Tourist Offices 111
  transport 110–11
  University 111, 112
Salardú 262
salaries 33
Salazar 243
Salinas, Pedro 22
Sallent de Gallego 254
Salobreña 181
Salou 203
San Andrés de Teixido 75
San Antonio de Calonge 235
San Bernardo, monastery of 118
Sancho the Strong, King of
    Navarre 247
Sancho IV, King of Castile 148–
    9
San Cristobal (mountain) 162
San Feliú de Guixols 234
San Fermín bullrunning festival
    240, 241–2
San Fernando 74
Sangenjo 303
San Isidro 287
San Lorenzo del Escorial 101–2
San Lorenzo de Sabucedo 74,
    297
Sanlúcar de Barrameda 57,

    157–8, 159
  bodegas 156
  fiesta 74–5
San Martin de Valdeiglesias,
    winery in 95
San Mauricio Lake 262
San Miguel in Excelsis
    Sanctuary 245
San Pedro Manrique 74, 122
San Pedro de Pinatar 74
San Sadurní de Noya 229
San Sebastián 269–73
  accommodation 272–3
  climate 41
  fiestas 73, 271
  history 270
  main areas 270
  nightlife 272
  Old Quarter 271
  restaurants 273
  San Telmo museum 271
  shopping 271–2
  Tourist Offices 270
  transport 269–70
Santa Cruz de Tenerife 73
Santander 86, 267, 283–6
  accommodation 285–6
  fiesta 285
  history 284
  main areas 284
  museum 284
  nightlife 285
  restaurants 286
  shopping 285
  sport 285
  Tourist Office 284
  transport 283–4
Santes Creus Abbey 202
Santiago de Compostela 16,
    245, 246, 267, 294, 299–302
  accommodation 301–2
  Cathedral 300–1
  restaurants 302
  Santa María la Real Del Sar
    301
  transport 300
Santiago de Lóquiz 243
Santillana del Mar 287–8
Santo Domingo de la Calzada
    278
Santoña 284
San Vicente de la Sonsierra 74,
    276
Saragossa 248–53
  accommodation 252
  Aula Dei Monastery 251
  Cathedral 250
  churches 250
  climate 41
  fiestas 75, 251
  history 250
  main areas 250
  museums 251

  nightlife 252
  restaurants 252–3
  shopping 251
  sport 251
  theatre 251
  Tourist Offices 250, 251
  transport 250
Scipio Aemilianus 121–2
Scipio Africanus 151
scorpions 78
scuba diving 164
sea nettles 66
Segóbriga 13, 126
Segovia 103–4
self-government, regional 25
Seo de Urgel 263
Sepúlveda 106
Serrano, Pablo 217
Seville 21, 145–54
  accommodation 153–4
  Alameda de Hércules 149
  Alcázar 147, 148
  ballet 151
  bullfights 58, 148, 151
  Calle Bustos Tavera 148–9
  Calle Cabeza del Rey Don
    Pedro 149–50
  Cathedral 147, 148
  churches 150
  climate 41, 145
  convents 150
  crime 11, 152–3
  Dance of the Seises 151
  fiestas 73, 74, 151–2
  history 147–8
  Hospital de la Caridad 148
  legends 148–50
  main areas 147
  María Luisa Park 148
  museums 148, 150
  nightlife 153
  palaces 150
  restaurants 147, 154
  Santa Cruz quarter 147, 148
  shopping 152
  tobacco factory 148
  Tourist Offices 147
  transport 145, 147
  Triana gipsy quarter 147
sharks 79
sherry 57, 60, 154, 155–6
shoeshines 75
shooting 67–8
shopping (see also under
    individual towns) 60–1
Sierra Cazorla 188
Sierra Nevada 175, 189, 194–5
siesta 31–2
Sigüenza 123–4
Sisebuto, King of the Visigoths
    16
Sitges 198
skiing